W9-CFF-318

Comparing Jewish Societies

THE COMPARATIVE STUDIES IN SOCIETY AND HISTORY BOOK SERIES

Raymond Grew, Series Editor

Comparing
Jewish Societies

TODD M. ENDELMAN, EDITOR

Ann Arbor
THE UNIVERSITY OF MICHIGAN PRESS

Copyright © by the University of Michigan 1997
All rights reserved
Published in the United States of America by
The University of Michigan Press
Manufactured in the United States of America
⊗ Printed on acid-free paper

2000   1999   1998   1997   4   3   2   1

A CIP catalog record for this book is available from the British Library.

Library of Congress Cataloging-in-Publication Data

Comparing Jewish societies / Todd M. Endelman, editor.
    p.   cm. — (The Comparative studies in society and history
book series)
    Includes bibliographical references and index.
    ISBN 0-472-09592-7 (cloth : acid-free paper). — ISBN
0-472-06592-0 (pbk. : acid-free paper)
    1. Jews—History—1789–1945.   2. Judaism—History.   3. Jews—
Social conditions.   4. Israel.   5. Cross-cultural studies.
I. Endelman, Todd M.   II. Series.
DS125.C536   1997
909'.04924—dc21
                                                        97-4811
                                                        CIP

Contents

Foreword

For nearly forty years the quarterly issues of *Comparative Studies in Society and History* have published articles about human society in any time or place written by scholars in any discipline and from any country. Those articles, inevitably reflecting the changing methods and interests within the specialized fields of research from which they grew, have presented new evidence and new techniques, challenged established assumptions, and raised fresh questions. Now this series of books extends and refocuses the comparisons begun in some of the most stimulating of those essays.

The editors of each volume identify a field of comparative study and then determine which essays from among all the articles that have appeared in *CSSH* best exemplify the range and excitement of their topic. In making their selections, they consider everything published from the first issue of *CSSH,* in October 1958, to the present (including scores of new manuscripts currently under consideration). The book thus builds on a group of articles that are part of a continuing dialogue among scholars formed in different disciplines, traditions, and generations. To this core the editors add essays never before published, essays they have commissioned in order to round out the book and to illustrate more fully the potential range of their topic and the new directions it is taking. The authors of the published articles are given the opportunity to revise their essays in the light of this project, and each volume is therefore a new work in the specific sense that its chapters are abreast of current scholarship but also, in its broader purpose, a cooperative enterprise reconsidering (and thereby reconstructing) a common topic.

Having established the theme to be addressed and identified the scholars to do it, the editors then invite these colleagues to join in exploring the ramifications of their common interest. In most instances this includes a conference in Ann Arbor, attended by contributors and by many other scholars, at which issues of conceptualization, interpretation, and method can be debated. Sometimes the volume's topic is made the basis of a graduate course, with contributors giving a series of lectures in a seminar lasting a term or more and attended by a variety of interested specialists. Thus, the books in this series, which in each case started from an indirect dialogue in the pages of *CSSH,* took form through direct exchanges. Individual manuscripts were criticized and new suggestions tried out through open-ended and lively discussions that identified common concerns and reflected on each particular study in light of different disciplines and the experience of different societies. Reshaped by the community it had created, each volume has become a statement of where scholarship currently stands and of questions that need to be pursued. Through the process in which individual chapters are reconsidered and revised, general problems can be better identified and usefully reformulated.

In this way this series extends the tradition that *CSSH* represents. A scholarly quarterly is a peculiar kind of institution, its core permanently fixed in print, its rhythmic appearance in familiar covers an assurance of some central continuity, its contents influenced by its past yet pointing in new directions. *CSSH* seeks to create a community without formal boundaries, a community whose membership is only loosely determined by subject, space, or time. Just as footnotes and references embed each article in particular intellectual traditions while stretching beyond them, so the journal itself reaches beyond editors, contributors, and subscribers, speaking in whatever voice unknown readers respond to, whenever and wherever they turn its pages. The resulting dialogues are not limited to any single forum, and the journal itself changes from within, while balancing between venturesomeness and rigor as old debates are refined and new problems posed.

The books in this series further in another form aspirations acknowledged in the opening editorial of the first issue of *CSSH,* in which Sylvia Thrupp declared her belief that "there is a definite set of problems common to the humanities, to history, and to the various social sciences." Changes in the way these problems are conceived and in the vocabulary for expressing them have not lessened the determination to reject "the false dilemma" between "error through insularity and probable superficiality." Insistence upon thorough, original research has been the principal defense against superficiality, emphasis upon comparison the means for overcoming insularity. Many of the articles published in *CSSH* are systematically comparative, across time and between societies, and that is always welcome—but many are not. Each published article was independently chosen for its qualities of scholarship and imagination as well as for its broader implications. For the contributors to and readers of that journal, comparison has come to mean more a way of thinking than the merely mechanical listing of parallels among separate cases. Articles designed to speak to scholars in many disciplines and to students of different societies are recognized as intrinsically comparative by the nature of the problems they pose, the structure of their argument, and the effect of their conclusions.

Every piece of research deserves to be seen in many contexts: the problems and concerns of a particular society, the immediately relevant scholarly literature with its own vocabulary and evidence, the methods and goals of a given discipline, a body of theory and hypotheses, and sets of questions (established, currently in vogue, or new). Nor can any prescription delimit in advance how far subsequent comparisons of similar problems in different contexts may reach. After its first decade *CSSH* began placing articles within rubrics that call attention to a central comparative theme among adjacent essays. In addition an editorial foreword in each issue notes other sets of connections between current articles and earlier ones, inviting further comparisons of broad themes, specific topics, and particular problems or methods. A variety of potential discourses is thus identified, and that open-ended process has culminated in this series of books. Some of the volumes in the series are built around established themes of comparative study, subjects known to require comparison; some address topics not always recognized as a field of study, creating a new perspective through fresh questions. Each volume is thus an autonomous undertaking, a discussion with its own purposes and focus, the work of many authors and its editor's vision of the topic, establishing a field of knowledge, assessing its present state, and suggesting some future directions.

The goal, in the quarterly issues of *CSSH* and in these books, is to break out of received categories and to cross barriers of convention that, like the residual silt from streams that once flowed faster, have channeled inquiry into patterns convenient for familiar ideas, academic disciplines, and established specialties. Contemporary intellectual trends encourage, indeed demand, this rethinking and provide some powerful tools for accomplishing it. In fact, such ambitious goals have become unnervingly fashionable, for it no longer requires original daring nor theoretical independence to attack the hegemony of paradigms—positivism, scientism, Orientalism, modernization, Marxism, behavioralism, and so forth—that once shaped the discourse of social science. Scholars, however, must hope that the effort to think anew can also allow some cumulative element in our understanding of how human societies work, and so these books begin their projects by recognizing and building upon the lasting qualities of solid scholarship.

With a pioneering spirit the essays in this volume track diverse ways to meet a long-recognized opportunity and a serious intellectual need. Written by scholars whose work is deeply embedded in Jewish studies, each of these essays makes use of substantive knowledge and sophisticated methods commonly associated with other areas of study. Jewish studies is an expanding field with rich traditions on which to build, and in a masterful first chapter Todd Endelman explains how its historiography, although aware of some of its possibilities, rarely gave comparative analysis central place. His regret at opportunities missed, a point with which the next chapter, by Stephen Sharot, begins, is echoed throughout the volume. Like Endelman's, many of the articles here suggest that now is a time when Jewish studies can take up the challenge of comparative analysis with renewed energy and promise.

These essays do that in a variety of ways. Many of them reach out to consider relevant aspects of Gentile societies, and this wider focus has a reciprocal effect. A closer look at societies and cultures that are not Jewish often helps sharpen the questions to be asked about Jewish communities at the same time that it stimulates fresh questions with regard to the structure and practices of the non-Jewish societies being compared. In both respects comparison thus facilitates the definition of significant historical problems (and leads sometimes to the recognition of overlooked evidence). Strikingly, these chapters touch on every continent save Australia (Europe, of course, is the focus of several, as are Israel and the Middle East; Nancy Green includes the United States; Dan V. Segre, Africa; and Leo Spitzer writes on Bolivia). In these studies the culture that migrants carry with them becomes a crucial, fascinating matter for deep reflection and for important observations about how permeable (and impermeable) cultural boundaries are—a consistent theme in Spitzer's tale of urban and rural, regional, ethnic, and class differences and a major issue as well in Zachary Lockman's chapter.

Comparison has another effect, for, done carefully, it tends to make methodological issues explicit, and these chapters are notable for the sophistication with which they do so. From Sharot's two chapters at the beginning to the final chapter by Shlomo Deshen, they reach toward theory and are thus connected to some of the most influential work in the social sciences. These studies note, and cause the reader to reflect upon, the extent to which the particular insights research achieves follow from the choice of what to compare. Considering the lot of East European Jews in New York, London, and Paris, Green compares men and women, forms of labor, economies, and urban structures as well as ethnic differences and similarities—and each points to different findings. In this book even the studies of specific Jewish communities are similarly explicit in concentrating on Sephardi and Ashkenazi traditions, on Jews as workers (which Lockman does), as minorities, and (in Hillel Kieval's comparisons) as victims.

There are essays that analyze social structures and others that emphasize ideas, ideologies, mysticism, and theology, as in Sharot's study of millennial and messianic movements, David Sorkin's thoughtful essay on the Enlightenment and Jewish emancipation, and Fishman's comparison of kibbutzim, in which ideology and structure intersect. Important in their own right, these comparative studies tend to break out of old frameworks, observing with a new eye how, for example, the literature on Jewish history has been shaped and narrowed by preoccupation with German culture and thus with opposition to modernity, an effect that Sorkin highlights and that Fishman similarly finds significant in Israel itself. For, as Segre also notes, the meanings of that state have been many and varied.

Escaping from established frameworks, even ones as important as the tension between preservation and assimilation, becomes one of the achievements of these studies. This breaking away from established assumptions does not require that the societies compared be distant from one another. Shlomo Deshen's close observation of North African Jews in Israel interweaves personal odyssey and a wide range of scholarly literature to construct an orderly account of the process by which religions change. Unfamiliar comparisons, such as Sorkin's study of Jewish and Catholic religious revival, can uncover similarities that recast the understanding of both. Giving religion central place, these chapters restore to social analysis a critical aspect of culture frequently slighted.

Once they are recognized, conceptual boundaries can be crossed, and that can lead to a new category of analysis, as in Sammy Smooha's attention to the problems of ethnic democracy, a concept that emerged from comparing Ireland and Israel and one that has sobering implications for the contemporary world. As in Kieval's close study of the Central European communities that staged ritual murder trials, comparison can also expose the complexity and diversity of local circumstances that challenge those sweeping generalizations that so easily engulf accounts of anti-semitism. Such attention to the complexity of context becomes another one of the themes that runs through this volume, one especially empha-sized in the chapters by Segre and Deshen.

Most fundamentally, of course, these essays are contributions to Jewish studies, and in their diversity they suggest a bit of the field's wide range while demonstrating the new light that theoretical sophistication, fresh research, and independent judgment always bring. They illustrate the use-fulness of comparative analysis as an aid in deploying theory, designing research, and probing received interpretations. Their call for comparison strengthens links to other fields of learning and builds bridges that bring fresh energies to Jewish studies. The intellectual traffic, however, will move in both directions, as scholars who have little familiarity with Jewish stud-ies (and who, incidentally, will be grateful for the useful glossary included here) realize that the experience of Jews has much to teach about how cul-tural boundaries can be shifting and all but invisible yet still lasting; about the social impact of religion; about, and this will surprise many, the forms of colonialism and ways of assessing their effects; about what minority sta-tus implies and how it comes into being; about the construction of modern identities, the meanings of ethnicity, and the uses of nationalism; and about the effects of migration. Thinking comparatively about Jewish his-tory helps us to see similarities often hidden behind walls of national his-toriography and to avoid mere folklore in explaining differences. The doors of many mansions are opened by *Comparing Jewish Societies.*

Raymond Grew

Introduction: Comparing Jewish Societies

Todd M. Endelman

In a programmatic essay in the *Jewish Journal of Sociology* in 1963, the distinguished American sociologist Seymour Martin Lipset lamented the paucity of comparative studies of Jewish communities and Jewish political and social behavior. In particular, he regretted that most communal studies focused on the "Jewishness" of communities, that is, their rejection or retention of religious rites and beliefs, while ignoring variations in the behavior of Jews around the world, which he believed were linked to the structures and values of the larger, Gentile societies in which they lived. The theme that ran through his essay was that "the comparative study of the Jew must be linked inseparably with the comparative study of the Gentile." Writing in *Comparative Studies in Society and History* in 1974, the English-born, Oxford-educated Israeli sociologist Stephen Sharot echoed Lipset's lament, noting how little change had occurred in sociological research on Jews in the eleven years since the publication of Lipset's article. Most studies were restricted to Jewish communities in the United States, he noted, their findings possessing "little generality beyond that society."[1]

If these observations are correct in regard to the sociology of the Jews, how much the more so in regard to the history of the Jews. Historians of the Jews and their religion have been a conservative lot in the way they go about their work, reluctant, if not averse, to introducing a comparative dimension to their writing. With few exceptions they have shown little enthusiasm for comparing Jewish communities across time and/or space (what I will call "internal comparisons") or comparing Jews with non-Jews either in the same place or in different national contexts (what I will call "external comparisons"). To be sure, noteworthy exceptions here and there address comparative themes, for example, the Leo Baeck Memorial Lectures of Gerson Cohen on Sephardi and Ashkenazi messianism and Yosef Yerushalmi on Spanish and German racial thinking.[2] But most contributions to Jewish historical writing either focus on Jews alone, usually within narrow geographical and chronological limits, or, at the other extreme, survey broad expanses of Jewish history, collapsing differences among communities and subcommunities in order to force their varied experiences into a uniform model or framework. The two now classic studies of Jacob Katz, *Tradition and Crisis: Jewish Society at the End of the Middle Ages* and *Out of the Ghetto: The Social Background of Jewish Emancipation,* are well-known examples of this latter approach. In *Out of the Ghetto,* for example, in defending his presentation of emancipation in Western and Central Europe as "one fabric" and "a meaningful whole," Katz acknowledges that this "entails the neglect of details and the omission of special features of development in each separate country" but maintains, nonetheless, that emancipation "followed a similar, if not identical, course" throughout the West.[3]

To be fair, few historians, regardless of their field, show much interest in comparative perspectives. Historians of England, for example, are notorious for their parochialism (an inheritance of Britain's now faded imperial power), their inability or unwillingness to see events within their small island kingdom in the context of events elsewhere. Moreover, given the trend toward increasing specialization (some would say balkanization) in academic life, there are professional and intellectual disincentives to venturing into unfamiliar territory, which comparative work requires. No historian, after all, wants to see his or her work dismissed as superficial or dilettantish, to be branded a dabbler or an amateur.

In this context, however, the writing of Jewish history is unlike the writing of most other group or national histories: it lacks territorial focus. From late antiquity to the present it is the history of a diaspora, of more or less discrete communities scattered about several continents. In historiographical terms this diffusion is both a blessing and a curse. It is a curse to the extent that it demands knowledge of a multitude of historical settings, far more than most persons can master. But it is also a blessing to the extent that it lends itself almost effortlessly to comparative treatment. Indeed, given its diaspora character, Jewish history is better suited to comparative treatment than more conventional territorially focused fields. Having unfolded in the most diverse settings—in the orbits of Islam and Christianity, under capitalism and communism, in liberal and absolutist regimes, amidst peasants and proletarians—it offers unique, almost laboratory-like opportunities for examining how communities with similar but not identical backgrounds and traditions adapt to different environments. Moreover, these kinds of comparisons reveal similarities and dissimilarities not only among Jewish communities but among the dominant or host societies in which Jews have lived as well. The heuristic benefits of this kind of comparative work, in other words, transcend the borders of Jewish historiography.

If so, why have historians of the Jews been reluctant to introduce a comparative dimension to their work? One could answer that their reluctance has been a function of the inward-looking, even "parochial" nature of the enterprise. But this explains little. In truth, the answer is both more complex and more instructive. It is rooted, first, in the circumstances in which modern Jewish historical consciousness developed and the political ends to which Jewish historical writing was dedicated from the start; second, in the institutional structure in which Jewish historical training and research took place (and to some extent still do); and, third, in the feelings and ideas with which the two great upheavals of recent Jewish experience—the destruction of European Jewry and the emergence of the State of Israel— have saddled historians.

Jewish Historical Consciousness

The textual foundation for Jewish self-understanding until the modern era was the Hebrew Bible, a body of writing in which historical narratives are conspicuous and awareness of the meaningfulness of history permeates even legal and prophetic texts. For the transmitters and redactors of these texts, however, history per se, in all its messy complexity and rich diversity, possessed no meaning or value. Their interest in the past was focused and selective: history was, above all, a vehicle for demonstrating God's relationship to his people, Israel, and, to some extent, why some groups within the people were to be entrusted with its leadership. History offered instruction; it was didactic; correctly understood, that is, as interpreted by the rabbis of antiquity and their heirs, it revealed God's will and purpose and what he required of humankind, in general, and the Jews, in particular.[4]

Given the critical role of historical narrative and consciousness in biblical Israel, one might assume that Jews would have continued to cultivate the writing of history in the centuries that followed. But, in fact, this was not so. After the redaction of the Bible, history ceased to be a characteristic genre of Jewish literary creativity. As Yosef Yerushalmi remarked in the prologue to *Zakhor,* "Although Judaism throughout the ages was absorbed with the meaning of history, historiography itself played at best an ancillary role among the Jews and often no role at all."[5] Amid the countless thousands of texts written by Jews in the postbiblical period, historical narratives number less than a few score. While one can cite notable examples—*The Jewish War* and *The Jewish Antiquities* of Josephus Flavius, the Crusade chronicles of the twelfth century, the *Shevet Yehudah* (The Scepter of Judah) of Solomon ibn Verga, the *Meor einayim* (Light for the Eyes) of Azariah de'Rossi, the *Tsemah David* (The Sprout of David) of David Gans, etc.—one cannot speak of schools or traditions of historical writing extending over more than one generation. In the sixteenth century, in the wake of the Spanish expulsion and the messianic hopes it fueled, there was a minor efflorescence of Jewish historiography—ten major works from this period survive—but their authors left no heirs. Jews remained indifferent to the writing of their history until the nineteenth century.

This indifference, however, should not be confused with an absence of historical consciousness. The history of ancient Israel, as presented in the Hebrew Bible and elaborated in rabbinic *midrashim* (homiletic texts), informed Jewish self-understanding.[6] In biblical narratives and their rabbinic retellings later generations found an explanation for their collective fate. From these texts they learned that God chose the Jews from all the nations of the earth to receive the Torah and that he covenanted himself to nourish and protect them, guiding their destiny from generation to generation, rewarding and punishing them according to their merits, using other, larger nations as instruments of his will. But, one must ask, if Jews were so alive to the idea of history, if they believed that past and present were different and that the record of the past was pregnant with meaning, why then did they cease to write history with the close of the biblical period? Why is historical writing between the ancient and modern periods so insignificant a part of Jewish literature?

The answer is that until the nineteenth century Jews believed that the critical, decisive events in their history, those chronicled in the Hebrew Bible, had already occurred and that subsequent events were mere repetitions or, better, elaborations of these earlier events.[7] For pre-modern Jews the larger-than-life events of biblical antiquity decided, clarified, and made meaningful Israel's collective fate for all time. These included, above all, the redemption from Egyptian bondage, the giving of the Torah on Mount Sinai, the conquest of the Land of Israel, the destruction of the First Temple and the Babylonian exile, the rebuilding and then destruction of the Second Temple, exile and dispersion. These events overflowed with meaning; they told Jews who they were and what their fate was and offered consolation and hope in difficult times. To be sure, subsequent events also were subject to divine direction, but they lacked the cosmic import and orienting meaning that biblical events possessed. Instead, pre-modern Jews tended to see in them the working out of fundamental patterns established at the start of Jewish history. Thus, when Jews suffered collective disasters such as expulsions and massacres, they viewed them through the filter of the rabbinic interpretation of biblical events: just as God exiled his people from their home as punishment for their sins, so too he continued to chastise them in their exile when they departed from his commandments.

In the first half of the nineteenth century, during the early decades of the struggle for political emancipation and social acceptance in Western and Central Europe, the writing of history once again became important to Jews.[8] As with so many other landmarks in the modernization of Jewish intellectual life, it was in the German states, where opposition to emancipation and integration was more bitter than elsewhere in the West, that "the turn to history" (Ismar Schorsch's apt phrase) occurred. It arose not from disinterested intellectual curiosity but as an ideological response to German opposition to emancipation. The first practitioners of *Wissenschaft des Judentums* (Science of Judaism), as the new history-minded critical scholarship came to be known, were acculturated, university-educated Jewish scholars, still steeped in traditional rabbinic learning but intoxicated as well with the academic canons of historical scholarship, who desired to combat the charge that Jews were unfit to be citizens. Since no German-language scholarship on Jewish beliefs, customs, and achievements existed (other than that written in an antisemitic or conversionist spirit), they proposed to create a body of work to correct Christian misperceptions and biases.[9] Their goal was to show that Jews had been central actors in human history—above all, as creators and bearers of the monotheistic idea but also as poets, statesmen, philosophers, grammarians, and men of science and medicine. They labored to show that so-called Jewish traits—their alleged clannishness, superstition, commercial immorality, lack of culture, concentration in marginal, low-status trades—were not a fixed part of an essentialized Jewish character but, instead, the result of centuries of persecution. In other words, historical circumstances, rather than their religion, had made Jews the way they were. They also wished to demonstrate that Judaism had a dignified, intellectually rich history that, like other religious civilizations, warranted scholarly investigation.

Leopold Zunz's landmark essay "Etwas über die rabbinische Literatur" (1818) first articulated the program of *Wissenschaft des Judentums*. It called for a historical study of the entire literary corpus of Jewish civilization (rabbinic literature in the widest possible sense of the term) in order to reveal its true character and extent. This enterprise was to be carried out in accord with current methods of scholarship, thus allowing the results to take their place as an integral part of the Western intellectual tradition. The finest and fullest flowering of the school was Heinrich Graetz's monumental work *Geschichte der Juden von den ältesten Zeit bis auf die Gegenwart,* which appeared in eleven volumes between 1853 and 1876 and continued to exert a profound influence on views of the Jewish past even in this century.

Internal religious conflicts within German Jewry at this period also fueled "the turn to history." In the campaign to modernize Jewish worship and belief, historical scholarship became a much-wielded tactical weapon.[10] Conservative, moderate, and radical reformers alike mined the historical record to demonstrate that growth and change were an ever-present dimension of Judaism. Armed with evidence of an evolutionary rather than a static past, they argued that, just as Judaism had adapted itself to new circumstances in earlier epochs, so too it should continue to do so now that a more tolerant age had dawned. More narrowly, they used historical research to find precedents for reforms that they wished to introduce, hoping thereby to depict innovative measures as time-sanctioned practices that had fallen into disuse and were now ripe for revival. Zunz's *Die gottesdienstlichen Vorträge der Juden* (1832), for example, by showing how the synagogue had functioned at all times as a forum for exegesis (*midrash*), worked to legitimate the introduction of German-language preaching in the face of opposition from traditionalists, who viewed it as assimilation to Christian practice. Reform theologians also turned to history to advance their program. Under the spell of German idealism they traced the evolution of Jewish religious consciousness in its forward march from biblical times to the present, from the primitive to the philosophical. Doing so also served two other ends as well: it refuted the common Christian claim that Judaism had become fossilized prior to the Christian era and had ceased to develop thereafter, and it allowed reformers to draw a distinction between the eternal theological core of Judaism and the temporal ritualistic shells that formed around it at different stages of its development.

For decades afterward the writing of Jewish history, which remained (and, to a large extent, still remains) in the hands of scholars who were themselves Jewish, bore the impress of the circumstances in which it had originated. Throughout the nineteenth and well into the twentieth century, both in Central and Western Europe, it was marked by an apologetic cast. Because the struggle for emancipation in Central Europe extended into the last third of the century and because new forms of antisemitism throughout Europe threatened to undo gains that had already been made, Jewish historical writing continued to serve defensive ends. It remained sensitive to the political context in which it was being read. In practice, this meant that scholars focused on those historical periods in which Jews seemed more like their neighbors (medieval Spain, renaissance Italy) and those cultural activities (philosophy, biblical studies, poetry) in which Jews and Christians shared a common interest. They created a sanitized (and distorted) picture of the Jewish past by emphasizing its rationalist and universalist dimensions and dwelling on its "outstanding" representatives and their "contributions." At the same time, they ignored, marginalized, or condemned the doings of those who offended or embarrassed them—wonderworkers, ascetics, mystics, messianists, alchemists, mintmasters, pawnbrokers, tax farmers, etc.[11]

The philosophical idealism that the earliest Jewish historians imbibed at university also left its mark. In a cultural setting in which intellectuals took ideas to be more "real" than material or corporeal realities, Jewish history was envisioned as a history of what Jews had thought (or, at best, a history of what they had suffered and thought). Even when the intellectual climate in Central Europe changed, Jewish history frequently continued to be written in this vein, in part because most historians came from a traditional milieu, in which their earliest and most intensive training was devoted to the interpretation of religious texts. External political pressure also contributed to this restricted notion of the content of Jewish history. In Central Europe, where emancipation was a long, bitterly contested process, Jews were under pressure to renounce or disclaim membership in a separate Jewish nation, for, the argument went, if they constituted a nation, they could not become members of the nation-states in which they were living. It became a commonplace in Jewish apologetics to claim that the Jewish people lost their collective national character after the destruction of Jerusalem in 70 C.E. This helps to explain why Jewish historians in the nineteenth century rarely endowed their subject with a political dimension, preferring to see the Jewish past largely as intellectual and religious history.

Yet, however much political pressures and academic canons influenced the writing of Jewish history, they failed to uproot one of the pillars of traditional historical consciousness among Jews: their central and distinctive place in the story of humankind. For centuries Jews had believed that their history was unique, different, exceptional, because God had chosen them alone to receive his law. Other nations were fated to decay and disappear, but the Jewish nation, however chastised, would endure and in the end reap its reward. In the nineteenth century, despite their professions of universalism, Jewish historians remained wedded to the idea of chosenness, albeit in a much transformed, universalized version. What set the Jews apart, they believed, was their historical role as bearers of the spirit and the idea of ethical monotheism. To them alone God entrusted the preservation of pure, universal truths. This variation on the uniqueness of Jewish history was especially characteristic of historical scholarship associated with the Reform movement, which, having de-emphasized Jewish behavioral particularism, needed to construct an ideological rationale for collective survival and continuity in the age of emancipation and beyond.

If Jewish integration into state and society before World War I had been more successful, this inclination to view Jewish history as unique—and thus not comparable in the end to other histories—would undoubtedly have weakened or perhaps even disappeared. The "normalization" of Jewish life in Europe would have been accompanied by the normalization of Jewish historical writing. This was, however, not to be the case. Throughout Europe the "Jewish Question" remained a matter of public concern, a topic of popular and intellectual debate, and, in some states, a lightning rod for deeply held political and cultural resentments. Not until the second half of the twentieth century did it cease to be so central an issue. In part because of this, the period from the 1870s through the 1940s was one of remarkable intellectual and political ferment in the Jewish world, with publicists, revolutionaries, and ideologues offering a rich spectrum of solutions to the Jewish Question, most of them variations on the themes of socialism, nationalism, and assimilationism. Since the Jews' fate and future[12] remained a matter of seemingly endless speculation, Jewish historical writing remained harnessed to ideological ends. It served both external, apologetic, defensive ends as well as internal, intracommunal, political ones. The work of every Jewish historian of note in this period—

Simon Dubnow, Yitzhak Baer, Ben Zion Dinur, Yehezkel Kauffman, Joseph Klausner, Gershom Scholem, Cecil Roth, Raphael Mahler, Maier Balaban, Jacob Shatzky—is infused with and shaped by his response to this ongoing debate. (The Galician-born, Viennese-educated Salo W. Baron, who spent most of his life in New York, teaching at Columbia University, is the one prominent exception.) Even in Great Britain and the United States, where the Jewish Question was less prominent than elsewhere, its impact on historical writing was still pervasive. For example, the agendas of the American Jewish Historical Society, which was established in 1892, and of its British counterpart, the Jewish Historical Society of England, which was founded the following year, reflected communal concerns about mass migration from Eastern Europe and the xenophobic, nativist storm it aroused in both countries. The publication programs of both institutions intended to demonstrate that Jewish settlement went back centuries (to Columbus's voyage, in the American case) and that Jewish contributions to the life of the nation were manifold and diverse.[13]

Because most Jewish historical scholarship before the midcentury mark was *engagé,* part and parcel of a passionate debate about the place of the Jews in the world and their future, it was in no position to view its subject in comparative perspective. It lacked the emotional distance needed to take a detached view of the historical process. With the fate of the Jewish people hanging in the balance, Jewish historians had immediate, pressing tasks: historical understanding for its own sake was a distraction or a luxury. And, for those scholars who believed that Jewish history was unique and timeless—that it, in Yitzhak Baer's words, "follows its own laws"[14]—a comparative approach was beside the point.

The Making of Jewish Historians

The indifference, even aversion, to comparative perspectives that has characterized the writing of Jewish history is also rooted in the institutional marginalization of the field from its origins until recent decades. Modern Jewish historiography developed outside the academy and remained there for several generations. Before World War II Central and West European universities did not teach postbiblical Jewish history (with one exception, which will be noted); indeed, the former were notorious for denying professorial appointments to Jews, whatever their subject. The writing of Jewish history fell to university-educated persons who found employment as communal and congregational rabbis, administrators of charities, teachers in Jewish schools, librarians, instructors in rabbinic and teachers seminaries, journalists and editors, and, from the 1920s, researchers in a handful of Jewish research institutes, such as YIVO in Vilna and the Akademie für die Wissenschaft des Judentums in Berlin. Cecil Roth, for example, worked as a free-lance writer and lecturer from the time he completed his doctoral dissertation in 1925 until he was appointed to a privately funded readership in postbiblical Jewish studies at Oxford in 1938, and even then the refusal of his alma mater, Merton College, to make him a fellow kept him on the periphery of university life. Moreover, those few Jews who held academic history posts were not inclined to draw attention to their origins by exhibiting professional interest in Jews. Their intellectual curiosity and career hopes were focused elsewhere—in better plowed, less "parochial" fields.

In the United States the situation differed only marginally.[15] Jewish history was taught at the Reform and Conservative rabbinical seminaries and at Hebrew colleges in Baltimore, Chicago, Boston, and Philadelphia but made no inroads into the academic mainstream until the appointment of Salo Baron to the Department of History at Columbia University in 1930. His appointment augured well for the normalization of Jewish historiography, at least in the United States. In the first issue of *Jewish Social Studies,* in 1939, he attacked what he called the idealistic approach to Jewish history, the view that an autonomous "inner" force (religious spirit or national will or character) was driving and shaping Jewish destiny. There was a growing feeling, he observed, that "historical explanations of the Jewish past must not fundamentally deviate from the general patterns of history which we accept for mankind at large or for any other particular national group."[16] Baron's appointment was a landmark, but his impact on the conceptualization of Jewish history, both in the United States and abroad, was limited before World War II and for several decades thereafter; in fact, it was not until the 1960s and 1970s, when his own doctoral students first received teaching positions in secular universities, that his influence began to be felt more widely.

In Israel the opening of the Hebrew University in Jerusalem in 1925 and other universities after 1948 provided an unprecedented institutional foundation for the teaching of Jewish history in an academic setting. Yet from the start the subject was considered part of the larger enterprise of the teaching of Jewish studies and was divorced, both in an intellectual and institutional sense, from other fields of historical research. In the decade following the appointment of Yitzhak Baer to the Hebrew University in

1930, which formally introduced Jewish history to the curriculum, the Jewish and "general" historians deliberated about where the former should be housed. Because the faculty of the Institute of Jewish Studies insisted that Jewish history deserved institutional recognition of its own, two separate departments were created.[17] To this day, with the exception of the smallest and newest of Israel's universities, Ben-Gurion in Beersheba, the academic study of Jewish history remains within a ghetto of its own making—in autonomous departments of Jewish history—isolated from broader trends in the profession, a situation that has strengthened inward-looking tendencies inherited from prewar European historiographical traditions.

These tendencies also received powerful reinforcement from the nationalist ideology that undergirded Israel's creation. The founding fathers of the Jewish historical establishment in Israel and their immediate successors were ideological Zionists of one stripe or another. While they rejected the assimilationist biases of *Wissenschaft des Judentums* and celebrated rather than erased Jewish particularism, they did not repudiate the traditional view that Jewish history was different, that it was the outcome of autonomous forces, that, to quote Baer again, there was "a power that lifts the Jewish people out of the realm of all causal history."[18] Where they differed was in their conviction that these forces were national and social rather than spiritual and religious.[19]

In the United States, however, the writing of Jewish history in the postwar period moved in a different direction, one foreshadowed in Baron's prewar views. Beginning in the 1970s, with the extraordinary expansion of Jewish studies courses in both liberal arts colleges and research universities, Jewish historical research and writing became increasingly integrated into mainstream academic life. Secular, not Jewish, educational institutions became home to most persons writing Jewish history. More secure, more "at home," in the United States than their predecessors, postwar historians were less inclined to engage in special pleading. The harsh political realities that nourished and long afterward continued to shape modern Jewish historiography softened or disappeared altogether, thus losing their immediate relevance to American Jews.[20] Indeed, in the last half-century the status and level of acceptance of American Jews soared to unimagined heights. In line with this unprecedented change the Jewish historians in their midst ceased to address overarching questions of Jewish existence and destiny (which is not to say that they were immune to the impact of extra-academic concerns and anxieties, such as those provoked by the Holocaust and Jewish demographic decline).[21]

Nonetheless, one must not exaggerate the extent of change. Old habits die hard. While Jewish historiography has lost much of its older ideological flavor, it still retains traces of its past. The inclination to view the history of religious ideas and movements as the privileged core of Jewish history is still strong, though not dominant, in part because substantial numbers of those who enter the field have received a traditional religious education, whose central feature is the interpretation of rabbinic texts. For them it is natural to view Jewish history as a vertical continuum of text-based ideas and scholarship. Moreover, their own immersion in communal life and religious practice, however strong their commitment to academic standards, inclines them to view the Jewish experience as somehow different, endowed with profound if not totally unique meanings and resonances. From this point it is a short step to the questionable conclusion that to compare the Jewish experience is to diminish or trivialize it somehow. (This does not explain, of course, a reluctance to pursue internal comparisons.)

Recent political trends in the United States also reinforce old habits of thinking about Jewish history. In some universities the teaching of Jewish history remains institutionally segregated, housed in a Jewish studies rather than history department, an arrangement echoing its departmental isolation in Israeli universities. In the American case this arrangement is often the outcome of pressures associated with the politics of ethnic, racial, and gender assertiveness that have buffeted campuses in recent decades. On urban campuses on which African-American and other student groups regularly make use of antisemitism, autonomous Jewish studies departments serve a symbolic political purpose, signaling public recognition of Jewish suffering and achievements. (In other cases university administrators, out of ignorance or shortsightedness, have placed Jewish historians in departments of religion.)

The politics of victimization, an outgrowth of the politics of ethnic assertiveness, also feeds this tendency to think about Jewish history in isolation from other histories. In an atmosphere in which groups link their cohesion and self-understanding to their prior mistreatment (slavery, the Holocaust, internment, patriarchalism), there is a disincentive to suggest comparing the experiences of victimized groups. The fear is that such comparisons will blur public awareness of past suffering and thus reduce the sympathy and support that this knowledge is believed to arouse. (This fear inevitability surfaces in discussions of the "uniqueness" or "comparability" of the Holocaust.) In the end, of course, any assertion of the historical uniqueness of a particular experience must rest on a comparative perspective, even if implicit, since the very idea of uniqueness implies dissimilarity, a quality that can be apprehended only through comparison.[22]

Comparing Jewish Societies

This volume is programmatic in intent: it seeks to make a case for viewing Jewish history in a comparative perspective. The essays collected here illustrate what is gained from making comparisons as well as, to be honest, what is lost. Their authors are a diverse group of historians and social scientists, some of whom do not see themselves as working in Jewish studies. What all have in common is their willingness to view Jewish data in a comparative context. For the social scientists in this group this comes naturally: it is integral to their training and their method. For the historians, on the other hand, the comparative perspective is an outlook acquired at a later stage in their careers, after their dissertations have become their first books and articles. It is no coincidence that the essays in this volume that appeared initially in *Comparative Studies in Society and History*—between 1970 and 1993—are the work of social scientists (with one exception), while those commissioned for the volume are the work of historians, who have come to the comparative method relatively recently. The essays of the latter group, drawn from larger projects on which they are currently working, reflect the changes in Jewish historical writing in the United States described in the previous section. (Again, it is no coincidence that the historians are American-trained and, with one exception, Nancy Green, teach in American universities.) Their work, however, is in no sense representative of the field as a whole, which remains methodologically conservative, indifferent or averse to making comparisons.

The logic of the comparative method comes from the biological and physical sciences, but, as William Sewell wrote in 1967, in historical research this experimental logic is adapted "to inquiries where a true experiment is impossible."[23] Indeed, at an earlier period social scientists commonly used macrosocial comparisons to demonstrate the validity of broad theoretical arguments as if there were little difference between their research and that of experimental lab-based scientists. They searched for— and found, of course—similarities and consistencies in a range of case studies from different historical contexts to prove the fruitfulness and correctness of theoretical insights. In one sense this kind of work gave the comparative method a bad name, especially among historians, who reproached it with generating forced analogies and arbitrary parallelisms. But, in fact, as Marc Bloch emphasized in a seminal statement in 1928, "the comparative method, rightly conceived, should involve specially lively interest in the perception of differences" as much as similarities.[24] It has the potential to expose what is individual, specific, and unique as much as what is more general.

Two basic methodological decisions undergird all comparative work: how the comparison is to be constructed and what scale of comparison is to be made. On both counts the essays here form a diverse collection. The first, most basic distinction is between those that make "internal" and those that make "external" comparisons. Representative of the former category is the first contribution of Stephen Sharot, a wide-ranging comparison of pre-modern Jewish communities in Europe, the Middle East, and Asia. Rejecting the notion that there is one universal, authentic Jewish pattern and that different historical communities embodied mere variations of that pattern, Sharot uses the comparative method and its ability to enhance differences to explore the influence of non-Jewish cultural and social environments on Jewish religious practices. By comparing the behavior of Jews across space and time, his internal comparison foregrounds external influences as explanations for variations in ritual behavior and religious syncretism. In her study of East European immigrants in New York, London, and Paris, Nancy Green takes a similar tack, seeking to understand the impact of different turn-of-the-century settings on immigrants from more or less similar backgrounds. Her exploration of the divergent paths taken by East European immigrants challenges, like Sharot's contribution, assumptions about the similarity of Jews the world over. At the same time she also indicates how the "divergent" comparative method differs from comparative perspectives more commonly used in discussions of Jewish immigration: "linear" studies, which compare the "before" and the "after" of the migration experience and thus invoke New World circumstances to explain change; and "convergent" studies, which explore differences among ethnic groups in the same locale and thus look to the Old World cultural baggage that accompanied them to explain these differences.[25]

Green makes explicit what is implicit in all internal comparisons: internal comparisons highlight external differences, that is, differences in the economic, cultural, and political conditions of the states or regions in which Jews live or lived. In his essay Hillel Kieval uses the ritual murder accusation against Jews in fin-de-siècle Europe to explore social and cultural tensions in four Central European towns. Seeking to understand why formal murder trials were staged in these four towns—at a time when the ritual murder accusation was resurgent in much of Central and Eastern Europe—Kieval brings into close view the cultural geographies of the trials, describing in detail local politics, social structures, intergroup relations, linguistic and nationalist tensions, and commercial activities. Comparing these cases allows him to distinguish between sufficient and necessary causes in the genesis of blood libel trials and to raise new questions about the relations between Jews and their neighbors in fin-de-siècle Europe. The sheer number and diverse character of the variables that he brings into play make clear, however, that the comparative method is at best an approximate, messy business, that, despite its debt to the experimental method in the physical and natural sciences, it is in no sense scientific in its results.

The contributors to this volume who make external comparisons—those between Jews and other groups living in more or less similar circumstances—highlight differences of another order, differences residing more within than without the group. Leo Spitzer's evocative account of the encounter between the indigenous Amerindian people of Bolivia and Central European Jewish refugees and his discussion of how each regarded the other brings into focus the pivotal role of cultural baggage. In a similar vein David Sorkin's essay on German Jewry in the years 1770–1830, in which he compares *haskalah,* emancipation, and assimilation to homologous developments within Germany or other Western states, introduces a breath of fresh air into discussions of Jewish modernization. In viewing German *haskalah* and Central European Reform Catholicism as parallel efforts to renew religious traditions in the light of the new science and philosophy of the eighteenth century, he brings into focus the specific character of the German *haskalah,* a much-debated issue in Jewish historiography. And, by pointing to differences between the two reform movements in terms of their relationship to the state and the nature of their support, Sorkin implicitly responds to those who fear that the comparative method blurs differences, running roughshod over the unique features of particular cases in order to demonstrate the universality of a theory. Indeed, his essay and others in this collection, such as Sammy Smooha's comparison of the handling of conflict in Northern Ireland and Israel, show how, in competent hands, the comparative method in no way compromises the historical integrity of individual cases.

In regard to the second methodological issue, the scale or level of comparison, a range of approaches, from carefully observed microsocial accounts to sweeping comparisons in the manner of Max Weber and his successors, are included here. At one extreme are the contributions of Aryei Fishman and Zachary Lockman, in which the units being compared—orthodox Zionist pioneers of East European and German background, in the first instance, and Arab and Jewish railroad workers under the British Mandate, in the second—are numerically small and their territorial and chronological boundaries limited. In studies like these, comparison is a more manageable, precise exercise than when carried out on a broader historical canvas. Yet the downside of carefully constructed small-scale comparative exercises is that their yield is more modest than macrohistorical studies in the grand manner. Their conclusions, however illuminating, reveal their true value only in combination with the results of countless other microstudies. At the opposite extreme from the Fishman and Lockman contributions are the two essays of Sharot, who brings to the study of Jewish religious behavior and movements the methods of classical historical sociology. The boldness of his approach, his willingness to weigh evidence from several epochs and continents in order to reveal the variables and relationships that determined patterns of religious behavior, tends to make historians uncomfortable, especially those who work on a more modest scale and hesitate to venture, at least in print, outside their own bailiwicks. In the nature of things comparative work on this scale cannot provide the nuanced explanations and finely shaded descriptions that characterize more narrowly conceived comparative studies. Still, in historical writing, as in life, it is hard to have one's cake and eat it too.

Shlomo Deshen's article, an analysis of the presentation of a Torah scroll in an Israeli development town during the 1965 general election, might seem at first reading to be out of place in a volume devoted to comparing Jewish societies, since, in fact, it is not overtly comparative in method. It has been included, however, because it adds another dimension to thinking about the study of Jewish societies in a comparative context. The conceptual tools that Deshen deploys in this essay grew from his disenchantment with once regnant sociological and anthropological approaches to religion. In comparing their assumptions about the workings of religion to the actual practice of traditional Judaism among North African Jews in Israel, he realized that there was an enormous gap—that comparison was not illuminating because these approaches were too ethnocentric, too tied to Christian European culture. So, in their place he developed a situational method employing abstract concepts of analysis that are not rooted in a particular religious culture. In the context of this volume his contribution demonstrates the fruitfulness of comparison in revealing the hidden assumptions in the established, "canonical" texts of history and the social sciences.

Conclusion

The institutional isolation in which Jewish historians worked from the start of the modern period began to weaken two or three decades ago. The creation of Jewish history positions in departments of history in universities across North America encouraged a process of historiographical normalization or assimilation, broadening the concepts and paradigms with which Jewish historians worked. The writing of Jewish history became livelier and more sophisticated, attracting the interest even of practitioners beyond its own borders. It would, however, be misleading to talk of the triumph of the new over the old. For one thing, much Jewish history continues to be written in institutional settings that are detached from the usual academic units in which historians are housed—in seminaries, departments of Jewish studies, and, in the Israeli context, departments of Jewish history. In addition, nonacademic commitments and well-entrenched modes of thinking about Jews and their religion continue to hold sway.

Thus, however profound the impact of institutional integration, it is fair to characterize the field *as a whole,* even at present, as intellectually conservative, that is, as less sensitive to the concerns and issues that dominate other, more mainstream historical fields. This has led some critics and reviewers, outsiders to the field in most cases, to brand Jewish historians as parochial, old-fashioned, and self-absorbed. By now this kind of criticism, which often reveals more about the reviewer than about his or her familiarity with the field, has become stale. In this introduction I have tried to avoid this kind of morally charged criticism and to explain, rather than damn or defend, how the writing of Jewish history came to be what it has been and how it has started to be transformed. In doing so, and in collecting the articles in this volume, my intent has been to stimulate those who do Jewish history to think about their field in new ways. To avoid being misunderstood, let me make clear that I harbor no overblown illusions about the redemptive powers of comparative history. It is not my contention that comparing Jewish societies will usher in a new age of historical wisdom or reveal hitherto unknown secrets. My hopes and claims are more modest: to suggest that Jewish history, with its lack of territorial focus, offers laboratory-like opportunities for making comparisons and that doing so can generate new, intellectually engaging questions and provide sharper, more finely tuned answers to new and old questions. Each essay in this collection can stand alone as a contribution to its own discrete field of inquiry; together they demonstrate the fruits of thinking in comparative terms about the development of Jewish societies across time and place.

NOTES

I completed the editing of this volume during the academic year 1995–96 while holding the Steelcase Research Professorship at the Institute for the Humanities at the University of Michigan. I am grateful to the institute's director, James Winn, and its wonderful staff for providing me with such congenial surroundings in which to work on this and other projects. I also want to express my heartfelt thanks to Amy Hamermesh of the Frankel Center for Judaic Studies for helping me with a host of computer-related problems. Without her assistance my task would have been far more onerous. Ray Grew, Rainer Liedtke, and Maud Mandel—themselves practitioners of comparative history—took time from their own work to read and comment on this introduction, for which I am most grateful.

1. Seymour Martin Lipset, "The Study of Jewish Communities in a Comparative Context," *Jewish Journal of Sociology* 5 (1963): 157–66, reprinted in *The Ghetto and Beyond: Essays on Jewish Life in America,* ed. Peter I. Rose (New York: Random House, 1969), 21–32; Stephen Sharot, "Minority Situation and Religious Acculturation: A Comparative Analysis of Jewish Communities," *Comparative Studies in Society and History* 16 (1974): 329–54. A revised version of Sharot's article is published in this volume.

2. Gerson D. Cohen, *Messianic Postures of Ashkenazim and Sephardim,* Leo Baeck Memorial Lecture 9 (New York: Leo Baeck Institute, 1967); Yosef H. Yerushalmi, *Assimilation and Racial Anti-Semitism: The Iberian and the German Models,* Leo Baeck Memorial Lecture 26 (New York: Leo Baeck Institute, 1982).

3. Jacob Katz, *Out of the Ghetto: The Social Background of Jewish Emancipation, 1770–1870* (Cambridge, MA: Harvard University Press, 1973), 3–4.

4. The best introduction to Jewish historical writing from its biblical origins to the present is Yosef Hayim Yerushalmi, *Zakhor: Jewish History and Jewish Memory* (Seattle: University of Washington Press, 1982). See also Amos Funkenstein, *Perceptions of Jewish History* (Berkeley: University of California Press, 1993).

5. Yerushalmi, *Zakhor,* xiv.

6. In the introduction to *Perceptions of Jewish History* Amos Funkenstein writes that "a modicum of historical awareness" also existed among the creators of

and commentators on *halakhah*, who, for juridical reasons, maintained clear distinctions of time and place in the commentaries, codes, novellas, and responsa that they produced.

7. It has been argued that in the absence of a Jewish state (between 70 and 1948) the political foundation for a national historiographical tradition was missing. But on reflection this turns out to explain little, for, while it is true that in recent centuries nationalism has stimulated the writing of history, much historiographical work in the past occurred outside the framework of (1) nation-states, (2) nationalist movements, and (3) strong political units of any kind. Moreover, the absence of political sovereignty after 70 did not impede Jews from thinking of themselves as a nation.

8. On the emergence of modern Jewish historical scholarship, see Ismar Schorsch, *From Text to Context: The Turn to History in Modern Judaism* (Hanover, NH: University Press of New England, 1994).

9. At the outset of the emancipation struggle, the only comprehensive postbiblical history of the Jews in a European language was that of the Huguenot minister Jacques Basnage. *L'Histoire et la religion des Juifs depuis Jésus Christ jusqu'à présent* appeared in Rotterdam in seven volumes between 1706 and 1711. A revised edition, in fifteen volumes, was published in The Hague between 1716 and 1721. An English translation was published in London in 1706 and a condensed, two-volume English edition in 1708. The only sympathetic European-language guide to Judaism was Leon Modena's *Historia de' riti hebraici*. Written in Venice in Italian in 1614 and 1615, it was first published, in Paris, in 1637. An English edition appeared in 1650. On Basnage, see Miriam Yardeni, "Yahadut ve-yehudim be-einei ha-golim ha-protestantiyim ha-tsarfatiyim she-be-holland (1685–1715) (Judaism and the Jews in the Eyes of the French Protestant Exiles in Holland), in *Mehkarim be-toldot am-yisrael ve-erets yisrael le-zekher zvi avneri* (Studies in the History of the Jews and the Land of Israel in Memory of Zvi Avneri), ed. A. Gilboa et al. (Haifa: Haifa University Press, 1970), 163–85; "New Concepts of Post-Commonwealth Jewish History in the Early Enlightenment: Bayle and Basnage," *European Studies Review* 7 (1977): 245–58.

10. See especially Ismar Schorsch's essay "Scholarship in the Service of Reform" in his collection *From Text to Context.*

11. On the impact of *Wissenschaft des Judentums* on the agenda of modern Jewish historical scholarship, see Gershom Scholem, "Mi-tokh hirhurim al hokhmat yisrael" (Reflections on the Science of Judaism), in *Devarim be-go: pirkei morashah ve-tehiyyah* (Essays on Heritage and Revival), 2 vols. (Tel Aviv: Am Oved, 1976), 2:385–403; Ismar Schorsch "The Myth of Sephardi Supremacy," *From Text to Context,* 71–93.

12. This phrase is taken from the title of a work by the early Zionist sociologist Arthur Ruppin, *The Jewish Fate and Future,* trans. E. W. Dickes (London: Macmillan, 1940).

13. David Cesarani, "Dual Heritage or Duel of Heritages? Englishness and Jewishness in the Heritage Industry"; and Tony Kushner, "The End of the 'Anglo-Jewish Progress Show': Representations of the Jewish East End, 1887–1987," in *The Jewish Heritage in British History: Englishness and Jewishness,* ed. Tony Kushner (London: Frank Cass, 1992), 29–41, 78–105; John J. Appel, "Hansen's Third Generation Law and the Origins of the American Jewish Historical Society," *Jewish Social Studies* 23 (1961): 3–20.

14. Yitzhak F. Baer, *Galut,* trans. Robert Warshow (New York: Schocken Books, 1947), 122.

15. On the development of Jewish studies in general in American universities, see Paul Ritterband and Harold S. Wechsler, *Jewish Learning in American Universities: The First Century* (Bloomington: Indiana University Press, 1994).

16. Salo W. Baron, "Emphases in Jewish History," *Jewish Social Studies* 1 (1939), reprinted in *History and Jewish Historians: Essays and Addresses,* ed. Arthur Hertzberg and Leon A. Feldman (Philadelphia: Jewish Publication Society, 1964), 77–78.

17. David N. Myers, *Re-Inventing the Jewish Past: European Jewish Intellectuals and the Zionist Return to History* (New York: Oxford University Press, 1995), 112.

18. Baer, *Galut,* 120.

19. The weakening of ideology in Israeli public life, a trend that can be traced back to the invasion of Lebanon in 1982, if not earlier, has also had an impact on Israeli historiography, in particular on work concerning Zionism and the early years of the state. See the special issue "Israeli Historiography Revisited" of *History and Memory: Studies in Representations of the Past* 7, no. 1 (Spring–Summer 1995). The growing presence of American-trained Jewish historians in the ranks of Israeli universities also has contributed to diluting the strong ideological character of Israeli-based Jewish historiography.

20. Today, as in the past, most historians of the Jews are themselves Jews. Only in Poland and Germany, where few Jews remain, is the writing of Jewish history in non-Jewish hands and thus disconnected from broader communal concerns. But in these cases, of course, it is linked to and shaped by powerful and complex emotions deriving from German and Polish treatment of Jews in the past. As Jewish historical writing in the United States, however, becomes less an ethnic enterprise and more a disinterested academic one, the composition of its practiners seems destined, at least in the long run, to become more mixed.

21. For one example of the impact of the Holocaust on recent scholarship about earlier periods in American and European history, see Todd M. Endelman, "The Legitimization of the Diaspora Experience in Recent Jewish Historiography," *Modern Judaism* 11 (1991): 195–209.

22. This receives confirmation in Steven T. Katz's work on the phenomenological and historical uniqueness of the Holocaust. At the heart of this ongoing, multivolume project is an intensive exercise in comparative history. For a summary, see

Steven T. Katz, *The Holocaust and Comparative History,* Leo Baeck Memorial Lecture 37 (New York: Leo Baeck Institute, 1993).

23. William H. Sewell Jr., "Marc Bloch and the Logic of Comparative History," *History and Theory* 6 (1967): 209.

24. Marc Bloch, "A Contribution towards a Comparative History of European Societies," *Land and Work in Medieval Society,* trans. J. E. Anderson (Berkeley: University of California Press, 1967), 58.

25. See also Nancy L. Green, "The Comparative Method and Poststructural Structuralism—New Perspectives for Migration Studies," *Journal of American Ethnic History* 13, no. 4 (Summer 1994): 3–21.

Religious Syncretism and Religious Distinctiveness: A Comparative Analysis of Pre-Modern Jewish Communities

Stephen Sharot

The Comparative Approach and Jewish Communities

The revival of comparative historical sociology in the last two decades has had little influence on the study of Judaism and Jewish communities. When Jewish historians make comparisons, it is generally in order to highlight the uniqueness of a particular community on which their studies are focused, rather than to demonstrate and explain similarities and differences among a number of communities.[1] Comparative studies of Jewish communities by sociologists have tended to be of two types: comparisons of pre-emancipation European communities with communities of the modern era, often taking the United States as the model of modernity and emphasizing that "America is different";[2] and comparisons of the Judaism and the Jewishness of the communities of the United States and Israel.[3] Sociological comparisons of traditional, or pre-modern, Jewish communities have been one of the lacunae in the narrow span of comparative Jewish studies.

The infrequency of the explicit application of the comparative perspective in Jewish studies might, at first, appear surprising because the fact that Jews have lived in many different societies would seem to invite the comparative approach. Yet among Jewish historians and social scientists of traditional Jewish communities there has been a tendency to assume the existence of a basic Jewish pattern and to characterize the different communities as variations of that pattern. This tendency is linked to the presupposition that the survival of the Jews as a distinctive people in pre-mod-

23

ern contexts is to be explained by their religious separatism. The commitment and devotion of traditionalist Jews to their religion and the nature of that religion, its ritualism and halakhic regulation, is frequently put forward to account for Jewish continuity and the singularity of Jewry wherever Jews were found. The Jewish religion is said to account for the survival of the Jews, "despite persecution," as in Europe, and "despite tolerance," as in traditional China and precolonial India.[4] One implication of this argument is that secularization, the decline in the social significance of religion, poses a threat to the continuation of diaspora Jewish communities in the modern era. An alternative argument, that Jews survived into modern times because they constituted a "people-class" of merchants and financiers and that their problems in the modern era are a consequence of the loss of their economic niche, has attracted little support outside certain Marxist circles.[5]

An emphasis on the universal, unifying functions of the Jewish religion for Jewish communities has inhibited the application of a comparative approach that seeks to relate variant cultural and religious developments among Jewish communities to non-Jewish social and cultural environments. Such a comparative approach was advanced over thirty years ago by S. M. Lipset, who wrote that "the comparative study of the Jew must be linked inseparably with the comparative study of the Gentile." Lipset gave little indication of how comparative studies of Jewish communities should systematically be carried out, and he somewhat confused his case by contrasting the comparative approach with studies that investigated the extent to which Jewish communities were losing or retaining their Jewishness. He wrote that a study of the Jews organized around the maintenance or decline of Jewishness may be justified from a religious perspective but could not be justified from an intellectual perspective.[6] It is not clear, however, why studies of varying degrees of Jewish religious or cultural distinctiveness should be opposed to the comparative approach. Lipset related how differences in the cultural practices and organization of Jewish communities may be accounted for by differences in the cultures and organizations of Gentile environments, but he made no explicit reference to the fact that Jewish adoption of Gentile culture and organizational forms is itself problematic. In other words, Lipset did not pose the question of why some Jewish communities are more like their Gentile neighbors than others. Asking this question does not presuppose an authentic or essential Jewish culture or Judaism that provides a benchmark for comparative purposes and in relationship to which the Judaism of different communities can be judged as more or less Jewish. Like all religions, Judaism has never stopped changing, and it may be argued that all changes, whether they are in a syncretistic or separatist direction, are in part responses and adaptations to non-Jewish environments.

A comparison of Jewish communities with respect to their relative cultural similarities to, and differences from, non-Jewish societal contexts requires a consideration of cultural items in terms of the distinctiveness that they lend to the communities. Comparative statements regarding differences in food, dress, etiquette, folklore, games, language, religion, and so on are not easy because the distinctiveness of the item will depend on its meanings and symbolic values, which are likely to vary among societies and among different contexts in a single society. Religion is one of the most important symbolic foci that provide the bases for the identity of minorities and ethnic groups, and in traditional societies, in which the social significance of religion extends to most institutions, religious differences are likely to be the bases of cultural distinctiveness. In modern societies the extent to which Jewish communities are distinctive from, or similar to, the wider environment is related to the degree of secularization. With few exceptions the Jewish communities of the modern diaspora that have retained a high level of cultural distinctiveness are those sectarian communities, such as the *hasidim* and other ultraorthodox groups, who have fought against the intrusion of secularization and have continued to make little differentiation between religion and culture. All traditional societies are characterized by the pervasiveness of religion, and a comparison of pre-modern Jewish communities with respect to variations in cultural distinctiveness does not, therefore, involve comparisons of the relative importance of religion. A comparison of cultural distinctiveness among pre-modern Jewish communities cannot be separated from a comparison of their religious syncretism with, and distinctiveness from, coterritorial non-Jewish religions, and it is on these religious differences that this essay will focus.

Dispersal

The migration of Jews in the ancient and medieval periods brought them to societies that differed greatly in religion and social structure. Jewish communities in four geographical-cultural areas will be compared in this essay: the communities of the Islamic Middle East (understood here to include North Africa), China, India, and the region known in Hebrew as

Ashkenaz, principally Central and Eastern Europe. The conquests of the Arabs brought about 90 percent of the Jewish population under Islam, and, although some Jews converted to Islam, the number of Jews increased in the centuries after the conquests, and Jewish communities spread throughout the Middle East.[7] Communication among the communities was precarious in the first centuries of Arab political unification, improved between the tenth and the thirteenth centuries, and declined thereafter. The political divisions of the Islamic Middle East separated the Jewish communities from one another, and many developed religious customs independently of the others. A number of subcultural areas of Middle Eastern Jewry have been distinguished: Morocco, the Fertile Crescent (including Egypt, Palestine, Syria, and Iraq), Turkey, Yemen, Kurdistan, and Persia.[8]

From the area of the first diaspora, the Middle Eastern and Mediter-ranean territories, the Jews dispersed farther north and west into Europe, while a smaller number settled farther south in the Sahara and farther east in the Caucasus, Turkistan, Afghanistan, India, and China. There is evi-dence of a Jewish community in Cologne in the first half of the fourth century C.E., and it is likely that Jews settled in several other localities in the Rhineland in Roman times, but evidence of the uninterrupted settle-ment of Jews who came to be known as Ashkenazim begins only from the ninth century. Jews remained concentrated on the Mediterranean coast in the early Middle Ages, and it is between the eleventh and thirteenth cen-turies that new Jewish settlements were established in the heartlands of Germany, France, and England. Expulsions from the end of the thir-teenth century resulted in the migration of the Ashkenazim eastward, and from the seventeenth century Eastern Europe was the major center of Ashkenazic Jewry.[9]

The presence of Jews in China is documented from the eighth century C.E., and there are indications of settled Jewish communities in China from the ninth century. Various sources, Chinese, Christian, and Arab, refer to Jews living in a number of Chinese towns in the thirteenth and fourteenth centuries, but after 1342 there are no further reports until the middle of the sixteenth century, when Jesuit missionaries began to report on their meet-ings with Chinese Jews in the city of Kaifeng. At the beginning of the sev-enteenth century the seven hundred or so Jews in Kaifeng made up the sole remaining Jewish Chinese community, and when the last synagogue was demolished, around 1860, there remained only a few impoverished indi-viduals who identified themselves as Jews.[10]

The existence of the Cochin Jews on the Malabar coast of southwestern India from the tenth century is firmly established, but the origins and date of settlement of the more numerous Bene Israel in the Konkan region, close to Bombay, are obscure: a reference by Maimonides suggests that a Jewish community, other than the Cochinis, existed in India in the twelfth century, but the earliest written mention of Jews permanently settled in the Konkan region appears only in 1738. The Indian communities retained their demographic viability, and the majority migrated to Israel after the foundation of the state.[11]

Initial Dispositions and Minority Situations

In whatever part of the world Jews found themselves, it is a reasonable assumption that they were initially disposed to maintain the distinctiveness of their religion and some degree of social distance from non-Jews. Although ancient Judaism had been syncretistic in its formative stages, it developed relatively distinctive forms with clearly defined boundaries that set it off from other religions. A great emphasis was put on the maintenance of monotheism and its protection from the "idolatrous" beliefs and practices of non-Jews. The Bible and the *aggadah* provided the records that accounted for the distinction of Jewry from other nations, and the consciousness of election governed the development of talmudic Judaism, which multiplied the precepts and prohibitions intended to separate Jews from Gentiles.

The Talmud developed at a time when the demographic concentration of Jews in a few areas enabled them to maintain communities that were largely self-sufficient in economic and social life. Babylonia was the most important center of Jewry from at least the third century, and the Babylonian Talmud, which was codified about 500 C.E., was accepted by most Jewish communities as authoritative, rather than the Jerusalem Talmud. Babylonian Jewry continued to be the center of talmudic study until the eleventh century, and from Persia the authority of the Babylonian Talmud came to be accepted by most Jews under Islam and, in the last centuries of the first millennium, by the growing Jewish communities in Europe. The Jews who founded communities as far east as India and China were most likely to have come from Persia or from other talmudic communities of the Near East.[12] Thus, at the time of widespread settlement over many parts of the world Judaism had become clearly identified with a particular people, and the Talmud was widely diffused.

Judaism was a boundary-maintaining religion and relatively intolerant toward other religions, but Jews migrated to societies with religions that differed considerably in their permeability or insularity and in their tolerance or intolerance toward other religions. These religious differences were likely to affect the extent to which Jews maintained or strengthened their religious distinctiveness or, alternatively, developed in a more syncretistic direction. In addition to their religious differences the societies to which Jews migrated differed also in their social, economic, and political structures. It has been argued that the Jews' religion produced their social separation even though they lived with non-Jews in common socioeconomic and political structures, but it may also be argued that the extent to which Jews emphasized their religious separation depended on the characteristics of the social structures of the host societies and the positions that the Jews held within those structures.

The social structures and the structural locations of the Jews determined the types and possibilities of social interaction between Jews and Gentiles. The dependence of Jews on the products and economic services of non-Jews made total social isolation impossible, but this left a wide range of possibilities, from minimal contacts, restricted to highly formal secondary relationships, to an extensive and wide variety of contacts, including friendship and intermarriage. The range and nature of social contacts with Gentiles would in turn affect Jewish religious orientations. The central argument of this essay is that an explanation of variations in Jewish religious distinctiveness and syncretism is to be found by a comparison of the non-Jewish religions and the social structures of the societies in which Jews lived.

The process by which Jews adopted into their own religion the religious beliefs and practices of the wider society and the process by which Jews strengthened and elaborated their religious distinctiveness can enter into a dialectical relationship; the religious influences from the wider society may be met by countervailing forces that seek to oppose those influences and insulate the minority religion. Syntheses may emerge whereby borrowings from the environment are reinterpreted and judaized in a way that restates Jewish religious distinctiveness. The emergent practices might at the same time express the linkages with the non-Jewish society and Jewish distinctiveness.

The transformation of beliefs and practices from the Gentile environment into distinctive Jewish forms was accommodated by the centrality of religious texts in talmudic Judaism and the availability of religious elites to interpret them. Popular rites that were shared with Gentiles could be refashioned and made more distinctively Jewish by interpreting them through the mediation of authoritative texts.[13] Jewish religious distinctiveness was more likely to be attenuated where the religious texts were absent or lost and where there was no scholarly elite to shape syncretism into separatism.

The problems involved in explaining variations in Jewish religious separatism and syncretism among widely different societies have to be acknowledged. A comparative analysis of Jewish communities within societies that share important characteristics is likely to be more fruitful than a comparison within societies that differ in fundamental ways. Within a narrower range of comparison it would be possible to "control" common factors, treating them as parameters, and then proceed to examine the influence of the factor or factors that are not held in common. A comparison of Jewish communities in traditionalist settings restricts the comparison to societies in which religion, whether insular or permeable, is socially significant throughout the society. Pre-modern Jewish communities were situated, however, in societies (Middle East, India, China, and Europe) that differed greatly in the characteristics of their religions and social structures. The cultural and social environments are different in so many respects that it is impossible to control each of the possible influences in order to show their relative importance. My approach has been to begin by comparing communities that differ very widely with respect to their non-Jewish sociocultural environments and then go on to compare communities in sociocultural environments that are similar in a number of significant respects. As the range of comparisons becomes more restricted, as in a comparison of Western Jewish communities, certain factors relevant to the wider range, such as different world religions, can be treated as parameters. It is hoped that a comparison of communities in vastly different environments will at least point to the most significant factors accounting for very gross differences in religious distinctiveness and syncretism.

Religious Syncretism and Distinctiveness

An obvious place to begin a comparison of religious syncretism and distinctiveness among Jewish communities is the Middle East. In contrast with the Far East and Europe, Jews had not transplanted their culture to an alien environment but were, from the outset, very much part of the indigenous culture. The expansion of the Arab empire facilitated the widespread dispersion of Jews over the Middle East, but in many areas they were established long before the advent of Islam. In its formative stages Islam incorporated many religious, legal, and moral conceptions from the Jews, and, although the boundaries between Islam and Judaism were clearly drawn by both religions, Jews and Muslims continued to share many beliefs and practices. It is often difficult to know the direction of the influence of the two religions on each other, but the general tendency is for a dominant majority to influence a subordinate minority.

Outwardly, there was little to distinguish Jews from Muslims: Jews developed variants of the local forms of Arabic but basically they spoke the same language, and, despite occasional regulations seeking to differentiate Muslim and Jewish dress, their styles in clothes were similar or identical. It has been said that the Middle Eastern Jews were "Arab in all but religion," but this phrase assumes that a clear distinction between religious and secular areas of culture can be made in pre-modern societies. In fact, a minority's adoption of the dominant language was bound to have implications for its religion. By about 1000 C.E. the majority of Middle Eastern Jews had, like the rest of the population, adopted Arabic,[14] and this involved the adoption of religious concepts and ways of thinking that were expressed in Arabic. The Jews used Arabic for translating and teaching the Bible as well as discussing Jewish law and ritual.

There was considerable overlap between the religious little traditions of Jews and Muslims. One central cult, which had many pre-Islamic elements but which was brought into the framework of both Islam and Judaism in the Middle East, especially in North Africa, was that of pilgrimage to the tombs of saints. Both Muslims and Jews sought the intercession and protection of saints (sometimes the same saints), placing candles and oil lamps on their shrines and performing rituals by their tombs. Family pilgrimages were made when important family events occurred, and collective pilgrimages were made on the anniversary of the death of the saint. Other shared supernaturalist beliefs and practices were associated with sorcery, divination, ecstatic prophecy, demons, the evil eye, the magical significance of numbers, and the protective power of amulets. Jews were also influenced by more "orthodox" Islamic practices: the short, intense features of Muslim prayer impressed Jews, whose own religious services displayed far more decorum than the services of European Jews.[15]

Extensive cultural borrowing did not necessarily detract from attachment to great tradition Judaism as written in the sacred books and interpreted by religious specialists. An analysis of Jewish wedding ceremonies in Tripolitania has shown that, while there were clear Muslim cultural influences, Jews would draw upon the sacred texts of Judaism to interpret and reinterpret the wedding customs in a way that would assert their Jewishness. The *mimuna,* a festival particular to Moroccan Jews that celebrates the end of Passover, demonstrates a complex dynamic between the cultural influence of the environment and the cultural expressions of Jewish particularity. The themes and symbols of the festival, expressing fertility and renewal, had their counterpart in a Muslim festival, and Muslims contributed to the Jewish festival by selling or providing bread and greenery as gifts. The Passover, celebrating the exodus from Egypt, involved practices, such as the eating of unleavened bread, that represented a withdrawal of Jews from non-Jews, while the *mimuna* represented a reintegration into the wider milieu, with Jews indicating their commonality with the wider population by wearing the costumes of Muslims. The concentration of Jews in urban occupations meant that they were dependent on Muslim peasants for agricultural produce. The Muslims, in turn, would approve those Jewish rituals involving fertility. The various Jewish interpretations of the festival that sought to find its origins in Jewish tradition may have served to camouflage its obvious links with the Muslim cultural environment.[16]

The distinctiveness of Middle Eastern Jewish communities as religious minorities varied greatly, even among those who had little or no contact with other Jewish communities. There are few anthropological studies of traditionalist Middle Eastern Jewish communities outside Israel before their disintegration after 1948, but two studies, one of Jews in northeastern Iraq and the other of Jews in the northwestern Sahara of Algeria, provide interesting cases for comparison, especially since both communities had no significant contact with other Jewish communities. In the former case the Jewish culture demonstrated many similarities with the Kurdish Muslim culture: in addition to sharing values with respect to marriage, family, and honor, they also held common magical beliefs and worshiped at the same holy graves. The Jews observed the Sabbath, dietary regulations, and laws of family purity, but their religion was maintained mostly by oral tradition; they had virtually no knowledge of the Talmud, and religious learning was not important.[17] In contrast, the Jewish community in Ghardaia in the northwestern Sahara shared few religious practices with neighboring Muslims. They adhered rigidly to traditional Jewish values and practices, prayed in the synagogue three times a day, and highly valued religious learning. Integrated with the great tradition were local magicoreligious practices whose historical origins were often lost, but only a few of them were held in common with Muslims. The customs peculiar to the Ghardaia Jews sometimes functioned to uphold great tradition values; for example, at the age of five every boy had to undergo an elaborate ceremonial initiation that served to dramatize the importance of religious learning for Jewish males.[18]

Although the Middle Eastern communities varied greatly in their religious distinctiveness and syncretism, most of them were neither as highly syncretistic as the communities of China and India nor as highly distinctive as the pre-emancipation European communities. The first Jews to settle in Kaifeng had probably been merchants from Persia,[19] and there is little doubt that they were familiar with talmudic Judaism. Many of the community's texts, possibly including talmudic tractates, were destroyed by a flood in 1642, but salvaged texts, including Torah scrolls, were transcribed, and the prayer books that survived into the nineteenth century included liturgies for the Sabbath and festivals.[20] It appears, however, that Chinese influences entered the Jews' beliefs and practices at an early stage, and visitors from the West in the seventeenth and eighteenth centuries found highly acculturated Jews who dressed like other Chinese, spoke the same language, ate the same food, worked in the same occupations, and married non-Jewish Chinese, absorbing the non-Jewish women into the community. The religion of the Chinese Jews combined certain distinctively Jewish beliefs and practices with beliefs and practices from the Confucian, Buddhist, and Taoist religions.

The Jesuits, whose reports have to be interpreted with care, took note of the Chinese Jews' impaired knowledge of Hebrew and of Jewish religious law and custom, but they reported on beliefs that were regarded as Jewish such as belief in one God, judgment in the hereafter, and the resurrection of the dead and on practices such as observance of the Sabbath and some festivals, circumcision, and abstinence from pork. The influence of the religious environment was clearly visible in the architecture of the Jewish temple, the use of non-Jewish ritual objects, the observance of Chinese seasonal festivals, ancestor worship, the absorption of Chinese rituals into rites of passage, and the use of inscriptions written on stone tablets for the transmission of religious beliefs. Although the temple did not contain images or statues of ancestors and gods, the Chinese Jews burned incense and made offerings to their ancestors as well as to biblical figures and Confucius. The inscriptions on stone tablets and temple archways were written in Chinese, used Chinese terms for God, contained quotations from Confucian writings, and proclaimed that the principles of Confucianism and the religion of the Chinese Jews were the same. Expressions of the common and parallel elements in Judaism and Confucianism were already evident on a stele from the year 1489, and this message was reiterated in subsequent inscriptions with many favorable references to the literature and doctrines of Confucianism. Such moral precepts as devotion to parents and the emperor, reverence for ancestors, and the pursuit of learning were held to demonstrate the commonality of the two religions.[21]

Unlike the Chinese Jews, who were totally assimilated into the non-Jewish population in the end, the Cochin and Bene Israel communities in India remained demographically viable, but during their periods of isolation from other Jewish communities their Judaism lost much of its distinctiveness. They adopted many Hindu customs and were assimilated into the caste system. The isolation of the Cochin Jews was much less complete than that of the Bene Israel, but it is evident from thirteenth-century tombstones that the Cochin Jews had at that time an imperfect knowledge of Hebrew and the Bible, and evidence from more recent times shows that they shared folk symbols, heroes, and folksongs with neighboring Hindus, Muslims, and Christians.[22] The Cochin were divided into subcastes of "white" and the more numerous "black" Jews; the latter were probably descendants of converts from and intermarriages with the indigenous population. Taboos on intermarriage and free social contacts, as well as outbursts of antagonism, characterized the relationships between the two subcastes.[23] The white Cochinis had more contacts with, and were consequently more influenced by, the European, mainly Sephardi, Jews who arrived with the European colonial powers. At the end of the seventeenth century a Sephardi Jew from Amsterdam recorded that Cochini rites were similar to those of his own community, but he noted certain unusual features, such as the congregation going barefoot in the synagogue.[24]

The Bene Israel in the Konkan occupied a low caste position of oil pressers, and they were known as Saturday Oilmen because they rested their oxen on Saturday, as opposed to the Hindu Monday Oilmen, who rested their oxen on Monday.[25] Little is known of the religion of the Bene Israel prior to their "discovery" by Christian missionaries and Cochini Jews. The missionaries taught them to read and understand Hebrew and provided them with the Jewish Bible in Marathi, and the Cochinis introduced them to the liturgy and laws of talmudic Judaism. Prior to these influences the Bene Israel did not have the Bible, the Talmud, or Hebrew prayer books. Their only Hebrew prayer was the *shema,* which was repeated on many ritual occasions, including circumcision, marriage, and death. What appeared to outsiders to be the remnants of Judaism included the observance of Saturday as a day of rest, circumcision on the eighth day, some dietary restrictions, and the celebration of certain festivals that were similar in content and time of observance to Jewish festivals.

If the forebears of the Saturday Oilmen had been talmudic Jews, their Judaism had clearly undergone extreme attenuation over time, and there had been massive acculturation to the religious beliefs and practices of their Hindu and Muslim neighbors. Shared customs included ceremonial food offerings, certain marriage and funeral rites, and refraining from the remarriage of widows and from eating beef. In those places in which they did not have their own cemeteries, the Bene Israel buried their dead in Muslim cemeteries. The relative influence of Muslims and Hindus on the Bene Israel cannot be estimated because the Muslims were themselves heavily influenced by Hinduism, and all religious groups in India were incorporated into the caste system.[26] The Bene Israel were divided into two subcastes, the Gora (white) and the Kala (black). The Gora, who claimed they were the pure descendants of the original Jewish settlers, were considered to be higher in caste than the Kala, but, in contrast to the subcastes of the Cochin Jews, the Bene Israel subcastes did not differ in skin color, the Gora were more numerous than the Kala, and the Kala were permitted to pray in Gora places of worship.[27]

The fasts and festivals of the Bene Israel had Marathi names, and their observances point to considerable syncretism: the Feast of the New (Year) and the Holiday of the Closing of the Doors corresponded to Rosh Hashanah and Yom Kippur; the Feast of (partaking of) Khir corresponded to the Feast of Tabernacles; the Feast of Holi, a Hindu festival of a carnival nature, synchronized with Purim; the Festival of Jar Closing, in which a jar containing a sour source mixture was covered up and opened after eight days, corresponded to Passover (but with no reference to the deliverance from Egypt); and the Fast of Birda, which was broken at the end of the day by the partaking of Birda curry, corresponded to the Ninth of Av.[28] A complex of beliefs and rituals unique to the Bene Israel was centered on Eliyohu (Elijah), and an annual pilgrimage was made to a village where Elijah was said to have appeared and then ascended to heaven.

A ceremony that paralleled similar ceremonies among both Hindus and Muslims was that of Malida, the Feast of Eliyohu, which was undertaken to show thanks and fulfill obligations to the divine on such occasions as recovering from an illness or completing a journey.[29] The origins of the Malida ceremony are unknown, but it appears to have involved some judaization of Hindu ceremonies in which offerings are made to gods or divine patrons. In comparison, the Holiday of the Closing of the Doors involved the adaptation of a Jewish holiday, Yom Kippur, to the ritual framework of the caste system and the expansion of Jewish motifs through the incorporation of Hindu modes. On the day of the holiday the Bene Israel atoned for their sins by living like Hindu ascetic-renouncers and secluding themselves behind locked doors, thereby avoiding all contact with, and pollution from, non–Bene Israel. They expressed their purity by dressing in white, fasting, and bathing. The holiday reaffirmed their exclusivity as a community, uniting all its members, including their dead ancestors, who were believed to have returned and become reunited with the living on the day. Following the termination of the fast the ancestors were believed to depart from the world, and the Bene Israel would resume contact with their Hindu and Muslim neighbors, giving alms to low-caste Hindus. By becoming like pure ascetics and Brahmin for a day, the Bene Israel were affirming both the distinctiveness of their group and the legitimacy of the hierarchical caste system.[30]

Although most Jewish communities under Islam retained a greater religiocultural distinctiveness than the Jews of China and India, it is the Jewish communities in medieval and early modern Christian Europe that provide the strongest contrast with the Jewish communities of the East. The medieval Jewish communities under Christendom can be divided into four cultural units: Christian Spain, Mediterranean France (the Midi), Italy, and the northern European communities, especially central France and Germany, usually called Ashkenaz. The Ashkenazim, who in the early modern period came to be concentrated demographically in Eastern Europe, provide us with the clearest example of the reinforcement of religious distinctiveness.[31]

The Ashkenazim came to put a great emphasis on the strict interpretation of the religious law and the stringent observance of religious ritual. Most European Jewish communities in the Middle Ages were small, unlike the talmudic-era Babylonian communities, whose size and occupational differentiation made economic self-sufficiency possible; their dependence on non-Jews for produce and services required lenient interpretations of some of the religious laws. For example, the eating of bread made by Gentiles was permitted because Jews were not able to produce sufficient quantities. The drinking of wine made by non-Jews remained forbidden, but, because Jews were not able to have their own vines, a solution was formulated through a division of labor: Gentiles were engaged in the preparatory stages, while Jews would prepare the wine for Jewish use. These necessary compromises were accompanied by a multiplication and hardening of halakhic rules in those areas in which economic dependence was not the issue. This elaboration of the *halakhah* reinforced religious distinctiveness and set Jews apart from Christians and from Christianity, which Jews passionately repudiated.[32]

Religious practices such as the donning of *tefillin* and the wearing of *tsitsit,* which in the early Middle Ages were neglected in some communities, were revived from the twelfth century and came to be strictly observed.[33] The extension of halakhic regulations by religious elites, such as the Franco-German *tosafists* in the twelfth and thirteenth century, were gradually accepted by the majority of Jews. For example, a few lines in the Talmud about salting meat were transformed into a comprehensive set of regulations that, together with other extended rules of *kashrut,* came to govern minutely the preparation and cooking of food within Jewish kitchens.[34]

Stricter precepts concerning contacts with non-Jews were extolled by Hasidei Ashkenaz, an elite group of ultra-pious Jews in thirteenth-century Germany who combined strenuous halakhic standards with pietistic mysticism. It has been argued that their forms of penitence were influenced by Christian pietistic movements, including those of mendicant friars, but, if this were the case, they succeeded in transforming these influences into distinctive Jewish forms. These Jewish pietists permitted contact with Christians only when Jews were in a hierarchically superior position, as they were when they employed Christian servants. Otherwise, contacts with non-Jews were to be avoided. Resistance to their religious innovations by other Jews led the pietists into a somewhat sectarian stance even within the Jewish community, but features of the movement were eventually incorporated in somewhat less radical forms into the religion of Ashkenazi Jewish communities.[35]

The ever-growing commentaries on the Talmud were codified in the sixteenth century in the *Shulhan arukh,* which was adopted by Jewish communities as their major guide to ritual observances, the regulation of social, economic, and familial relationships, and personal appearance. The extension of the religious meanings of Jewish cultural distinctiveness to clothes became especially evident in Eastern Europe. The long black caftans and large hats, which had been the costume of Polish nobles in the seventeenth century, became distinctively Jewish in the eighteenth century, and, after the inroads of secularization in the nineteenth century, they became the outward sign of the religious as opposed to secular Jew.

Like Middle Eastern Jewry, the religious particularism of Ashkenazi Jewry was expressed through a distinctive sacred language, Hebrew, but the Ashkenazim reinforced their distinctiveness through the Yiddish language, which differed far more from the environmental vernaculars of non-Jews than the Jewish variants of Arabic. Yiddish developed as a fusion of Hebrew, German, and, at a later stage of its development, Slavic languages to become an indigenous Jewish language. Not only did Yiddish become the major Jewish vernacular; it also became the vehicle of oral religious studies, from the elementary school to the *yeshivah.* Most religious scholarship continued to be written in Hebrew, but rabbis conducted their oral discussions in Yiddish, preaching was in Yiddish, many prayer books came to include large portions of text in Yiddish below the Hebrew text, and supplicatory prayers appeared in Yiddish.[36]

The way of life regulated by the *halakhah* that made for the all-encompassing distinctiveness of Ashkenazim was related to a central religious value that also contributed to it: the study of the Torah. The study of the Torah made full observance of the *mitsvot* possible, and its influence was apparent in the patterning of gender relationships, the institutions of education, and the determination of status. Torah study was important primarily for men; the role of women was to assist men in living according to this value. The ideal was that not only the scholarly elite but all Jewish men would study the Torah, perhaps on a certain day of the week or for a fixed time each day. For those who lacked the intellect or education necessary for this study, the rabbis introduced selections from the major religious texts into the synagogue services, so that all could obey the commandment to study, if only symbolically. Status and prestige in the community depended on the level of scholarship. Wealth was not sufficient in itself to achieve the highest status, although wealth and scholarship often went hand in hand. A number of educational institutions provided at least an elementary religious education for most males, but their major aim was to produce scholars who would study at the *yeshivot.* Marriages were often arranged according to the religious scholarship of the prospective bridegroom, and it was not unusual for a wealthy man to support his son-in-law while the latter devoted his time to study. The wife of a scholar often managed the family business, thereby giving her husband time to study.[37]

The Ashkenazi communities were more culturally insular than other Jewish communities, but no Jewish minority has been immune to the influences of the dominant religion and culture. The influence of the architectural styles of cathedrals and churches is evident in many synagogues, illustrations in Hebrew books were similar to those in non-Jewish art, and games with Hanukkah tops and excursions on Lag b'Omer were similar to customs among non-Jews.[38] The custom of giving Jewish children a second name in German communities, which was especially prevalent in smaller towns, stemmed from German folk influences.[39] Many magicoreligious beliefs and customs were shared with the non-Jewish population. Beliefs in demons and witches, the invocation of spirits, dreams as portents, the reading of the stars, and the use of amulets, incantations, and all kinds of folk medicines to cure illnesses were shared by Jews and Christians or were similar in many ways. Much of this folk magic was adopted by Jews from Christians, but influences were not always in one direction: the magical properties of kabbalistic signs were incorporated into the folkways of German Christians.[40]

Although Jews adopted magical devices from Christians, the symbolic meanings they attributed to those devices often differed. For example, both Jews and Christians in Germany protected children from the assaults of the devil or demons by lighting twelve small candles and one large one, but, whereas for Christians the candles symbolized the beneficent presence of the Twelve Apostles and Jesus, for Jews the candles symbolized the twelve tribes of Israel and the Patriarch.[41] Rabbis tended to take a permissive, pragmatic attitude toward such folk magic and sometimes defined magical practices as techniques that did not violate the *halakhah.* Scholarly Jews who extended their knowledge to astrology and kabbalah would be regarded as potent prophets and miracle makers. Popular customs did not escape the textual orientations of the Ashkenazim, and exegetical discussions of magical beliefs tended to blur the lines between learned and popular medieval culture and reduce the impression of a shared popular culture among Jews and Christians. The cultural influences of the non-Jewish milieu were always active, but they were little recognized because the rabbis always legitimated their customs by references to the indigenous criteria of Jewish religious texts or the immutability of age-old Jewish customs.

Environmental Culture and Social Structure

An explanation of differences among Jewish communities with respect to religious syncretism and distinctiveness must take into consideration the demographic distribution and communication networks of world Jewry. Urban concentration did not guarantee, and rural distribution did not necessarily weaken, continuing religious distinctiveness, but the number of

Jews within a geographical-cultural area and the possibilities of contacts with Jews in other cultural areas were significant factors. Small Jewish communities within large, broadly homogeneous cultural areas, with little or no contact with denser Jewish concentrations elsewhere, were more susceptible to non-Jewish influences.

A study of the memorial book of the Kaifeng community suggests there were between seven hundred and seven hundred and fifty Jews in the seventeenth century, and this was in a city whose population in the Sung era may even have exceeded one million. With the possible exception of Hangchow there had probably been fewer Jews in other Chinese cities.[42] In the first centuries of its existence the Kaifeng community no doubt had contacts with other Jewish communities in China and with non-Chinese Jews who traveled to China along the Silk Route and by sea, but by the beginning of the seventeenth century it had been cut off from contact with and knowledge of other Jewish communities for several centuries.

Jewish communities in India also had little or no contact with other Jewish communities for a long period. The Cochin Jews, whose existence on the Malabar coast of southwestern India from the tenth century is firmly established, may never have fully lost contact with other Jewish communities, but for many centuries such contacts were sparse and infrequent. Travelers from the West, including Jewish travelers, reported on them from the twelfth century, and the arrival of the Portuguese at the end of the fifteenth century introduced some Jews from the Iberian Peninsula, who intermarried with the Cochin Jews. Dutch rule in the second half of the seventeenth century greatly facilitated contact with the Amsterdam Jewish community, and from that time the Judaism of Cochin Jews was heavily influenced by Europe.[43]

The number of Cochin Jews in the 1940s, prior to the emigration of most Indian Jews to Israel, was no more than three thousand, and they were greatly exceeded by the Bene Israel, who numbered from fifteen to thirty thousand at that time. Prior to their settlement in Bombay, beginning in the mid-eighteenth century, the Bene Israel had lived scattered in many villages in the Kulaba district of Konkan. The number of Bene Israel in the middle of the eighteenth century has been estimated as no more than five thousand, and the number of families in each village was probably no more than twelve to fifteen. Migration to Bombay, the influence of Christian missionaries, and intensified contacts with other Jews, Cochini and European, brought the Judaism of the Bene Israel more into line with that of other communities.[44]

Geographical mobility was not common in pre-modern communities, but Jews were more mobile than most, and, although often irregular, the network of contacts and ties among the European and the Middle Eastern communities supported knowledge of, and identification with, a people whose boundaries stretched far beyond the immediate community. There was probably no Jewish community in the Middle East or Europe that was cut off from other Jewish communities for such an extended period as those in China and India, but there were Jewish communities under Islam, such as those in the Grand Atlas of southern Morocco, the Algerian desert, Yemen, Kurdistan, the Caucasus, and Afghanistan, that were isolated for long periods. There was little or no contact between the majority of Jewish communities under Islam and those in Christendom up to the nineteenth century. Many of the Jews who were expelled or migrated from Spain and Portugal at the end of the fifteenth century settled in and influenced the cultural development of communities in North Africa and the Ottoman Empire, but there were many communities under Islam that remained untouched by Sephardi influence.[45]

The number of Ashkenazim rose slowly in the later medieval period, and at the end of the seventeenth century, when there were about one million Ashkenazim in Europe and one million Jews in the Middle East, the former began to outstrip the latter demographically. The Ashkenazi communities forged a denser network of contacts than those in the Middle East but constituted small minorities scattered in many small communities within Europe's many states. There was no medieval state in which the Ashkenazim constituted more than 1 percent of the population, and in no medieval city did their number exceed one and a half thousand.[46] Polish Jewry became by far the largest in Europe, and a census of the half-million Polish Jews in 1763–64 found that nearly one-third lived in villages and that a larger proportion lived in small towns with fewer than five hundred Jews. Only twelve towns had more than two thousand Jews.[47]

Although the Jewish communities with the most syncretistic religious systems were to be found among those isolated for long periods from the denser settlements of Jewry, there were also examples of isolated communities that retained high levels of religiocultural distinctiveness, while the history of Western Jewry since the eighteenth century has shown that large numbers, extensive communication, and a sense of identity with a far-ranging people do not prevent substantial acculturation. An explanation of variations in Jewish religious syncretism and distinctiveness requires, therefore, an analysis of the religious cultures and social structures of the wider Gentile societies that would influence barriers between Jews and non-Jews.

The social significance of religion was extensive in traditionalist societies, playing an important part in the dominant groups' orientations to religious minorities. The major religions in China were both permeable and pluralistic; they combined and reconciled diverse beliefs and practices, and little or no attempt was made to demand the exclusive allegiance of worshipers. In adopting non-Jewish practices, Chinese Jews followed the general Chinese practice of observing sacraments from a number of religious traditions—Buddhist, Taoist, etc.—side by side.

Confucianism, the official Chinese state doctrine, was neither a state religion nor a church in the Western sense; the literati espoused a doctrinal orthodoxy and emphasized the necessity of performing certain rites, but there was little or no attempt to coerce others. The Chinese political elite permitted and encouraged religious syncretism if it was politically efficacious to the state. Max Weber wrote that "the most important and absolute limit to practical tolerance for the Confucian state consisted in the fundamental importance of the ancestor cult and this-worldly piety for the docility of the patrimonial subject."[48] Like Muslims, with whom they were often confused, the Chinese Jews found that there was little or no formal constraint on them to conform to non-Jewish beliefs and practices as long as they recognized the ancestral cult and the religious status of the Chinese emperor.

The Chinese ruling strata perceived their empire as the universe, composed of concentric circles, becoming increasingly barbarous the further they lay from the Chinese core.[49] Their disdain for barbarian foreigners was occasionally expressed in restrictive edicts of a temporary nature against people, mainly Muslim, of recognizable foreign extraction. The Chinese Jews were frequently called "blue-capped Muslims" because of the color of their headgear during prayer, but their long-term residence, appearance, and behavior made them indistinguishable from other Chinese. Resident in Kaifeng, the cultural and political center of the Sung Dynasty, the Jewish community was at the core of the Chinese universe. There was, therefore, no cultural basis to subject them to any differential legal, political, economic, or social treatment.

The important elements of the Chinese social structure—the extended family, clan, and political rule by a centralized bureaucracy—did not dispose the Jews to enter a peculiar structural niche in the society. The original Jewish settlers in Kaifeng were probably specialists in the manufacture, dyeing, or pattern printing of cotton fabrics, but economic diversity among native Kaifeng Jews is illustrated by a 1512 inscription that mentions degree holders, civil and military officials, farmers, artisans, traders, and shopkeepers. In the fifteenth, sixteenth, and seventeenth centuries a number of Jews attained high political and military posts, and others were successful as physicians and scholars.[50]

The majority of Kaifeng Jews were members of the small Chinese merchant-artisan class that occupied a social position between the mass peasant base and the literati, but from the beginning of the fourteenth century Kaifeng Jews entered the scholar-official class in increasing numbers, some coming to hold important positions. In contrast to the free towns of Europe, Chinese towns were seats of the mandarinate, and the ambition of most merchant families in the towns was to break into the scholar-official class.[51] The literati were not a completely closed class, and in the large, wealthy, imperial city of Kaifeng Jews, as much as others, could take advantage of the limited opportunities for mobility.

Song Nai Rhee has argued that the civil service system transformed Jewish intellectuals into Confucian literati, a transformation that affected their total philosophical and religious perspective. Some members of the Jewish community, those who were more conscious of their religious distinctiveness, disapproved of the confucianization of the community's intellectuals, but, as members of the Chinese elite, the Jewish scholar-officials were bound to have an important influence on the whole community. Participation in the civil service also contributed to intermarriage and assimilation; the Jewish literati had to leave Kaifeng because, like all other civil servants, they were prohibited from holding official positions in the place of their birth.[52] It may be hypothesized, therefore, that the substantial religious syncretism of Chinese Jews was related not only to the permeability and pluralism of Chinese religion but also to the Chinese social structure, which permitted the socioeconomic integration of the Jews in Chinese society.

Like the Chinese religions, Indian Hinduism was absorptive and pluralistic toward minority religions. The dominant Hindus tolerated religions that did not threaten the caste system and the supremacy of the Brahmins, but, although they were pluralistic in the sense that they did not actively attempt to enforce a Hindu monopoly, the assimilative character of the caste system and the permeable boundaries of the Hindu religion resulted in a virtual monopoly of Hinduism over much of India.[53] Although the Bene Israel had only acquired the status of a low caste, it had presumably been to their advantage to accept voluntarily certain Hindu rituals and the caste system; it was difficult for an alien and therefore impure group that was not economically self-sufficient to exist outside the Hindu community. Once the Jews had adopted the caste system and some principle practices of Hinduism, their own distinctive beliefs and rituals were tolerated within the Hindu community itself. Indian Jews constituted small *jatis* (castes) within an ocean of thousands of other *jatis,* which varied greatly with respect to their gods, rituals, and customs.

Although the general orientations of Hinduism favored a syncretic Jewish religion, the Indian social structure did not induce substantial assimilation. There were two opposed bases of social solidarity in traditional Indian society: the solidarity of village and the solidarity of caste.[54] Indian villages were largely autonomous units; there were no large-scale, interregional religious institutions in India, while the authority of secular leaders rarely extended to the internal affairs of the village. It is clear that the close association of the Bene Israel with Hindus and Muslims in the villages of Konkan occasionally resulted in intermarriage, but the solidarity of caste reinforced their social boundaries and enabled them to survive as a distinctive group. As in China, Jews were not singled out for differential treatment as Jews, but, unlike China, their very integration into the Hindu religiosocial system contributed to their social preservation.

In contrast to the religions of the East, Islam developed out of a monotheistic tradition, inheriting from it strong dispositions to religious boundary maintenance. Islam was flexible in incorporating folk beliefs and practices of nominally Muslim populations, but its permeability was slight in comparison with Eastern religions, and the dominant Islamic groups were consistent in their rejection of distinctive Judaic beliefs and practices. Again, in contrast with Eastern religions, which were generally content to coexist peacefully with other religions, Islam has often been markedly monopolistic; it has sought, often with success, to establish itself as the only religion in a particular area by converting or eliminating non-Islamic religious groups. Islamic monopolism was, however, mainly directed toward "pagans" or nonmonotheists; its disposition toward Jews and other "peoples of the book" was, in general, more pluralistic than monopolistic. Mohammed established the general principle that adherents of non-Islamic monotheistic faiths should be allowed to live under Muslim rule, and, although in its early warrior phase this principle was not consistently upheld, religious pluralism became firmly established once the Arabs had conquered vast territories containing large non-Islamic populations.

The broad pluralist disposition of the dominant Arabs toward other monotheists was formulated in a number of decrees that provided for the protection of the persons, property, and religious observances of subordinate minorities and imposed additional taxes to be paid by the communities to the Islamic rulers. References to Judaism in Islamic writings were mostly negative, but hostility toward Jews rarely had a religious basis. In contrast to Christianity, Islam arose in an area peripheral to Judaism; it did not present itself as the divine fulfillment of Judaism and gave no special place to the Jews in its sacred history. Islam presented both Judaism and Christianity as deviations from the pure monotheism that it claimed to be reviving, but it did not propound central religious doctrines that related specifically to the Jews. Muslim polemicists concerned themselves more with Christians than with Jews, who were neither a religious nor a military threat.[55] During the medieval period outbreaks of persecution, usually against Christians as well as Jews, were infrequent and limited. The most serious occurred in Egypt and Palestine-Syria from 1012 to 1019 under the Fatimid caliph al-Hakim, in the 1140s in North Africa and Spain under the Berber Almohads, and in 1172 in Yemen. After the persecutions subsided, Jews and Christians who had been forced to convert to Islam were allowed to revert to their original faiths.

The treatment by Islamic regimes of Jews and other non-Muslim minorities varied greatly from one region to another and from one period to another. The absence of Christians in Morocco after the Almohad persecutions left the Jews as the only religious minority, and from the late Middle Ages and into modern times Morocco was among the least tolerant of Islamic countries. The two other comparatively intolerant countries during that period were Iran and Yemen. The militant Shiite dynasty in Iran, which was enthroned at the beginning of the sixteenth century, subjected its religious minorities, including the Jews, to persecutions and occasionally forced conversions. Shiite rule in Yemen also made for oppressive conditions, but the Sunni Islamic regimes at the center of the Islamic Near East tended to be more tolerant. The conditions of non-Muslims declined under the rule of the "barbarian" military regimes in the fourteenth and fifteenth centuries, revived under the Ottoman Turks in the sixteenth and seventeenth centuries, and then deteriorated again, but over long periods and up to recent times the Jews under Islam enjoyed a comparatively secure existence, free from persecution.[56]

Within the framework of general religious pluralism the Jews were subject to a certain amount of differential treatment, although, again, this varied considerably between periods and provinces. Fiscal discrimination was heavy in many cases, but with a few exceptions, such as Yemen, other forms of discrimination were slight. Some of this differential treatment was motivated by a desire to secure the monopoly of Islam over its nominal adherents and to protect Islam from other religions. In order to demonstrate the superiority of Islam over other religions numerous restrictions on non-Muslims were introduced concerning such matters as modes of dress, size of buildings, and the carrying of arms. These measures were introduced not to exclude the Jews and other *dhimmis* from Islamic society but, rather, to establish the "correct" hierarchical distinctions. The hierarchical scheme, based on religious principles, was subject to economic and political exigencies; restrictions on *dhimmis* were seldom enforced consistently, and discrimination was intermittent.[57]

Middle Eastern Jews underwent a transformation from an agricultural people to one of merchants and artisans in the seventh and eighth centuries, and the absence of restrictions in the economic sphere enabled them to enter a great variety of occupations and to remain economically undifferentiated from urban Muslims. The positive attitude of Islam toward urban life and trade contributed to the status and integration of the predominantly urban-dwelling Jews. In contrast to Europe, commercial and craft guilds limited to members of the dominant faith did not exist in the early Islamic period, and the incorporation of Jews into unified economic communities, little affected by religious boundaries, continued into modern times. Although Muslims devised legal means to circumvent the religious prohibition on usury and engaged extensively in credit transactions, Islamic restrictions on handling money and fashioning gold and silver objects for sale provided special occupational niches for Jews in some countries. In many cases positions in the military and the state bureaucracy were not open to Jews, but Jews did serve in some state bureaucracies in middle and lower ranks, and under certain sovereigns a few Jews reached positions of power and influence. The Jewish poor were mostly small artisans and petty traders, although there were a few Jewish agricultural settlements in some areas, such as Morocco.

In the Ottoman Empire in the fifteenth and sixteenth centuries the Jews were prominent as traders, manufacturers, tax farmers, and customs officials. The Turkish ruling elites were concentrated in government, religious institutions, and the military, and, with respect to those economic activities that they regarded as beneath them, they preferred Jews over Christians, whose loyalty was suspect. The decline of the Ottoman Empire was accompanied by reduced tolerance, growing segregation, and increased poverty, with Jews losing their former privileged position and being replaced by Christian minorities.[58]

Towns were fully integrated into the broader political systems of Islamic societies, and the absence of municipal autonomy meant that there was no corporate structure or urban law that might have differentiated Jews from others. In most cases the residential concentration of Jews was voluntary: predominantly homogeneous religious quarters were customary in Muslim towns, and there was no degradation associated with living in one. There were, however, exceptions. The *mellah* established in Fez, Morocco, in 1438 was intended to protect the Jewish community following attacks on its members. It became the prototype of the Moroccan "ghetto." Those established from the middle of the sixteenth century on were intended to isolate Jews rather than to defend and protect them. The *mellah* was often separated by walls from the Muslim quarters, and there were restrictions on Jews when moving outside the *mellah*. In Iran and the Yemen the stigmatization of Jews as ritually unclean was used to justify residential restrictions, and in seventeenth century Yemen Jews were forced to live in special areas on the outskirts of towns. Such forced residential segregation had no parallel in the Ottoman Empire, and during its heyday the behavior and attitudes of the Turkish authorities toward Jews tended to be very favorable.[59]

Comparisons of conditions among the Muslim states have to be qualified by noting the range of circumstances that prevailed within a single country. These variations have to be understood in relation to the social structures of the Islamic Middle Eastern societies that were characterized by a division between the administrative cities and towns of the sultans and the fragmented tribal structures that provided the basis of social and political ties in the countryside and desert areas. In Morocco, in particular, there was no single pattern of Jewish-Muslim relations, and there were considerable differences among the Jewish communities living in the imperial cities, where the Jewish population could be many thousands, the smaller trading and administrative centers, and the oasis towns and mountain villages, with perhaps just a few isolated Jews. The sultan did not have effective control over the whole country, and many inland communities, in the desert oasis and mountainous areas, were dependent for their security on tribal and local patrons, to whom they paid tribute.[60]

The Jews under the sultans had their own semiautonomous community organizations to which the Islamic rulers delegated substantial political authority, including the task of collecting taxes. One later version of this community organization was the Ottoman *millet* system, which was extended from the Greek and Armenian communities to the Jews and allowed each religious community to control matters of religion and personal status.[61] In Morocco the ties between Muslim patrons and Jewish clients could interfere with the loyalty of Jews to their community and obstruct the operation of Jewish autonomy. Attempts were made by the Jewish community to limit the sphere of influence of non-Jewish institutions and to insist on the exclusive jurisdiction of the Jewish courts of law in matters of litigation between members of the community. But, even where the Jewish institutions were corporate, elaborate, and pervasive, highly personalistic relations could develop between Jews and Muslims, and close and intimate associations were not uncommon.[62]

A comparison of the syncretistic Kurdish Jews and the more distinctive Ghardaia Jews of the northwestern Sahara shows a considerable difference in the level of social interaction with Muslims. The majority of Kurdish Jews were manual laborers, living in villages and small towns of Islamic Kurds. In the small towns they lived by choice in separate quarters adjacent to the Muslim quarters, but many Muslims lived in the Jewish quarters, some even in Jewish households as lodgers or workers. Jews and Muslims visited one another and ate in one another's houses. In contrast, the Ghardaia Jews were highly segregated both from the neighboring Arabs, who belonged to the Malekite sect, and the neighboring Berbers, who belonged to the puritanical Ibadite sect. The Ghardaia Jews lived in a ghettolike quarter, performed specialized economic functions, and interacted with Muslims only in impersonal relationships.[63] In general, however, the social boundaries enclosing the Jews under Islam were limited and took mainly voluntary forms.

Like Islam, Christianity was an insular religion: while flexible in incorporating pagan folk beliefs and practices that did not present articulate religious alternatives or challenges, it was consistent in establishing clear boundaries with alternative religious systems, such as Judaism. Church authorities differed from Islamic authorities insofar as they were less disposed to take a pluralistic stance toward other monotheistic faiths.

The fact that Jews were the only deviant religious group whose existence was tolerated by the central organs of the church is important to understanding the situation of the Jews in medieval Europe. Muslims were not tolerated except on a temporary basis in Spanish and Italian areas, while Christian heretics were bloodily suppressed. The Jews were the sole recognized representatives of religious deviance, the only group to fall outside the otherwise complete religious monopoly of the church. Ecclesiastical authorities were willing to tolerate Jews in a submissive state until the end of days, at which time their conversion would herald the Second Coming of Jesus. The church taught that the exile and degraded state of the Jews was a divine penalty for their repudiation of Jesus and could thus be regarded as evidence for the truth of Christianity. This doctrine did not mean that Christians should not attempt to evangelize Jews, but forced conversion was officially prohibited.

This policy of limited pluralism was upheld relatively consistently by the papacy and the church hierarchy throughout the medieval period; with a few exceptions they counseled tolerance and restraint during intolerant periods, and they sought to protect Jews and safeguard their property. The church had little executive power outside the papal states and individual bishoprics, but its attitudes toward Jews influenced the policies of secular rulers, who often found that the existence of a Jewish community was congruent with their economic and fiscal interests. Even if they were aware of it, lower church officials and ordinary Christians were less likely to appreciate the official church policy of limited tolerance; local and regional clerics, particularly parish priests and wandering monks, often led or encouraged anti-Jewish outbreaks. During periods of unrest, such as the Crusades and the Black Death, neither church nor most secular authorities were able or willing to prevent massacres of Jews.

Outbreaks of persecution were more frequent under Christianity than under Islam, and, although the church was rarely directly responsible for such acts, its teachings about Jewish guilt and unworthiness provided the perpetrators with encouragement and justification. The first major massacres of Jews in Europe occurred at the end of the eleventh century, when the lower stratum of the crusaders extended the quest of purifying the Holy Land from the pollution of Muslims to purifying Christian territories from the pollution of Jews. In the thirteenth century the accusation that Jews murdered Christian children for ritual purposes replaced the crusading ideology as a justification for killing Jews. By the fourteenth century the popular image of the Jew had become demonized: as "deliberate unbelievers," Jews were accused of being Satan's associates on earth, and widespread large-scale massacres followed accusations that Jews had caused the Black Death by polluting wells. The destruction of the depersonalized followers of Satan was seen as part of a cosmic battle that would herald Christian salvation.[64]

The tragic side of European Jewish history should not obscure the fact that there were long periods when a limited tolerance, sanctioned by the church, did prevail. But in order to safeguard its virtual religious monopoly the church found it necessary to segregate and restrict that group over which its religious authority did not extend. The segregation and subservience of the Jews began in the early centuries of the current era, when the church was having little success in converting the Jews and when it regarded Judaism as a dangerous proselytizing competitor. Yet the church continued to exclude and restrict Jews long after Judaism had ceased to be a threat. During the early Middle Ages there appears to have been considerable socializing between Jews and Christians, and, as late as the eleventh century, church councils were still complaining of Christians partaking of meals and sharing accommodations with Jews. The establishment of clear boundaries between Christians and Jews was, for the church, a necessary adjunct to its acceptance of the Jewish presence as a personification of the absence of true belief and its punitive effects. The protective policy of the church toward the Jews weakened from the thirteenth century, and in the later Middle Ages church regulations providing for Jewish segregation were extended and elaborated in minute detail.

Although voluntary residential separation was common throughout the medieval period, the ghetto did not become a state-enforced institution until the fifteenth century. Jews did not oppose the legal institution of separate quarters and, like other corporations, accepted distinctive dress and markings. They did object to the Jewish badge, which was first instituted by the church in the thirteenth century; intended as a sign of humiliation, it took one and a half centuries to become firmly established. The church's increased emphasis on Jewish segregation in the latter part of the medieval age may have been a response to challenges to church power by heretical movements and secular rulers. Some churchmen expressed the view that Jews encouraged, directly or indirectly, the development of Christian heterodoxies and deviations, and through their segregation and submission the church could pretend that it continued to dominate a Christian order.[65]

As self-proclaimed protectors of the church and guardians of Christian piety, secular rulers were influenced by its segregationist policies, but they were not totally determined by them. Political and economic interests could outweigh religious considerations. The existence of an independent secular law allowed for the evasion of church policies, and Jews were sometimes able to play off secular authorities against the church and to form strategic alliances with both secular and religious powers. The religious orientation of the dominant group cannot alone account for the clear legal, economic, and social separation of the Jews in medieval European society, and it is appropriate to consider the Jews' social position and economic functions in European feudal societies.

The prohibition on Jews owning serfs prevented them from establishing large estates, but European rulers welcomed them in the early Middle Ages as merchants who could provide valuable services in international and wholesale trade. In return for substantial fiscal contributions and economic services, princes protected the Jews and their property, applied the most tolerant features of the available legal traditions, facilitated Jewish economic enterprises, and sometimes authorized certain economic functions, such as moneylending, to be performed exclusively by Jews. Jewish occupational structure was at first diversified in trade, crafts, and credit facilities, and, despite early medieval disdain for merchants and church antagonism, many Jewish communities achieved social prestige and political influence by their association with secular rulers. From the period of the Crusades a class of Gentile wholesale merchants grew, and Jews were increasingly restricted to moneylending, which was forbidden to Gentiles by the canonical prohibition of the church and suited the Jews because it was both profitable and allowed them time for religious study.

Jewish participation in agriculture constantly declined; their lands were expropriated; their insecure position put a premium on owning property that could be moved. As competitors of Christian merchants, Jews did not gain from the more favorable view of commerce that developed in Europe in the twelfth and thirteenth centuries. They were squeezed out of commercial markets, while the prohibition on joining guilds and other discriminatory practices prevented their participation in many crafts. Rulers encouraged Jewish moneylending in order to ensure a continual source of taxable income, and by the end of the twelfth century the word *Jew* had come to mean moneylender. Christians associated usury with heresy and the devil; their dependence on Jewish moneylenders could only compound already existing antipathy toward Jews.[66]

In addition to their economic specialization Jews were further separated by the corporate structure of medieval society. The early Jewish settlers in some areas received rights and privileges as individuals or as families, but these arrangements gradually took corporate forms as the societies became increasingly feudal. The legal status of the Jewish estate or corporative entity came to be denoted by the term *serfdom,* and, although the popes of the twelfth and thirteenth centuries proclaimed the perpetual serfdom of the Jews to the church, jurisdiction over Jews passed to secular rulers. The

Jews were, in many respects, chattels of the sovereign power but, in the feudal context, were comparatively free because they lived under the sovereign's protection and enjoyed a considerable measure of corporate autonomy. Their legal status in some regimes was considerably better than that of enserfed peasants: they were free to move, held municipal offices in the towns, had the right to bear arms up to the thirteenth century, and contributed to the armed defense of the towns. Yet, although their rights and privileges approached in some places those of Christian nobles and burghers, they were less protected than Christian dependents by set rules governing feudal bonds, and their rights and conditions of residence depended more on the will and interests of rulers.

In addition to the religious factor, which prohibited Jews from taking the oath of the Christian burghers, the continued dependence of Jews on royal or baronial authorities prevented them from becoming part of the burghers' corporation. More generally, their subjection to authorities with divergent interests meant that their corporate status remained abnormal within medieval European society. Jews constituted one of many corporations within the European corporate system, but theirs was also perceived to be outside that framework. They were civilly unique, living under a law that applied only to them, and in the later Middle Ages, when other corporations and estates were being amalgamated into the states through common legal bonds, the civil isolation of Jews came to parallel their religious isolation, and they were expelled from a number of Western and Central European states.[67]

The first Jewish communities in Poland benefited from the special relationship with the Polish monarchy, but from about 1580, with the decline of the monarch as a centralizing force, the Jews came increasingly under the control of feudal lords. The strengthening of feudal structures in Poland and the absence of a native merchant class provided economic opportunities for Jews, many of whom became lease holders who paid fixed sums to noble landowners in return for managing and profiting from their estates. As a result, peasant animosity toward noble landowners was deflected toward Jews and was made worse by their humiliation at being placed under the authority of a religiously despised group. Living in small towns and villages, Polish Jews lived in closer contact with Gentiles than ghetto Jews in Italy and Central Europe, but intimate contact was made rare by the interpenetration of religious and economic tension. Hatred burst out in the widespread massacres of Jews in 1648; with the economic decline of Poland in the eighteenth century, the persecution of Jews increased.[68] The Jewish population in Eastern Europe increased rapidly in the nineteenth century, but, although Jews held a comparatively wide range of occupations, they remained a distinctive economic stratum of traders and artisans, mediating between the nobles and peasant masses. Up to the Holocaust Jews continued to be regarded as strangers in Polish society.[69]

The corporate status of the Jews in medieval European states and early modern Poland not only contributed to their separation from non-Jews; it also provided the framework for an autonomous Jewish community in which Jews organized their lives and exercised social control in accord with their distinctive religion. The collection of taxes by the communities, their appointment of leaders and salaried officials—such as rabbis, cantors, ritual slaughterers, beadles, and scribes—and their control of wide areas of daily life, including education, social welfare, and other religious services, often amounted to more autonomy than what existed within the medieval cities in which the communities were located. The development of absolutist monarchies was accompanied by the dismantling of medieval corporations, including those of the Jews, who, unlike other groups, were often expelled rather than incorporated into the more centralized polities. Many Jews migrated to Eastern Europe, and from 1500 to 1648 the Polish Jews created the largest network of communal and educational institutions of any European Jewry. Following the partitions of Poland (1772–95), the legal foundations of community autonomy were either weakened or abolished, but under Russian rule the majority of East European communities continued to retain a high level of autonomy.[70]

Jewish leaders could enforce their will by fines or corporal punishment and could make use of the *herem* (ban), whose severity ranged from threatened, and temporary, to permanent excommunication. The excommunicant was excluded from all religious facilities and might also be excluded from economic and social relationships. Since this meant exclusion from all society, the excommunicant was forced into a terribly isolated situation. It was not, of course, possible for a Jew to be unaffiliated with the community and yet remain a Jew: Jewish identity was a corporate identity. This extensive social control within the boundaries of highly autonomous communities inhibited deviation from Jewish religious distinctiveness.

Conclusions

The sparseness of historical data on some Jewish communities means that explanations of gross differences in levels of Jewish religious syncretism and distinctiveness in pre-modern societies must necessarily be tentative. It is not possible to trace the religiocultural developments of the Chinese, Indian, and many Middle Eastern communities over the centuries because most of our information derives from Europeans who visited and described the communities after they were "discovered." In certain cases we can only compare a number of static portrayals of communities at the end of their periods of isolation and from these attempt to reconstruct their histories. Where the distinctiveness of the Jews' religion had become highly attenuated, it would appear that the process occurred over a long period and that it cannot be explained by the characteristics and orientations of the first generation of Jewish settlers. If the original Jewish settlers had been predisposed to accept other religions and be socially absorbed by the host society, the communities would not have survived centuries of isolation from other Jewish communities, even in a highly attenuated form.

The size of the Jewish populations and their distance from major centers of Jewish settlement are important factors but should not be overemphasized. Comparatively small numbers, and lack of contact with other Jewish communities, could only make a community particularly malleable to its cultural and social environments. One important cultural dimension was the degree of boundary maintenance by the dominant religions. Jewish religious syncretism was more extensive in those societies in which the dominant religion was permeable than in those societies in which it was insular. Although the differences between Judaism and the dominant religious systems were initially much greater in China and India than in the Middle East and Europe, the permeability of the Eastern religions contributed to the much greater loss of Jewish religiocultural distinctiveness in the East.

Religions with permeable boundaries are more disposed to pluralism, to tolerate other religions alongside themselves, while insular religions are more disposed to monopolism, to demand allegiance within a defined territory. The greater the tendency of the dominant group to coerce the Jews into accepting the majority religion, the more the Jews emphasized their religiocultural distinctiveness. The greater the tendency of the dominant group to accept the existence of Judaism, the more likely the Jews would adopt elements of its religion into their own.

Both religiocultural and social structural dimensions influenced the extent to which Jews were separated socially from non-Jews. Where Jews were separated, they were less likely to adopt elements from the non-Jewish religioculture. Where Jews were not so separated and social contacts with non-Jews were more frequent and intimate, extensive syncretism was more likely. The extent to which Jews were separated within a society was related to the dominant groups' disposition to monopolism or pluralism. A totally monopolistic policy, if successful, would have resulted in the disappearance of Jews, but, although there were periods of massacres, forced conversions, and expulsions in Europe, periods of pluralism were generally longer. Variations in social separation have, therefore, to be considered within the framework of pluralism, although it is obvious that Jews were more likely to be separated from non-Jews in those societies whose pluralist stance was of a comparatively limited form. In some cases segregation of the Jews was motivated by the dominant group's desire to impose or reinforce its religious monopoly over the non-Jewish population.

Some spheres of separation of Jews from non-Jews were little related, at least in any direct way, to the religious motives and orientations of the dominant group. Differences in the social structures of host societies were also relevant. The European feudal structure of estates and corporations made for Jewish separation in the economic, social, and political spheres, and the special nature of the Jewish corporations resulted in their marginalization within European states. Jews were less segregated in the looser social structures of Middle Eastern societies, but the convergence of religion and state under Islam made for some administrative separation and partial communal autonomy for Jews as well as Christians. In China and India Jews were not politically separate, and corporate Jewish polities did not develop. The Indian caste system made for some social separation, but, in contrast to the Middle East and Europe, Jews were separated within the dominant religious system and not outside it. The social separation of Jews as a caste in India implied a substantial Jewish syncretism, whereas in the Middle East and Europe the greater the social separation of Jews from non-Jews, the greater the tendency of Jews to retain or reinforce their religiocultural distinctiveness.

The factors determining either religious syncretism or religious distinctiveness tend to cluster together. In the East infrequent contact with other Jewish communities, permeable environmental religions, the dominant groups' pluralistic orientations, and lack of structural differentiation between Jews and non-Jews cluster together, resulting in a substantial Jewish syncretism. In the West frequent contact among Jewish communities, insular environmental religions, dominant groups' monopolistic orientations, and substantial structural differentiation from non-Jews cluster together, resulting in a limited syncretism or, in some cases, a reinforced distinctiveness. To some extent this clustering is a result of the exigencies of logical compatibility of the dimensions. For example, it is more likely that dominant groups adhering to an insular religion would segregate members of another religion than that dominant groups adhering to a permeable religion would. But, although it is not possible to distinguish entirely the determining dimensions, none of them can be entirely reduced or collapsed into the others. For example, it is not possible to predict on logical grounds the extent to which dominant groups adhering to an insular religion will be disposed to segregate members of a minority religion. In other words, the cluster, or convergence, of dimensions accounting for syncretism and distinctiveness is, to some extent, empirically fortuitous; the clustering could not be predicted from a knowledge of the relevant dimensions alone.

This empirical clustering means, however, that the comparative method does not enable us to determine the relative importance of each of the dimensions affecting the level of syncretism and distinctiveness. It has been suggested that the demography of Jewish communities and their level of contact with other Jewish communities were less important than either the religiocultural orientations of the dominant groups or the social structures of the host societies, but there is no attempt to state the relative importance of the cultural and social dimensions. There is not a sufficient number of empirically divergent cases to enable us to hold each determining dimension constant. This is a limitation that most broad cross-cultural studies using more than one causal factor or variable have to accept, and it is hoped that it will be regarded as sufficient if the major social and cultural dimensions affecting differences in syncretism and distinctiveness of the communities under study have been accurately delineated.

NOTES

1. A welcome exception, comparing Jewish-Gentile relations in medieval Europe and Islamic countries, has recently been published: Mark R. Cohen, *Under Crescent and Cross: The Jews in the Middle Ages* (Princeton, NJ: Princeton University Press, 1994).

2. Steven M. Cohen, *American Modernity and Jewish Identity* (New York: Methuen, 1983); Calvin Goldscheider and Alan S. Zuckerman, *The Transformation of the Jews* (Chicago: University of Chicago Press, 1984). The latter work does include some comparisons of German and French communities in the nineteenth century. Wider comparisons of Jewish communities in the nineteenth and twentieth

centuries were made in my book *Judaism: A Sociology* (Newton Abbot: David and Charles, 1976).

3. Charles S. Liebman and Steven M. Cohen, *Two Worlds of Judaism: The Israeli and American Experiences* (New Haven: Yale University Press, 1990).

4. Religious separatism was incorporated into Max Weber's notion of the Jews as a pariah people. Max Weber, *Ancient Judaism* (New York: Free Press, 1952), 3, 336–55.

5. Abram Leon, *The Jewish Question: A Marxist Interpretation* (New York: Pathfinder Press, 1970).

6. S. M. Lipset, "The Study of Jewish Communities in a Comparative Context," *Jewish Journal of Sociology* 5 (1963): 157–66.

7. Salo Wittmayer Baron, *A Social and Religious History of the Jews,* 18 vols. (New York: Columbia University Press, 1952–80), 3:99–114.

8. Andre N. Chouraqui, *Between East and West: A History of the Jews of North Africa* (Philadelphia: Jewish Publication Society, 1968), 86–97; S. D. Goitein, *Jews and Arabs: Their Contacts across the Ages* (New York: Schocken, 1955), 109–15, 122–23; Walter P. Zenner and Shlomo Deshen, "Introduction: The Historical Ethnology of Middle Eastern Jews," in *Jewish Societies in the Middle East: Community, Culture, and Authority,* ed. Walter P. Zenner and Shlomo Deshen (Washington, DC: University Press of America, 1982), 1–34.

9. Kenneth R. Stow, *Alienated Minority: The Jews of Medieval Latin Europe* (Cambridge, MA: Harvard University Press, 1992), 6–7.

10. Michael Pollak, *Mandarins, Jews, and Missionaries: The Jewish Experience in the Chinese Empire* (Philadelphia: Jewish Publication Society, 1980), 260–66, 317–19.

11. Benjamin J. Israel, *The Bene Israel of India: Some Studies* (New York: Apt Books, 1984), 11, 61–64, 71; Carl Mark Gussin, "The Bene Israel of India: Politics, Religion, and Systematic Change" (Ph.D diss., Syracuse University, 1972), 7.

12. Baron, *History of the Jews,* 2:191–209, 5:3–20, 6:16–27. The Beta Israel in Ethiopia are excluded from this comparative analysis because the evidence suggests that the development of their distinctive Jewish identity occurred from the fifteenth century and that their religious system was an outgrowth of the Ethiopian tradition. Steven Kaplan, *The Beta Israel (Falasha) in Ethiopia: From Earliest Times to the Twentieth Century* (New York: New York University Press, 1992).

13. Harvey E. Goldberg, "Anthropology and the Study of Traditional Jewish Societies," *AJS Review* 15 (1990): 1–22.

14. Most Middle Eastern Jews spoke Aramaic before they adopted Arabic, but only in the mountains of Kurdistan and Armenia did Jews retain the Aramaic dialect. Goitein, *Jews and Arabs,* 131–40.

15. Ibid., 177–92; Chouraqui, *Between East and West,* 67–79; H. Z. (J. W.) Hirschberg, *A History of the Jews in North Africa,* 2 vols. (Leiden: E. J. Brill, 1974), 1:175, 165–76; Cohen, *Under Crescent and Cross,* 135–36.

16. Goldberg, "Anthropology"; "The Mimuna and the Minority Status of Moroccan Jews," *Ethnology* 17 (1978): 75–87.

17. Dina Feitelson, "Aspects of the Social Life of Kurdish Jews," *Jewish Journal of Sociology* 1 (1959): 201–16; Yona Sabar, *The Folk Literature of the Kurdistani Jews* (New Haven: Yale University Press, 1982), xxv–xxxii.

18. L. C. Briggs and N. L. Guele, *No More For Ever: A Saharan Jewish Town* (Cambridge, MA: Peabody Museum of Archaeology and Ethnology, Harvard University, 1964). Another example of a relatively isolated community whose religious culture remained very distinct from that of its Muslim neighbors was the Yemenite community. S. D. Goitein, "Jewish Education in Yemen as an Archetype of Traditional Jewish Education," in *Between Past and Present,* ed. C. Frankenstein (Jerusalem: Szold Institute, 1953), 109–46. A study of the Jewish communities of Jerba, Tunisia, has also shown a very high level of religiocultural distinctiveness that has continued up to the present. Abraham L. Udovitch and Lucette Valensi, *The Last Arab Jews: The Communities of Jerba, Tunisia* (Chur, Switz.: Harwood Academic Publishers, 1984).

19. The reasons for postulating a Persian origin are mostly linguistic: the repeated use of Judeo-Persian rubrics in the religious manuscripts. Pollak, *Mandarins, Jews, and Missionaries,* 267.

20. Ibid., 286–87, 296.

21. W. C. White, *Chinese Jews: A Compilation of Matters Relating to the Jews of Kaifeng Fu,* 3 vols. (1942; reprint, New York: Paragon Book Reprint Corporation, 1966); Donald Daniel Leslie, *The Survival of the Chinese Jews: The Jewish Community of Kaifeng* (Leiden: E. J. Brill, 1972), chaps. 7–9; Pollak, *Mandarins, Jews, and Missionaries,* 274, 292–307.

22. David G. Mandelbaum, "The Jewish Way of Life in Cochin," *Jewish Social Studies* 1 (1939): 23–60; Shalva Weil, "Symmetry between Christians and Jews in India: The Cnanite Christians and the Cochin Jews of Kerala," in *Jews in India,* ed. Thomas A. Timberg (New York: Advant Books, 1986).

23. J. B. Segal, *A History of the Jews of Cochin* (London: Vallentine Mitchell, 1993), 17, 22–26, 71–88.

24. Ibid., 39–45.

25. Ezekiel Barber, *The Bene-Israel of India* (Washington, DC: University Press of America, 1981), 10, 13.

26. Israel, *Bene-Israel,* 54, 58, 60; Shirley Berry Isenberg, *India's Bene Israel: A Comprehensive Inquiry and Sourcebook* (Bombay: Popular Prakashan, 1988), 110–43; Gussin, "Bene Israel," 2, 26; Joan G. Roland, *Jews in British India* (Hanover, NH: University Press of New England, 1989), 12–13.

27. Israel, *Bene Israel,* 35–36.

28. Barber, *Ben-Israel,* 61–65.

29. Ibid., 63, 66; Gussin, "Bene Israel," 135, 147–48; Isenberg, *India's Bene Israel,* 115, 117.

30. Shalva Weil, "Yom Kippur: The Festival of Closing the Doors," in *Between Jerusalem and Benares: Comparative Studies in Judaism and Hinduism,* ed. Hananya Goodman (Albany: State University of New York Press, 1994).

31. Comparisons of the Ashkenazim with the Sephardim of Christian Spain and the Italian communities of the Renaissance and Counter-Reformation are to be found in my article on messianism in this volume. For the comparative purposes of this essay, it also makes sense to focus on the Ashkenazim. Cohen writes that the pervasive influence of Islamic and Arabic culture on medieval Christian Spain spoils the clarity of a comparison between Christian and Islamic countries. He notes that Italy is too special a case for comparison, but, by bringing Mediterranean France (the Midi) into his comparison, he is able to show that divergent socioeconomic and political conditions could temper religious intolerance. Cohen, *Under Crescent and Cross,* xx–xxi. I find that Cohen's work supports my own perspective of distinguishing between the effects of cultural, mainly religious, factors and social structural factors.

32. Jacob Katz, *Exclusiveness and Tolerance: Studies in Jewish-Gentile Relations in Medieval and Modern Times* (Oxford: Oxford University Press, 1961), 22–23, 29–46.

33. L. Rabinowitz, *The Social Life of the Jews of Northern France in the XII–XIV Centuries,* 2d ed. (New York: Hermon Press, 1972), 174–78.

34. Haym Soloveitchik, "Religious Law and Change: The Medieval Ashkenazic Example," *AJS Review* 12 (1987): 205–21.

35. Ivan G. Marcus, "Hierarchies, Religious Boundaries and Jewish Spirituality in Medieval Germany," *Jewish History* 1 (1986): 7–26; *Piety and Society: The Jewish Pietists of Medieval Germany* (Leiden: E. J. Brill, 1981), 64, 77–83, 89–97; Stow, *Alienated Minority,* 121–34; Katz, *Exclusiveness and Tolerance,* 93–105.

36. Max Weinreich, *History of the Yiddish Language* (Chicago: University of Chicago Press, 1980), 255–62. On the characteristics of religious literature in Yiddish for women, see Chava Weissler, "The Religion of Traditional Ashkenazic Women: Some Methodological Issues," *AJS Review* 12 (1987): 73–94.

37. For detailed accounts of the traditional Jewish community in early modern and modern times, see Jacob Katz, *Tradition and Crisis: Jewish Society at the End of the Middle Ages* (New York: Free Press, 1961); and Mark Zborowski and Elizabeth Herzog, *Life Is with People: The Culture of the Shtetl* (New York: International Universities Press, 1952).

38. Weinreich, *History of the Yiddish Language,* 182, 186.

39. Herman Pollack, *Jewish Folkways in Germanic Lands (1648–1806): Studies in Aspects of Daily Life* (Cambridge, MA: MIT Press, 1971), 27–28.

40. Ibid., 49, 113–45; Joshua Trachtenberg, *Jewish Magic and Superstition* (Philadelphia: Jewish Publication Society, 1961).

41. Theodor H. Gaster, *The Holy and the Profane: Evolution of Jewish Folkways* (1955; reprint, New York: William Morrow, 1980), 60–63.

42. Pollak, *Jewish Folkways,* 318–19.

43. Segal, *Jews of Cochin,* 8–13, 21, 37–45.

44. Israel, *Bene-Israel,* 11, 61–64, 71; Gussin, "Bene Israel," 7.

45. Chouraqui, *Between East and West,* 86–97; Goitein, *Jews and Arabs,* 109–15, 122–23.

46. Stow, *Alienated Minority,* 6–7.

47. Arieh Tartakower, "Polish Jewry in the Eighteenth Century," *Jewish Journal of Sociology* 2 (1960): 110–14; Raphael Mahler, *A History of Modern Jewry, 1780–1815* (London: Valentine Mitchell, 1971), 279–85.

48. Max Weber, *The Religion of China* (New York: Macmillan, 1964), 213–14.

49. Etienne Balazs, *Chinese Civilization and Bureaucracy* (New Haven: Yale University Press, 1964), 22.

50. White, *Chinese Jews;* Leslie, *Survival of the Chinese Jews,* 108–11.

51. Balazs, *Chinese Civilization and Bureaucracy,* 41–42, 70–78.

52. Song Nai Rhee, "Jewish Assimilation: The Case of the Chinese Jew," *Comparative Studies in Society and History* 15 (1973): 115–26; Pollak, *Mandarins, Jews, and Missionaries,* 307–9, 325–32, 338–43.

53. Max Weber, *The Religion of India* (New York: Free Press, 1958), 9–29.

54. M. N. Srinivas, *Religion and Society among the Coorgs of South India* (Oxford: Clarendon Press, 1952), 31–32.

55. Bernard Lewis, *The Jews of Islam* (Princeton, NJ: Princeton University Press, 1984), 85–88; Cohen, *Under Crescent and Cross,* 23–27, 52–55, 161.

56. Lewis, *Jews of Islam,* 52, 125–53; Cohen, *Under Crescent and Cross,* 67–74, 163–69, 174–77; Norman A. Stillman, *The Jews of Arab Lands: A History and Source Book* (Philadelphia: Jewish Publication Society, 1979), 41–53, 64–77, 87–92; Bat Ye'or, *The Dhimmi* (Rutherford, NJ: Fairleigh Dickinson University Press, 1985), 52–79.

57. Baron, *History of the Jews,* 3:120–72; Chouraqui, *Between East and West,* 42–55; Cohen, *Under Crescent and Cross,* 112; Nissim Rejwan, *The Jews of Iraq: Three Thousand Years of History and Culture* (London: Weidenfeld and Nicolson, 1985), 87–91.

58. Amnon Cohen, *Jewish Life under Islam: Jerusalem in the Sixteenth Century* (Cambridge, MA: Harvard University Press, 1984), 140–219; Lewis, *Jews of Islam,* 28–29, 90–91, 129–39, 142–46; Stillman, *Jews of Arab Lands,* 62–63, 86; Cohen, *Under Crescent and Cross,* 88–103, 125–28.

59. S. D. Goitein, *A Mediterranean Society: The Jewish Communities of the Arab World as Portrayed in the Documents of the Cairo Geniza,* 6 vols. (Berkeley: University of California Press, 1967–93), 2:290–93; H. Z. Hirschberg, "The Jewish Quarter in Muslim Cities and Berber Areas," *Judaism* 17 (1958): 405–21; Lewis, *Jews of Islam,* 135–39, 148–53; Stillman, *Jews of Arab Lands,* 78–91; Cohen, *Under Crescent and Cross,* 125–28.

60. Allan R. Meyers, "Patronage and Protection: The Status of Jews in Precolo-

nial Morocco," in Deshen and Zenner, *Jewish Societies in the Middle East,* 85–104; Moshe Shokeid, "Jewish Existence in a Berber Environment," in ibid., 105–22; Harvey E. Goldberg, *Jewish Life in Muslim Libya* (Chicago: University of Chicago Press, 1990), 38–39.

61. Lewis, *Jews of Islam,* 125–26.

62. Lawrence Rosen, *Bargaining for Reality: The Construction of Social Relations in a Muslim Community* (Chicago: University of Chicago Press, 1984), 153–62; Shlomo Deshen, *The Mellah Society: Jewish Community Life in Sherifian Morocco* (Chicago: University of Chicago Press, 1989), 27; Goitein, *Mediterranean Society,* 2:298–99; Hirschberg, *History of the Jews in North Africa,* 1:174; Cohen, *Under Crescent and Cross,* 132–34.

63. Feitelson, "Social Life of Kurdish Jews"; Briggs and Guele, *No More For Ever.*

64. Baron, *History of the Jews,* 4:5–12, 89–149; 9:3–54; 10:122–91; Leon Poliakov, *The History of Anti-Semitism from the Time of Christ to the Court Jews,* trans. Richard Howard (New York: Vanguard Press, 1965), chaps. 2–7; Joshua Trachtenberg, *The Devil and the Jews* (Philadelphia: Jewish Publication Society, 1961); Stow, *Alienated Minority,* 102–20, 232–40; Cohen, *Under Crescent and Cross,* 17–24, 139, 169–74.

65. Baron, *History of the Jews,* 9:3–96, 11:77–121; Stow, *Alienated Minority,* 10–40, 232–59; Cohen, *Under Crescent and Cross,* 32–42, 129–31.

66. Baron, *History of the Jews,* 6:150–277, 12:25–197; Guido Kisch, *The Jews in Medieval Germany: A Study of Their Legal and Social Status* (Chicago: University of Chicago Press, 1949), 318–22, 327–29; David Biale, *Power and Powerlessness in Jewish History* (New York: Schocken Books, 1986), 60–66; Cohen, *Under Crescent and Cross,* 77–87. Cohen writes that the greater heterogeneity of Jewish economic activities in Mediterranean Christian areas appears to have tempered anti-Jewish feeling. Ibid., 102–3.

67. Baron, *History of the Jews,* 9:135–236, 10:41–117, 11:3–76, 192–283; Biale, *Power and Powerlessness,* 74, 62–66; Stow, *Alienated Minorities,* 97–101, 273–77, 281–308; Cohen, *Under Crescent and Cross,* 45–51, 121–24.

68. Hillel Levine, *Economic Origins of Antisemitism: Poland and Its Jews in the Early Modern Period* (New Haven: Yale University Press, 1991).

69. Zborowski and Herzog, *Life Is with People,* 66–67, 151–58; Celia S. Heller, *On the Edge of Destruction* (New York: Columbia University Press, 1977).

70. Stow, *Alienated Minorities,* 155–95; Biale, *Power and Powerlessness,* 77–82; Mahler, *History of Modern Jewry,* 229–58, 370–423; I. Levitats, *The Jewish Community in Russia, 1772–1844* (New York: Columbia University Press, 1943).

Jewish Millennial-Messianic Movements: A Comparison of Medieval Communities

Stephen Sharot

The Millennial-Messianic Heritage of Medieval Jews

Historians of the Jews have rarely made a distinction, common in the social scientific literature on religious movements, between millenarian, or millennial, movements and messianic movements. Millenarian movements look forward to an imminent, collective salvation to occur in a transformed world that will be brought about by, or take place under, the auspices of supernatural beings or processes. The present world will be replaced by a perfectly good and happy one, in which the terrestrial and transcendental realms will be united. The meaning of the millennium is not necessarily limited to the literal sense of a thousand years but is often perceived as an eternal age. In a messianic-millennial movement it is believed that a savior figure will accomplish, or take a leading part in, the collective salvation and transformation of the world. Not all millenarian movements have messiahs, and some messianic movements may have visions of the future that are not strictly millenarian in the sense of an expected transformation in nature as well as society.[1]

In ancient Judaism the development of millennial beliefs preceded the development of a messianic figure. While many of the prophecies of the preexilic prophets were based on supernatural premises, they did not present a view of the future as an essentially different order from that of the present. The dualistic conception of two worlds, in which the future hope would be realized in transcendental as well as terrestrial realms, was essentially a postexilic development. Its beginnings may be traced to Deutero-Isaiah, who is believed to have prophesied in the last years preceding the conquest of Babylon by the Persians, in 539 B.C.E. Deutero-Isaiah's belief that the climactic events in history would presage not a new historical era but a transformation of the world on a cosmic scale was followed by most later prophets. During the classical period of Jewish apocalyptic works, from the second century B.C.E. to the second century C.E., their writers moved toward a view of the future world that was removed from historical reality. Whereas the ancient prophets knew only a single world in which the events of "the Day of the Lord" would occur, the apocalyptic works made a radical distinction between this world and the next, the reign of darkness and the reign of light, and between sin and holiness, impurity and purity. Concrete hopes for political redemption remained a central feature of mil-lenarian hopes, but from the early third century C.E., with the transfer of Jewish leadership from Palestine to Babylon, concrete hopes of political redemption became increasingly subordinate to mythic and cosmic fan-tasies. The dominant millenarian tradition, inherited and extended by medieval Jewry, was one in which supernatural elements about the millen-nium were the most prominent. Not only the Jewish masses but most scholars as well thought of the millennium as an entirely new world.[2]

The majority of medieval Jews expected a transitional period of cata-strophic events prior to the reign of the messiah. The preexilic prophets threatened the destruction of the kingdom of Judah and the terrible pun-ishments of the Day of the Lord, but they differed over whether the pun-ishments would be imposed on Israel alone, on other peoples alone, or on both Israel and other nations. The later preexilic prophets added cosmic disturbances such as earthquakes, fire, great noise, and whirlwinds. These elements became more pronounced in later Jewish eschatalogical writings, especially those written under Roman domination, which referred to the events preceding the millennium (monsters, demons, plagues, famines, floods, falling stars, earthquakes, wars, revolutions, and so forth) as the "birth pangs of the messiah." The belief arose that the messiah would come at the time of the deepest catastrophe of the Jewish people. This apocalyptic literature, which was further elaborated against a background of political upheavals, wars, and exile, provided subsequent generations with a frame of reference for interpreting the crises they experienced as signs of the coming of the messiah.

In the medieval period expectations about the nature of the messianic age varied among rabbis and scholars. The "rationalist" position was clas-sically stated by Maimonides, who wrote that the "only difference between this world and the Days of the Messiah is the subjection of Israel to the nations." The messiah was to restore the kingdom of David, rebuild the Temple, reinstate the ancient laws and sacrifices, and gather the Jews from their dispersion, but there were to be no miracles, no changes in nature, no innovations in creation, and no end to history. The rationalist viewpoint was opposed by Jewish scholars who were millenarians as well as messianists: the revival of the kingdom of David was to be accompanied by changes in nature, in the cosmos, and in humankind's moral character.[3]

In Israelite and early Judaic literature the concept of a messiah was either absent or of little importance beside that of eschatological salvation. During the Second Temple period Jewish writings continued to refer to eschatological salvation without a messiah; still a variety of savior figures were envisioned during that period. The most prominent messianic image was the this-worldly, warrior-king of Davidic origin who would die when his kingdom ended. After the failure of the last revolt against the Romans, apocalyptic writers began to make a distinction between the warrior messiah of the House of Joseph, who would die in the final battle against Gog and Magog, and the more spiritual messiah of the House of David, who would rule the future kingdom.[4] Rabbinic literature presented the messiah as the redeemer, the instrument by which the kingdom of God was to be established as well as the future ruler of that kingdom. It included, however, many contrasting views, and the Middle Ages did not inherit a coherent, unified conception of the messiah.

The Talmuds and collections of scriptural exegesis presented the age of the coming of the messiah as the end of time, but Jacob Neusner argues that the messiah was incorporated into talmudic or rabbinic Judaism through a process that neutralized imminent expectations and activist forms of messianism. The messianic hope was incorporated into an eternal sanctification of life to be attained by religious observance and study. Jews were encouraged to accept their suffering and resign themselves in a humble and passive manner to political subordination. It was not rebellion but repentance that would bring the messiah. Thus, the coming of the messiah and dramatic change were dependent on obedience and keeping things as they were.[5]

Although the dominant rabbinical tendency did not encourage imminent expectations of the coming of the messiah, it was nevertheless an article of faith among Jews in the medieval and early modern periods to hope constantly for the advent of the messiah. The twelfth principle of the best-known formulation of Jewish religious doctrine, Maimonides' "Thirteen Principles of the Jewish Faith," reads: "I believe with complete faith in the coming of the messiah, and even though he should tarry, nevertheless, I shall wait for his coming every day." Affirmation of this belief was a persistent theme in Jewish prayers: in a number of daily benedictions, in the prayers after meals, during the wedding ceremony, and on festivals and fast days. Family and business letters, holiday wishes, and expressions of congratulations often concluded with the wish that the correspondents would witness the advent of the messiah and the ingathering of the exiles. Belief in the coming of the messiah and the collective salvation of the Jews in a future, this-worldly, perfect age may, therefore, be described as normative in traditional Judaism.

The question is: under what circumstances were millennial-messianic beliefs activated in the form of millennial-messianic movements? Crises have been a common explanation among historians and social scientists for the outbreak of messianic and millennial movements, not only with respect to Judaism but also in other religious traditions. Millennial movements have been interpreted as responses to the disruption of social and cultural patterns. One acute instance of disruption is a disaster such as an epidemic, famine, war, or massacre. Following a disaster, people feel vulnerable, confused, and full of anxiety and thus turn to messianic beliefs in order to account for otherwise meaningless events. They interpret the disaster as a prelude to the millennium; thus, their deepest despair gives way to the greatest hope.[6]

Small, local, short-lived messianic outbursts have occurred in Jewish communities that did not directly experience a serious crisis; the news of an event or series of events elsewhere in the world was often sufficient to activate messianic beliefs. Crises do appear to be among the necessary causes of large and widespread messianic movements, but a crisis is not a sufficient cause. Given the importance of the belief in the messiah in Judaism and the number of disasters and crises in Jewish history, it may be thought surprising that there have been so few important Jewish messianic movements. This may be understood, in part, by the influence of a tradition that opposed activist forms of messianism and warned against attempts to calculate the timing of redemption.

In the diaspora, messianic movements were rarely militaristic, but still they represented a challenge to passive forms of messianism: the messiah was said to have appeared or was about to appear, imminent dates of redemption and the return to the Holy Land were announced, and believers were assigned an important role in speeding these processes. The fact that messianic movements broke from the dominant rabbinical opinion meant that they were likely to emerge only in exceptional circumstances. Disasters and crises were among those circumstances, but these events have to be understood in wider cultural and social frameworks.

Millennial-Messianic Movements in the Medieval Period

The analysis of early millennial movements in the diaspora is hampered by the absence of historical information both on the movements themselves and on the circumstances in which they arose. This is the case of a messianic incident in Crete, sometime in the second half of the fifth century, a series of movements in Persia in the eighth century, and seven millennial outbursts from about 1060 to 1172.[7] The series of incidences in the late eleventh century and the twelfth century occurred in places as distant from each other as Spain and Yemen, but it has been argued that they were all connected in some way with the Crusades. In fact, an examination of the location and the timing of the movements shows that the connection with the Crusades was tenuous at best. In those areas where Jews were massacred by the hordes following the crusading armies, the survivors interpreted their sufferings within a Jewish religious framework, but they did not turn to active messianism. Some Jews did view the persecution in a millennial context,[8] but among the Ashkenazim this did not become the dominant trend, and they took no steps to prepare for such an event.

Jewish chronicles of the period show that Jews understood the persecutions of the Crusades as a continuation of the seemingly endless sufferings that God had chosen them to endure.[9] They saw precedents to the massacres in biblical narratives, and this archetypal mode of thought possibly militated against any tendency to view the events as signifying an end to history. They believed that their suffering was a just retribution for the sins of the Jewish people and their failure to uphold the law of God. While some declared that their own sins were being justly punished, self-accusation was more a conventional formula than a deeply held belief. Medieval Ashkenazim found little in their own behavior to warrant such punishment, and some concluded that they were being punished for the sins of their ancestors.[10] For them suffering was a test of faith; it was imposed on a religiously qualified generation that was able to withstand the cruel tests and thereby fulfill the hopes of God. Compensation was to come in the form of an immediate personal afterlife in which proof of religious merit was to be rewarded by happiness in heaven.[11] Ashkenazi rabbis also stressed that the righteous would be resurrected and enjoy the splendors of

the ultimate redemption, but they did not introduce any apocalyptic interpretations of contemporary events into their millennial conceptions.[12]

Millennial movements remained very rare among the Ashkenazim.
During the medieval period most instances of millenarianism occurred
among the Jews of Spain and, after the expulsion of 1492, in Italy. In
Castile in 1295 considerable excitement centered on two messianic
prophets in the town of Avila and the village of Ayllon. In Avila a reputed
illiterate claimed that angels had dictated to him a treatise revealing the
imminent future kingdom, while in Ayllon a prophet announced that on a
specified day of that year a blast of the messiah's horn would summon
Jews from exile. Many prepared themselves by fasting, praying, and giving
to charity, and on the day they rose early, dressed in white, and went to the
synagogue to await the signal.[13] Nearly a century later, in 1391, a number
of prophets predicting the imminent coming of the messiah appeared in
Spain, but the fragmentary records of these events do not allow us to
establish the extent of the messianic enthusiasm.[14]

Millennial fervor in 1391 occurred at a time of widespread attacks on
Jews, who were often given the choice of death or conversion. Some of
those who converted tried to leave Spain for the Land of Israel, believing
that their migration would help bring the messiah.[15] A further migration
of converts, also stimulated by messianic hopes, occurred after the conquest of Constantinople by the Turks in 1453. The eschatological interpretation of this event also stimulated messianic hopes among Jews in
Palestine, Italy and its colonies, Sicily, and Spain.[16] Messianism became
more widespread after the expulsion of the Jews from Spain in 1492. Jewish exiles expressed a strong belief in the imminent coming of the messiah,
seeing in the Christian-Islamic wars a sign of their own coming redemption. They expected that their expulsion would be fully revenged, but they
also believed that the expulsion was a means of redemption, since it
resulted in the concentration of Jews in the Turkish empire, closer to the
Land of Israel.[17]

It is difficult to know how many Jews chose conversion rather than exile
from Spain, but one generous estimate is that 160,000 went into exile, while
another 240,000 converted and remained in Spain.[18] The first recorded
millenarian incident in postexilic Spain among the conversos occurred in
1500 in the small town of Herrara in northern Castile, which in the
fifteenth century had contained a Jewish community of substantial size
and wealth. Ines, the daughter of a shoemaker, proclaimed that she had
been led by her mother, a boy who had just died, and an angel to heaven,

to a place where she had heard the voices of souls who had been burnt "in sanctity of the name [of God]." The majority of conversos in Herrara believed her, and many came from elsewhere to see her. They ceased work, fasted, and prepared themselves in holiday clothing for the imminent arrival of the messiah. Some said that a town created in heaven would be brought down to earth and that the converts would dwell there, eating off golden plates.

There were similar occurrences elsewhere. Maria Gomez, a prophetess in Chillon, a small provincial town in Ciudad Real, claimed that she had ascended to heaven, where she had been told that all the conversos who fasted, observed the Sabbath, and kept other commandments would be taken to the Holy Land. In the same province another prophet claimed that he had ascended to heaven, where he had met God, Elijah, the messiah, and the prophetesses of Herrara and Chillon. He said that Elijah would come to Spain to collect all the conversos who gave alms to the poor, believed in the law of Moses, and kept the Sabbath and other precepts. His followers dressed in holiday garb in readiness for the messiah.

Popular prophecy among the New Christians occurred in other parts of Spain, such as Córdoba and Valencia. Signs in the sky, political events, and wars were taken as evidence that 1500 was the year of redemption. Most prophetesses and prophets who appeared at the time predicted that Elijah and the messiah would soon appear and take the converts who believed in redemption to Israel on clouds or the wings of angels. Several communities of converts in Castile lived for weeks in a state of exaltation and excitement, leading ascetic lives, fasting regularly, and adhering as rigidly as possible to Jewish observances. The Inquisition learned of the movements and imprisoned and burned many of those involved.[19]

About nine thousand Spanish exiles settled in Italy, which, in the sixteenth century, became the center of messianic speculation and activity.[20] The most important propagator of an imminent millennium among the Iberian exiles in Italy was the widely respected Isaac Abravanel (1437–1508). In a trilogy on the messianic theme, published in Italy in 1496–98, he collected the messianic beliefs common at the time and, on the basis of his interpretations of biblical and talmudic literature, historical events, and astrological calculations, predicted that the process of redemption would begin in 1503 and be completed by 1531. He noted some disillusionment among Jews that the messiah had not come despite the massacres and expulsions but argued that the low state of the Jews indicated that salvation was imminent. The messiah, who had been born before the expulsion, would appear in Rome following a series of wars among Muslims, Christians, and the ten lost tribes of Israel. In the face of his supernatural powers all nations would either yield and pay homage to him or be destroyed. The ingathering of the exiles and the resurrection of the dead would follow, and nature would come to approximate its state at the beginning of creation. The change in nature would be especially felt in Israel, where the Jews, the spiritual elite, would spend their time in worship and the study of the Law, while their material needs were met by other nations.[21]

That belief in the imminent coming of the messiah was not confined to Iberian exiles in Italy was demonstrated by the widespread acceptance among Italian Jews of the messianic prophecies of Asher Lemlein in 1502. Lemlein, an Ashkenazi, announced in Istria, near Venice, that the messiah would come within six months if the Jews repented and prepared for their redemption. Disciples carried his prophecy to many parts of Italy; widespread episodes of repentance were recorded, and long after 1502 the year was known as the year of repentance.[22]

Disappointment over the failure of Lemlein's prophecy did not stop others from announcing an imminent coming, and millennial expectations continued among Jews in Italy. Some perceived the upheavals within Christendom as portents of the coming millennium. The activity of Lutherans was incorporated into the apocalyptic prophecies of Abraham ben Eliezer ha-Levi, who believed that, beginning in 1520, the process of redemption would unfold with the coming of the messiah in 1530 and the rebuilding of the Temple in 1536–37. Intense messianic hopes were also expressed in the Hebrew poems of the time.[23]

The activities of David Reuveni and Solomon Molcho also stirred messianic hopes. Arriving in Venice in 1524, Reuveni claimed that he was a prince from one of the ten lost tribes in the "Wilderness of Harbor" and that he had been sent to seek assistance from the pope and the European powers to conquer Palestine. Through the influence of a Jewish banker, Reuveni received an audience with the pope, who in turn gave him a letter of recommendation to the Portuguese king. The king received Reuveni, but the enthusiastic reception given to him by conversos compelled him to leave Portugal. Three years after his return to Italy, Reuveni went with Molcho to the Imperial Diet in Ratisbon to ask the emperor to arm Jews in order to regain Palestine from the Turks. The emperor imprisoned them, and Reuveni was taken back to the Iberian Peninsula, where he died, probably in an auto-da-fé.

Reuveni's intentions, at least at first, were not messianic: he claimed to be neither the messiah nor his prophet but, rather, a statesman with political and military proposals. Nevertheless, some Jews saw his mission in a messianic light, an interpretation to which he gave some encouragement. While to Christians he spoke of joint military action against the Turks, to the Jews he spoke of returning to Jerusalem as part of the process of salvation. He maintained that God had ordained him to wage war to redeem the Jews but upheld the traditional view that the final act of redemption would be achieved by a miracle.

The romantic nature of Reuveni's career and his contacts with high Christian dignitaries have led many to exaggerate his influence on Jews and his importance in Jewish millenarianism. His appearance in Portugal caused great excitement among the conversos there, but his influence among Italian Jews was not as great. He appeared at a time when rumors about the ten lost tribes were common in Italy, but many Italian Jews regarded him as an imposter or a madman. In both Venice and Rome the Jewish communities were divided about how to treat him. In Rome the leaders refused to support him, but he did convince some wealthy Jewish families, who gave him their patronage and financial support. His influence peaked after his audience with the pope, but, after failing in Portugal, support and belief among Italian Jews waned.[24]

While Reuveni's influence was declining, Solomon Molcho was gaining a considerable reputation as a messianic prophet. Born into a converso family in Lisbon, Diogo Pires took the Hebrew name Molcho, circumcised himself, and fled to Salonika, where he studied kabbalah. His prophecies, which included the destruction of Rome and the beginning of redemption in 1540, became known in Italy, and, following the sack of Rome in 1527, which appeared to give credence to them, he went to Italy. He came to believe that he was the messiah, and, in conformity with a talmudic legend about the sufferings of the messiah, he sat as a beggar for thirty days at the gates of Rome. Molcho met opposition from leaders of the Jewish community but gained an audience with the pope; his reputation was further strengthened when certain prophecies that he was said to have made—a flood in Rome and an earthquake in Portugal—did, in fact, occur. He went to Venice, where he gained the support of a large section of the community, but his opponents denounced him to the Inquisition in Rome, and only the protection of the pope saved him at that time from the fire. He was burned in 1532 in Mantua after the failure of his mission with Reuveni to the emperor.[25]

Messianic expectations appear to have declined after Molcho's death, but they were renewed in Italy in the 1560s. A number of dates for the imminent coming of the messiah were announced, but the year that was most widely and strongly believed to be the year of redemption was 1575. When that year passed, a leading believer in imminent redemption recalculated the year to be 1608, but he expressed himself with less certainty than before.[26]

Explanations

Gerson D. Cohen's contention that no discernible connection existed between the persecution of the Jews and their messianic movements and that all such movements appeared in areas and periods of relative stability has to be questioned.[27] It is true that among the Ashkenazim persecution was not followed by millenarianism. Among the Sephardi and Italian communities, however, some instances of millenarianism did follow persecution, although here disaster was not a necessary condition for a messianic outburst.

Disaster did not immediately precede the incidents in Castile in 1295; in fact, there is no clear historical or social factor that can account for these events. Some Castilian Jews had fears concerning their future. The last years of the reign of Alfonso X (1252–84) had been marked by the execution and jailing of a number of Jewish courtiers who had become involved in court intrigues, and in 1281 the king had many Jews arrested in their synagogues. Sancho IV (1284–95) reinstated the Jewish notables and gave them important positions as tax farmers and financiers, but the Crown was under continual pressure to eliminate Jews from state positions and various economic activities. With the death of the king in 1295 many Jews feared that they would now be exposed to the persecution of their enemies.[28] Demands were made on the new rulers to exclude Jews from their official positions, but it is not known whether the death of the king aroused great fears among the poorer stratum of Jews, who supported the prophets of Avila and Ayllon.

Avila had a Jewish population of about fifty families, mainly small shopkeepers and artisans who had some land under cultivation and owned small herds of sheep and cattle.[29] In a village such as Ayllon the economic character of the Jews could not have been very different. Millenarianism did not appear in the larger urban Jewish communities, which were dominated by wealthy Jewish families.

The millenarianism in 1391 had a clear background of disaster: violent attacks on Jews began in Seville and then spread to the rest of Spain. In large part the disturbances represented a social protest on the part of the Christian poor; they singled out Jews for attack since they provided a large proportion of the tax farmers and receivers acting on behalf of the Crown and the aristocracy. The majority of Jews were neither tax farmers nor wealthy, but the mobs attacked the Jews as a group, making no distinction between rich and poor. The riots continued for about a year, and the Spanish Jewish community may have lost as many as 40 percent of its members to murder, emigration, and conversion. Thousands more converted in the following decades under the pressures of a conversion campaign, anti-Jewish legislation, and occupational exclusion.[30]

The concern of the Spanish rulers that the presence of Jews had a corrupting influence on the New Christians and was thus an obstacle to their policy of Christian unification was possibly the most important factor in bringing about the greatest disaster to befall Spanish Jewry: the expulsion of 1492. The Jews were given four months to leave Spain, and those who remained were either forcibly expelled or baptized. They were forced to sell their property for very little and forbidden to take gold, silver, precious stones, and other specified goods. Pillage on land and sea accompanied the expulsion: thieves and pirates murdered many; others died of hunger and disease; and some were turned away from the lands where they had hoped to find refuge. The majority of exiles migrated to Portugal, but the Portuguese king, John II, admitted them on the condition that they leave the country within eight months. When the time ran out, he began to sell them as slaves. John's successor, Manoel I, freed them, but in 1497, as a result of an agreement with Spain, ordered them converted by force.[31]

Spanish exiles provided an important focus for millennial excitement among Italian Jews at this time,[32] but, since Italian Jews had not directly experienced any great disaster or persecution, their millenarian excitement requires further explanation. When Jews have been persecuted and segregated, non-Jewish millennial movements have not stimulated Jewish millenarianism, but during the Renaissance, when social and cultural contacts between Jews and their neighbors were greater, Italian Jews shared in the widespread millenarianism of the Italian population. Many Christian millennialists knew of the expulsion from Spain, assigned Jews a cosmic role in their eschatologies, and shared with their Jewish counterparts millennial interpretations of astrological portents and historical events. Millennial tension and expectations built up in Italy in the 1480s and 1490s, when a number of prophets appeared in various parts of the country, including

Venice, proclaiming imminent destruction and the end of the world. This excitement was related to expectations of invasion and the actual French invasion in 1494 by Charles VIII. In France Charles VIII was seen in the millennial role of a second Charlemagne, and Charles saw himself as an apocalyptic reformer of the church, a new crusader who would conquer the Islamic world. The prophecy that Charles VIII would conquer the Muslims and convert them to Christianity circulated in Italy as well as in France, and at first his Italian conquests did appear to fulfill the prophecies.[33]

The invasion had a particular impact on Jews. The second entrance of the French into Rome in 1495 was accompanied by an anti-Jewish outbreak, but once Charles assumed control in the city he put the Jews under his protection. This, together with the fact that the pope and his cardinals had fled Rome, gave rise to the belief among some Jews that a new era was about to begin. The arrival of the French in Naples in 1495 brought with it the pillage of its numerous and influential Jews, but one Jewish prophet saw Charles's entry into the city as a sign of the imminent advent of the messiah. In a somewhat confused fashion he calculated that 1490 had been the beginning of the period of sufferings, that 1495 ended this period, and that 1503 would mark final deliverance.[34]

The most important focus of millennial excitement in Italy was Florence, where Savonarola, prior of the Dominican convent of San Marco, preached the coming advent to enthusiastic crowds. Before the French invasion Savonarola had preached great suffering for Florence and Italy, and following the invasion, when he talked more of the coming millennium, he spoke with the authority of a prophet whose former predictions had come true. For Savonarola the tribulations of Florence were a sign of its election as the chosen city, the new Jerusalem, the center of the millennium, and the Florentines as latter-day Israelites who would reach new spiritual heights and enjoy great riches, power, and a large empire.[35] We do not know how much impact Savonarola's campaign had on Italian Jews, but B. Netanyahu argues that Abravanel, a courtier at Naples who had to flee the French, must have been aware of Savonarola.[36]

The millenarianism of Italian Jews in the first decades of the sixteenth century was not the result of direct experience with disaster or persecution; it reflected, rather, the influence of Spanish exiles and Christian messianists and their messianic interpretation of major historical events. The revival of millenarianism among Italian Jews in the last decades of the sixteenth century coincided with the anti-Jewish measures of the Counter Reformation. From the 1560s an increasing number of harsh restrictions were imposed on Italian Jews: they were expelled from many areas, their occupations and economic pursuits were severely limited, they were forced to wear a distinctive badge and live in ghettos, and the Talmud was publicly burned and prohibited. Reduced to poverty and a precarious existence, many emigrated from Italy.[37] Of those who remained many appear to have found compensation in millenarianism and mysticism.

Localized messianic incidents, such as those in Avila and Ayllon in 1295, were not immediately preceded by acute crises, but among the Sephardim and the conversos and in Italy the most active messianic incidents followed major tragic events: the massacres of 1391, attacks on the conversos from the 1440s and their persecution by the Spanish Inquisition from 1480, the expulsion of 1492, and the persecutions of the Italian Counter Reformation. Yet active messianism was almost unknown among the Ashkenazim, who experienced a greater number of disasters and periods of persecution. Ashkenazim were massacred in large numbers during the Crusades, at the time of the Black Death, and on a number of other occasions. They were subject to a number of expulsions, particularly in the fourteenth, fifteenth, and sixteenth centuries, and their livelihoods were increasingly restricted by anti-Jewish decrees.[38] While the faith of the Ashkenazim in the eventual coming of the messiah was often strengthened during these periods of persecution, there were no influential predictions of, or preparations for, his imminent coming.

Most of the popular prophets in Spain were unscholarly men who found support from their own socioeconomic stratum, but the differences between Sephardim and Ashkenazim extended also to the elite rabbinical level. Sephardi rabbis tended to condemn messianic pretenders and prophets, but they often seemed preoccupied with calculating the date of the coming of the messiah. Ashkenazi rabbis were influenced by injunctions that prohibited such calculations, and this orientation penetrated to the masses: speculation on the matter remained esoteric and limited to narrow circles. In Spain scholars felt no inhibition about discussing in public the date of the coming of the messiah, which they made the subject of a long series of tracts.[39] The millenarianism that followed the expulsion of 1492 infected all strata of Iberian Jewry, the wealthy and scholarly as well as the poor and unscholarly.

Millenarianism was not the only response of the Sephardim to persecution; other responses included hopeless despair, self-blame for the failure to keep the religious law, and acceptance of Christianity. Nevertheless, millenarianism was one significant response to disaster: through it their sufferings became the birth pangs of the messiah, while they, the victims of persecution, believed that they would soon find happiness in the millennial kingdom.

The contrast in the responses of Ashkenazim and Sephardim to persecution reflects more general differences in their cultural and religious orientations. The Ashkenazim emphasized sin, guilt, humility, and asceticism; their quiescence and passivity were not conducive to millenarianism. The Sephardim emphasized pride, nobility, self-assertiveness, and, in some cases, epicureanism. They put great emphasis on the noble status of their families. As among the Ashkenazim, descent from scholars was important, but Sephardic notions of nobility were closer to those of Christians: nobility was seen to be inherent in the families themselves, and claims were made of descent from the nobility of ancient Jerusalem including, toward the end of the Middle Ages, the house of David.

In general, the Ashkenazim were stricter in their religious practice. Religious laxness and indifference were not uncommon among rich Sephardim, especially courtiers who found that Jewish religious requirements were not always compatible with court life.[40] Averroism, which stressed the superiority of reason over faith, spread among some wealthy Sephardim, while at the same time other wealthy Sephardim were engaged in the study of kabbalah. Some of the kabbalists attacked their peers for their rationalism and accommodation to the non-Jewish world.[41]

Secular tendencies among the Sephardim explain, in part, why they often acted differently from the Ashkenazim when faced with the alternative of conversion or death. Many Ashkenazim, including entire communities, converted under such pressure, but the majority remained faithful, believing that they ensured their path to heaven by the choice of death. Martyrdom became an ideology and an institutionalized ritual: for the "sanctity of the name" those Jews faced with the threat of forced conversion first recited benedictions and then killed their children and themselves. This phenomenon did not appear among the Sephardim until the end of the fourteenth century, and even then only a small minority pursued martyrdom; the great majority preferred to submit to conversion.[42] Perhaps the Sephardim were able to make choices more frequently, for in Germany the mob was intent on pillage and killing, whereas in Spain conversion was the long-range goal of the rulers.[43] Nevertheless, even when faced with similar situations, Ashkenazim and Sephardim chose different paths.

Cohen traced the differences between Ashkenazi passivity and Sephardi self-assertion to their different beginnings. He argued that Palestine provided the cultural roots of the Ashkenazim and that, after the failure of the Bar Kochba revolt, Jews in Palestine remained relatively quiescent: its leaders taught submission and passive waiting for the intervention of God. On the other hand, the cultural roots of Iberian Jews were in Babylonia; there they held two political stances: the cooperation of Jewish leaders with the Gentile rulers and the rebellion of dissatisfied groups.[44]

This, however, is not a convincing argument. It is true that in the early Middle Ages Franco-German Jewry came under the influence of Palestine, by way of Italy, while Spanish Jewry had links with Babylonia through North Africa. It is also true that differences between Ashkenazi and Sephardi rituals stemmed, in part, from their separate beginnings in Palestine and Babylonia, respectively.[45] But there is no evidence of a transmission of different political and cultural orientations to the wider society, and it is clear that these orientations developed over time, becoming distinctive only in the later Middle Ages.

Mention has already been made of the development of kabbalah among Sephardi Jews. The possibility that these religious innovations stimulated millenarianism deserves consideration. Certain Spanish kabbalists, such as Abraham Abulafia, were also messianists, but, while their mystical experiences and prophetic announcements were closely related, their messianism was not a logical outgrowth of their kabbalistic doctrines.[46] The major part of the most important kabbalistic work of the period, the *Zohar,* was probably completed between 1280 and 1286,[47] and it is interesting to note that Moses de Leon, its author, lived in Avila at the time of the messianic prophet.[48] The *Zohar* contains a number of eschatological passages that allude to the later Crusades and the collapse of the palaces of Rome and apocalyptic calculations that predict that the exile would end at the beginning of the fourteenth century.[49] These passages, however, are only a small part of a vast work, actually a collection of several books, concerned with mystical interpretations and secret meanings of the whole world of Judaism. Furthermore, the influence of the *Zohar* and the kabbalah in general is not evident until the last decades of the fifteenth century, and for some time it remained the esoteric preoccupation of small circles of mystics who had no apparent influence on the millenarianism of the masses.[50]

Asher Lemlein was influenced by certain kabbalistic doctrines,[51] but in Italy only in the second half of the sixteenth century were there indications of a close interrelationship between millenarianism and kabbalah.[52] Mordecai Dato wrote on millennial themes around the year 1575,[53] and a group of kabbalists tried to hasten the coming of the messiah by introducing new significance into the midnight prayer for Israel's restoration.[54] Many kabbalists in Italy in the last decades of the sixteenth century were also millenarians, but, in contrast to Lurianic kabbalah, which became the dominant form in the seventeenth century, nothing in the kabbalistic system of the period would inspire millenarianism. Moreover, it can be argued that the spread of mysticism was itself a response to the deteriorating situation of Italian Jews.

The different cultural orientations of Sephardim and Ashkenazim have to be seen, in turn, in relation to the differences in the societies in which they lived and, in particular, to differences in their relationships with them. Until the second half of the tenth century the number of Jews in Germany and northern France was very small, and Franco-German Jewry became firmly established only around the year 1000. Prior to the first Crusade, apart from some minor incidents, the Ashkenazim lived in peace, and, although there was a general disdain for merchants in early medieval Europe, Jews were able to achieve a reasonable economic position. This period of economic advance and relative security was, however, of comparatively short duration. From the first Crusade, in 1096, the economic and social position of the Ashkenazim in Western and Central Europe declined: attacks became more frequent; Jews were limited to a narrow range of occupations, especially moneylending, and increasingly segregated from the non-Jewish population. This is not to say that no Ashkenazim ever lived peacefully or that friendly relations with Christians never existed but that violence and segregation took their toll, strengthening Ashkenazi cultural distinctiveness and feelings of separateness from the dominant society.[55]

In contrast, large-scale persecution of the Sephardim began after a very long period of relative peace and prosperity. Apart from a temporary setback as a result of the invasion of the Almoravides in the 1080s, Spanish Jews under Muslim rule enjoyed prosperity and high status. This lasted until the invasion of the Almohades in 1147, when many Jews migrated north to Christian Spain, where, from the beginning of the Christian reconquest in the second half of the eleventh century, their already favorable position improved further. The reconquered territories were characterized by greater religious and ethnic diversity than other Christian societies in which Jews had settled. Iberia's Christian princes adopted in some measure the Muslim model of "protected peoples," providing their Muslim and Jewish minorities with legal safeguards, group autonomy, and access to relatively high-status occupations. The Christian kings referred to themselves as the "kings of the three religions," and a pluralistic structure evolved in which a comparatively high level of tolerance characterized relations among the three religious collectivities.

The Christian princes of the reconquest found the Jews reliable allies, while Jewish familiarity with the newly conquered territories was a useful asset. Kings and nobles appointed Jews to important positions as diplomats, financiers, tax farmers, administrators, scholars, and physicians. In Castile, which was often in a state of political disturbance, kings felt that they could trust their Jewish counselors, who were not subject to the conflicting loyalties of their Christian vassals. Jews occupied a wide variety of professions and occupations and, unhampered by economic discrimination, were of great importance in the economy of the country: they constituted a large section of the urban population and bourgeoisie, controlling a significant part of Spanish commerce, industry, mining, and viticulture. The ruling elements saw Jewish land ownership as being in the royal interest and put no restrictions on their acquisition of estates. Some wealthy Jews owned castles and villages and even exercised feudal rights in the thirteenth and fourteenth centuries. Secular leaders often ignored or opposed decrees of the church that were intended to segregate and discriminate against Jews. Some popes complained about the important positions given to Jews in Spain, but in Spain itself churchmen employed Jews to lease, administer, and collect taxes from ecclesiastical properties.

The majority of Spanish Jews lived in their own quarters, but up to the latter part of the fourteenth century this was entirely voluntary, and it was not unusual to find Jews living outside and Christians living inside the Jewish quarters. There were no clear external differences between Jews and Christians: they spoke the same language, took similar names, and wore the same style of clothes. The lifestyle of wealthy Jews, who carried arms, mixed freely in royal courts and noble mansions, and conspicuously displayed great riches and luxury, had no counterpart among the Ashkenazim. The Jewish community itself was split socially between a minority, the rich and powerful, and the majority, small merchants and artisans, but cordial relations between Jews and non-Jews were not limited to the upper stratum. Jewish and Christian burghers had friendly professional and personal relationships; Jewish advocates represented Gentile clients in secular courts; Jewish artisans had Christian customers or worked for Christian employers; Jewish textile merchants employed Christian workers; Jews and non-Jews joined in common processions, shared the public baths, exchanged gifts on holidays and family occasions, and ate occasional meals together. Jews performed the roles of godfather and godmother at Christian baptisms, while Christians performed similar roles at Jewish circumcisions.[56] This is in sharp contrast to the precarious position of the Ashkenazim, their low status as despised moneylenders, and their segregated existence.

Feelings of superiority among the Sephardim stemmed not only from their Judaism and Jewishness, as was the case among the Ashkenazim, but also from their status and power within the larger society. Since they felt secure in and strongly identified with the dominant culture, any reversal in their situation was bound to create disorientation. Among the Ashkenazim, who rarely identified with the host society and culture, pogroms and expulsions created suffering but less fundamental disorientation: their tradition of martyrdom reminded them that persecution was an integral part of their history and that it was sensible to keep their assets in liquid form, ready to move.

Indications that the position of Spanish Jews was not inviolable were already present at the end of the thirteenth century. With the reconquest nearly completed and most of the Iberian Peninsula united into a few large kingdoms, churchmen and secular rulers began to treat the Jews more as they were being treated in the rest of Christian Europe. In Aragon the change in church policy began in the middle of the thirteenth century, but in Castile, where Jewish influence in the state, and especially in its financial administration, was greater, the status of the Jews remained high, and relations between Jews and Christians remained good.[57]

The spread of anti-Jewish sentiment in the fourteenth century was related to a number of factors: the success of the reconquest; the decline in the pluralistic orientation of the Spanish princes; the increasing influence in Spain of common European cultural and religious patterns; and the growth of the Christian bourgeoisie. In Aragon the Jews lost much of their political influence and socioeconomic status, while in Castile, despite increasing demands by clergy, burghers, and nobles for the removal of Jews from positions of state, the Jews were not seriously affected until the second half of the fourteenth century. A civil war in Castile in 1366–69 ruined a number of Jewish communities and marked the beginning of the decline of Jewish power in the state. In the last decades of the century discriminatory and segregative measures began to be put into effect.[58]

The pogroms of 1391 were followed, in 1412–15, by discriminatory measures that excluded Jews from certain trades, barred them from service in the royal and urban governments, and reduced their social interaction with Christians. The Spanish kings soon abolished many of these anti-Jewish edicts and tried to restore the Jews to their former status. While this brought some improvement in their situation, it did not restore them to their pre-1391 situation: many communities were not reestablished, the Jews' political rank and influence declined, fewer wealthy Jews remained, some discriminatory measures were instituted, and the center of Jewish life moved from the large cities to the small towns, where Jews continued as small merchants, shopkeepers, and artisans. Nevertheless, up to the expulsion of 1492 the situation of Spanish Jews remained considerably better than that of the Ashkenazim of Western and Central Europe. Despite an official ban on office holding in the royal and urban administrations, Jews remained important as financiers, tax farmers, physicians, and surgeons, and these rich Jews continued to mix in court and government circles. Although occasional outbreaks continued, popular discontent was directed more against Jewish converts to Christianity than against Jews. The aristocracy may have felt threatened by the rise of wealthy converts, but its members were not especially hostile toward Jews, who continued to be protected by the rulers of Aragon and Castile until the expulsion.[59]

Thus, even in the fifteenth century the strong contrast between the Ashkenazim and Sephardim remained: the Sephardim were not confined mainly to moneylending but were found in a wide range of occupations, including the most prestigious; they were not segregated in ghettos but were allowed to mix freely with non-Jews; and they did not feel an enormous cultural gulf between themselves and the non-Jewish population but identified with many aspects of Spanish culture. During the second half of the fifteenth century the sermons and writings of Jewish scholars continued to express a high respect for Iberian Christian culture.

A number of discriminatory measures and unauthorized local expulsions in Castile preceded the expulsion edict of 1492, but it came as an unexpected and enormous blow.[60] Its effects on the lives and self-image of Spanish Jewry were devastating, far greater than those of any other expulsion of Jews. One reason for this, perhaps, was that it was on a far greater scale than other expulsions: those in Germany or France had been either partial or carried out in stages, and the total expulsion of Jews from England in 1290 had affected a much smaller community.[61] More important, however, the Sephardim felt that they were being torn, violently and cruelly, from their homeland. For the Ashkenazim expulsion was a tragedy in the sense that they lost their property and were forced to migrate and resettle, but it little affected their attachment to a particular society and culture or focal elements of their identity. For the Sephardim, who regarded themselves as among the cultural elite and who took great pride in their history and achievements in Spain, exile was a great blow to their identity and pride and gave rise to enormous resentment and a desire for revenge. Some exiles expressed their concern that they had accepted expulsion without attempting armed resistance; some found consolation in the belief that the punishments of the "end of time" were near.[62]

It would appear, therefore, that messianism was a response to disaster among people whose leaders had enjoyed wealth, status, and power and who had been rejected by a society into which they had formerly been highly integrated, culturally and socially. To illustrate this with an individual case: Isaac Abravanel, who served as diplomat and financier to six kings, associated freely with kings and nobles and participated comfortably in both Jewish culture and the culture of the Christian upper stratum. On three occasions, in Portugal, Spain, and Naples, Abravanel was separated from his property, stripped of his honor, and forced into exile. He shared the false optimism of Spanish Jewry, and, although his immediate reaction was to despair of redemption, he came to interpret the expulsion as part of the birth pangs of the messiah. In his messianic works he emphasized revenge: the redemption of the Jews would emerge from the punishment of the Gentiles, especially of the Christians.[63]

The change in the situation of Italian Jewry in the sixteenth century replicates, in many respects, the change that had occurred earlier in Spain. During the Renaissance, in the fifteenth century and the first half of the sixteenth, Italian Jews mixed freely with Christians and adopted aspects of the dominant culture. Christians, including clergymen, visited synagogues to hear Jewish preachers, and friendships sometimes developed between rabbis and priests. As had been the case in Spain, Gentile friends served as godfathers at circumcision ceremonies. The Jews of Renaissance Italy emphasized courage and self-esteem; attracted to pomp and solemnity, they concerned themselves with titles, coats of arms, and the right to bear arms.[64] Counter Reformation measures in the second half of the century represented a sharp reversal for Italian Jews; like the Spanish Jews before them, they experienced a sudden fall from wealth and honor and the rejection of a society that had formerly accepted them and whose culture they had, in many respects, accepted. Once again the sufferings were interpreted as the birth pangs of the messiah.[65]

All European Jews experienced persecution, but Spanish and Italian

Jews underwent a deeper disruption of their social expectations and cultural order. They experienced a greater deprivation, relative to their past state, in their economic position, social status, and political influence.

Conclusions

Crises have preceded messianic movements in Jewish history, but not all crises have given rise to messianic movements. In fact, only a few did so. An analysis of the relationship of crises and messianic movements requires an examination of the nature of the crises and of the cultural framework in which they were understood. Many widespread messianic outbursts arose during or following instances of acute persecution, massacre, or exile, but the influence of these disasters on messianic outbursts was variable, dependent on other factors. One important cultural dimension influencing the association between persecution and messianism was the presence or absence of other established explanations of, and compensations for, persecution. Messianic beliefs were as much a part of the religious tradition of Ashkenazim as they were of that of Sephardim, but in the medieval period the former were far less prone to use those beliefs to account for the disasters that befell them. Ashkenazim attributed their fate to the sins of the Jewish people and found solace in the belief that in accepting death rather than conversion they were proving their righteousness and would be rewarded by a blissful afterlife. Sephardim and Italian Jews explained the exile from Spain and their persecution as part of the birth pangs of the messiah and looked forward to the revenge that would be exacted by his forces.

The responses of Sephardim and Ashkenazim to persecution were related to more general differences in their cultural orientations toward the countries in which they lived and to the whole notion of *galut*. During most of the medieval period the situation of Jews in the Iberian Peninsula was considerably better than elsewhere, and, although Sephardim accepted exile from the Holy Land as part of their religious tradition, they formed a strong attachment to the Spanish kingdoms and their culture. Exile was less prominent in their consciousness, and thus they turned to messianism when their pride and identity were shattered. On the other hand, Ashkenazim felt little or no attachment to their host societies, and thus, precisely because they felt in exile, seeing it as normative, they were less attracted to active messianism. Exile was a state of being to which they had to adjust so that sometime in the unforeseen future they would be redeemed.

The types of crises that have engendered Jewish messianic movements are those that have threatened or destroyed important elements of previously held identities, and messianic movements have represented attempts to reintegrate identities by focusing on a single core element. Prior to the crises identities may have contained ambiguous and possibly contradictory elements, and the crises have motivated Jews to adopt beliefs in an imminent redemption that cancels ambiguity and stands for a wholly Jewish identity. The expulsion from Spain had made meaningless what for many Sephardim had been an important part of their identity, and their messianism expressed both an absolute rejection of the Spanish culture and society from which they had been cast out and an absolute affirmation of the reason for their predicament—their Judaism.

NOTES

1. Yonina Talmon, "Pursuit of the Millennium: The Relation between Religious and Social Change," *Archives europennes de sociologie* 3 (1962): 125–48; "Millenarian Movements," *Archives europennes de sociologie* 7 (1966): 159–200; Maria Isaura Pereira de Queiros, "Messianic Myths and Movements," *Diogenes* 90 (1975): 78–99.

2. On the development of Jewish millenarianism and messianism in the ancient period, see Joseph Klausner, *The Messianic Idea in Israel: From Its Beginning to the Completion of the Mishnah* (New York: Macmillan, 1955); Sigmund Mowinckel, *He That Cometh,* trans. G. W. Anderson (Oxford: Blackwell, 1956); Sheldon R. Isenberg, "Millenarianism in Greco-Roman Palestine," *Religion* 4 (1974): 26–46; Ellis Rivkin, "The Meaning of Messiah in Jewish Thought," *Union Seminary Quarterly Review* 26 (1971): 383–406; *Encyclopaedia Judaica,* s.v., "eschatology" and "messiah." On the talmudic period, see Leo Landman, ed., *Messianism in the Talmudic Era* (New York: Ktav Publishing House, 1979). On the medieval period, see Joseph Sarachek, *The Doctrine of the Messiah in Medieval Jewish Literature* (New York: Hermon Press, 1968); Gershom Scholem, "Toward an Understanding of the Messianic Idea in Judaism," *The Messianic Idea in Judaism* (London: Allen and Unwin, 1971), 1–36; Nahum N. Glatzer, "Zion in Medieval Literature: Prose Works," in *Zion in Jewish Literature,* ed. Abraham S. Halkin (New York: Herzl Press, 1961), 83–100. Collections of texts are found in Raphael Patai, ed., *The Messiah Texts* (New York: Wayne State University Press, 1979); and George Wesley Buchanan, ed. and trans., *Revelation and Redemption: Jewish Documents of Deliverance from the Fall of Jerusalem to the Death of Nahmanides* (Dillsboro: Western North Carolina Press, 1978).

3. Sarachek, *Doctrine of the Messiah,* 301–3; Scholem, "The Messianic Idea in Judaism," 30–33; Yitzhak Baer, *A History of the Jews in Christian Spain,* 2 vols., trans. Louis Schoffman (Philadelphia: Jewish Publication Society, 1961), 1:249.

4. See the collection of articles in Jacob Neusner, William Scott Green, and Ernest S. Frerichs, eds., *Judaisms and Their Messiahs at the Turn of the Christian Era* (Cambridge: Cambridge University Press, 1987). See also items listed in n. 2.

5. Jacob Neusner, *Messiah in Context* (Philadelphia: Fortress Press, 1984).

6. Michael Barkun, *Disaster and the Millennium* (New Haven: Yale University Press, 1974).

7. These movements and their background are discussed in my book *Messianism, Mysticism, and Magic: A Sociological Analysis of Jewish Religious Movements* (Chapel Hill: University of North Carolina Press, 1982). See also Aaron Zev Aescoly, *Ha-tenuot ha-meshihiyyot be-yisrael* (Jewish Messianic Movements) (Jerusalem: Mosad Bialik, 1956); Jacob Mann, "Ha-tenuot ha-meshihiyyot be-yamei masaei ha-tslav ha-rishonim" (Messianic Movements at the Time of the First Crusade) *Ha-tekufah* 23 (1925): 243–61, 24 (1928): 335–58.

8. Shlomo Eidelberg, *The Jews and the Crusades: The Hebrew Chronicles of the First and Second Crusades* (Madison: University of Wisconsin Press, 1977), 13.

9. Ibid., 10.

10. H. J. Zimmels, *Ashkenazim and Sephardim: Their Relations, Differences, and Problems as Reflected in the Rabbinical Responsa* (London: Oxford University Press, 1958), 233–50; Moses A. Shulvass, *Between the Rhine and the Bosporus: Studies and Essays in European Jewish History* (Chicago: College of Jewish Studies Press, 1964), 5–13.

11. Robert Chazan, "The Hebrew First Crusade Chronicles," *Revue des études juives* 133 (1974): 235–54.

12. Gershom Scholem, *Major Trends in Jewish Mysticism* (New York: Schocken Books, 1969), 87–90.

13. Baer, *Jews in Christian Spain,* 1:277–80.

14. Ibid., 1:159–62; Gershom Scholem, *Kabbalah* (Jerusalem: Keter, 1974), 65–66; *Encyclopaedia Judaica,* s.v., "Botarel, Moses ben Isaac"; Aescoly, *Ha-tenuot ha-meshihiyyot,* 226.

15. Benzion Dinur, "Tenuat aliyah mi-sefarad le-erets Yisrael aharei gezeirat [5]151" (Emigration from Spain to the Land of Israel after the Disorders of 1391), *Zion* 32 (1967): 161–74.

16. Joseph R. Hacker, "Links between Spanish Jewry and Palestine, 1391–1492," in *Vision and Conflict in the Holy Land,* ed. Richard I. Cohen (Jerusalem: Yad Izhak Ben-Zvi, 1985), 111–39.

17. H. H. Ben-Sasson, "Galut ve-geulah be-einav shel dor golei Sefarad" (Exile and Redemption in the Eyes of the Spanish Exiles) in *Yitzhak F. Baer Jubilee Volume,* ed. S. W. Baron et al. (Jerusalem: Historical Society of Israel, 1960), 216–27; Isaiah Tishby, *Meshihiyyut be-dor gerushei Sefarad u-Fortugal* (Messianism in the

Time of the Expulsion from Spain and Portugal) (Jerusalem: Merkaz Zalman Shazar, 1985).

18. Julio Caro Baroja, *Los Judios en la Espana moderna y contemporanea,* 3 vols. (Madrid: Ediciones Arron, 1961), 1:189–90. Baroja estimates that in 1541 there were 250,000 converts in a Spanish population of 7.4 million.

19. Baer, *Jews in Christian Spain,* 2:356–58; "Ha-tenuah ha-meshihiyit be-Sefarad be-tekufat ha-gerush" (The Messianic Movement in Spain in the Period of the Expulsion), *Zion* 5 (1933): 71–77; Haim Beinart, "The Converso Community in Sixteenth and Seventeenth-Century Spain," in *The Sephardi Heritage,* ed. R. D. Barnett (London: Vallentine Mitchell, 1971), 457–78; Haim Beinart, "Anusei Halia ve-tenuah shel ha-neviah Ines" (The Conversos of Halia and the Prophetess Ines of Herrera), *Zion* 53 (1988): 13–52.

20. Cecil Roth, *The History of the Jews of Italy* (Philadelphia: Jewish Publication Society, 1946), 179; Moses A. Shulvass, *Roma vi-Yerushalayim* (Rome and Jerusalem) (Jerusalem: Mosad Ha-Rav Kook, 1944), 41–67.

21. B. Netanyahu, *Don Isaac Abravanel* (Philadelphia: Jewish Publication Society, 1953), 200–240; Isaac E. Barzilay, *Between Reason and Faith: Anti-Rationalism in Italian Jewish Thought, 1250–1650* (The Hague: Mouton, 1967), 122–23; Baer, "Ha-tenuah ha-meshihiyit."

22. Shulvass, *Roma vi-Yerushalayim,* 44–45; *The Jews in the World of the Renaissance* (Leiden: E. J. Brill, 1973), 9, 210; A. Marx, "Le Faux messie Ascher Laemmlein," *Revue des études juives* 61 (1911): 135–38.

23. Shulvass, *Roma vi-Yerushalayim,* 45–48; Aescoly, *Ha-tenuot ha-meshihiyyot,* 250; Lionel Kochan, *Jews, Idols and Messiahs: The Challenge from History* (Oxford: Basil Blackwell, 1990); Isaiah Tishby, "Acute Apocalyptic Messianism," in *Essential Papers on Messianic Movements and Personalities in Jewish History,* ed. Marc Saperstein (New York: New York University Press, 1992), 267–69.

24. Aescoly, *Ha-tenuot ha-meshihiyyot,* 251–78; "David Reuveni in the Light of History," *Jewish Quarterly Review* 28 (1937–38): 1–45; Shulvass, *Roma vi-Yerushalayim,* 54–64; Cecil Roth, "A Zionist Experiment in the Sixteenth Century," *Midstream* 9, no. 3 (1963): 76–81; Azriel Shohat, "Le-farashat David ha-Reuveni " (Notes on the David Reuveni Affair), *Zion* 35 (1970): 96–116.

25. Aescoly, *Ha-tenuot ha-meshihiyyot,* 266–78; Shulvass, *Roma vi-Yerushalayim,* 61–64.

26. Ibid., 79–82; David Tamar, "Ha-tsippiyah be-Italyah li-shenat ha-geulah [5]335" (Messianic Expectations in Italy for the Year 1575), *Sefunot* 2 (1958): 61–88.

27. Gerson D. Cohen, "Messianic Postures of Ashkenazim and Sephardim (Prior to Sabbatai Zevi)," in *Studies of the Leo Baeck Institute,* ed. Max Kreutzberger (New York: Frederick Ungar, 1967), 117–56.

28. Baer, *Jews in Christian Spain,* 1:129–31, 137; Abraham A. Neuman, *The*

Jews in Spain: Their Social, Political, and Cultural Life during the Middle Ages, 2 vols. (Philadelphia: Jewish Publication Society, 1942), 2:244–47.

29. Baer, *Jews in Christian Spain,* 1:198.

30. Ibid., 2:97–112; Léon Poliakov, *The History of Anti-Semitism,* vol. 1: *From the Time of Christ to the Court Jews* (London: Vanguard Press, 1975), 157–58; Philippe Wolff, "The 1391 Pogrom in Spain: Social Crisis or Not," *Past and Present,* no. 50 (1971): 4–18; Jane S. Gerber, *The Jews of Spain: A History of the Sephardic Experience* (New York: Free Press, 1992), 113–17; Bernard F. Reilly, *The Medieval Spains* (Cambridge: Cambridge University Press, 1993), 199–201.

31. Baer, *Jews in Christian Spain,* 2:434–49; Poliakov, *History of Anti-Semitism,* 200–201; Jacob S. Minkin, *Abrabanel and the Expulsion of the Jews from Spain* (New York: Behrman's Jewish Book House, 1938), 143–51; Gerber, *Jews of Spain,* 129–42.

32. Lemlein's prophecies also spread among Ashkenazim who had been expelled from parts of Germany and had settled in Istria and other towns of the Venetian Republic. Shulvass, *Jews in the Renaissance,* 12.

33. Marjorie Reeves, *The Influence of Prophecy in the Later Middle Ages* (Oxford: Clarendon Press, 1969), 354, 358, 430–35; Donald Weinstein, *Savonarola and Florence* (Princeton: Princeton University Press, 1970), 62–63, 112–15, 166; David B. Ruderman, "Hope against Hope: Jewish and Christian Messianic Expectations in the Late Middle Ages," in *Essential Papers on Jewish Culture in Renaissance and Baroque Italy,* ed. David B. Ruderman (New York: New York University Press, 1992), 299–323.

34. Samuel Krauss, "Le roi de France Charles VIII et les espérances messianiques," *Revue des études juives* 51 (1906): 87–96. Krauss speculates that the unknown prophet made his calculations during Lemlein's movement.

35. Weinstein, *Savonarola and Florence,* 142–47, 167–69, 374–76.

36. Netanyahu, *Isaac Abravanel,* 247–78. Netanyahu notes the parallels between the prophecies of Savonarola and Abravanel. Often the only substantial difference is that one is referring to the Florentines and Florence, while the other is referring to the Jews and Jerusalem. The parallels are, however, common features in millenarianism and are not sufficient to conclude that Savonarola had a direct influence on Abravanel.

37. Roth, *History of the Jews of Italy,* 289–94; Salo Wittmayer Baron, *A Social and Religious History of the Jews,* 18 vols. (New York: Columbia University Press, 1952–83), 14:114–46.

38. Stephen Sharot, *Judaism: A Sociology* (New York: Holmes and Meier, 1976), 25–29; Poliakov, *History of Anti-Semitism,* vol. 1, chaps. 2–7.

39. Cohen, "Messianic Postures," 125–42.

40. Zimmels, *Ashkenazim and Sephardim,* 188–267.

41. Baer, *Jews in Christian Spain,* 2:245–46, 253–59.

42. H. H. Ben-Sasson, "Kiddush Ha-Shem," *Trial and Achievement: Currents in Jewish History* (Jerusalem: Keter, 1974), 209–16; Robert Chazan, "The Hebrew First Crusade Chronicles," *Revue des études juives* 133 (1974): 235–54; Cohen, "Messianic Postures," 148–56; Poliakov, *History of Anti-Semitism*, vol. 2: *From Mohammed to the Marranos* (London: Routledge and Kegan Paul, 1973), 73–95.

43. Isaiah Sonne, "On Baer and His Philosophy of Jewish History," *Jewish Social Studies* 9 (1947): 61–80.

44. Cohen, "Messianic Postures," 144–47.

45. Zimmels, *Ashkenazim and Sephardim*, 12–15.

46. The "practical" kabbalah of Abulafia, stressing the mystical qualities of sacred names, numbers, and letter combinations, was highly magical. Scholem, *Kabbalah*, 53–55; Aescoly, *Ha-tenuot ha-meshihiyyot*, 194–213; Abraham Berger, "The Messianic Self-Consciousness of Abraham Abulafia," in *Essays on Jewish Life and Thought Presented in Honor of Salo Wittmayer Baron*, ed. Joseph L. Blau et al. (New York: Columbia University Press, 1959), 55–61.

47. Scholem, *Major Trends in Jewish Mysticism*, 188.

48. Baer, *Jews in Christian Spain*, 1:198.

49. Scholem, *Major Trends in Jewish Mysticism*, 186; Baer, *Jews in Christian Spain*, 1:249, 269. Baer notes similarites between the kabbalah and the works of the Franciscan Spirituals.

50. The *Zohar* glorified poverty as a religious value, making it a quality of the *shehinah* (divine presence). This was a striking innovation in Judaism and possibly reflects the influence of the Christian environment. Poliakov is wrong, however, to link kabbalah with the poor (2:243). Baer wrote that among the foremost masters of the kabbalah were men of wealthy families as well as from the lower social strata (1:243). He noted the parallels between the Franciscan Joachimites of the thirteenth century, who attacked the worldliness of the church, and the kabbalists, who attacked Jewish communal leaders for their neglect of the Torah and their exploitation of the poor (1:261–77, 367–73). Like the Franciscans, the kabbalists did not themselves come from the poor but were from comfortable families who rejected involvement in the world. On the Franciscans and Joachimist prophecy in Spain, see Reeves, *Influence of Prophecy*, 221–24, 247, 446.

51. Marx, "Le Faux messie," 135–38. The influence of the kabbalah is seen in Lemlein's arguments that the sinner has to be reincarnated to provide him with the opportunity to become righteous and that the messiah has to come to repair the sin of the first man, of whom the messiah was the last reincarnation.

52. Tamar, "Ha-tsippiyah be-Italyah," 61–88; Barzilay, *Between Reason and Faith*, 63–65.

53. Scholem, *Kabbalah*, 76.

54. Shulvass, *Jews in the World of the Renaissance*, 212. Elior argues that kabbalah became infused with messianic tendencies after the expulsion from Spain. Rachel Elior, "Messianic Expectations and Spiritualization of Religious Life in the

Sixteenth Century," *Revue des études juives* 145 (1986): 35–49. Idel, in contrast, questions the importance of the expulsion on developments in the kabbalah, including the Lurianic kabbalah. He argues that the expulsion made an overwhelming impression only on Iberian Jews and that it was not mentioned or was given little prominence by messianists such as Asher Lemlein and Abraham Eliezer ha-Levi. Moshe Idel, "Particularism and Universalism in Kabbalah, 1480–1650," in Ruderman, *Essential Papers,* 324–44.

55. For further analysis of the situation of the Ashkenazim and their religious responses, see my other article in this collection, "Religious Syncretism and Religious Distinctiveness: A Comparative Analysis of Pre-Modern Jewish Communities."

56. Poliakov, *History of Anti-Semitism,* vol. 2, chaps. 5–7; Neuman, *Jews in Spain,* 1:161–69, 2:182–274; Americo Castro, *The Spaniards* (Berkeley: University of California Press, 1971), 532, 544–47; Thomas F. Glick, *Islamic and Christian Spain in the Early Middle Ages* (Princeton: Princeton University Press, 1979), 168–69, 207.

57. Baer, *Jews in Christian Spain,* 1:177–80.

58. Ibid., 1:308, 364–68, 2:24–25, 31; Poliakov, *History of Anti-Semitism,* 2:140–56.

59. Baer, *Jews in Christian Spain,* 2:244–51; Poliakov, *History of Anti-Semitism,* 2:163–68; Wolff, "The 1391 Pogrom in Spain," 4–18; Gerber, *Jews of Spain,* 129, 137.

60. Baer, *Jews in Christian Spain,* 2:322, 433; Poliakov, *History of Anti-Semitism,* 2:189–99; Stephen H. Haliczer, "The Castilian Urban Patriciate and the Jewish Expulsions of 1480–92," *American Historical Review* 78 (1973): 35–58.

61. Baer, *Jews in Christian Spain,* 2:434–49.

62. Ben-Sasson, "Galut ve-geulah"; Tishby, *Meshihiyyut be-dor gerushei Sefarad u-Fortugal;* "Acute Apocalyptic Messianism"; H. H. Ben-Sasson, "Dor golei Sefarad al atsmo" (The Generation of the Spanish Exiles and Its Fate), *Zion* 26 (1961): 23–64.

63. Netanyahu, *Isaac Abravanel,* 87–88, 226–34.

64. Shulvass, *Jews in the Renaissance,* 195–99, 207–10, 328, 333–36, 346–47, 350.

65. Tamar, "Ha-tsippiyah be-Italyah," 63, 70–72. Some Jewish historians have come to question the "idealized" portrait of Jewish culture during the Renaissance and have reevaluated the effects of ghetto segregation. In place of the former emphasis on cultural decline, ghettoization is seen as releasing new cultural energies. This reevaluation has not disputed that the majority of Italian Jews underwent a deterioration in their socioeconomic situation. Robert Bonfil, "Change in the Cultural Patterns of a Jewish Society in Crisis: Italian Jewry at the Close of the Sixteenth Century," in Ruderman, *Essential Papers,* 401–25. See also Ruderman's intro., 1–39.

Enlightenment and Emancipation: German Jewry's Formative Age in Comparative Perspective

David Sorkin

Every historiographical tradition has its characteristic preoccupations. This is especially true for the revolutionary age of the late eighteenth and early nineteenth centuries. French historians remain preoccupied with the causes of the revolution, especially the role of the Enlightenment.[1] American historians continue to analyze the nature of the American Revolution, seeking to ascertain whether it was fundamentally novel and, if so, in what ways.[2]

Historians of European Jewry have a related preoccupation. In the years 1770–1830 German Jewry underwent a revolution in culture, politics, and social relations normally subsumed under the rubrics of *haskalah,* emancipation, and assimilation. These developments have long been associated with Berlin, and the "Berlin *haskalah"* has in fact become a shibboleth for the end of "traditional" and the beginnings of "modern" Jewish society. As a result, the scholarship on European Jewry has been peculiarly "germanocentric," with German Jewry being deemed the locus of the "origins of the modern Jew" or the "mirror of modernity" as well as a paradigm for understanding the transformation of the Jews of other countries.[3]

In studying these developments, historians have been attentive to the impact of events in the larger society, for example, how the breakdown of estate society encouraged the *haskalah* or how the French Revolution furthered emancipation. Many of them have nonetheless continued to treat the developments themselves as somehow singular, the peculiar result of the Jews' passage from the margins to the center of German society. Characteristic of this parochial outlook are studies that examine the three developments of *haskalah,* emancipation, and assimilation in relationship to one another with at best passing reference to the larger society or other religious and ethnic groups.[4]

The purpose of this essay is to test the idea of singularity, treating it is a claim that must be established rather than an assertion that can simply be stated. The historian must first endeavor to show similarity and commonality before he or she can speak with any conviction about difference, let alone singularity. This essay will undertake comparison of two kinds. External comparison will enable us to explore the ways in which there were parallel or homologous developments among other religious, national, and minority groups. We will first compare the three developments of *haskalah,* emancipation, and assimilation to different groups. Internal comparison will allow us to understand the ways in which German Jewry differed from other Jewries. We will attempt to see what set Berlin and German Jewry apart from Jewish communities elsewhere. By first establishing what, if anything, German Jewry had in common with other groups and other Jewries, we will be in a position to argue with some precision about the ways, if any, in which it was singular.[5]

External Comparison

Haskalah

Haskalah is a highly ambiguous term. It has been used to designate the specific cultural movement that emerged in Berlin and Königsberg in the 1770s and 1780s, as well as the movement that began to crystallize in Eastern Europe in the 1820s, but also as a virtual equivalent for the modernization of European Jewry or for any group or movement favoring such a process.[6] This ambiguity is not accidental: *haskalah* first gained widespread use as an equivalent for the German term *Aufklärung* (enlightenment) in the closing decades of the nineteenth century, when East European proponents of a range of postliberal ideologies (autonomism, socialism, Zionism) began to question the "liberal" ideals it represented and to hold the original exponents of those ideals (the *maskilim* proper) responsible for the larger changes, and alleged failures, that European Jewry had experienced in the past century.[7]

This ambiguity aside, the *haskalah* of the eighteenth century would seem to designate an internal, exclusively Jewish phenomenon. In fact, the *haskalah* belongs to the larger development of a "religious" Enlightenment in Western and Central Europe. Common wisdom has long had it that the

Enlightenment either recast the fundamental questions of religion or attempted to liberate secular culture from it. In fact, the relationship of religion to the Enlightenment was more complex and varied. Especially if we look at the issue from the side of the established religions, then we find that all of them had influential representatives who welcomed the new science and philosophy of the Enlightenment as a means to renew and reinvigorate faith.

This attempt to put the Enlightenment in the service of revealed religion was at the heart of the religious Enlightenment. As a movement, it represented a kind of golden mean. For Protestants this was usually so in two senses: at first, as a middle way between an older orthodoxy and a form of "enthusiasm" or inspirational faith; later, between the secular Enlightenment and belief. Thus, in England, after the Act of Toleration (1689), a moderate Anglicanism used key notions of the Enlightenment (Lockean reasonableness, Newtonian science, ideas of natural religion and toleration) to provide a broadly Arminian alternative, stressing the role of free will in the attainment of grace, to rigid Calvinism, which stressed predestination, on the one side, and inner light enthusiasm, like Puritanism, on the other. Subsequently, it served as a middle ground between deism and unreconstructed orthodoxy.[8] For Catholics in Central Europe and Italy "reform Catholicism" meant a middle ground between baroque piety, scholasticism, and Jesuitism, on the one side, and a highly charged reform movement, like Jansenism, on the other, which enabled them to recover neglected aspects of their textual heritage as well as to absorb contemporary science and philosophy.[9] What these representatives of religious enlightenment sought was a way to enlist substantial portions of Enlightenment thought to support, renew, and reinvigorate belief.

The *haskalah* was the Jewish version of the religious Enlightenment. It was an effort to correct the historical anomaly of a Judaism out of touch with central aspects of its textual heritage as well as with the larger culture. Throughout most of the Middle Ages in Europe, and especially during most periods of heightened religious creativity, Jews had sustained a balanced view of their own textual heritage as well as a beneficial and often intense interaction with the surrounding culture. In the post-Reformation, or baroque, period, in contrast, Ashkenazi Jewry had increasingly isolated itself in a world of talmudic casuistry and kabbalah, neglecting the Bible, Jewish philosophy, and the Hebrew language within and the vast changes in the general culture without.

The nature of Judaism in this period merits discussion. It has become common practice to use the label "traditional" to designate the Judaism that existed from the rabbinic period until the eve of the *haskalah*. To be sure, the Judaism of the sixteenth through eighteenth centuries was the authoritative interpretation that was defended and reproduced by rabbis and courts, schools and talmudic academies. Yet the sanction of power should not mislead us into thinking that this was an immutable form of Judaism eternally endowed with normative status. Rather, baroque Judaism was a version that arose at a specific time in a specific community, namely, the Ashkenazi Jewry of early modern Europe. It represented a valid interpretation of Judaism but not Judaism per se. Isadore Twersky has characterized it as a form of "monolithic Talmudism," which, while able to accommodate kabbalah, excluded the other "meta-halakhic" disciplines of Hebrew philosophy and biblical studies.[10]

The *haskalah* began as an effort to revive and introduce into baroque Judaism those neglected intellectual traditions that promoted a reasonable understanding of Jewish texts, thereby permitting engagement with contemporary science and philosophy. In opposition to a monolithic Talmudism based on casuistry and supported by kabbalah, it offered the literal interpretation of Talmud combined with the study of Hebrew language and philosophy and the literalist exegesis of the Bible. When the *haskalah* emerged as a movement in the last third of the eighteenth century (1770s), it borrowed many forms and categories from the Enlightenment, but its contents were largely derived from these hitherto neglected medieval Jewish traditions. For example, Moses Mendelssohn (1729–86) attempted to revive the tradition of philosophy in Hebrew in the 1750s, while in the 1770s and 1780s he tried to revive the tradition of literalist biblical exegesis.[11]

For a number of reasons the *haskalah* can profitably be compared with Reform Catholicism. Both movements emerged about a generation or so after similar developments in English and German Protestantism. Both were largely motivated by a sense of having lost important, if not some of the best, aspects of their heritage as well as not having kept pace with science, philosophy, and the Protestants. For them, unlike for Anglicans or German Protestants, the Enlightenment represented a science and philosophy of largely foreign, Protestant origins.

The *haskalah* and Reform Catholicism began as autochthonous efforts at religious and intellectual renewal. The *haskalah*'s effort to broaden the curriculum drew on criticism of Ashkenazi education dating back to the sixteenth-century Prague rabbi Judah Loew. The earliest *maskilim* were drawn from three social groups. Autodidacts such as Israel Zamosc (1700–1772), Moses Mendelssohn, and Naphtali Herz Wessely (1725–1805) made their reputations by using their secular learning to revive the disciplines of biblical exegesis and philosophy in Hebrew. Physicians trained at German universities, such as Tobias Cohen (1652–1729), Abraham Kisch (b. 1728), and Aaron Solomon Gumpertz (1723–69) tried to convey their knowledge of contemporary science and philosophy to their coreligionists by writing popular works or aiding the autodidacts. Finally, rabbis such as David Frankel (1707–62), Jacob Emden (1697–1776), and Hirschel Lewin (1721–1800) studied science and philosophy, Hebrew, and vernacular languages.[12]

Reform Catholicism represented a second humanist reform, or counter–Counter Reformation.[13] It offered science (Newton), philosophy (Leibniz-Wolff, Locke), and historical study (scripture, patristics, church history) as intellectual alternatives to scholastic speculation and a new pastoral ideal (*Seelsorge*) as a practical alternative to cults, brotherhoods, and processions. In its earliest phase it was confined almost entirely to Benedictine and Augustinian monasteries. In the 1740s it began to emerge in university curricula (Würzburg, Salzburg) in the form of the study of historical sources and Wolffian philosophy, which was the philosophical idiom of the Enlightenment in Central Europe to an even greater extent than Locke's philosophy was the philosophical idiom of the Enlightenment in England. And it also emerged in the academies (Bavaria), where it informed the research agenda.[14]

In this early stage there was no demarcation between religious enlighteners and "traditionalists"/"orthodox," since the *maskilim* and reform Catholics were traditional or orthodox. The *haskalah* and Reform Catholicism became factions only with the politicization of intellectual and religious life in the closing decades of the eighteenth century and the state sponsorship that subsequently resulted.

The *haskalah* emerged as a movement in the 1770s and 1780s in consequence of a convergence of intellectual and political factors.[15] On the one side, the *maskilim* began to use the categories and media of the Enlightenment to systematize and present their ideas. Some of the movement's major productions appeared in these decades: Mendelssohn's *Book of the Paths of Peace* (1783), a German translation of the Pentateuch, printed in Hebrew letters, with a commentary and introduction; and the Hebrew journal *Ha-meassef* (The Assembler [1784]). On the other side, the *maskilim* received the sponsorship of the mercantile elite, who were the leaders of the Berlin Jewish community, since these men saw the *haskalah* as a solution to the galling contradiction between their economic standing (they had attained great wealth during the Seven Years' War) and political status (they still suffered from numerous degrading and expensive disabilities). At this point the tools the *haskalah* had created for the intellectual renewal of Judaism began to be enlisted for a reform of the Jews. The mercantile elite created the Free School in Berlin (1778) in order to transform the Jewish poor through education, and elsewhere *maskilim* tried to rally support for similar projects.[16] Nonetheless, the *haskalah* was moderate in its conceptions and was not considered a distinct faction. That factionalization occurred only after 1786 with the onset of the struggle for emancipation after the deaths of Frederick the Great and Mendelssohn. A new community leadership ceased to see the *haskalah* as an answer; a younger generation of *maskilim* began to embrace more radical ideas; and an open break with the rabbis made them into a faction.[17]

Reform Catholicism was transformed into a faction by growing state sponsorship. After the accession of a conservative pope opposed to reform in 1758 (Clement XIII), Central European states adopted Reform Catholicism as a religious and ideological justification for etatist reform. In this period Reform Catholicism achieved some of its greatest victories, beginning with the abolition of the Jesuits. By the 1770s Wolffian philosophy was firmly in place at both older universities and new foundations. In the Habsburg lands Stephan Rautenstrauch (1734–85) put theological studies on a historical basis by revising the curriculum of the seminaries in 1774.[18]

Reform Catholic programs in this period combined social and political aims with intellectual and religious ones. Ignaz Felbiger (1724–88) revamped elementary education by adapting Pietist methods, which were seen as a model of piety, industry, and discipline, to Reform Catholic ideas and needs. Felbiger implemented the state's policy of using compulsory education as a means to inculcate internal discipline. The curriculum was designed according to estates, attempting to educate the children of peasants and artisans to be more productive and moral subjects of the state. Felbiger's reforms included a German translation of the Bible (1767) that aimed to acquaint schoolchildren directly with the sources of their faith.[19]

During the Co-Regency (1765–80) the baroque piety of pilgrimages, public holidays, and brotherhoods, which was seen as religiously retrograde and economically unproductive, was reduced. Joseph II introduced additional reforms in his decade of sole rule, including the Toleranzpatent of 1781, which extended civil equality and the right of private worship to

Lutherans, Calvinists, and orthodox Christians as well as extending some rights to Jews.[20]

All these victories were the result of an alliance with the state that went under the name of Febronianism, a doctrine that advocated Episcopalianism and the Gallican model in opposition to the monarchical papacy.[21] Reform Catholicism became a distinct faction, and the battle between it and the orthodox was fought out in a burgeoning public sphere of journals, pamphlets, and books.

Comparison of the early stages of the *haskalah* and Reform Catholicism shows that the effort to renew tradition was not peculiar to German Jewry but represented a common response of established religions to the new science and philosophy of the eighteenth century. Elements of German Jewry were far less segregated and far more a part of the surrounding culture than has usually been assumed.[22] In addition, the politicization of both movements in the closing decades of the eighteenth century suggests that the earlier phase of the *haskalah* (religious renewal) should not be confused with the later one (reform of the Jews and emancipation). Sponsorship from above diverted the movement from its original religious-intellectual agenda to political tasks. This diversion occurred prior to the French Revolution and was accelerated by events of the revolutionary era, if not necessarily by the Revolution itself.[23] Yet this diversion was characteristic of the religious Enlightenment and not specific to German Jewry.

The interesting similarities between Reform Catholicism and the *haskalah* should not be allowed to obscure fundamental differences. Absolute numbers or critical mass altered the very nature of the phenomena. Reform Catholicism, or for that matter all Christian forms of the religious Enlightenment, were the work of numerous people working within an array of established institutions. In fact, such a large number of people was involved that there was a clear division between clerical or religious enlighteners on the one side and lay or secular enlighteners on the other. This was not the case in the *haskalah,* which was the work of a score or two of individuals. Here no division existed between lay and clerical enlighteners. Indeed, this lack of division might be a major source of confusion in understanding its nature.

Scholars have previously distinguished between the *maskilim* on the basis of language (Hebrew vs. German), generation (an earlier generation born between 1720 and 1750, a later one after 1750) and stance (radical vs. moderate) and have identified some correlation between the three factors: for example, the older *maskilim* (Wessely, Mendelssohn) tended to write in

Hebrew and to be more moderate, whereas the younger ones (born after 1750) tended to write in German and to be more radical.[24] Perhaps the underlying distinction is between religious enlighteners and secular ones. The generation of Mendelssohn and Wessely was primarily concerned with the religious and intellectual renewal of Judaism and only later diverted into politics. The younger generation was primarily concerned with the reform of the Jews; radicalism on religious matters was but one issue in a larger agenda.

This analysis suggests that, while there is a basis for comparison between the *haskalah* and religious Enlightenment as religious and intellectual phenomena, there may well be an irreducible difference between them as social and political phenomena. The religious Enlightenment among majority groups that had a state and among minority groups without a state may well have been structured, and functioned, in fundamentally different ways. We will have no control for such a hypothesis, however, until we have studies of the religious Enlightenment among other stateless minority groups such as the Armenians and the Greeks in the Hapsburg and Ottoman Empires.[25]

Emancipation

The process of political emancipation was not confined to Berlin, German, or European Jewry. Rather, the Jews' experience belonged to the emancipation of various groups, including peasants and dissident or nonconformist religious minorities throughout Western and Central Europe. This process often had enduring consequences for the self-understanding of the minority group. An obvious example for comparison with German Jewry are Catholics in England. The two were linked through the term *emancipation:* while the term appeared in documents in some German states as early as 1817–18, it became popular and predominant after the "emancipation" of the Catholics in England in 1829.[26]

For English Catholics and Berlin Jews the achievement of emancipation mirrored the imposition of disabilities in that both were protracted incremental processes. Catholics suffered civil and religious disabilities that had accumulated since the mid-sixteenth century. The original Acts of Supremacy and Uniformity of the Elizabethan Settlement (1559) were augmented whenever there was a real or perceived threat of Catholic subversion, which occurred with some frequency: 1570s and 1580s (recusancy fines, oath of loyalty for lower-grade officials), 1590s (Five Mile Act),

1606 (Penal Laws), 1678 (exclusion from House of Lords), 1692 (Double Land Tax), 1695 (Disabling Act). Emancipation occurred over a period of a half-century, beginning with the First Relief Act of 1778, which gave Catholics religious equality (persecution of priests was abolished) and the right to purchase and inherit land, and continuing with the Second Relief Act of 1791, which gave them entrance to the professions, to the final act of 1829.[27]

Jews had been admitted to Berlin in 1671 under favorable circumstances. Their situation had deteriorated in the first half of the eighteenth century. Residency laws were tightened between 1713 and 1740 both in terms of the actual numbers of Jews allowed as well as the conditions their children had to meet to establish households of their own. Between 1728 and 1769 old taxes were increased and additional taxes added, including the burden of "collective responsibility" (*solidarische Haftung*) in 1728, in which the community became responsible for the financial fate of its members. And between 1718 and 1750 the occupations open to Jews were progressively restricted.[28]

These disabilities were removed in stages. Minor reforms took place in the late 1780s, when the transit tax (*Leibzoll*) was eliminated and the requirement to purchase state-made porcelain (Moses Mendelssohn had porcelain monkeys adorning his fireplace) was waived in favor of a one-time payment. The Emancipation Law of 1812 granted freedom of residence and occupation (with the exception of the civil service), abolished all special taxes, and imposed duties of citizenship, including military service, but still left Judaism and its adherents as second-class citizens.[29] The decree of 1847 confirmed that status. Full emancipation was achieved only in 1869.

The protracted emancipation process accelerated and shaped the cultural adjustment, since in both cases emancipation was contractual: both groups were required to reciprocate for the rights they received. German Jews were expected to regenerate themselves through reforms in education, occupational structure, and religion in exchange for rights. English Catholics were to show that they would not threaten the constitution by providing "securities" of their loyalty, for example, government "veto" of episcopal candidates and the "exequatar," the right to inspect papal documents. Reciprocity entailed a rethinking of the nature of the minority community and its relationship to the majority society. The process of emancipation was by definition ideological.

Despite this similarity, there were fundamental differences between the two cases that should not be overlooked. First and foremost was the legal framework in which emancipation occurred. English Catholics functioned within a minimalist state whose legal system discriminated against dissenting or nonconformist Christians yet vouchsafed them basic rights of residence and occupation. Catholics were not able to hold public office, but they were Englishmen. In contrast, Jews in Berlin faced a highly regulated tutelary state (*Polizeistaat*) that did not recognize basic rights: everything from residence to occupation was a privilege to be negotiated.

Second, the reciprocity at issue was not the same. The reciprocity demanded of Jews in the German states was comprehensive, involving occupations, education, and religion. Yet it was also elusive: the actual demands were frequently ambiguous, and the terms often shifted, a situation exacerbated by the incremental nature of the emancipation process. In fact, the lack of clarity about what emancipation required was a crucial feature of the entire process, and some historians have claimed that the misunderstandings and tensions to which this ambiguity gave rise were in part responsible for the subsequent emergence of opposition to Jewish participation in German society and political antisemitism.[30] For English Catholics, in contrast, the reciprocity was clearly defined and limited in scope.

We have already seen the radicalizing effect on the *haskalah* of the politicization of the 1770s and 1780s. From the first decade of the nineteenth century that process of radicalization was extended. A new group of preachers, teachers, and publicists (born in the 1770s and 1780s) turned the ideas of the *haskalah* into an ideology of emancipation—a program of regeneration understood as a contract or quid pro quo. They formulated and disseminated this ideology in a new German-language public sphere of journals and sermons, books and pamphlets. The ideologues aimed to enlist support for emancipation from non-Jews as well as to proclaim and foster the efforts of their fellow Jews toward regeneration. In addition, they wished to subdue the opposition to emancipation of an emerging Orthodoxy.[31] This ideology was the seedbed of all movements for change in Judaism, whether Reform, Positive-Historical, or Neo-Orthodox.

Among English Catholics the Cisalpines enlisted the ideas of Continental Reform Catholicism, or Catholic Enlightenment, to persuade English Protestants of their trustworthiness and loyalty. To show that they were "rational Catholics" who believed in "liberality," they embraced such ideas as reasonable observances (including a vernacular liturgy), the Febronianist view of ecclesiastical democracy, toleration of other religions, and renunciation of conversion. They disseminated these ideas in sermons, pamphlets, books and periodicals.[32]

Scholarship and historical research and writing played a role for both groups as well. The critical, "scientific" study of Judaism (*Wissenschaft des Judentums*) emerged from the conviction that the emancipation of the Jews required the prior emancipation of Judaism. Scholars such as Leopold Zunz (1794–1886) and Isaac Markus Jost (1793–1860) believed that only if Judaism were first shown to have a worthwhile literature and history throughout its dispersion could it then be treated as equal to Christianity. Once Judaism had gained equality the emancipation of the Jews would follow.[33] Joseph Berington (1746–1827), John Lingard (1771–1851), and Alexander Geddes (1737–1802) wrote history to vindicate the sort of reasonable Catholicism they advocated. They believed that they needed to dispel jaundiced views of the church if they were to gain emancipation and succeed in imposing their own understanding of a reasonable Catholicism.[34]

Here, again, we should not overlook important differences. Catholics in England numbered about eighty thousand in the late eighteenth century.[35] Their emancipation followed that of nonconforming Protestants and belonged to the political process that established a confessional pluralism whereby membership in the Church of England ceased to be the criterion for inclusion in the body politic. But the Catholic cause was also significantly advanced by territorial-demographic changes. By adding an additional five million Catholics to the population of Great Britain, the Union with Ireland in 1800 made the issue central to the politics of the day. Catholic emancipation averted a major constitutional crisis, and for that very reason the Tories acquiesced to the change. Yet it should also not be forgotten that the newly emancipated Irish Catholics were quickly disenfranchised when new property requirements were enacted.

In contrast, territorial change worked to the disadvantage of Berlin Jewry. The final partitions of Poland in 1793 and 1795 brought the province of Posen, with an additional 125,000 Jews, under Prussian jurisdiction. The Prussian authorities considered these Jews, who on the whole were far poorer than those who had been admitted to Berlin, to be backward, benighted, and unworthy of rights. Their presence thus served as a brake on the emancipation process.[36]

Assimilation

In the period from 1770 to 1830 Berlin Jewry experienced what one historian called a "conversion epidemic." The most recent and thorough research suggests that some sixteen hundred individuals converted in the

period. Yet these figures are deceptive. Some four hundred of these converts were not born to Jewish mothers and thus were not converts according to Jewish religious criteria but only according to Nazi racial criteria. In
addition, many of those who converted in Berlin in this period were not
natives but were attracted to the city because of their desire to convert. The
number of native Berliners who converted was probably about two hundred and fifty persons. This low number is also deceptive since it does not
show the magnitude of the phenomenon: conversion was not spread evenly
among all groups but was concentrated among the young. One in seven of
those born after 1800 in fact converted.[37]

How are we to understand this phenomenon? Was it an anomaly or part
of a long-term process? The evidence seems to suggest that it was a one-
time occurrence that arose because of the specific circumstances of Berlin.
Haskalah and emancipation had both failed. The *haskalah* had not offered
a cultural or institutional alternative to traditional Judaism. Its language
(Hebrew) and concerns (cultural reform, secular education) kept it from
addressing a broader audience; it remained the preserve of a coterie of
intellectuals. It had also not been much of an aid in the struggle for emancipation. The efforts at emancipation begun in the late 1780s had stalled,
yielding few results and leaving the ignominious position of the Berlin Jewish elite largely unchanged.

Some of the conversions were a response to this situation. Others were
part of a general decline of morals manifest in extramarital affairs, illegitimate births, and financial irresponsibility. Still others were the result of
opportunism, the effort to gain access to academic and bureaucratic
careers, which remained closed to Jews. There were also conversions out of
love and even some out of conviction.[38]

These conversions were a new phenomenon in Jewish history in number
and in kind. In the Middle Ages and early modern period there had been
some conversions from conviction, and in the early modern period there
was also a pattern of indigent Jews converting for material benefit.[39] What
was obviously new and shocking in Berlin was that members of the community's elite left the fold in significant numbers and that such behavior
became something of a fashion, whether as a form of social climbing or
social conformism.

If we see conversion as a social rather than, or as well as, a religious phenomenon, then it was not restricted to Jews, who were only one among a
number of foreign colonies in Berlin. The Great Elector's policy of reli-

gious toleration extended to numerous dissident religious groups. With the revocation of the Edict of Nantes, French Huguenots were invited to Berlin. The Huguenot community that developed became a significant part of the Berlin landscape, amounting to some five thousand persons in the 1780s. This "colony" (the Jews of Berlin were also known as a colony) also experienced leakage in the second half of the eighteenth century. Seventy percent of marriages in the French colony between 1748 and 1806 were "outmarriages." This development seemed to follow a generational pattern. The first generation married almost entirely within the colony. The second generation sought eligible partners at home and in other colonies of the Huguenot diaspora but also began to marry fellow Berliners. In the third generation the number of outmarriages to fellow Berliners increased dramatically, though there was differentiation among social groups. The lower classes seemed readier to marry out, whereas the wealthy and influential made endogamy and the maintenance of tradition a source of pride and distinction.[40]

We should not overlook the basic difference between the French and Jewish colonies in Berlin. The Huguenots' religion linked them to, rather than separated them from, the rest of Berlin. To be sure, as Calvinists the Huguenots belonged to a small minority of the Prussian populace: in 1740, 90 percent of Prussians were Lutherans, 7 percent Catholics, and 3 percent Calvinists. Yet in Berlin the colony significantly affected the proportions: 80 percent were Lutherans, 19 percent were Calvinists (when one includes the Huguenots), and only 1 percent Catholics.[41] The barriers between the Protestant groups were obviously not as high as between Jews and Christians. For a Jew to marry a Christian required a leap; for a Huguenot to marry a German Calvinist or Lutheran took little more than a hop.

These differences notwithstanding, the experience of the French colony suggests that in order to gain a proper understanding of Berlin Jewry's "conversion epidemic" it must be seen as part of a larger phenomenon of social assimilation in a highly regulated though religiously tolerant absolutist society. The social regulation of the Frederician *Polizeistaat* cannot be underestimated; neither can its religious toleration. That religious toleration created the possibility of "assimilation." To what extent was the Jewish experience simply an aspect of the Prussian pattern? Or to what extent was it part of the breakdown of the Frederician state and its estate society? Without detailed comparison we cannot begin to answer such questions.

In addition, the question of assimilation should not be limited to those who converted or left the fold. After all, the converts were the minority. Assimilation, or to use a less-charged and more current term, *acculturation,* could take other forms.

The nineteenth century saw the emergence of a new German Jewish middle class imbued with the ideology of emancipation. In the period from 1780 to 1870 German Jews made the transition from an impoverished, geographically dispersed, and socially differentiated community to an increasingly affluent, urbanized, homogeneous bourgeoisie. This transformation was made largely through the commercial expansion that accompanied the industrial revolution. Jews at the extreme ends of the economic scale disappeared: poor Jews either emigrated or achieved economic success, the old elites either lost their fortunes and influence or abandoned Judaism. The result was that by 1870 the bulk of the community was concentrated in the middle.[42]

Already in the Vormärz era this middle class began to assert itself in communal politics on the basis of the ideology of emancipation. It advocated reforms in education, liturgy, and occupations. Moreover, it created a network of secondary associations to support these efforts as well as a new form of middle-class sociability. The ideology of emancipation thus became an additional form of cohesion. It was not the *haskalah* that had succeeded, then, but a radicalized version of it based on the contract of regeneration for rights.

The English Catholic community provides an important contrast. In the period from 1770 to 1850 it was "transformed beyond recognition." A rural community of agricultural laborers and domestics grouped around the seigneur and his priest gradually gave way to an urban community of artisans, merchants, and nonagricultural laborers, who, in cooperation with the mission, made provisions for their religious needs. Like German Jews, English Catholics experienced change at a brisker pace than the general population. These social changes combined with the "decline of the gentry"—from demographic thinning and some defection to the Church of England—to deprive the gentry of its prior predominance.[43]

Yet, unlike German Jewry, the English Catholic middle classes failed to assert their will. English Catholicism witnessed the triumph of the clerical hierarchy. The Catholic third estate did not impose the congregationalism that would have enabled it to succeed the gentry and become an equal partner to the clergy. Instead, the bishops gained control. Although the Cisalpines pressed their version of "rational" Catholicism and "liberality" throughout the era of emancipation and thereafter, it was the episcopalists and finally the ultramontanes who gained the upper hand.[44]

The success of the German Jewish middle classes and the failure of their English Catholic counterparts can be ascribed to developments in the larger society. In Germany the Protestant middle classes accumulated significant power in social and religious institutions in the Vormärz; laicization proceeded apace in the churches, and in general the democratic impulses that erupted in the Revolution of 1848 had often first been tested in the struggle for control of ecclesiastical institutions.[45] In England, in marked contrast, there was a general failure of middle-class ecclesiastical aspirations: the democratic principle of "congregationalism" failed among Protestant dissenters, and the clergy reasserted itself in the Anglican Church as well.[46]

The fate of the emancipated, or emancipating, minority hung on that of the larger society. Yet this points to a paradox. Did the German-Jewish middle classes succeed to the extent they did in part because the German middle classes also managed to gain power in similar institutions, even if they did not gain political power at the highest levels? If such middle-class triumph is characteristic of German Jewry's experience, how is it to be reconciled with the clichéd view of German history in which its "peculiarity" is the result of a weak, apolitical middle class?[47]

The method of external comparison suggests that what distinguished Berlin or German Jewry was not its singularity but, rather, the extent to which its transformation was part of larger historical developments. The *haskalah* was the Jewish version of the religious Enlightenment—an effort to use the philosophy and science of the Enlightenment to renew religious faith that governments then adopted to support a program of reform from above or political stability. Emancipation was a process that religious minorities in general experienced when the states in which they lived began to redefine themselves on the basis of individual rights, when they shifted from being confessional to dynastic, administrative, or political bodies. Assimilation was also a trend characteristic of a dissolving estate society on its way, however hesitantly, to becoming a bourgeois civil society.

To be sure, Berlin or German Jewry's experience of these developments and processes had individual features. These were, however, variations within a family of examples. The question is, then, how do we account for the fact that this Jewry was so intimately involved in the processes of the larger culture? Why Berlin and Germany? To assay an answer to this question we must turn to the method of internal comparison.

Internal Comparison

Berlin represented a specific type of Jewish settlement in Europe. It belonged to the new, northern towns (Vienna, Königsberg, Copenhagen) in which Jews were first permitted to settle, or resettle, after the Peace of Westphalia. Central Europe had largely been emptied of Jews in the post-Reformation period. They were allowed to return both to urban and rural areas during and after the Thirty Years' War.[48] The urban settlements were associated with the Court Jews, whom the princes invited to settle in their lands to aid in the consolidation of state or dynastic power through fiscal reform and economic development.

These new Jewish settlements brought to the fore the tensions of the larger society. The Central European states were attempting to graft mercantilist, commercial policy onto primarily agrarian societies. The tension was greatest in Prussia, which was an agrarian and military society (a "state with an army" or, as some would have it, "an army with a state"). The result was that the Jews lived with a series of overt contradictions. They were the exemplars of an economic utility that the state both prized and condemned. Wealthy Jews were given new economic opportunities but suffered restrictive legislation, while poor Jews were excluded altogether. While the state's economic policy favored commerce, the medieval image of the debased "money" Jew still prevailed. These tensions had their counterparts within the Jewish community: new economic opportunities led to new cultural and social ones, yet the baroque Judaism of Ashkenazi Jewry dictated an isolated, exclusive religious culture. Enlightened absolutism and *haskalah* were the ideological responses that emerged to address and redress these tensions. These were the cultural creations of agrarian societies attempting to adjust to commerce, individual rights, and religious toleration.

In contrast to the northern settlements founded by Court Jews, what Lois Dubin has called the "port" Jews of London, Amsterdam, Bordeaux, Trieste, and, slightly later, Odessa underwent a very different experience.[49] Rather than agrarian societies adjusting to commerce, here were either societies in which powerful groups had wholeheartedly adopted commerce (England, Holland) or else cities built on commerce (Bordeaux, Trieste, Odessa). The tensions characteristic of the northern settlements did not plague them. Those communities founded by Sephardim fleeing the Iberian Peninsula were never constituted as autonomous communities subject to a developed body of Jewry laws. In consequence there was little or no need for a reforming ideology in the society as a whole or among the Jews themselves. Rather than *haskalah,* many of the elements of *haskalah* (e.g., knowledge of vernacular languages and secular studies, study of Hebrew and the Bible) became part of the fabric of everyday life, a fact encouraged by the flexible Sephardi or Italian traditions that prevailed within the community.[50]

The third type of urban settlement, the cities in which Jewish residence had been continuous since the Middle Ages (Frankfurt am Main, Hamburg, Prague), did not experience the same tensions as the northern court settlements, since they underwent a slower transformation from the older Jewish occupations (moneylending) to the newer ones (commerce) and were not as closely linked to the state. The initial opposition to the *haskalah* was concentrated in these cities, though a generation or two later they were to become centers of the movement.[51]

Internal comparison allows us to focus on the northern settlements of Court Jews and to ask, why Berlin and not Vienna, Königsberg, or Copenhagen? In fact, the question is, why Berlin-Königsberg? since Königsberg also played an important role in the *haskalah* and the struggle for emancipation. On the one side, clearly, Berlin-Königsberg, and not Vienna, was the center of the German-speaking Enlightenment and also epitomized the tensions of an agrarian society in transition. On the other, the Jewish community of Vienna was too small, settlement there largely restricted to wealthy court and commercial Jews, to serve as a cultural center: as a result of strict residence regulations, the community numbered some 570 Jews in 1780 and some 840 a decade later.[52] Similarly, Copenhagen neither served as a center of Enlightenment nor possessed a large and diverse Jewish community.

The characteristic tensions of the northern settlements were at their height in Berlin. The tensions between an older way of life (autonomous community, baroque Judaism) that could not continue and a new one (religious and civil equality) that was only partially, and reluctantly, being allowed to emerge set the Jews of Berlin and Germany apart from Jews elsewhere and brought to the fore their revolutions in culture, politics, and social relations. The port Jews were able to lead different sorts of lives with less struggle and without an explicit ideology. It was the explosive friction between old and new, between intimate involvement in the larger society and enforced distance from it, that made Berlin and German Jewry so much a part of the developments in European society yet also so visible among European Jewries. What was singular about German Jewry was not the developments themselves but the concentration and heightened expression of so many aspects of European life among a minority group in such a brief period.[53]

It is not surprising that the witticism "the Jews are like the people among whom they live, only more so" has always been attributed to a German Jew, usually the poet Heinrich Heine. In the case of Berlin and German Jewry in the period of Enlightenment and emancipation, the witticism seems apt.

NOTES

1. For a recent summary of the scholarship, see Roger Chartier, *The Cultural Origins of the French Revolution* (Durham: Duke University Press, 1991).

2. For a recent example, see Gordon Wood, *The Radicalism of the American Revolution* (New York: A. A. Knopf, 1992).

3. Michael Meyer, *The Origins of the Modern Jew: Jewish Identity and European Culture in Germany, 1749–1824* (Detroit: Wayne State University Press, 1967); Gerson Cohen, "German Jewry as Mirror of Modernity," *Leo Baeck Institute Year Book* 20 (1975): ix–xxxi. For a review of this issue in the scholarship of the last decade and a half, see Trude Maurer, *Die Entwicklung der jüdischen Minderheit in Deutschland, 1780–1933* (Tübingen: M. Niemeyer, 1992), 1–12. In an earlier work I argued that German Jewry should not be treated as paradigmatic for European Jewry, since its experience was the exception rather than the rule. David Sorkin, *The Transformation of German Jewry, 1780–1840* (New York: Oxford University Press, 1987), 8, 173–77.

4. For a recent example see Steven M. Lowenstein, *The Berlin Jewish Community: Enlightenment, Family and Crisis, 1770–1830* (New York: Oxford University Press, 1994). Lowenstein shows parallels between the crisis of the *haskalah* and the Enlightenment in Germany (69f.) and makes some comparison to the French Revolution (187). For additional literature, see Maurer, *Die Entwicklung der jüdischen Minderheit in Deutschland.*

5. This essay draws on materials from two of my earlier essays: "From Context to Comparison: The German Haskalah and Reform Catholicism," *Tel Aviver Jahrbuch für deutsche Geschichte* 22 (1991): 23–58; "Juden und Katholiken: Deutsch-jüdische Kultur im Vergleich, 1750–1850," in *Deutsche Juden und die Moderne,* ed. Shulamit Volkov (Munich: R. Oldenbourg, 1994), 9–30.

6. A striking use of the term as an equivalent for *modernization,* including *acculturation, assimilation,* and *social integration,* is found in Shmuel Ettinger, "The Modern Period," in *A History of the Jewish People,* ed. H. H. Ben-Sasson (Cambridge: Harvard University Press, 1976), esp. 826–46. Ettinger belongs to what has

been called the "East European school" of Jewish historiography. For this school, see Jonathan Frankel, "Assimilation and the Jews in Nineteenth-Century Europe: Towards a New Historiography?" in *Assimilation and Community: The Jews in Nineteenth-Century Europe,* ed. Jonathan Frankel and Steven Zipperstein (Cambridge: Cambridge University Press, 1992), 1–37. The more limited use of the term is found in Jacob Katz, *Tradition and Crisis: Jewish Society at the End of the Middle Ages,* trans. B. D. Cooperman (New York: New York University Press, 1993), 214–36, though the opposition here between "traditional" Jewish society or "traditional" Judaism and *haskalah* once again suggests identification of *haskalah* with modernity or acculturation.

7. On the history of the term, see Uzi Shavit, "Ha-'haskalah' mahi?" (What Is the "Haskalah"?), *Mehkerei Yerushalayim be-sifrut ivrit* 12 (1990): 51–83. While this study breaks new ground, there is room for additional work. A thorough investigation of the term's history should be undertaken that uses the method of *Begriffsgeschichte* to study the relationship between shifts in meaning and social and political change.

8. For England, see Mark Pattison, "Tendencies of Religious Thought in England, 1688–1750," *Essays and Reviews* (London: Longman, Green, Longman and Roberts, 1861), 254–329; J. G. A. Pocock, "Clergy and Commerce: The Conservative Enlightenment in England," in *L'Eta dei lumi: studi storici sul settecento Europeo in onore di Franco Venturi,* 2 vols. (Naples: Jovene, 1985), 1:523–62; Norman Sykes, *Edmund Gibson: Bishop of London, 1669–1748* (London: Oxford University Press, 1926).

9. Adam Wandruszka, "Der Reformkatholizismus des 18. Jahrhunderts in Italien und in Oesterreich," in *Festschrift Hermann Wiesflecker zum sechzigsten Geburtstag,* ed. Alexander Novotny and Othmar Pickl (Graz: Historical Institute of the University of Graz, 1973); Eduard Hegel, *Die Katholische Kirche Deutschlands unter dem Einfluss der Aufklärung des 18. Jahrhunderts* (Opladen: Rheinischwestfaelische Akademie der Wissenschaften, 1975); Bernard Plongeron, "Was ist katholische Aufklärung?" in *Katholische Aufklärung und Josephinismus,* ed. Elisabeth Kovacs (Vienna: Verlag für Geschichte und Politik, 1979); T. C. W. Blanning, "The Enlightenment in Catholic Germany," in *The Enlightenment in National Context,* ed. Roy Porter and Mikulas Teich (Cambridge: Cambridge University Press, 1981), 118–26.

10. "Talmudists, Philosophers, Kabbalists: The Quest for Spirituality in the Sixteenth Century," in *Jewish Thought in the Sixteenth Century,* ed. Bernard Dov Cooperman (Cambridge, MA: Harvard University Press, 1983), 431–59. For a recent study of the formation of baroque Judaism, see Jacob Elbaum, *Petihut vehistagrut: ha-yetsirah ha-ruhanit-sifrutit be-Folin u-ve-artsot Ashkenaz be-shilhei ha-meah ha-sheish esrei* (Openness and Insularity: Literary-Spiritual Creativity in Poland and Central Europe at the Start of the Sixteenth Century) (Jerusalem: Magnes Press, 1990). For a survey of the literature, see Joseph M. Davis, "The Cul-

tural and Intellectual History of Ashkenazic Jews, 1500–1750: A Selective Bibliography and Essay," *Leo Baeck Institue Year Book* 38 (1993): 343–90.

Perhaps scholars have been reluctant to see Ashkenazi Judaism of this period as a distinct formation because of the *haskalah*'s and the early *Wissenschaft des Judentums*' denigration of it. Leopold Zunz, for example, argued that European Jewry's "dark ages" did not coincide with that of Christian Europe but, rather, came in the sixteenth through eighteenth centuries as a result of persecution and isolation. See his book *Die Gottesdienstlichen Vorträge der Juden* (Berlin: A. Asher, 1832), 437f.

11. The works in which he tried to revive Hebrew philosophy were the first journal in modern Hebrew, the *Kohelet musar,* and the commentary to Maimonides' logical primer, the *Biur milot ha-higgayon.* The exegetical works were his commentary to the book of Ecclesiastes (*Biur le-megilat Kohelet* [1770]) and his translation, introduction to, and commentary on the Pentateuch, *Sefer netivot ha-shalom* (1779–83). See my book *Moses Mendelssohn and the Religious Enlightenment* (Berkeley: University of California Press, 1996).

12. Isaac E. Barzilay, "The Background of the Berlin Haskalah," in *Essays on Jewish Life and Thought Presented in Honor of Salo Wittmayer Baron,* ed. Joseph L. Blau (New York: Columbia University Press, 1957); J. Eschelbacher, "Die Anfänge allgemeiner Bildung unter den deutschen Juden vor Mendelssohn," in *Beiträge zur Geschichte der deutschen Juden: Festschrift zum siebzigsten Geburtsage Martin Philippsons,* (Leipzig: G. Fock, 1916); Azriel Shohet, *Im hilufei tekufot: bereishit ha-haskalah be-yahadut Germanyah* (The Beginning of the *Haskalah* in German Jewry) (Jerusalem: Mosad Bialik, 1960). On Jews studying medicine at German universities in the seventeenth and eighteenth centuries, see Monika Richarz, *Der Eintritt der Juden in die akademischen Berufe: judische Studenten und Akademiker in Deutschland, 1678–1848* (Tübingen: J. C. B. Mohr, 1974), 23–42.

13. R. J. W. Evans, *The Making of the Habsburg Monarchy, 1550–1700* (Oxford: Clarendon Press, 1979), 449.

14. Robert Haass, *Die geistige Haltung der katholischen Universitäten im 18. Jahrhundert* (Freiburg: Herder, 1952); Notker Hammerstein, *Aufklärung und katholisches Reich: Untersuchungen zur Univeritätsreform und Politik katholischer Territorien des Heiligen Römischen Reichs deutscher Nation im 18. Jahrhundert* (Berlin: Duncken and Humblot, 1977); Ludwig Hammermayer, *Geschichte der Bayerischen Akademie der Wissenschaften, 1759–1807,* 2 vols. (Munich: C. H. Beck, 1959–83).

15. Some scholars see the *haskalah* emerging as a full-blown movement without accounting for its origins within Judaism or Jewish society. See, for example, Katz, *Tradition and Crisis,* 214–25; *Out of the Ghetto: The Social Background of Jewish Emancipation, 1770–1870* (Cambridge, MA: Harvard University Press, 1973), 28–41; Mordechai Levin, *Erkhei hevrah ve-khalkalah ve-idiologiyah shel tekufat ha-haskala* (Social and Economic Values in the Ideology of the *Haskalah*) (Jerusalem:

Mosad Bialik, 1975), 39f. Others see the movement of the 1770s and 1780s as the *haskalah* proper and the period from 1720 to 1770 as the early *haskalah;* that is, they think the early *haskalah* prepared the way for, and came to fruition in, the ideological movement that aimed to reform the Jewish community and lay claim to leadership of it. For this view, see Shmuel Feiner, "Isaac Euchel—'Entrepreneur' of the *Haskalah* Movement in Germany" (Hebrew), *Zion* 52 (1987): 427–69. In contrast, I see the early *haskalah* as an independent tendency that was dedicated to intellectual and religious renewal and that was diverted into social and political issues by the politicization of the larger society in the 1770s and 1780s. The competing interpretations result from a difference in perspective. Shmuel Feiner's view is based on an understanding of the phenomenon in Central and Eastern Europe in the century 1770–1870, mine on the comparison of the *haskalah* with other forms of religious Enlightenment in the eighteenth century.

16. In a forthcoming article Shmuel Feiner questions whether the Free School should be seen as an institution of the *haskalah*. For the traditional account, see Mordekhai Eliav, *Ha-hinukh ha-yehudi be-Germanyah bi-yemei ha-haskalah ve-ha-emantsipatsiyah* (Jewish Education in Germany in the Period of the Enlightenment and Emancipation) (Jerusalem: Jewish Agency, 1960), 71–79. Isaac Euchel attempted to rally support for the foundation of a similar school in Königsberg. See his book *Sefat emet* (Königsberg, 1782).

17. For this periodization, see Sorkin, "From Context to Comparison." Lowenstein shows the change in the community leadership in *Berlin Jewish Community,* 25–32, 69–72, 89–104.

18. Josef Mueller, "Zu den theologiegeschichtlichen Grundlagen der Studienreform Rautenstrauchs," *Tübinger Theologische Quartalschrift* 146 (1966): 62–97.

19. Richard van Duelmen, "Die Prälaten Franz Toepsl aus Polling und Johann Ignaz von Felbiger aus Sagan. Zwei Repräsentanten der katholischen Aufklärung," *Zeitschrift für bayerische Landesgeschichte* 30 (1967): 731–823; James Van Horn Melton, *Absolutism and the Eighteenth-Century Origins of Compulsory Schooling in Prussia and Austria* (Cambridge: Cambridge University Press, 1988), 94–105, 209–30.

20. Derek Beales, *Joseph II: In the Shadow of Maria Theresa* (Cambridge: Cambridge University Press, 1987).

21. Herbert Raab, "Episcopalism in the Church of the Empire from the Middle of the Seventeenth Century to the End of the Eighteenth Century," in *The Church in the Age of Absolutism and Enlightenment,* ed. Wolfgang Müller, trans. Gunther Holst (London: Burns and Oates, 1981).

22. This argument has been made by Shohet, in *Im hilufei tekufot,* but has not received the attention it deserves.

23. The evidence Steven Lowenstein has presented suggests that internal changes within the Berlin Jewish community, rather than the impact of the revolution, were the driving force of radicalization. See his book *Berlin Jewish Commu-*

nity. Shmuel Feiner has recently made this point in a controversy with Reuven Michael. See his essay "Between the French Revolution and the Changes in the 'Berlin Haskalah'" (Hebrew), *Zion* 57 (1992): 89–92.

24. Isaac E.Barzilay emphasized the role of language in distinguishing between moderate and radical *maskilim.* See "The Ideology of the Berlin Haskalah," *Proceedings of the American Academy for Jewish Research* 25 (1956): 1–38; "The Treatment of Jewish Religion in the Literature of the Berlin Haskalah," *Proceedings of the American Academy for Jewish Research* 24 (1955): 39–68. Moshe Pelli also used the categories of radical versus conservative or moderate. *The Age of Haskalah* (Leiden: E. J. Brill, 1979). Michael Meyer, in *The Origins of the Modern Jew,* emphasized generational shifts.

25. Professors Benjamin Braude (Boston College), David Myers (UCLA), and Richard Hovannisian (UCLA) organized a conference on this topic at the Clark Library in Los Angeles in November 1995.

26. David Sorkin, "Emancipation and Assimilation: Two Concepts and Their Application to German-Jewish History," *Leo Baeck Institute Year Book* 35 (1990): 17–18.

27. Edward Norman, *The English Catholic Church in the Nineteenth Century* (Oxford: Clarendon Press, 1984), 34; *Roman Catholicism in England from the Elizabethan Settlement to the Second Vatican Council* (Oxford: Oxford University Press, 1985), 9–13.

28. For a useful summary of these laws, see Lowenstein, *Berlin Jewish Community,* 11–13.

29. Ibid., 78–79, 85–86.

30. Reinhard Rürup, "Jewish Emancipation and Bourgeois Society," *Leo Baeck Institute Year Book* 14 (1969): 67–91.

31. Sorkin, *Transformation of German Jewry,* 79–104, 124–34; Mordechai Breuer, "Emancipation and the Rabbis," *Niv ha-midrashah* 13–14 (1978–79): 26–52; Katz, *Out of the Ghetto,* 142–60.

32. Eamon Duffy, "Ecclesiastical Democracy Detected," *Recusant History* 10 (1969–70): 193–209, 309–31; and 13 (1975–76): 113–48. For the Cisalpines, see Joseph Chinnici, *The English Catholic Enlightenment: John Lingard and the Cisalpine Movement, 1780–1850* (Shepherdstown, WV: Patmos Press, 1980). For the press, see John R. Fletcher, "English Catholic Periodicals in England," *Dublin Review* 198 (1936): 284–310.

33. Ismar Schorsch, *From Text to Context: The Turn to History in Modern Judaism* (Hanover, NH: University Press of New England, 1994).

34. R. W. Linker, "English Roman Catholics and Emancipation," *Journal of Ecclesiastical History* 27 (1976): 166f.; Chinnici, *English Catholic Enlightenment.*

35. Norman, *English Catholic Church in the Nineteenth Century,* 6.

36. Herbert Strauss, "Pre-emancipation Prussian Policies towards the Jews, 1815–47," *Leo Baeck Institute Year Book* 11 (1966): 107–36.

37. Lowenstein, *Berlin Jewish Community*, 120–22.

38. Ibid., 122–33.

39. Jeremy Cohen, "The Mentality of the Medieval Jewish Apostate: Peter Alfonsi, Hermann of Cologne, and Pablo Christiani," in *Jewish Apostasy in the Modern World*, ed. Todd M. Endelman (New York: Holmes and Meier, 1987), 20–47; Shohet, *Im hilufei tekufot*, 174–97.

40. Juergen Wilke, "Zur Geschichte der französischen Kolonie," in *Hugenotten in Berlin*, ed. Sibylle Badstübner-Gröger et al. (Berlin: Nicolaische Verlagsbuchhandlung, 1988), 80. For an excellent comparison of the economic role of the two colonies, see Stefi Jersch-Wenzel, *Juden und "Franzosen" in der Wirtschaft des Raumes Berlin/Brandenburg zur Zeit der Merkantilismus* (Berlin: Colloquium-Verlag, 1978).

41. Wilke, "Zur Geschichte der französischen Kolonie," 54. These figures obviously do not take account of the Jews.

42. Sorkin, *Transformation of German Jewry*, 107–24; Maurer, *Die Entwicklung der jüdischen Minderheit*, 85–100.

43. John Bossy, *The English Catholic Community, 1570–1850* (London: Darton, Longman and Todd, 1975), 295–363.

44. Ibid., 337–90; Norman, *English Catholic Church in the Nineteenth Century*, 69–109.

45. Hans Rosenberg, "Theologischer Rationalismus und vormärzlicher Vulgärliberalismus," *Politische Denkströmungen im deutschen Vormärz* (Göttingen:Vandenhoeck und Ruprecht, 1972), 18–50; Robert Bigler, *The Politics of German Protestantism: The Rise of the Protestant Church Elite in Prussia, 1815–1848* (Berkeley: University of California Press, 1972).

46. W. R. Ward, *Religion and Society in England, 1790–1850* (London: Batsford, 1972).

47. David Blackbourn has in fact emphasized the extent to which the German middle classes asserted themselves in associational and religious life in the nineteenth century. See David Blackbourn and Geoff Eley, *The Peculiarities of German History: Bourgeois Society and Politics in Nineteenth-Century Germany* (Oxford: Oxford University Press, 1984), 160–292.

48. Jonathan Israel, "Central European Jewry during the Thirty Years' War," *Central European History* 16 (1983): 3–30. For the distinction between these newer settlements and the older ones, see Steven M. Lowenstein, "The Social Dynamics of Jewish Responses to Moses Mendelssohn," in *Moses Mendelssohn und die Kreise seiner Wirksamkeit*, ed. Michael Albrecht, Eva J. Engel, and Norbert Hinske (Tübingen: Niemeyer, 1994), 342.

49. Lois Dubin explores this concept at length in *Enlightenment, Absolutism, and the Jews of Trieste* (Stanford: Stanford University Press, forthcoming).

50. "Port" and Court Jews were not entirely distinct, since there were also Court Jews in the ports. Rather, the nature of the community and the surrounding society

were fundamentally different. For the example of Trieste, with its *haskalah avant la lettre,* see Lois Dubin, "Trieste and Berlin: The Italian Role in the Cultural Politics of the Haskalah," in *Toward Modernity: The European Jewish Model,* ed. Jacob Katz (New Brunswick: Transaction Books, 1987), 189–224. For London, see Todd M. Endelman, *The Jews of Georgian England, 1714–1830: Tradition and Change in a Liberal Society* (Philadelphia: Jewish Publication Society, 1979); and "The Englishness of Jewish Modernity in England," *Toward Modernity,* 225–46. For Bordeaux, see Frances Malino, *The Sephardic Jews of Bordeaux* (University: University of Alabama Press, 1978); and Richard Menkis, "Patriarchs and Patricians: The Gradis Family of Eighteenth-Century Bordeaux," in *From East and West: Jews in a Changing Europe, 1750–1870,* ed. Frances Malino and David Sorkin (Oxford: Basil Blackwell, 1990), 11–45. For Odessa, see Steven Zipperstein, *The Jews of Odessa: A Cultural History, 1794–1881* (Stanford: Stanford University Press, 1986).

51. On the opposition to the *haskalah* in Frankfurt and Prague, see Moshe Samet, "Mendelssohn, Wessley and the Rabbis of their Era" (Hebrew), *Mehkarim be-toldot am Yisrael ve-Erets Yisrael* 1 (1970): 233–57. For the later *haskalah* in Prague, see Hillel Kieval, "Caution's Progress: The Modernization of Jewish Life in Prague, 1780–1830,"*Toward Modernity,* 71–106.

52. Alfred Francis Pribram, ed., *Urkunden und Akten zur Geschichte der Juden in Wien,* 2 vols. (Vienna: Braunmüller, 1918), 1:liv, lvii, lviii.

53. David Blackbourn has argued that what distinguished Germany from other countries at the end of the nineteenth century was the "heightened version of what occurred elsewhere." *Peculiarities of German History,* 292.

The Modern Jewish Diaspora:
East European Jews in New York,
London, and Paris

Nancy L. Green

The Comparative Method

Who are more alike, a New York Jew and a Parisian Jew or a Jewish New Yorker and an Italian New Yorker? The comparative question itself shapes the answer in part.[1] In the first half of the question *Jew* is the noun, *New York* and *Paris* the points of comparison. In the second half the issue is one of comparative ethnicity within one city. The entire question asks, what is more important, ethnicity or acculturation, or, in other words, past or present?

In examining East European Jews at three "ports" of arrival, the analysis of the modern Jewish diaspora raises certain methodological issues from the outset. Migration studies of the last two decades have resurrected the immigrant community in ways crucial to reevaluating the nation-state. Most of these studies have been what can be called linear studies, following the emigrant/immigrant from Poland to Paris or from Italy to New York. The comparison is an implicit one, between past and present, the before and after of the migration experience.[2] A second type of migration study uses a more explicitly comparative approach—a convergent model. Jews and Italians have been the most frequently studied historical neighbors, understandably so, given their proximity both in time (of arrival) and space (the Lower East Side of New York).[3] The questions asked are typically those of comparative social mobility, or, more prosaically, success and failure over time. The city is the given, immigrant "baggage" the explanatory factor.

Each comparative model begins with certain assumptions about similarity and difference. The linear model, not surprisingly, situates difference (and the explanation of that difference) between the Old World and the New.[4] The convergent model postulates difference among ethnic groups at the point of arrival. A third model can be called divergent, tracing paths from Vilna to New York, Paris, and London. Less frequently employed, the divergent comparative study takes an immigrant group as the (at the) point of (literal) departure and examines the impact of various destinations on ethnicity. This approach, however, raises the problem of disaggregating the diaspora, an uncomfortable premise for some community scholars, as Dominique Schnapper has suggested with regard to Jewish studies.[5]

I would like to explore the divergent paths taken by East European Jewish emigrants. This comparison, like all comparisons, has the advantage of generalizing beyond a single linear case. It furthermore has the benefit of challenging an assumption that underlies much of Jewish studies: the similarity of Jews the world over. At one level East European Jewish *grine* (newcomers) may indeed be more similar to one another, whether in New York, London, or Paris, than they are to first-generation Italians in any of those locations. The divergent comparison suggests, however, another level of analysis, one exploring the differentiation of the East European Jewish "constant" throughout space. While the broad lines of Jewish migration from the 1880s on are well-known, the global description of change from East to West has to be nuanced by confronting variations on that theme.

Before turning to this tale of three cities, two final caveats must be added to the comparative method. First, the level of analysis also necessarily affects the "discovery" of similarity or difference. At a certain level of generality all East European Jews look alike (especially in comparison to native Jews, Polish immigrants, etc.); at a closer level of inquiry, however, differences are more apparent. This is the level that I propose to examine here. Second, particularly for questions of acculturation, the time frame chosen will also affect the comparison. If acculturation "works" over the *longue durée,* the comparative question will yield different answers depending on the time period chosen. For the first generation the category East European Jews has a greater degree of similarity than two or three generations later. Nevertheless, even by limiting the scope here to the 1880–1924 period, we can still explore the premises of the transformation of East European Jews into American, English, and French Jews.[6]

The Linear Paradigm

The movie *Fiddler on the Roof* illustrates the basic model of East European Jewish emigration for the period from 1880 to 1914. The final scene portrays the heartbreaking flight after a pogrom. The first step of the move to America is symbolized by a wooden wagon filled with belongings, most of which probably never reached Ellis Island. The popular paradigm of East to West Jewish migration begins with persecution and pogroms and ends with social mobility.[7]

Scholarship of the last two decades has, of course, nuanced that image, both with regard to the causes of emigration and conditions upon arrival. The forces of emigration were more complex than *Fiddler on the Roof* admits. Pogroms were but the most tragic and visible signs of the increasing divorce between Jews and the tsarist regime (although not everyone left, and some even returned).[8] Economic difficulties, due to the slow industrialization of the Pale of Settlement (to which the vast majority of Jews were confined), were seriously aggravated by legislation restricting Jews to a limited number of professions. As the employment market and geographic space became increasingly overcrowded, emigration occurred for work as well as for freedom. Consequently, the vast majority of emigrants had not only religion or ethnicity as a community bond but socioeconomic status as well. Poor, skilled, or semiskilled, most of them left with little but a trade *in der hand.*

Nor were the conditions of immigration that easy, as even Abraham Cahan's novel of ruthless success, *The Rise of David Levinsky,* showed.[9] Whether the destination was New York, London, or Paris, East European Jews (like other immigrants) confronted poverty and hardship upon arrival. They found work in what could be called "immigrant" as well as "Jewish" trades—small-scale commerce and small-scale industry, that is, as peddlers and tailors. They set up organizations for mutual aid and little *shtiblekh* for worship. They began publishing newspapers in Yiddish and debating fiercely, on street corners and in cafés, about the past, present, and future.

To be sure, differentiation within the immigrant communities occurred, as the myriad and often competing organizations that they created attest. Immigrant demands and destinies began to diverge economically, politically, and religiously. Immigrant bosses quickly emerged, although Jewish historians have been reluctant to explore the merciless David Levinskys of the immigrant middle class.[10] Politically, the immigrants imported and developed two ideologies initially problematic for native American, English, or French Jews: socialism and Zionism. Political differentiation took place within the immigrant "community."

Even in the religious realm conflicts occurred. While native Jews often characterized all immigrants as either obscurantist preachers or unrepentant anarchists, in fact, those who emigrated ran the gamut from tradition-alists to freethinkers, and clashes over religious space occurred in all countries of immigration. The desert island joke sums it up: a Jew stranded on a desert island builds a synagogue and then builds a second one. When he is finally saved, his amazed rescuers ask, "Why two?" "One to pray in and one that I never set foot in."

Other, cultural differences can be traced to immigrant origins. Even in the New World haughty Litvaks continued to turn down their noses at their uncultivated coreligionists from the south, the Galizianers. And we know that a Galizianer pot roast in the New World is still different than a Litvak one, even two generations removed.[11] Yet more work still needs to be done on the effect of premigration intra-ethnic differences on life in the New World.

We thus have a linear paradigm of East European Jewish communities in the West that, thanks to the last two decades of research, has been increasingly refined. Yet the increasing complexity of that model has not been at the expense of a general "East European" construct. On the contrary, it has contributed to enriching it. Differentiation has not seriously questioned the notion of a certain level of "community." As Joshua Fishman and others have suggested, "Jewish" and other ethnic identities were built in the New World as much or if not more so than in the Old.[12] That construction was part of the migration process itself. And, ultimately, institutional diversification gave way to tactical amalgamation, if not actual consolidation. Indeed, the point is that the composite East European model includes all *landsmanshaft* organizations. That each organization catered to a different group was a characteristic of the entire group. The ethnic community paradigm has emerged, thus, as one that posits a whole of diversified but not divisive parts.

The Divergent Challenge

Linear studies of immigrant "community" have thus not challenged the basic premise that the major difference in experience lies between East and West. In that respect both East (from Lithuania to Galicia) and West (from New York to London) have, at a certain level, been "homogenized," representing two poles that, like other migration narratives, chart the change from tradition to modernity. What happens when we "deconstruct" the West by examining the East European Jew in different diaspora locales? The point of differentiation shifts. It is no longer solely a comparison of

East and West nor even one of diversification within immigrant communities but, rather, an analysis of difference within New World experiences.

The divergent analysis can thus ask a number of comparative questions that focus on differences at the points of arrival. For example: (1) How do perceptions before departure influence the destination decision? (2) To what extent do the strength and timing of migration streams affect acculturation in different cities? (3) How did reception by the existing Jewish communities affect the adaptation of the newcomers? (4) And how did different political, cultural, and economic conditions in each country of immigration affect immigrant culture?

Images of Emigration

Roger Ikor, in his prize-winning novel about an immigrant Jewish cap maker in Paris, vividly evoked the late-nineteenth-century emigration question: Where to? His hero, Yankel Mykhanowitzki, crosses the Russian-German border still doubting his choice of a final destination. He reexamines his reasons for choosing France and, having eliminated Germany—due to Bismarck, Nietzsche, and Wagner—turns to England, the United States, and France:

> And England? Ah! England has a lot of good points. . . . But no, not England either. Why? He tried to beat around the bush. The English are rich men, you see, and the poor must not feel very comfortable among them; and they are known to be haughty, imperialist. . . . Liberals, you say? Sure, liberals! But full of prejudices, of tradition, full of dukes sporting monocles. . . . And first of all, why do they still have a king, even an ornamental one? What's his purpose, that parasite?
>
> And Yankel listed all the good reasons for avoiding England. But he forgot the only real one, that England is an island, and he absolutely didn't want to settle on an island. You can never get away from an island, and you never know when you might want to leave.
>
> That left the two Republics, America and France—America meant the United States, of course. Yankel had long hesitated between the two, and he still hesitated, or pretended to. News from New York was encouraging. Emigrant letters talked about masses of money to be earned. But Yankel worried little about money; he had modest needs. Riches as such didn't interest him, or only incidentally. He would easily claim, like his dear Tolstoy, that money corrupts men. What he wanted

was a gentle and humane existence. But he had heard of the harshness with which the American immigration officials greeted the newcomers; sure, that was just the first step which had to be gotten over; but it seemed a bad omen. Compared to France, ah! France. . . .

When the word was pronounced in Rakwomir, faces lit up. Victor Hugo, Voltaire, the Rights of Man, the Revolution, the barricades, liberty-equality-fraternity. . . . The tyrants that the French had overthrown! The generous causes for which they had become inflamed! Even their national hymn was that noble "Marseillaise" that democrats, nihilists, socialists and revolutionaries sing, in defiance of autocracy, under the whip of the Cossacks.[13]

Yankel's uncertainty is more suggestive than explanatory. But it raises the important question, to what extent did the predeparture *imaginaire* influence the migration streams? Although the overwhelming number of emigrants pursued the streets-paved-with-gold path, we know that there was also a negative flip side to the American myth. As Abraham Cahan observed in an editorial in 1911: "In Europe it has become the custom to view life in America condescendingly. A land of skyscrapers and yellow journalism, a huge circus of business dealing and bluffing—this is all people there [in eastern Europe] know about the United States."[14] The comparative study asks, How many people went elsewhere? How many were deterred from Ellis Island because of negative images or more encouraging ones about conditions elsewhere?

For England we, unfortunately, have little data. Few immigrant letters or emigrant guidebooks are extant, and the composite picture of immigration for economic opportunity and religious freedom drawn by Lloyd Gartner is not particularly specific to England, except for the symbolic role played by the English Rothschilds (as elsewhere). Indeed, Gartner insists that the emigrants came in spite of warnings about antisemitism and difficult working conditions.[15] With regard to France, however, there is testimony that an ideological component helped to draw immigrants there. French civilization and the French Revolution remained powerful images a good century after Louis XVI had been toppled. Polish exiles and Russian nobles went to France, in part, for linguistic reasons, French being spoken widely in cultured circles in the East. Russian revolutionaries, Italian anarchists, and socialists headed to Paris with 1789 in mind. For Jewish emigrants the fact that the Jews had been emancipated during the Revolution gave a particular content to the image of liberty, equality, and fraternity.[16]

While most emigrants followed family or friends to far-off places in what is now commonly called chain migration, each location had its own set of representations from which emigrants chose. Much more work needs to be done on the "destination question" from the perspective of departure. But the comparative emigration study first shows how alternative routes existed, that the United States was not the only choice. Furthermore, comparison shows that similar factors were at work in drawing emigrants westward. The United States, England, and France all represented two things that were severely restricted in the East: jobs and freedom. Yet each country also had its specific character and appeal, which have perhaps been overlooked in the emphasis on linear models of chain migration: Skyscrapers, Her and, after Victoria's death, His Majesty, and the Bastille are but symbolic shorthand for the emigration imagination. This is not to suggest that all dreamers and revolutionaries went to France and all go-getters to the United States. Nonetheless, it is important to understand how differentiation may occur even before emigration. Expectations and images, premigration political and cultural options, colored the divergent migration streams before any borders were crossed.

The Impact of Numbers

From 1830 to 1925 over seventeen million English, seven million Germans, and six million Italians migrated westward, as did four million Jews.[17] Nearly three million Jews moved in the 1881–1914 period alone. By 1925, according to Jacob Lestschinsky, three and a half million East European Jews had left their homes, heading primarily for the United States and Canada (2,650,000 and 112,000), England (210,000), Argentina (150,000), and France (100,000).[18]

The overwhelming size and mythic image of migration to the United States have led some historians to explain the development of the new Jewish communities in England and France as but by-products of the move across the Atlantic, "leaving behind the sick or more fortunate," according to Michel Roblin.[19] England, in particular, was a noted country of transmigration. According to Arthur Ruppin's calculations, 114,000 Jews left England for the United States from 1880 to 1930.[20] In 1886 an immigrant speculated that some 90 percent of those in England planned to continue to the United States.[21] France also served as an important transit point for emigrants going on to the United States and Argentina. There are stories of families passing through Paris on their way from Odessa to New York or even from Argentina back to Russia. In 1892, when the Hamburg port was closed due to a cholera epidemic and the United States slowed immigration for fear of typhoid, many transatlantic aspirants were routed through Paris, hoping to board the next boat out of Le Havre.[22]

The numbers of immigrants alone can in part explain subsequent differences in acculturation patterns. There were some 795,000 East European immigrants in New York City in 1910, 63,000 Russian and Russian-Polish immigrants in London in 1911, and 35,000 East European Jews in Paris before World War I.[23] The respective populations of these cities circa 1900 being 5.5 million, 6.6 million, and 2.7 million, Jews formed approximately 14 percent of the New York City population, less than 1 percent of the London population, and 1.3 percent of the Paris population. In comparison with other destinations, then, the massive nature of emigration to New York seems in itself to account for a de facto cultural pluralism in which Jews would play an important and visible role in the city. The smaller number of Jewish immigrants in London and Paris may thus help explain the greater tendency toward acculturation to the dominant cultural models in those cities.

The immigration story looks different, however, when viewed at the precinct level. In addition to comparing global Jewish migration patterns, we can look at the impact of immigration within various cities. First, immigrant neighborhoods, regardless of size, constituted a critical base for most newcomers' lives. It was within their borders that immigrant institutions formed (a desert island would have been sufficient). From the vantage point of local street corners, pubs, and cafés, the real or imagined boundaries of Yiddish-speaking enclaves were cohesive and comforting, encouraging continuity rather than cultural exchange, regardless of the actual geographic scope of the community. Second, from the perspective of the non-Jewish world, absolute size was not always a critical determinant either. The large Jewish Lower East Side of New York was perceived as one (albeit the largest) immigrant neighborhood among others;[24] the smaller East End of London, on the other hand, became a target of anger and resentment greatly out of proportion to its size; while the relatively circumscribed Pletzl of Paris was almost invisible to unknowing outsiders. Thus, numbers, while important, are also relative. The dimensions of emigration to New York clearly affected the nature of settlement there and the possibilities of an ethnic Jewish consciousness. But the smaller numbers of immigrants to London and Paris did not mean the absence of vibrant immigrant cultures in their time. Comparisons across space must also be situated within local political and social environments.

Uptown/Downtown, West End/East End, Juifs/Israélites

Jews attract Jews. In each city immigrant Jews were met by native Jews. The established communities influenced immigration in two ways: first, as an implicit (if largely unwilling) "pull"; second, as intermediaries in the acculturation process. The knowledge that Jewish communities existed in New York, London, and Paris was sufficient in and of itself to attract coreligionists. This pull took two forms, one almost mythical, the other more concrete. The most important, tangible pull, as for other immigrant groups, came in the form of letters, money, and boat tickets sent from West to East, "publicity" more powerful than any the boat companies devised. But this was a pull essentially between (earlier and later) immigrants. The native Jewish communities exercised a different kind of attraction, one that worked on the immigrants' imagination. Information about conditions in the West included larger-than-life images of wealthy coreligionists. Schiffs, Montefiores, and Rothschilds symbolized both material and social success; they were also code names for Jewish philanthropy, a safety net in case of need.

But Jewish solidarity had its limits. The Western communities did indeed extend help to East European Jews, in tsarist Russia as well as in immigrant quarters in New York, London, and Paris. Acculturated Western Jews were reluctant, however, to see large groups of poor, foreign Jews settle among them, creating too-visible *agglomérations* in their midst. Culture, economics, and even religious practice separated Western Jews from their Eastern brethren. Tradition versus modernity, informal religious fervor versus formal, top-hatted, decorous prayer, divided West and East in the first generation. Western Jews worried about resurgent antisemitism and community coffers strained to the limit by the impoverished newcomers. The New York, London, and Paris communities all tried various systems to distribute the newcomers throughout their respective countries but with little success.[25]

In each country, however, strategies and concerns differed. As Zosa Szajkowski commented, "The principle of every European committee was to facilitate the migration of refugees, but not to their own country."[26] As European committees tried to hasten the departures of emigrants to the

United States, the New York committee, in turn, worked to avoid the creation of concentrated "ghettos" on the East Coast. When the United States began to place restrictions on immigration in 1906, the French Jewish weekly *Archives Israélites* complained that this was unjust on the part of such a large, unpopulated country.[27]

More important, the Western communities' concerns were circumscribed by their relationship to the societies in which they lived. Immigrants from the East arrived in the United States as the debate over "old" versus "new" immigrants began to heat up. Conflicts between (native) German Jews and Russian Jews can be seen as a micro-version of the larger debate. Divisions and reciprocal hostilities between Uptowners (German Jews) and Downtowners (Russian immigrants) reflected not only the ways in which natives perceived immigrants but also the ways in which older immigrants saw the new arrivals.

In England the growth of the immigrant quarter intersected with worries over two larger issues gnawing at English society: the debate over the "uses of charity" and concern over unemployment. Anglo-Jewish charities, like English parishes before them, were concerned lest their largesse itself attract paupers; the "deserving" and "undeserving" poor had to be differentiated.[28] To ward off hardship cases and prevent increased unemployment the *Jewish Chronicle* issued warnings about the saturated labor market, while the Jewish Board of Guardians even placed notices in East European Jewish newspapers to discourage prospective job seekers.[29]

As for France, the response to the immigrants there, too, was couched in terms specific to the concerns of native Jews about their own precarious status within the larger society. The immigrants began to arrive within (and even during) the years of the Dreyfus Affair. To be sure, the antisemitism surrounding the affair focused more on rich Jews than on poor.[30] But the underlying hypothesis, repeated indefatigably by Edouard Drumont, author of the virulently antisemitic best-seller *La France Juive,* was that Jews were foreign to the French body politic. The arrival of really foreign Jews (*juifs*) only heightened the concerns of French Jews (*israélites*) about their place within French society. The immigrants arrived just as the *israélites* were reemphasizing their allegiance to the state and their identification with the republic.

In all three countries foreign and native Jews eyed one another warily. Yet beyond this similarity the specifics were rooted in the native communities' relationship to their surrounding environment. The solutions proposed by American, English, and French Jews took on a similar yet fundamentally dissimilar form in each country. Each community sought to socialize the newcomers. But that socialization was less in conformity to a universal Jewish model than to the local cultural one: to be American in the United States, English in England, more French than the French. The *Settlement Cookbook* not only provided recipes; it prescribed americanized norms of cleanliness for immigrant kitchens.[31] The Jewish Working Men's Club, founded in London in 1872 by Samuel Montagu, sought to eliminate foreign "speech, habits, and views" "repugnant to English feeling and to imbue the newcomers with English sentiments and notions."[32] Similarly, the French Jewish weekly *L'Univers Israélite* strongly suggested at the turn of the century that it was necessary "to give this population . . . a very suitable Parisian demeanor, to 'wash away' [*débarbouiller*] that which is exotic and too shocking. . . . We are not suggesting either makeup, nor a disguise, but a sort of material and moral adaptation."[33]

Native Jews, from Paris to London to New York, sought to remake the immigrants in their own image. They promoted the acculturation of the newcomers while protecting their own. In so doing, they provided a crucial first impetus to the subsequent differentiation of East European Jews into French, English, and American ones. Their actions reflected, in each case, their status as a minority group within a dominant society. And each society and state had a different perspective on the minority groups within its midst.

Politics and Timing

The American, British, and French contexts within which the native Jewish welcome was expressed also affected immigrant adaptation. Official and popular conceptions of citizenship and nationality, as well as the political climate at the time of arrival, all form part of what could be called the cultural contours of arrival. Legislation regulating arrival and entry could, in itself, partially condition subsequent settlement and acculturation. The timing of waves of immigration varied as a result of that legislation, from 1870 to 1905 in England, 1870 to 1924 in the United States, and 1881 to the 1930s in France. That timing and the duration of the wave, like the numbers of those who came, were ultimately factors of differentiation. The politics of migration, which differed significantly from one country to another, reflected different political and social attitudes toward the acceptance of foreigners.

Two factors are particularly salient in the American case: the wide-open doors of the late nineteenth century and the closing of those doors in the 1920s. In no other country was schizophrenia about migration so apparent. The result was the creation of mass immigrant communities *before* the gates were closed. This meant three things. First, Jewish immigrants in New York settled into a situation of de facto cultural pluralism quite different from that encountered in England or France. The horizons of their acculturation were not set only by the already americanized German Jewish social workers whom they met in settlement houses but also by the first-generation Italians with whom they shared the Lower East Side. Ethnic identities were being forged in all of the new immigrant communities. Second, the cut-off of immigration that occurred in the 1920s hastened the americanization of those who had already arrived, since it halted the human resources of cultural continuity, that is, new, unamericanized arrivals from the Old World. Nonetheless, I would also argue, third, that this very suspension of the renewal of tradition via new immigrants from the Old World served to consolidate the East European cohort into a turn-of-the-century model. The construction of East European Jewish identity before 1924 would become the reference point for later representations of Jewish ethnicity, especially from the 1960s on.

The English case was quite the opposite. Immigration was halted earlier than anywhere else, by the Aliens Act of 1905. Although the act was perhaps more effective as a psychological deterrent than a legal one, it still had an important, twofold impact. First, particularly after it was reinforced in 1914, it limited Jewish immigration before massive and multiple immigrant communities had formed. Second, and more important, it expressed a political culture that rejected the notion of England as a country of immigration. Through the legislation and debates surrounding its passage England drew an image of itself as a country of *em*igration, one with more than enough internal immigrants, from Ireland, to fill unskilled jobs. But through the 1905 law Russian and Polish Jews were specifically targeted as undesirables in a culture that dismissed aliens altogether.[34]

France represents an intermediary position. Contradictory currents of immigration policy were always present, but the legal apparatus remained the most generous of all, until the 1930s. By the late nineteenth century the country was caught in a double demographic bind, wanting more inhabitants but unsure how to go about it. Visions of demographic drought led to a largely unheeded prescriptive literature encouraging French female fertility. It also led to debates about which national groups were most likely to assimilate French mental and cultural habits. An open immigration policy was thus underwritten by conflicting tendencies: the need for "arms" to "fill the void" along with concern about which "races" were most appropriate. While the antisemitism surrounding the Dreyfus Affair attacked Jews as outsiders in the French context, it was not as immigrants per se. In Drumont's imagery the foreignness of the Jews was more symbolic, in the sense of a foreign graft onto an otherwise healthy body.[35] The East European immigrants thus arrived in France as worries about the "Frenchness" of French society became increasingly predominant. Yet, at the same time, immigration was a de facto, indeed encouraged, part of public policy.

The impact of these differences in politics, political culture, and the timing of immigrant waves needs to be explored further. The different immigration policies not only circumscribed the numbers and timing of immigration but also expressed and reinforced the political cultures that had an impact on the immigrants after their arrival. At the most basic level the laws aimed at halting immigration into England and the United States perhaps changed the course of some migration routes. How many Russian Jewish revolutionaries went to France after 1905, rather than to England or the United States, hoping to return eventually to Russia? How many Polish Jews went to France instead of the United States in the 1920s?

Over the long run politics and timing may help explain the strength of the American Jewish immigrant community compared to those in Europe. The emergence and persistence of a strong ethnic community in the United States was due not only to sheer numbers but, ironically, also to the restrictive laws of the 1920s. Comparison with England suggests that the later date of the cut-off in the United States, coming after the arrival of so many immigrants, consolidated an East European ethnic model, which in turn imparted a more specific character to the americanization that followed. The formation of an immigrant culture was halted earlier in England, amid great hostility to immigration in general, an important factor in setting the tone for adaptation to English manners. In France, where the progressive opening of French doors was preceded and accompanied by a theory of assimilation, Jewish immigration continued into the 1920s and 1930s, with the arrival of new cohorts of Polish, Turkish, and German Jews.[36] The Jewish immigrant population, although still predominantly East European, thus also became more diversified.[37]

Comparison forces us to analyze acculturation differently. It is not just a question of a linear story of adaptation and change from East to West in which, globally, the immigrants to America, England, and France gradually adopted many of the sociocultural characteristics of their new homes.

As we have seen, different political cultures as well as specific laws shaped migration streams. As a result, the notion of melting pot has to be relativized both within the United States and without. Israel Zangwill's bubbling cauldron was not peculiar to the city of skyscrapers. Indeed, we can ask whether it was not even more effective in London or Paris, where smaller communities in different political and legal environments created their own forms of hyphenated identities.

The Economics of Divergence

Finally, we can compare East European Jews at work in these three cities. To be sure, there is much similarity in the activities of the Russian and Polish immigrants at home and abroad. The emigrants headed toward economic opportunity in the industrializing West, and, as they congregated in major cities, they entered those light industrial and petty commercial trades that offered easy access to newcomers. In this respect Jewish immigrant activity in New York, London, and Paris looks much the same. There were lots of tailors and countless peddlers.

Table 1 provides some tentative data for a divergent analysis. These figures must be interpreted with care, however, since they are based on census and survey data whose categories are not easily comparable. The absence of certain categories (clerks and domestics in London, 1895–1908, e.g.) may be due to the ways in which the data were obtained or tabulated. In comparing the base population in Russia with the emigrants, however, two basic characteristics emerge. First, tailors left in much greater numbers than grocers. That is, the emigration from the East was marked by a particularly high number of skilled workers, who left in numbers proportionally far greater than their percentage in Russia. This corresponds both to the reality of stifled opportunity in the East and to expectations of potential opportunity in the West. The "settled" figures bear out the fact that there was opportunity for skilled workers in the manufacturing and artisanal trades in the New World.

Second, merchants left in numbers significantly smaller than their proportion in the East (although declarations upon arrival may be deceiving, if not deceitful—biased in function of expectations and rumors about what to answer). The disappearance of commercial activity in the "arrival" statistics undoubtedly reflects the greater difficulty of transferring capital stock and clientele (rather than a trade skill) abroad. The reemergence of a commercial sector as immigrants settled in indicates

	Base Population	Declaration upon Arrival			Settled		
	Russia (1897)	U.S.A. (1889–1914)	London (1895–1908)	Paris (1906–12)	Manhattan (1890)	London (1891)	Paris (1910)
				A: All Occupations			
Agriculture	2.8	2.3	2.3	0.6	0.0	—	0.0
Manufacture and artisanal trades	37.7	64.0	75.0	76.8	76.9	—	62.1
Commerce	31.4	5.5	22.7	6.6	15.5	—	32.7
Labor and domestic service	18.6	21.0	0.0	3.4	0.0	—	0.0
Professions and white collar work	5.0	1.3	0.0	12.6	7.6	—	4.0
Other	4.5	5.9	0.0	0.0	0.0	—	1.2
Total	100.0[a]	100.0[a]	100.0[b]	100.0[c]	100.0[d]	—	100.0[e]
				B: Artisanal Trades			
Clothing	37.6	52.2	—	36.3	78.0	32.1	47.2
Animal products	17.6	8.5	—	22.8	0.5	34.6	16.8
Wood manufacture and construction	16.2	15.2	—	12.8	6.1	5.6	15.9
Food industry	8.4	6.2	—	6.1	9.6	25.0	0.5
Metal industry	7.1	4.6	—	12.7	5.0	0.9	15.5
Other	13.1	13.3	—	9.3	0.8	1.8	4.1
Total	100.0[a]	100.0[a]	—	100.0[c]	100.0[d]	100.0[f]	100.0[e]

[a] Simon Kuznets, "Immigration of Russian Jews to the United States: Background and Structure," *Perspectives in American History* 10 (1976): 101–2, 110. Kuznets adjusted the Russian figures to conform to the U.S. immigration categories. I have adjusted all other figures to Kuznets's: gainfully employed only; peddling combined with commerce; boots and shoes, as leather goods, are classified as animal products; cigars and cigarettes as food products.

[b] Lloyd Gartner, *The Jewish Immigrant in England, 1870–1914* (London: Simon Publications, 1973), 57–58. Derived from declarations made upon arrival at the Poor Jews' Temporary Shelter (*Annual Reports*).

[c] Société philanthropique de l'Asile Israélite de Paris, *Rapports des exercises*, 1906–7, 1909–12; see list in Nancy Green, *The Pletzl of Paris* (New York: Holmes and Meier, 1986), app. C.

[d] Adapted from Moses Rischin, *The Promised City: New York's Jews, 1870–1914* (New York: Corinth Books, 1964), 272. Derived from Baron de Hirsch study, published in *Geshikhte fun di idishe arbeter bavegung in di feraynikte shtatn*, ed. E. Tcherikower (New York; 1943–45), 1:258–59.

[e] Wolf Speiser, *Kalendar* (Paris: n.p., 1910), 78–80; see list in Green, *The Pletzl of Paris*, app. D.

[f] Derived from Léonty Soloweitschik, *Un prolétariat méconnu* (Brussels: Henri Lamertin, 1898), 47–48.

perhaps less a direct carryover from Eastern Europe than entrance into a new field of activity, easy for the newcomer with little capital to undertake—peddling.

While these characteristics mark the immigrant Jewish communities of the Lower East Side, the East End, and the Pletzl, a closer look at the figures reveals a greater diversity of opportunity in the West than myth allows. They show that an East European Jew in New York was more likely to become a tailor; in London, a shoemaker; and in Paris, a woodworker. The figures reflect the specific urban economies of each city. The garment industry, while important in all three metropolises, was, without contest, the major factor of economic life for Jews in Manhattan. By contrast, while there were certainly no lack of Jewish garment workers in London and Paris as well, Jewish occupations were more evenly distributed in these two cities. Jews became boot and shoe makers ("animal products") in large numbers in London. (There were also some two hundred Jewish umbrella stick makers—to each city its specialty.)[38] They were also cigar and cigarette makers ("food industry") in a country in which the trade was not, as in France, a state monopoly. In Paris many immigrants became cabinetmakers, working in and for the faubourg St. Antoine furniture district (where the less expensive end of the trade was centered). There were a significant number of goldsmiths and tinsmiths ("metal industry") as well. The other distinguishing characteristic of Paris was the large number of "professionals," that is, students and revolutionaries, who headed there. Yet, as we see in the "settled" figures, they did not necessarily find jobs in their fields.

These varied outcomes, which if interpreted within the context of a single country may pale under the predominance of garment making, take on greater importance in comparative perspective. The economic data clearly show how differentiation can reflect the structures on arrival more than the culture of departure. And the importance of these differences is in their challenge to the causality of a linear model. Skill transfer alone is not sufficient to understand either the large numbers of garment workers or the diversification of job opportunities from one city to the next. Local factors once again served to orient immigrant destinations and destinies.

Conclusion

A divergent comparative study thus shifts the analysis from one concerned with difference between East and West to one interested in variations within the immigrants' New Worlds. While at one level (compared to other immigrants or natives) East European Jews may look alike in the modern diaspora, at another important level the emigrants' itineraries, and their ultimate transformation into American, English, and French Jews, were inscribed in the migration project from the very beginning. Self-selection and representations of immigration started the process even before emigration.

More important, the divergent comparison locates differentiation and change within the receiving countries. Acculturation occurred everywhere, but, if the process was the same, the results were not. In this respect the divergent analysis complements the linear one while bringing into question certain assumptions about culture and skill transfer. Such transfers were affected, from the very first generation, by different opportunities in New York, London, and Paris, just as they were mediated by the specific receiving societies, their political cultures, their attitudes toward immigrants and Jews, and the native Jewish communities. From this perspective the "East European Jewish community" in emigration is a construct dependent as much upon divergent as upon linear change.

The diasporic analysis is also ultimately extendable. What we have explored here is, in fact, at a very general level, a construct within a fairly homogeneous model of migration to the urban economies of the industrializing West. What if we compare East European Jews in Buenos Aires or Palestine during the same period? New dimensions of difference appear. The East Europeans also became cowboys (gauchos) and farmers. And even within England alone, for example, the experience of a Jewish garment worker in (a factory in) Leeds or Manchester was in many ways quite different from that of his or her compatriot in a small workshop in London.[39] To study the modern diaspora raises important questions about ethnic unity that need to be addressed. As one anthropologist has commented, to study community is to find it.[40] By the same token, I would add, to study diversity is also to find it. Both approaches are complementary, and both need to be addressed in order to compare properly Jewish communities around the world.

NOTES

1. Nancy L. Green, "L'histoire comparative et le champ des études migratoires," *Annales, E.S.C.* 45 (1990): 1335–50. I would like to thank Phyllis Albert and

Judith Friedlander for their comments on previous drafts of this essay. An earlier version of this piece appeared in *European Migrants: Global and Local Perspectives,* ed. Leslie Page Moch and Dirk Hoerder (Boston: Northeastern University Press, 1995).

2. John W. Briggs is one of the few to have questioned explicitly this implicit comparison in "Fertility and Cultural Change among Families in Italy and America," *American Historical Review* 91 (1986): 1129–45; see Virginia Yans-McLaughlin, *Family and Community: Italian Immigrants in Buffalo, 1880–1930* (Ithaca, NY: Cornell University Press, 1977).

3. Thomas Kessner, *The Golden Door: Italian and Jewish Immigrant Mobility in New York City, 1880–1915* (New York: Oxford University Press, 1977); Joel Perlmann, *Ethnic Differences: Schooling and Social Structure among the Irish, Italians, Jews, and Blacks in an American City, 1880–1935* (New York: Cambridge University Press, 1988); Dominique Schnapper, "Quelques réflexions sur l'assimilation comparée des travailleurs émigrés italiens et des Juifs en France," *Bulletin de la Société française de sociologie* 3 (July 1976): 11–18; Judith Smith, *Family Connections: A History of Italian and Jewish Immigrant Lives in Providence, Rhode Island, 1900–1940* (Albany: State University of New York Press, 1985). See also Josef Barton, *Peasants and Strangers: Italians, Rumanians, and Slovaks in an American City, 1890–1950* (Cambridge, MA: Harvard University Press, 1975); Ronald H. Bayor, *Neighbors in Conflict: The Irish, Germans, Jews, and Italians of New York City, 1929–1941* (Baltimore: Johns Hopkins University Press, 1978); Donald B. Cole, *Immigrant City: Lawrence, Massachusetts, 1845–1921* (Chapel Hill: University of North Carolina Press, 1963); Ewa Morawska, *For Bread with Butter: The Life-Worlds of East Central Europeans in Johnstown, Pennsylvania, 1890–1940* (New York: Cambridge University Press, 1985); Gary Mormino and George Pozzetta, *The Immigrant World of Ybor City: Italians and their Latin Neighbors in Tampa, 1885–1985* (Urbana: University of Illinois Press, 1987).

4. *New World* here designates the country of immigration, be it transatlantic or trans-European. On the importance of integrating these different migrations into one conceptual model, see Dirk Hoerder, "An Introduction to Labor Migration in the Atlantic Economies, 1815–1914," in *Labor Migration in the Atlantic Economies: The European and North American Working Classes during the Period of Industrialization,* ed. Dirk Hoerder (Westport, CN: Greenwood Press, 1985), 3–31.

5. Dominique Schnapper, "Jewish Minorities and the State in the United States, France, and Argentina," in *Center: Ideas and Institutions,* ed. Liah Greenfeld and Michael Mertin (Chicago: University of Chicago Press, 1988), 186–209. There are few examples of the divergent approach applied to the Jewish diaspora: Karin Hofmeester, *Van Talmoed tot Statuut: Joodse Arbeiders en Arbeiders-bewegingen in Amsterdam, Londen en Parijs, 1880–1914* (Amsterdam: IISG, 1990); Andrew S. Reutlinger, "Reflections on the Anglo-American Jewish Experience: Immigrants, Workers, and Entrepreneurs in New York and London, 1870–1914," *American Jewish Historical Quarterly* 66 (1977): 473–84; Jack Wertheimer, *Unwelcome Strangers:*

East European Jews in Imperial Germany (New York: Oxford University Press, 1987), conclusion. Concerning Italians, see: Samuel L. Baily, "The Italians and the Development of Organized Labor in Argentina, Brazil and the United States, 1880–1914," *Journal of Social History* 3 (Winter 1969): 123–34; "The Adjustment of Italian Immigrants in Buenos Aires and New York, 1870–1914," *American Historical Review* 88 (1983): 281–305; John Briggs, *An Italian Passage: Immigrants to Three American Cities, 1890–1930* (New Haven: Yale University Press, 1978); Donna Gabaccia, *Militants and Migrants: Rural Sicilians Become American Workers* (New Brunswick, NJ: Rutgers University Press, 1988); Herbert S. Klein, "The Integration of Italian Immigrants in the United States and Argentina: A Comparative Analysis," *American Historical Review* 88 (1983): 306–46; Dominique Schnapper, "Centralisme et fédéralisme culturels: les émigrés italiens en France et aux États-Unis," *Annales, E.S.C.* 29 (1974): 1141–59. And, for a study of Portuguese and West Indians by two anthropologists, see: Caroline B. Brettell, "Is the Ethnic Community Inevitable? A Comparison of the Settlement Patterns of Portuguese Immigrants in Toronto and Paris," *Journal of Ethnic Studies* 9 (Autumn 1981): 1–17; Nancy Foner, "West Indians in New York City and London: A Comparative Analysis," *International Migration Review* 13 (Summer 1979): 284–97.

6. In France, for example, the categories of Jewishness have changed continually since the nineteenth century. The "Portuguese" and "German" Jews of the eighteenth century became the "French (and Alsatian) Jews" of the nineteenth century, especially from the perspective of the East European newcomers ("Pollaks" to the unkind). Since World War II the "French (and Polish) Jews" have become the "Ashkenazi" Jews in contrast to the "Sephardi" newcomers from North Africa. (That the latter term is a misnomer is another issue.) To an American Jewish visitor, of course, they're all "French." I explored this evolution in the naming of "community" in greater detail in "Jewish Migration to France in the Nineteenth and Twentieth Centuries: Community or Communities?" *Studia Rosenthaliana* 23 (1989): 135–53.

7. Sholem Aleichem's *Tevye the Dairyman,* on which *Fiddler* was based, is somewhat ambiguous with regard to the "destination question." One of the last lines reads: "tomorrow may find us in Yehupetz, and next year in Odessa, or in Warsaw, or maybe even in America." *Tevye the Dairyman,* trans. Hillel Halkin (New York: Schocken, 1987). Furthermore, as Sholem Aleichem wrote the story in installments over a decade, subsequent translators have sometimes chosen different episodes for the ending. See, for example, Edmond Fleg's translation, *Un violon sur le toit* (Paris: Albin Michel, 1962), which ends with Tevye going to Israel; and Halkin's discussion of the issue (xix–xx).

8. Jonathan Sarna, "The Myth of No Return: Jewish Return Migration to Eastern Europe, 1881–1914," Hoerder, *Labor Migration,* 423–34; Zosa Szajkowski, "Deportation of Jewish Immigrants and Returnees before World War I," *American Jewish Historical Quarterly* 67 (1978): 291–306.

9. Abraham Cahan, *The Rise of David Levinsky* (New York: Harper, 1917).

10. See Bill Williams, "'East and West': Class and Community in Manchester Jewry, 1850–1914," in *The Making of Modern Anglo-Jewry,* ed. David Cesarani (Oxford: Basil Blackwell, 1990), 15–33.

11. Judith Friedlander, "Jewish Cooking in the American Melting Pot," *Revue française d'études américaines* 11 (February 1986): 87–98.

12. Joshua Fishman, ed. *The Rise and Fall of the Ethnic Revival* (Berlin: Mouton, 1985); Stephen Steinberg, *The Ethnic Myth* (Boston: Beacon, 1981).

13. Roger Ikor, *Les fils d'Avrom: les eaux mêlées* (Paris: Albin Michel, 1955), 92–94. The suspension points are Ikor's.

14. Editorial by Abraham Cahan in 1911, cited in Ronald Sanders, *The Downtown Jews* (New York: New American Library, 1976), 344–45. Much has been written on East European Jews in New York; two classics are Moses Rischin, *The Promised City: New York's Jews, 1870–1914* (New York: Corinth Books, 1964); and Irving Howe, *World of Our Fathers* (New York: Simon and Schuster, 1976).

15. Lloyd P. Gartner, *The Jewish Immigrant in England, 1870–1914,* 2d ed. (London: Simon Publications, 1973), 26–30. It is a curious historiographical footnote that the supposedly most literate of emigrant groups left no good stock of letters. On Jewish immigration to England, see also: Eugene C. Black, *The Social Politics of Anglo-Jewry, 1880–1920* (Oxford: Basil Blackwell, 1988); Cesarani, *Modern Anglo-Jewry;* David Feldman, *Englishmen and Jews: Social Relations and Political Culture, 1840–1914* (New Haven: Yale University Press, 1994); William J. Fishman, *East End Jewish Radicals, 1875–1914* (London: Duckworth, 1975); Bernard Gainer, *The Alien Invasion: The Origins of the Aliens Act of 1905* (London: Heinemann, 1972); Tony Kushner, "The End of the 'Anglo-Jewish Progress Show': Representations of the Jewish East End, 1887–1987," in *The Jewish Heritage in British History: Englishness and Jewishness,* ed. Tony Kushner (London: Frank Cass, 1992), 78–105; Vivian D. Lipman, *Social History of the Jews in England, 1850–1950* (London: Watts and Company, 1954); Robert S. Wechsler, "The Jewish Garment Trade in East London, 1875–1914" (Ph.D. diss., Columbia University, 1979); Jerry White, *Rothschild Buildings: Life in an East End Tenement Block, 1887–1920* (London: Routledge, 1980).

16. I have examined this imagery at greater length in "La révolution dans l'imaginaire des immigrants juifs," in *Histoire politique des Juifs de France,* ed. Pierre Birnbaum (Paris: Presses de la Fondation Nationale des Sciences Politiques, 1990), 153–62; and in Nancy Green, Laura Frader, and Pierre Milza, "Paris: City of Light and Shadow," in *Distant Magnets: Expectations and Realities in the Immigrant Experience,* ed. Dirk Hoerder and Horst Rössler (New York: Holmes and Meier, 1993). On East European immigrants in France, see Nancy Green, *The Pletzl of Paris: Jewish Immigrant Workers in the Belle Epoque* (New York: Holmes and Meier, 1986); Paula Hyman, *From Dreyfus to Vichy: The Remaking of French Jewry* (New York: Columbia University Press, 1979); and David Weinberg, *A Community on Trial: The Jews of Paris in the 1930s* (Chicago: University of Chicago Press, 1977). For the war period, see Jacques Adler, *The Jews of Paris and the Final*

Solution: Communal Response and Internal Conflicts, 1940–44 (New York: Oxford University Press, 1987).

17. Jacob Lestschinsky, *Di yidishe vanderung far di letste 25 yor* (Jewish Migration in the Last Twenty-Five Years) (Berlin: HIAS-Emigdirekt, 1927), 2.

18. Ibid, 6; Arthur Ruppin, *Les Juifs dans le monde moderne* (Paris: Payot, 1934), 69.

19. Michel Roblin, *Les Juifs de Paris: démographie, économie, culture* (Paris: A. et J. Picard et Cie., 1952), 65. See Wechsler, "Jewish Garment Trade," 231–33, for the effects of transmigration on the Jewish immigrant labor movement in London.

20. Ruppin, *Les Juifs dans le monde moderne,* 69. Some migrants simply passed through English harbors. Others stayed a while (how long?) before moving on. Transmigration and step-migration are subjects that merit further study in themselves. Aubrey Newman has suggested the importance of studying the efforts of shipping companies in regulating the migration flow. See his essay "Trains, Ships and the Jewish Question" (paper delivered at the International Center for University Teaching of Jewish Civilization, Jerusalem, 10 July 1990).

21. Gartner, *Jewish Immigrant in England,* 44.

22. Green, *Pletzl,* 43, 221–22.

23. Rischin, *New York's Jews,* 271; Wechsler, "Jewish Garment Trade," 57–58; Green, *Pletzl,* 45. Statistics on Jews are notoriously difficult to establish. The *Encyclopedia Judaica* cites two different figures on the same page (albeit in two different articles) concerning Jews in the East End: 125,000 at the beginning of the twentieth century; 85,000 after World War I (s.v., "London"); it estimates only 540,000 Jews on the Lower East Side of New York for 1910 (s.v., "New York City"). No figures are given for Paris.

24. By 1910 Jews had become the largest immigrant group in New York City, constituting 41 percent of all foreign born. The next largest group were Italians, representing 17.5 percent of all foreign born, followed by Germans (14 percent) and Irish (13 percent). Rischin, *New York's Jews,* 271.

25. The Industrial Removal Office was set up in the United States specifically for this purpose. See ibid., 54; Green, *Pletzl,* 56–58; Gartner, *Jewish Immigrant in England,* 148–50; and Black, *Social Politics of Anglo-Jewry,* chap. 9.

26. Zosa Szajkowski, "The European Attitude to Eastern European Jewish Immigration (1881–1893)," *Publications of the American Jewish Historical Society* 41 (1951): 127–62.

27. *Archives Israélites,* 29 November 1906.

28. See, for example, Gareth Stedman Jones, *Outcast London* (Oxford: Clarendon Press, 1971), 266; David Owen, *English Philanthropy, 1660–1960* (Cambridge, MA: Harvard University Press, 1964), chap. 8; Peter Mandler, ed., *The Uses of Charity: The Poor on Relief in the Nineteenth-Century Metropolis* (Philadelphia: University of Pennsylvania Press, 1990); Gartner, *Jewish Immigrant in England,* 49–56.

29. See, for example, ibid., 25; Wechsler, "Jewish Garment Trade," 178–79,

187–88. Seasonal unemployment in the garment trades aggravated the issue. From 1872 to 1906, 30 to 40 percent of the casual relief recipients at the Board of Guardians were garment workers. Ibid., 180, 298.

30. Nancy Green, "Transformation de l'ennemi héréditaire: le cas du Juif en tant qu'étranger chez Drumont," *Vers des sociétés pluriculturelles: études comparatives et situation en France* (Paris: ORSTOM, 1987), 143–49; see also Hyman, *From Dreyfus to Vichy;* and Michael Marrus, *The Politics of Assimilation* (Oxford: Oxford University Press, 1971).

31. For example, Rischin, *New York's Jews,* 99–103, on americanization of immigrants.

32. Cited in Wechsler, "Jewish Garment Trade," 208–9. See also Black, *Social Politics of Anglo-Jewry,* chap. 9; Gartner, *Jewish Immigrant in England,* 182. Anglicization was so effective that after World War I the Jewish community began to concern itself with judaicization. Ibid., 240; Lipman, *Social History of the Jews,* chap. 7.

33. *L'Univers Israélite,* 15 February 1907.

34. See Gainer, *Alien Invasion;* J. A. Garrard, *The English and Immigration 1880–1910* (London: Oxford University Press, 1971); Colin Holmes, *John Bull's Island: Immigration and British Society, 1871–1971* (London: Macmillan, 1988). As Roy B. Helfgott wrote, comparing Jewish immigrants to England and the United States, "legislation affected the quality as well as the quantity of the immigrants." "Trade Unionism among the Jewish Garment Workers of Britain and the United States," *Labor History* 2 (1961): 202–14.

35. Edouard Drumont, *La France juive* (Paris: Librairie Blériot, 1888), 27.

36. Annie Benveniste, *Le Bosphore à la Roquette: la communauté judéo-espagnole à Paris, 1914–1940* (Paris: L'Harmattan, 1989); Edgar Morin, *Vidal et les siens* (Paris: Seuil, 1989).

37. The massive deportations of foreign Jews in particular and the post–World War II immigration of North African Jews have, however, done more than anything else to change the internal composition of the French Jewish community.

38. Léonty Soloweitschik, *Un prolétariat méconnu* (Brussels: Henri Lamertin, 1898), 48.

39. See, for example, Anne J. Kershen, "Trade Unionism amongst the Jewish Tailoring Workers of London and Leeds, 1872–1915," in Cesarani, *Modern Anglo-Jewry,* 34–52; cf. Joseph Buckman, *Immigrants and the Class Struggle: The Jewish Immigrant in Leeds* (Manchester: Manchester University Press, 1983); and, for the earlier period, Bill Williams, *The Making of Manchester Jewry, 1740–1875* (Manchester: Manchester University Press, 1976).

40. Brettell, "Is the Ethnic Community Inevitable?" 1.

The Importance of Place: Comparative Aspects of the Ritual Murder Trial in Modern Central Europe

Hillel J. Kieval

Introduction

At the close of the last century, from 1882 to 1902, the societies of Central Europe breathed new life into a cultural artifact thought to be both dormant and unappealing to the modern temperament. Hundreds of accusations of Jewish ritual murder appeared in newspapers and other mass-market publications; the parliaments of Budapest, Berlin, and Vienna debated the topic in open session; emerging antisemitic political parties attempted to exploit this reconstructed knowledge of Jewish ritual criminality in order to counter the effects of Jewish emancipation.[1] In the course of two decades the governments of Hungary, Austria, and Germany conducted four sensational murder trials against (multiple) Jewish defendants in which a motive of ritual enactment or religious compulsion was a central feature of the prosecution's case.

It is possible, of course, that what appears to be a new cultural phenomenon is in reality simply the by-product of a popular press that had not been in place before this time. Mass-market newspapers, in other words, were slow in taking notice of something that had been around for quite a while. The problem with this argument is that the distribution of reported cases was not constant over time. In fact, mass-market newspapers had appeared in Germany and the Hapsburg monarchy already in the 1860s, following the liberalization of press and censorship laws, yet interest in Jewish "ritual criminality" was hardly visible before the 1880s. More remarkable is the degree to which the topic of ritual murder saturated popular culture in Central Europe in the following decade. And the fact that magistrates and prosecutors in Germany and Austria-Hungary broke with nearly three centuries of legal and political precedent by reintroducing the charge of Jewish ritual murder to the criminal and legal proceedings of the state is of particular interest. Studying the modern ritual murder trial in Europe also provides an excellent opportunity to consider the role of competing systems of knowledge and power in the elaboration of social conflict. While the trials and the debates that swirled around them seem to argue for the convergence of myth, irrationality, traditional wisdom, and rational discourse in the production of social knowledge, they offer at the same time a rare perspective on social relations between Jews and Gentiles in the decades following political emancipation. Such confrontations appear to have impinged unexpectedly upon the political and cultural landscape, disrupting the equilibrium of Jewish social and communal life, revealing a significant domain of cultural misunderstanding and suspicion, and calling into question the liberal assumptions on which Jewish emancipation rested.

The trials in question took place in Tiszaeszlár, Hungary (1882–83); Xanten, in the Prussian Rhineland (1891–92); Polná, Bohemia (1899–1900); and Konitz, West Prussia (after 1918, Poland) (1900–1901); they were sandwiched between two other trials originating in the Russian Empire: Kutaisi (1878–79) and Kiev (1911–13), the famous Beilis affair.[2] Because the modern ritual murder accusation involved the virtually simultaneous occurrence of a peculiar phenomenon in different political and geographic settings, any explanation of it must necessarily be comparative. What did the settings have in common? What political, economic, or social factors predominated in each case? Are we dealing with similar or dissimilar Jewish communities, similar or dissimilar patterns of Jewish-Gentile interaction? In this essay I wish specifically to address the role that place, or locality, assumed in these affairs. Of what importance were local culture and geography, the intrinsic patterns of social relations versus extrinsic forces and factors? Finally, were bad relations between the two groups at the local level a prerequisite to a serious allegation of Jewish ritual murder or to a trial?

Toward a Cultural Geography of Place

A cultural geography of place is interested in specificity: the physical landscape of a village or a town, local patterns of economic exchange, the distribution of power, the creation of knowledge. There is tension in such an enterprise between the drive to compare—and hence to emphasize pattern—and the appreciation of uniqueness. A geography of place seeks to uncover the texture of local experience. It wishes to capture the perspectives of local actors and often relies on impressionistic surveys and personal accounts of varying provenance and points of view. The hope is that eventually both detail and overall shape come into focus, but there is no escaping the fact that the original impulse comes from a desire to celebrate the particular over the universal.

At the level of direct experience accusations of ritual murder emerge from social interactions and the ensuing moral constructions that imbue events with meaning. They are the products of face-to-face encounters, which are scripted in part by cognitive expectations and which add in their wake to the local complex of social knowledge. Ritual murder accusations, in other words, are born of, and nurtured by, community. It makes sense, from this perspective, to look closely at the villages and small market towns of the Central European countryside to uncover the dynamics of this process. These tended to be tranquil places whose traditional economic and social structures stood at some remove from the wide-ranging transformations associated with the industrial age. Tiszaeszlár, our first example, is also the only true village among them. Nestled in the northeastern stretch of Hungary's Great Plain—in what was then Szabolcs county in East-Central Hungary—on the left bank of the Tisza River, Tiszaeszlár stands between two large towns: to the south the city of Debrecen, to the east—before 1918—Szatmár (Satu Mare in Romanian).[3]

Nationalist historiography in many countries claims to have discovered in the village the cradle of national values, and no less a figure than the British historian C. A. Macartney, observing Hungary in the 1930s, described the villages of the Hungarian Plain as incorporating "the social and economic ideals of the true Magyar." His portrait stresses the tranquillity and banality of the Hungarian village as well as the regularity of its physical features:

The village itself is a regular pattern of very wide streets, most of them unpaved, the basking-place of pigs and poultry and geese, geese, endless geese; and bounding the street, rows of little whitewashed, one-storied houses, each with its narrow end turned to the street, while between its verandahed face and its neighbor's back, is a sandy courtyard, a well, a few sunflowers. Behind, opening straight onto the fields, are byres, barn, and stable. It is a community which reeks of the soil. Every man in it, from the local magnate downward, lives by, on, and from the soil. The fields stretch up to the very doors, and the fruits of them are scattered in the courtyards. The few craftsmen, who advertise their skill by a painted sign of smock, boot, or scythe, the cobbler, smith, and tailor, are themselves most often peasants who ply their trade in their spare hours.[4]

For subsequent ritual murder accusations small to mid-sized market towns served as the setting. The actual criminal investigation and subsequent trial of the Tiszaeszlár case occurred in such a town as well—Nyíregyháza, the district capital. Market towns, according to Macartney, differed from villages only in degree:

The business of local administration may be imposing enough to require a town hall and a police barracks; there are branches of the local banks, a resident doctor, dentist, and vet. There are many inns to quench the thirst of the market-day crowd, and above all, the market itself—a great dusty space, empty and desolate save at due season, when it fills to overflowing with a vociferous multitude of men and beasts.[5]

Even the largest of these towns, he argues, remained essentially "glorified villages." A high proportion of their inhabitants down to the 1930s were still landowners; many were peasants who went out by day into the fields; others were owners of country estates on which they spent much of their time.

Xanten, located on the Lower Rhine plain in the Rhineland province of Prussia (Rheinprovinz), seems appropriately to fit this characterization of town as oversized village. Once a Roman river crossing located on the main road that ran from Cologne to Cleves and Nijmegen, Xanten lost much of its economic importance with the subsequent shifting of the course of the river.[6] In 1910 its population stood at just under 4,300; Düsseldorf, in contrast, the seat of the main administrative subdivision (*Regierungsbezirk*) to which Xanten belonged, had almost 360,000 inhabitants; Cologne, the capital of the neighboring *Regierungsbezirk,* had a population of 600,000.[7]

The Lower Rhineland consists largely of isolated farmsteads and towns whose political status dates back to the thirteenth century. Forty years ago a geographer commented that the only flourishing towns in the region were those that enjoyed both rail transport and direct contact with the Rhine. Xanten was not one of these. With no industry of its own and no direct link to the river's traffic, it remained a local market center and appeared to preserve much of its historic character.[8] Paul Nathan, a Berlin journalist sent to cover the Xanten trial, said as much when he drew a picture of the town that contrasted starkly with his own (and his readers') urban milieu. Xanten hovered before him in the distance, in a kind of suspended animation, a combination of bucolic serenity and Catholic severity:

> Xanten—it lies so beautiful. Lost in greenery, the small, neat houses surround the mighty cathedral, the gothic St. Victor's Church, a towering presence, one of the most serious and memorable medieval constructions on the Lower Rhine. As one stands on the gently rising Fürstenberg and looks over the landscape at the clusters of green trees, the small patches of forest, the farms and villages, the gentle hills and the wide, flat plains, through which the Rhine flows wide and steel gray; and as one's eye is drawn again and again to the powerful mass of the cathedral, it seems as though the ruling power of the Middle Ages stands there as a bodily presence.[9]

Polná, the site of the Hilsner case, offers a variation on the theme of the small town left behind by industrialization. Situated along what was once an important road to Hungary, Polná rests in the Bohemian-Moravian highlands (Ceskomoravská vysocina), an extensive, wooded plateau that straddles the border between Bohemia and Moravia. Two larger, neighboring towns—Jihlava (Iglau) and Havlickuv Brod (Deutschbrod)—achieved fame as centers of silver mining beginning in the thirteenth century. Polná itself was, in the words of a recent historical guide, a "typical feudal town," owned by a succession of noble families from the thirteenth to the nineteenth century. The late-sixteenth and early-seventeenth century owners, the Zejdlic of Senfeld family, were Protestants who lent their support to the unsuccessful revolt of the Czech estates of 1618–20. In 1623 the bishop of Olomouc, Frantisek (Franz) of Dietrichstejn, acquired the feudal rights to the town from Emperor Ferdinand II for 150,000 zlaty. The Dietrichstejn family ruled Polná (from a distance) until 1848 and maintained large tracts of land there until 1922.[10]

Though technically part of Bohemia, Polná lies to the east of the closest large town in the region, Jihlava (Iglau), which belongs to Moravia. This geographic curiosity suggests a remoteness from Prague, the cultural and political center of Czech life. In 1871, when the first rail lines were opened connecting Prague, Jihlava, and Znojmo, they bypassed Polná altogether, coursing five kilometers from the outskirts of the town, as if to underline its geographic isolation.[11] In 1890 one could find a five-grade lower school (*obecní skola*) for boys and one for girls; a three-grade *mest'anská skola* (*Bürgerschule*) for each of the two sexes, geared toward trade and commerce; and a two-grade Jewish school. Polná's population at the time stood at 9,102, of whom 8,801 were Catholic, 247 Jewish, 44 Protestant, and 10 "other." The village of Malá Veznice, which featured prominently in the events of 1899 to 1900, lay to the northwest of the town. Its forty homes housed a population of 218, who were served by a one-grade school.[12]

Konitz (Chojnice), which is to be found in the former German province of West Prussia, is the largest of the towns that produced ritual murder trials around 1900. Before 1772 the territory of West Prussia, then known as "Royal Prussia," was administered by the Polish Crown. Following the first Polish partition it was attached to the Kingdom of Prussia, and both "Royal Prussia" and its neighbor to the east, the province of "Prussia," were renamed. From the 1820s to 1878 East and West Prussia were combined administratively; from 1878 to the end of World War I they were again organized as separate entities, with Danzig (Gdansk) serving as the West Prussian capital and Königsberg (Kaliningrad) as that of East Prussia. Since 1918 Konitz/Chojnice has been part of Poland.[13]

West Prussia understandably possessed a mixed German and Slavic population. In 1858 69.1 percent of its inhabitants were counted (by language) as Germans, 30.9 percent as Slavs. By 1910 the number of Germans had declined somewhat to about 65 percent (about 1,100,000 individuals). Of the 35 percent who claimed Slavic ethnicity 475,000 indicated Polish as their mother tongue and 107,000 Kashubian. About 22,000 people were listed as bilingual.[14] The town of Konitz itself was somewhat larger than Polná and more than twice the size of Xanten: 10,656 people in 1895, of whom 480 (4.5 percent) were Jews; 12,185 in 1910, of whom only 256 (2.1 percent) were Jews.[15]

The Dimensions of Time and Historical Change

The descriptions of Macartney and Nathan notwithstanding, the towns and villages of Central Europe hardly were frozen in time. Their populations may not have grown appreciably, their economies may indeed have declined since the onset of industrialization, but they were all deeply marked by the historical transformations of the eighteenth and nineteenth centuries. They were themselves artifacts of modern history. In the Hungarian countryside traditional patterns of social life began to give way in the 1860s in the face of impressive growth in the agricultural sector of the economy, an expansion that both preceded and accompanied the political gains of the 1867 Compromise (*Ausgleich*). In fact, important transformations in politics and the economy dated to the Revolution of 1848 and continued throughout the period of neo-absolutism. These included the emancipation of the peasants and the cancellation of feudal services and dues; the removal of the landowner's patrimonial rights and police powers; the introduction of the Austrian criminal code and legal procedures; improvements in schooling; reform of the tax system; the removal of internal tariffs; and uniform regulation of banking and commerce.[16]

With the establishment of the Dual Monarchy in 1867 new industrial firms, in the words of one historian, "sprang up like mushrooms after a spring rain."[17] Again, it was the agricultural sector (mainly grain production) that led the expansion and encouraged intensive, foreign capital investment. In 1867–68 alone 170 new industrial corporations and 552 credit institutions were established, and twenty-five hundred miles of new rail lines were built. With increased market-oriented management in agriculture thousands of new acres of land were devoted to grain production. For several decades industrial growth complemented developments in agriculture: the milling of flour soon emerged as Hungary's leading large-scale industry. The number of steam-driven mills grew from 146 in 1863 to 1,843 in 1895; in the 1860s Hungary exported as much flour as all other European states combined.[18]

Hungary's economy before World War I also showed signs of structural weakness and vulnerability. The stock market crash of 1873 resulted in a severe curtailment of foreign investment, and a prolonged decline in world grain prices in the 1870s and 1880s induced the government to abandon its previous free-market, laissez-faire policies in favor of increased protectionism.[19] Moreover, while the magnate families appeared to thrive in the transition to commercial agriculture, many members of the gentry found it necessary to sell their ancestral holdings. Sons of the lesser nobility, discouraged for cultural and psychological reasons from commercial pursuits, increasingly sought employment in urban professions and the civil service. Thus, the economy and the bureaucracy, though formally bifurcated, were mutually dependent. Andrew Janos has described Hungary's liberal elite as "a political class living off public revenue." It relied on a constantly expanding bureaucracy for its livelihood and so did all it could to encourage economic growth and development. National consolidation, in turn, depended on the state's ability to recruit non-Magyar economic elites and encourage their linguistic and cultural assimilation.[20]

In the German Rhineland the dukedoms and bishoprics that had made up the region before 1800 were consolidated under Prussian rule in the aftermath of the Revolutionary and Napoleonic wars (and after a period of annexation to France). After 1871 the Rhineland became the site of a prolonged political struggle, the *Kulturkampf,* that pitted imperial centralism and national liberal ideology against regionalism, Catholic culture, and minority rights. By the end of the decade Bismarck had forged a long-term alliance with heavy industrialists and large East Elbian landowners, and German Catholics ceased to be identified as enemies of the state; this ignominious role now passed to the Social Democrats and, increasingly, to liberalism itself.

In the intervening years, however, the *Kulturkampf* had engendered a strong, antiliberal ideology among Catholic intellectuals and church leaders in western and southern Germany. The German state was viewed as a creation of the National Liberal Party, a reflection of the three-pronged influence of liberalism, capitalism, and "Jewish" culture. Liberalism had led to unbridled material interest and the corruption of the social fabric, it was believed. It had produced demands for the separation of church and state and for the reduced influence of the church generally in society. In the opinion of Barbara Suchy the *Kulturkampf* itself came to be seen as the cultural counterpart to "Jewish" capitalism. "Its single goal was to set aside Christian spirit and ecclesiastical authority, the only obstacle[s] to Jewish power."[21]

Suchy's work on anti-Jewish attitudes and policies in the Rhineland inevitably attributes much of the hostility toward Jews to the power and influence of the Catholic Church. Historically, Catholic culture had implanted in the popular imagination lasting images of Jewish deicide, host desecration, and the spreading of plague—as well as ritual murder.[22] And it was from Münster, in neighboring Westphalia, that the theology professor August Rohling issued his notorious publication, *Der Talmudjude,* in 1871, a libelous work claiming to discover in the Talmud the prescriptive basis for a wide variety of Jewish criminal behavior. Rohling's book enjoyed much popularity: it went through six editions by 1878 and was frequently reissued thereafter. In Westphalia alone thirty-eight thousand copies of the book were distributed free of charge by the Bonifacius association.[23]

According to British and German newspapers, which reported on the

Xanten trial in 1892, children in Catholic schools in Germany were taught about Jewish ritual murders as historical fact.[24] The chief culprits in this educational exercise appear to have been children's readers dealing with the lives of the saints. One example, *Katholischer Kindergarten oder Legende für Kinder,* compiled by Franz Hattler, a Jesuit, was published under the patronage of local ecclesiastical authorities in Freiburg. Among the many saints whose lives it chronicled were three boys who, purportedly, had been murdered by Jews: Werner of Wesel (1287), Andreas of Rinn (1462), and Simon of Trent (1475). Since each of these children had been memorialized (and, eventually, sanctified) by the church as martyrs of Christianity, the Jesuit narrator, in transmitting to schoolchildren the lives of the saints as exempla of holiness, repeated the supposed circumstances of their deaths. No recounting of their lives and deaths could call into question the facticity of the ritual murder charge without, at the same time, raising doubt about the basis for their respective sainthoods. Perhaps Hattler had this in mind when he introduced the story of Simon of Trent with the observation that "reliable evidence shows that Jews are in the habit of stealing, buying and murdering Christian children."[25]

In the eastern parts of the Prussian state, where West Prussia—despite its name—is located, the *Kulturkampf* incorporated elements of national as well as religious struggle. Bismarck found that he could quash Polish nationalist activities by applying the legal and political provisions of the *Kulturkampf* against Polish culture in Prussia. Thus, the educational reform of 1871 reduced the influence of Polish Catholic clergy in the schools. By order of the Prussian Oberpräsident in 1873 German was declared the sole language of instruction in all schools except for classes in religion and choir at the lower levels. In 1876 German was made the sole commercial language (*Geschäftssprache*) for government officials; the following year all legal proceedings had to be held in German only.[26] In the 1880s anti-Polish activity moved in the direction of large-scale land purchases by and for Germans and the establishment of credit and employment associations. The Law for the Promotion of German Colonization in Posen and West Prussia was passed in 1886; its provisions allowed for one hundred million marks to be set aside by the Prussian Landtag to assist in the settlement of German peasants and workers.[27] The psychological tone of the anti-Polish campaign may have been more real than the outcome, however. Most land purchases in West Prussia, it turns out, came at the expense of other Germans. The Poles, moreover, met the challenge of Prussian "colonization" programs by setting up a rival network of banks and credit associations and instituting an economic boycott against German merchants.

In both Konitz and Tiszaeszlár the Christian population included Protestants as well as Catholics; hence, one must be cautious when assessing the role of religious institutions in general—and the Catholic Church in particular—in the turn-of-the-century trials. And, whereas Prussia's anti-Polish policies clearly form a backdrop to the history of West Prussia under the Second German Empire, it is not clear to me that the Polish-German conflict strongly influenced the Konitz affair. The Jews of the town identified politically and linguistically with Germany; the murder victim in the case was a German gymnasium student; and the role of Polish Catholics in the accusation and trial appears to have been minimal. Ethnic conflict and repression were certainly present in the Kingdom of Hungary after 1867. But Szabolcs county was not ethnically mixed, and, although the Jews of the high Tisza region tended to be Orthodox in practice, they were also largely Magyar speakers.[28]

Only in Polná do the twin themes of Catholicism and national conflict come together in a significant way. That is to say, since the Counter Reformation Bohemia and Moravia were overwhelmingly Catholic, and from the mid-nineteenth century Jews tended to be regarded as persistent carriers of German language and culture and defenders of Austrian centralism.[29] On a superficial level religious difference could be equated in Czech national consciousness with ethnic treason, as the "otherness" of the Jews apparently coincided with the power and ubiquity of the Germans. Thus, we read in Bretislav Reyrich's local history of Polná that the town's Jewish population colluded with district officials (i.e., representatives of the government in Vienna) in 1874 to convert what had been a privately supported "German-Jewish" school into a *public* German elementary school: "At the time of Czech political expansion, this school stood as a symbol of civic discord in Polná for a quarter of a century. Because of declining numbers of Jewish children, Czech children were also accepted there, and thus the school was given the name 'surplus storage' [*prebejvárna*]." In his printed guide to the town Reyrich noted with some bitterness that this two-grade German-Jewish school had been better endowed in the 1870s than both of the five-grade Czech schools.[30]

Religion could never be an unambiguous gauge of national affiliation, however. To begin with, Catholicism itself was deeply implicated in the German power structure in Bohemia-Moravia, since the seventeenth-century Counter Reformation had taken place in concert with an anti-Czech campaign that resulted in the forced exile or execution of scores of noble families. In many respects to be Catholic was to be loyal to the Hapsburg conception of Austria. And this implication was not lost on at least one important faction of Czech nationalist intellectuals—among whom stood Tomás Masaryk—who preferred to equate Czech culture with the Protestant Reformation (remembering that it had been the Protestant Czech estates that rose in revolt in 1618–20) or with the pre-Reformation Hussite movement.[31]

Moreover, the linguistic and national loyalties of Bohemian Jews could not be so easily predicted. The countrywide system of German-Jewish elementary schools, which derived from the educational reforms of Joseph II in the 1780s, had to a large extent been imposed on the local Jewish communities. In subsequent decades Jews used these schools to their advantage in the drive for economic and social advancement and political enfranchisement. From them they entered the classical gymnasia and universities or moved into the economic mainstream. The Jewish graduates more than accomplished the goal of the project's originators, that is, that they become fluent in the high culture of the Hapsburg state: they virtually became emblems of the imperial state and its "universal" language.[32]

But the ethnic loyalties of Bohemian Jewry did not remain fixed, nor were they ever free of ambiguity. This is a point on which Czech and German antagonists at the turn of the century often erred. Small-town and village Jews went through the same demographic and cultural transformations that produced middle-class Czech nationalism in general; they were neither immune to historical processes nor blind to the benefits that could accrue to Czech speakers who enjoyed a modicum of cultural and political autonomy. Jews who grew up in provincial cities and towns in the 1860s, 1870s, and 1880s entered Czech gymnasia in increasing numbers and thereby spent their formative years in what might be called the incubator of modern Czech politics. As more and more Jews abandoned the countryside for the cities, especially Prague, fewer and fewer Jewish children remained to fill the German-Jewish schools. This demographic imperative, combined with growing political pressure from the Czech national movement, resulted in the gradual elimination of this type of school between 1885 and 1900. Bohemian Jews, moreover, were rarely monolingual. Though they may have sent their children to German schools and found German avenues of mobility to be the most rewarding, they frequently came from Czech-speaking environments themselves, spoke Czech in the workplace and the market, and interacted constantly with Czech speakers.[33]

Jews could, and did, change declarations of national affiliation depending on political conditions or other circumstances. The census of 1900, for example, recorded what appeared to be a startling "change of heart" for Bohemian Jews. Over 54 percent of both Bohemian Jewry in general and Prague Jewry specifically declared their "language of daily use" (the only indicator of ethnic affiliation recognized by the Austrian census) to be Czech. Only ten years earlier about two-thirds of Bohemian Jewry—and three-fourths of the Jews of Prague—had indicated German as their language of choice. Were Jews employing simple political expediency? Perhaps. But the more compelling argument, it seems to me, is that the Austrian census did not (or would not) ask the questions that would more accurately capture their sense of ethnic belonging. The census consciously omitted the categories "ethnic group" and "nationality," opting instead for the more obtuse rubric "everyday language." Nor were Austrians given the opportunity to distinguish between political loyalty—citizenship—and ethnic loyalty.[34] And "everyday language," for a bilingual (if not multilingual) minority group that was often buffeted by political pressures from different directions, was not a good indicator of much of anything. Yet it is worth noting that the Jewish community of Polná had broken with the general pattern of linguistic declaration earlier than most of Bohemian Jewry. Already in the census of 1890 198 (approximately 59 percent) of the Jewish respondents declared themselves to be Czech; 140 (41 percent) indicated German as their primary tongue.[35]

Jewish-Gentile Relations

It goes without saying that the ritual murder accusations of the late nineteenth century and the ensuing investigations, trials, public debate, and riots revealed tensions and strains in the relationship between Jews and non-Jewish Europeans. Accusations of ritual murder, however, tended to be widely, if not uniformly, distributed across Central Europe, while only a handful of trials actually took place. Does this pattern mean that relations between Jews and Gentiles were uniformly in crisis or differentially bad? Were bad relations between the two groups at the local level a prerequisite to a formal investigation and trial?

Although there is no simple way to correlate the occurrence of a ritual murder trial in a given town or village to patterns of Jewish-Gentile interaction, one thing does seem certain: it is not necessary to have hostile interethnic relations to produce an accusation of ritual murder. Hungary, of all the territories of East Central Europe in the 1860s, 1870s, and 1880s, was quite possibly the least conducive to serious anti-Jewish agitation. The economic and political foundations of the state, as well as the reigning political culture of the Magyar gentry, encouraged rapid Jewish accultura- tion and social and economic integration while restraining expressions of hostility toward Jews. William McCagg wrote in this regard of a "collabo- ration" between Hungary's "Jewish capitalists" and the "nobiliary old regime."[36] Andrew Janos locates the defining features of the economic and political order in post-1867 Hungary in what he calls the "ethnic division of labor," in which the Magyar gentry dominated the bureaucracy, parlia- ment, and the judiciary and Jews monopolized the liberal professions and fed the capitalist economy.[37] The most likely sources of anti-Jewish feeling, according to C. A. Macartney, were to be found in the Catholic Church, among the lesser gentry—who began to see some of their lands "pass into Jewish hands"—and in the towns. Magnates may have looked upon the Jews "with that benevolent and contemptuous patronage which was the traditional relationship between the two classes."[38] On the whole, however, Jews and Magyars in Hungary had established a firm political and eco- nomic relationship that offered both security and opportunity for Jews. The general position of Jews in Hungarian society compared favorably with that of any other European country before 1914.

In Tiszaeszlár itself relations between Jews and non-Jews typically have been characterized as "friendly" and "intimate," even if defense attorney Károlyi Eötvös took pains in his memoirs to add that Christians tended to look down upon the Jews with "a certain old-fashioned, accustomed sense of superiority."[39] The picture offered by Paul Nathan, who completed a book-length study on Tiszaeszlár in 1892 (the same year that he was sent to cover the trial in Xanten), is more nuanced but basically positive. Rela- tions between the two groups appear to have been cordial and cooperative on an everyday level, as would befit life in a village. Tiszaeszlár had no Jew- ish quarter or ghetto. Jews lived side by side with their Gentile neighbors, and social contacts seem to have been marked by familiarity, even affec- tion, as well as by jealousy, resentments, and petty conflicts.[40]

The nobleman Géza Onody, part of whose hereditary estate lay in the vicinity of Tiszaeszlár, articulated the anti-Jewish perspective on intereth-
nic relations. In a polemical tract published in 1883 he described Tiszaes- zlár as "a small, modest village . . . with 1,200 to 1,400 inhabitants, among whom are 200 Jews, who with indefatigable diligence and tireless persever- ance work toward the exploitation and both the material and moral ruin of

the Christian citizenry."[41] To achieve the desired rhetorical effect of depicting "Christian" civilization as a vulnerable island besieged by swarming masses, Onody both underestimated the dimensions of the village and exaggerated the size of the Jewish population. Andrew Handler has placed the population of Tiszaeszlár at 2,700, including approximately 25 Jewish families. If one accepts 6 as a reasonable multiplier, the total number of Jews in Tiszaeszlár would have been approximately 150, or 5.5 percent of the general population.[42]

Among the extraordinary characteristics of Hungarian Jewry in the nineteenth century were its exponential growth and its immigrant origins. In 1785 the number of Jews stood at approximately 75,000—less than 1 percent of the general population—most of whom had migrated to Hungary from Bohemia and Moravia. The size of the Jewish community grew by 70 percent over the next twenty years (128,000 in 1805) as the result of large-scale immigration from Galicia, made possible by the attachment of Galicia to the Austrian crown in 1772, followed by the Josephinian toleration edicts of 1781 and 1789.[43] The Jewish population continued to climb steeply through the rest of the century thanks to the combined effects of immigration and a high rate of natural increase. By 1850 there were 369,000 Jews in Hungary (2.8 percent of the population); 932,000 Jews (4.5 percent) resided there in 1910. Thus, at the start of the twentieth century nearly 10 percent of the world Jewish population lived in the Kingdom of Hungary.[44]

Onody's polemic exploited the Galician origins of a large part of Hungarian Jewry to create an image of a fundamentally alien and uncivilized population:

They are the same bigotted fanatics today as [they were] when they migrated in droves to Hungary from the mass warehouse of European Jewry, Galicia. Inspired by the pernicious teachings of talmudic ethics, they are rigidly separated by dress, mores, life principles, and racial characteristics from the other elements of society—as are their coreligionists and the members of their race on the other side of the Carpathians, the Polish Hasidim.[45]

In a similar vein he described the neighboring town of Tisalök as "a nest of bigotted, Jewish fanaticism and a genuine Little Jerusalem, where the Christian population is—in the fullest meaning of the word—threatened in its existence."[46] As a political figure and writer, Onody was to play a major part in creating the vocabulary and iconography of the modern ritual murder accusation, but his voice was not representative of Hungarian opinion at large. His own "fanaticism" made him an oddity; his politics operated at a level that was far removed from the everyday life of the village. For, if there was a Mrs. Soos in Tiszaeszlár, who challenged the wife of Joszef Scharf (one of the defendants), saying, "Why do you need a goose anymore? The Jews will be driven out without them; I, too, will drive them out with a stick," there was also a Mrs. Batori, the Christian neighbor of the Scharfs, who on the day of the arrests brought lunch to their little son, Móric, and cared for him as a mother.[47]

The record of Jewish-Gentile interaction in Xanten during the nineteenth century is also shrouded in ambiguity, but here the theme of anti-Jewish behavior seems to be more continuous. Xanten had been the site of a massacre during the First Crusade (1096), in which some sixty Jews were either killed or committed suicide. As recently as 1834, anti-Jewish riots broke out in various places in the Lower Rhine, apparently in response to the murder of a boy, Peter Wilhelm Hoenen. Local suspicion for the crime rested on the Jews, despite the fact that the investigating magistrate held such views to be groundless. He opposed any discussion of Jewish ritual murder as "a barbarous superstition of centuries long past," but this did not prevent the widespread looting and destruction of Jewish homes and properties. The Prussian government eventually ordered security forces to go into the area to restore order, though not before the riots had spread throughout the countryside and even to Düsseldorf. In Xanten a crowd of about two hundred wound through the town throwing stones, shouting the anti-Jewish cry "Hep-Hep" and singing "disreputable" and "threatening" songs. The local police intervened without success, forcing the army and the Royal Hussars to be called in from Koblenz.[48]

It is doubtful that a single riot from the 1830s—much less an episode from the First Crusade—determined interethnic relations in the town at the close of the nineteenth century. On the eve of Xanten's ritual murder trial its Jewish community consisted of some eighty-five people, about 2 percent of the population at large, and there is little to indicate that life in the town was anything but peaceful and friendly.[49] Nor did the townspeople appear to harbor any grievances against the accused in the case, Adolph Buschhof: witnesses for the prosecution, as well as for the defense, testified to Buschhof's upstanding character.[50] When the Xanten population rioted against Jews and their property in the immediate aftermath of his arrest, the mayor, the district magistrate, and the provincial governor all came down hard against the rioters, threatening swift punishment. But surely, and almost inevitably, the riots had come, suggesting that popular violence had an important cultural component as a learned, historical response.[51]

The record of Jewish-Gentile relations in the Prussian "East" included its share of intolerance and persecution as well. The Teutonic Knights, who had colonized the lands of East and West Prussia, forbade Jewish settlement in their territories. During the centuries of Polish rule in Royal Prussia the size of the Jewish population was kept low through formal restrictions on their residence.[52] The Jews of nearby Poznan found themselves to be the target of a "host desecration" charge in 1399, whose implications reverberated down to the eighteenth century. In 1724 a resolution of sorts was reached when the Jewish community agreed to make annual payments to a local convent in atonement for the supposed crime. Jesuit seminarians launched sporadic riots against Poznan Jews in the late sixteenth and seventeenth centuries. One rampage, in 1687, lasted for three days, at the end of which the beleaguered Jews were rescued by forces of the local nobility.[53] Finally, the town magistrates staged a ritual murder trial against the Jews from 1736 to 1740, during which a number of Jews died under torture. The case was eventually dismissed by the royal court after much money had been spent and a number of Polish noblemen had come forward to affirm the innocence of the Jewish defendants.[54]

There are few explicit testimonies to the quality of Jewish-Gentile contact in West Prussia in general, or Konitz in particular, in the nineteenth century. The Jewish community of Konitz grew from 44 persons in 1816 to 425 in 1867 through a combination of internal migration from the West Prussian countryside and immigration from Russian Poland. The high point—563 individuals, or 5.6 percent of the town's population—was reached in 1885. Thereafter, following the pattern for West Prussia as a whole, the Jewish population declined as Jews migrated to other parts of the empire, especially to the industrializing cities. In 1895, 480 Jews lived in Konitz (4.5 percent of the general population), but by 1910 only 256 remained (2.1 percent).[55] A writer from the Viennese newspaper *Die Welt* claimed in 1900 that the Jews in Konitz had failed to reap any social benefits from emancipation, that they were effectively excluded from non-Jewish associational life and forced to create bourgeois institutions of their own that "shadowed" those of non-Jewish society.[56] This observation may be valid, but one should also keep in mind that local Jews did achieve a significant degree of cultural integration, entering the ranks of secondary and higher education in large numbers. Already by the 1850s Jews made up 6.4 percent of the student population at the Catholic Gymnasium.[57] Still, riots did break out in Konitz and in other towns in West Prussia in the spring and summer of 1900, as they had less than a decade earlier in the Rhineland, suggesting once again that, whatever the day-to-day relations, they were sufficiently tenuous so as to fail to contain popular passions that existed beneath the surface.

In Polná the ability of the Jewish community to enjoy relative stability and security depended on a combination of factors: the noble origins of the town, the impact of Catholic symbol and ritual on popular emotions, economic development, and the political tensions associated with the nationality struggle in the Czech lands. Polná's status as a noble town insulated the Jewish population from the burgher-instigated expulsions that had taken place in the so-called royal cities of Bohemia and Moravia in the fifteenth and sixteenth centuries. Jews who lived on noble domains could also often evade the effects of Counter Reformation imperial legislation, which sought to impose strict limits on Jewish family size, residence, and mobility.[58] Jews could and did seek guarantees of protection from powerful noble families in return for economic services and the payment of fees and taxes. It was under such circumstances in 1682 that Count Dietrichstejn laid the foundations for the growth of the modern Jewish community of Polná, when he set aside sixteen buildings behind the town's Upper Gate for permanent Jewish settlement.[59] Dietrichstejn's action had come about at the request of Polná's existing Jewish community, whose medieval settlement had been at the foot of the town's Calvary Hill. The hilltop, on which now rests the eighteenth-century Church of St. Barbara, had been the destination point of the annual Easter procession that commemorated Jesus' crucifixion. The pageant typically ended with the hanging of an effigy of Judas.[60] It is not clear to what extent, if any, the Jews sought new living conditions in order to remove themselves from proximity to this annual—and potentially dangerous—degradation. But the fact that they succeeded in finding both new quarters and long-term security through the agency of the Dietrichstejns points to a convergence of those political, economic, and religious factors that helped to shape local Jewish destiny.

Fifty-two Jewish families lived in Polná in 1724; by 1830 the number had grown to 128—or almost 770 individuals—despite the fact that so-called family laws, which since the 1720s had placed an absolute ceiling on the number of Jewish families allowed to reside in Bohemia and Moravia, had, in theory, rendered such growth impossible.[61] The revolutionary upheavals of 1848 spelled the end of noble influence in the town, the removal of some of the restrictions that had been placed on Jewish social and economic life, and the beginning of a political process that would lead eventually to full emancipation in 1867. It appears that the local Jewish population threw its lot in with the revolutionary movement of 1848 as evidenced by the fact that Jews formed their own company within the Polná National Guard.[62] Over the last three decades of the nineteenth century Jews from Polná did what most of their coreligionists in the Bohemian and Moravian countryside were doing: they left, leaving behind their village and small-town origins for the likes of Prague, Vienna, Brno, and New York. By 1890, as I have mentioned, the Jewish population stood at 247 (2.7 percent of the general population). Polná's last rabbi left the town in 1920; by 1930 only 51 Jews remained.[63]

Prosecutions in Polná

Both the Kutná Hora regional court (Krajsky soud Kutná Hora) and the Prague criminal court (Zemsky soud trestní—Praha) heard numerous cases in the 1880s and 1890s that involved anti-Jewish agitation of various types. The prosecutions dealt with libel, defamation of religion, disturbances of the peace, and "incitement" (*popuzování*) against a religious community—all punishable under Austrian law. Some of the charges were directed at newspaper editors who violated government censorship regulations; most related in some way to the broader political discourse of Czech-German national struggle. As a whole, these cases yield valuable information concerning the texture of daily life at the local level and offer a rare glimpse into the complex, highly symbolic world of Jewish-Gentile interaction.[64]

Two prosecutions in particular warrant special attention. They involve humorous, if somewhat bizarre, expressions of interpersonal antagonisms, point to the boundaries of "acceptable" defamation in Hapsburg political culture, and highlight the available institutional avenues of redress. The first concerns an indictment brought by State Prosecutor Schneider-Svoboda on 30 October 1892 against a thirty-two-year-old resident of Polná, the horse butcher Jan Chalupa.[65] Chalupa was accused of attacking religion (*rusení nábozenství*) by publicly ridiculing a recognized faith—namely, Judaism—repeatedly over a period of time between 1891 and 1892. On one level this was a totally mundane case, one of countless examples of the Hapsburg state's monitoring of—and intrusion in—the daily lives of its citizens, part and parcel of what Marc Raeff has called "the well-ordered police state."[66] It serves as a reminder, nevertheless, that Hapsburg officials regularly, if inconsistently, prosecuted individuals and institutions for making inflammatory statements about Jews and Judaism, inciting to violence, or, simply, publicly ridiculing the Jewish religion.

The prosecution of Jan Chalupa is also intriguing both for the details that it offers about daily life and the intricate social context of Jewish-Gentile interaction that it uncovers. The main witness against the accused, interestingly, was not himself a Jew but a Catholic named Josef Skála, who had been employed for the past six years by the Polná synagogue while, at the same time, serving as sexton (*kostelník*) of the Catholic Church. Skála testified that for nearly two years, whenever Chalupa came across him on the street, he would taunt Skála verbally, saying such things as: "What's that Jewish calf doing? What is he fed with? Is he given hay, dried grass and water?" Afterward Chalupa would admonish Skála, saying that he should not feed the calf grass, that it would burst. Yet at the same time he would call upon Skála to "go feed the calf," that the Jews would then make what he referred to as "*machalabeis.*"[67]

Although the precise words varied from incident to incident, this apparently formed the gist of Chalupa's frequent taunting of the unfortunate Skála. And, important for the prosecution's case, the teasing always occurred in public. Chalupa's bantering was as unrelenting as it was incomprehensible, and he, at least, considered it to be highly amusing. As for the church sexton, who doubled as a synagogue employee (his precise job is not given), he judged Chalupa's words to be slanderous. Though Skála himself did not issue a formal complaint, he spoke about the incidents to one Hermann Aufrecht (presumably Jewish), who in turn brought the matter to the attention of the court.

Aufrecht gave investigators his own account of the exchanges as told to him by Skála: "Skála, go fetch some hay and go to the Jewish synagogue; go feed the calf there, and the Jews will make '*machalabeis*' over it"; or, alternatively, "Bring straw and water; who will feed the Jewish calf, your wife or you?" After conferring with other members of the Jewish community, he issued a formal complaint to the court on the grounds that Chalupa's taunting constituted an insult to a recognized religion of the state. Three eyewitnesses offered testimony against Chalupa: a shop assistant named Julius Aufrecht, an acquaintance of Chalupa's named Karel Korotvicka, and Skála's wife, Katerina. She described an incident in which she and her husband were pulling grass in the vicinity of Chalupa's house.

He bounded out of the house and called to her, asking if she were pulling grass for the calf and who was feeding the calf, she or her husband? She told the court that she "immediately understood" what he was talking about because her husband frequently had relayed word of his teasings in the past. Chalupa's references to "feeding the calf," she explained, had to do with the fact that her husband worked for the synagogue; in her view, also, the remarks were defamatory.[68]

Schneider-Svoboda, the state's attorney, claimed in the writ of indictment that it was "as plain as day" that Chalupa's utterances constituted the belittling of a state religion. Just to be sure, however, he elicited the opinions of two rabbis: Philipp Polatschek, rabbi of Polná, and Dr. Nathan Ehrenfeld, chief rabbi of Prague. They appear to have concurred, although no one ventured an interpretation of just what Chalupa may have meant. The accused was sentenced in December 1892 to two months' imprisonment with a mandatory fast day every two weeks.[69]

As a document of social history, this case is remarkable on several counts. We learn, for example, not only that at least one Christian was in the employ of the Polná Jewish community but also that the Catholic Church and the synagogue shared a sexton. This feature of small-town life testified to a certain degree of intimacy between Jews and Gentiles. At the same time, however, it was received by at least one Polná resident as a provocation worthy of almost daily condemnation. The Christian synagogue employee may not have taken the initiative to issue a formal complaint against Chalupa, but he did sense that both his honor and that of his employers were at stake, and he did not take the insults with equanimity. Later neither he nor his wife hesitated to testify in court against his tormentor. Finally, we see evidence of a well-integrated Jewish community that "knows its rights" and does not shy away from bringing charges against one who would diminish them. And the state, represented by the prosecutor's office, sees it to be in its interest to defend the good name of the Jewish religion.

Chalupa's taunts themselves are fascinating if only because they are so obscure. They seem to revolve around a pair of mixed, or confused, images. The first pairing combines the image of a "fatted calf" with some other, specifically Jewish animal, perhaps an inarticulate allusion to the Golden Calf worshiped by the Israelites at the foot of Mt. Sinai. The words of derision carry a sting, as they imply not only that Skála, by his labor, is enriching the Jews ("fattening" their calf) but also that the Jews are making plans to slaughter the calf in some ritual. This ceremony or meal

Chalupa calls *machalabeis*. No one involved in the case knows what the word means; it is simply transcribed as heard by the several witnesses. At the same time, all concerned are convinced that this image, like that of the fatted calf, is defamatory. Here Chalupa seems to have fitted together Jewish-sounding words or syllables, which may have seemed genuine to him by reason of his relative proximity to Jewish life but whose meaning he could only guess at.

A number of possibilities exist about the meaning of Chalupa's punchline. The phoneme *beis* conjures a Jewish scene by virtue of the fact that it also stands for the second letter of the Hebrew alphabet (in northern European, or Ashkenazi, pronunciation). *Machala* calls to mind the Yiddish word *makhl,* or *maykhl,* which means "dish" or "treat." The fatted calf, then, is being prepared for a special, or second, meal. It is also possible that the word *machalabeis* represents a corruption of the Hebrew or Yiddish *aleph-beis* (alphabet/a . . . b . . .). Least likely, in my view, is the chance that Chalupa was aware of the Hebrew word *mahalah,* meaning "illness" or "disease." In the end the prefix *machala* may amount to little more than a three-syllable nonsense word that, when attached to the Yiddish *beis,* has the ring of a Jewish term—a farcical play that bears witness to Chalupa's simultaneous proximity to and distance from the Jewish world that lay outside his door. In all likelihood the term did not mean anything in particular. It simply formed a piece of Chalupa's manic humor, the point of which was to ridicule Jewish practices and humiliate Skála. The state's attorney unintentionally added to the joke by trying to get to the bottom of it; he needed precise definitions if he were to prove defamation; hence, the official consultations with the two rabbis. They were not of much help, but they agreed with all of the principals that there was an insult there somewhere.

If the case of Jan Chalupa reveals fissures in the Jewish-Gentile relationship in Bohemia, it nevertheless portrays a conflict that was relatively benign in its social and cultural repercussions, a far cry from the wrenching controversy over alleged Jewish ritual murder that would engulf the country less than seven years later. In 1897 a very different type of libel action took place, in which the image of Jewish ritual murder not only was present but also functioned as a rhetorical device in a political argument. The case involved Anna Vokrálová, age fifty, wife of a stove fitter who lived in the Bohemian town of Kolín, some fifty-five kilometers east of Prague. She was accused of having publicly insulted the emperor following the elections of 22 February 1897, in which representatives to the Imperial Diet from the fifth curia were chosen.[70] The winning party in the city were the Young Czechs, or National Liberals; in the suburbs the Social Democrats prevailed. Around 1 P.M. on the day of the elections a Jewish woman, Anna Finková, age forty-four, the wife of a peddler, and Marie Veselá, a Catholic, age sixty-two, the wife of a gravedigger, were walking through the main square in Kolín, when they passed a pharmacy next to the Grand Hotel. There they happened upon Anna Vokrálová, who had just emerged from the hotel; a brief conversation ensued, followed about a week later by a tip to the police and the arrest and trial of the unfortunate Mrs. Vokrálová.[71]

According to the formal indictment, which in general the statements of witnesses confirmed, Anna Vokrálová had joined the two women and said, in a voice loud enough for them and others to hear, "We won, we won!" "Who won?" Marie Veselá asked. Vokrálová responded with the first of two statements that were to get her in deep trouble with the authorities: "Not the Jews; they drink Christian blood, and the emperor chases Jewish girls [*Císar si namlouvá zidovky*]."[72] When Veselá admonished the other woman that she should not say such things, that it was, after all, "our lord and emperor [*nás Císar Pán*]" that she was talking about, Vokrálová is said to have answered: "He gives you shit, he gives you shit. He shits on you [*hovno vám dá, hovno vám dá, nasere vám*]." At her trial on 15 March 1897 Vokrálová received a verdict of guilty and a sentence of four months' imprisonment with a mandatory fast day every two weeks.[73]

As with the Chalupa case, the arrest and trial of Anna Vokrálová contain surprising bits of information and lend a unique perspective to the local dynamics of Jewish-Christian interaction in the Czech small town. The offended pair (excluding, of course, the emperor) included a Catholic and a Jew, both Czech speakers, who apparently had been attending the same funeral and who were at least friendly enough to enjoy each other's company on a leisurely stroll home. They, in turn, both knew the accused, who on her own initiative greeted the two in the town square. From Marie Veselá's sworn testimony we learn that Anna Vokrálová lived on the "Jewish street" in Kolín and that she worked as a domestic in Jewish households. We also learn that neither Veselá nor Finková denounced Vokrálová to the police. Veselá kept the incident to herself, she explains, except to tell a shopkeeper named Kantorová (whose religion was not given, but the name may well be Jewish). Could it be true, she wanted to know, what Vokrálová said about the emperor? It is not clear whether or not Veselá needed to be enlightened regarding the description of Jewish culinary habits. The shopkeeper, nevertheless, pronounced on both parts of the statement and assured Mrs. Veselá that what the accused had to say about both the emperor and the Jews was "ugly." Anna Finková revealed that at noon on the day in question she had been to a burial in the neighboring village of Zálobí and that she had walked back to town with Marie Veselá. She also identified the accused as a domestic worker who lived on the Jewish street. Vokrálová apparently came out of the hotel and accompanied the two women as far as the fountain. She then turned to them and shouted the incriminating sentences.[74]

A state police supervisor named Jan Musil testified that he was approached on 1 March (the day of an annual market fair in Kolín) by a youth of about twenty, who identified himself only as a shop assistant in the town (Veselá, meanwhile, claimed that Mrs. Kantorová had no assistant). The youth told Musil that Anna Vokrálová had insulted the emperor on 22 February and that he could get more information from the two female witnesses. Musil interviewed Veselá and Finková, and what he claims to have heard from the two differs in subtle ways from signed testimony of both women. According to the police supervisor's reconstruction, Vokrálová did not preface her remarks with the happy observation "We won, we won" but with the more ironic comment "the elections sure came off nicely [*to to pekne dopadlo, ty volby*]" followed immediately by "the Jews drink Christian blood and the emperor chases Jewish girls" (according to Veselá) or "the Jews drink Christian blood and the emperor *keeps* Jewish girls [*drzí se zidovkama*]" (according to Finková). Because he understood Vokrálová's introductory words to be ironic, he concluded that she was, in fact, disappointed with the results of the elections (allegedly, she harbored socialist sympathies) and verbally had equated one sorry state of affairs with another.[75]

That fact that Anna Vokrálová was charged only with insulting the emperor and not with defaming Jews is also intriguing. We cannot necessarily conclude from this, however, that accusations of Jewish ritual murder were held by the state to fall under the category of legitimate political discourse. Jan Chalupa learned that one could go to prison for a lot less. And the records of the Kutná Hora court alone reveal numerous criminal cases against newspaper publishers and editors on the charge of defaming a religious group or inciting to violence. What we may have in the Vokrálová case is a decision to prosecute what was considered to be the graver of two offenses. And, if the honor of the Jews meant less than the honor of the emperor, was there much cause for complaint? There is little doubt from the overall tenor of the proceedings—as well as from witnesses' accounts—that Vokrálová's outburst disturbed a sense of local order and propriety. In both the Chalupa and the Vokrálová cases non-Jews displayed a proprietary concern for Jewish sensibilities and collaborated successfully with Jewish residents to raise the alarm when the peace was disturbed.

A final observation concerning the two cases: the prosecutor (state's attorney) in each was Dr. Anton Schneider-Svoboda; Dr. Zdenko Aurednícek served as the defense attorney for Anna Vokrálová. The same two individuals were to face each other again in 1899 and 1900 in the murder trials against Leopold Hilsner, Schneider-Svoboda again as prosecutor and Aurednícek as defense attorney. Thus, the history of the modern ritual murder trial appears to be a lesson in irony. One man devotes nearly two years of his life to proving in a court of law that a Jewish defendant has committed murder according to a bizarre ritual that involves the use of the victim's blood, after having spent much of his career up to this point defending the state and its Jewish community against antisemitic agitation and group libel. Representing the Jewish defendant is a civil libertarian who, barely two years earlier, had worked for the acquittal of a woman whose public political diatribe was laced with ritual murder discourse.

One way to interpret this turn of events is to contrast it to the picture that has been presented in these pages of relative equilibrium in Jewish-Gentile relations. In other words, the prosecution of ritual murder trials against Jews represented a sea change in the attitude of the state toward its Jewish population, a tactical reversal of emancipation's social contract. Schneider-Svoboda's crossing of the barricades stood for that point at which the pursuit of respectability and the defense of order no longer worked in tandem with Jewish interests; worse still, these trials marked the beginning of a general criminalization of the Jews in modern European consciousness. But such an interpretation exaggerates the nature of the shift that we are observing. And it ignores the fact that, in the minds of the actors themselves, no change in attitude or bureaucratic ethos had taken place. People like Schneider-Svoboda were certainly convinced that their actions against the Chalupas, the Vokrálovás, and the Hilsners of the world reflected a single, coherent set of principles. Figuring out why a modern prosecution of Jewish "ritual murder" did not appear to disturb this set of assumptions, this commitment to modernity, order, and rationality, ultimately will explain more about the phenomenon than assuming that the world had suddenly turned upside down.

NOTES

1. About twenty years ago, in a study of German antisemitism before World War I, Stefan Lehr attempted to list all documented accusations of ritual murder against Jews that occurred during the last two decades of the nineteenth century. He counted 128 incidents from 1873 to 1900; all but 5 occurred in the single decade from 1891 to 1900. Presumably, if he had chosen to continue to the Beilis affair of 1911–13, he would have found at least a half-dozen more. Stefan Lehr, *Antisemitismus—religiöse Motive im sozialen Vorurteil: Aus der Frühgeschichte des Antisemitismus in Deutschland, 1870–1914* (Munich: Chr. Kaiser Verlag, 1974), 239–43.

Lehr essentially reproduced the list found in Georg Kalckert, *Die Haltung des deutschen Katholizismus zum Judentum im 19. Jahrhundert* (n.p., n.d.), which, in turn, had been based on Friedrich Frank's *Der Ritualmord vor den Gerichtshöfen der Wahrheit und Gerechtigkeit* (Regensburg: G. J. Manz, 1901). The cases were limited for the most part to Germany, Austria-Hungary, and the Balkan countries; the Russian and Ottoman empires received some attention; Western Europe was not represented.

2. Although monographs and article-length studies have been published for individual cases, there is to date no comprehensive study of the modern ritual murder trial in Europe. On the ritual murder accusation generally, see Daniil Khvol'son, *Die Blutanklage und sonstige mittelalterliche Beschuldigungen der Juden: Eine historische Untersuchung nach den Quellen* (Frankfurt a.M.: J. Kaufmann, 1901); and Hermann L. Strack, *Das Blut im Glauben und Aberglauben der Menschheit mit besonderer Berücksichtigung der "Volksmedizin" und des "jüdischen Blutritus,"* 8th ed. (Munich: Beck, 1900) (trans. as *The Jew and Human Sacrifice*). For the accusation in its medieval context, see Rainer Erb, ed., *Die legende vom Ritualmord: Zur geschichte der Blutbeschuldigung gegen Juden* (Berlin: Metropol, 1993); and Gavin Langmuir, *Toward a Definition of Antisemitism* (Berkeley and Los Angeles: University of California Press, 1990), chaps. 9–12.

3. Györgi Enyedi, *Hungary: An Economic Geography* (Boulder, CO: Westview, 1976); Tivadar Bernát, ed., *An Economic Geography of Hungary* (Budapest: Akadémiai Kiadó, 1989), 376–92.

4. C. A. Macartney, *Hungary* (London: Ernest Benn, 1934), 199.

5. Macartney, *Hungary,* 199–200.

6. Robert E. Dickinson, *Germany: A General and Regional Geography* (New York: E. P. Dutton, 1953), 466.

7. *Die Gemeinden mit 2000 und mehr Einwohnern im Deutschen Reich nach der Volkszählung vom 16. Juni 1925,* Sonderhefte zu Wirtschaft und Statistik, vol. 6 (Berlin: Statistisches Reichsamt, 1926), 48–49. This publication compares data from the 1925 census to that of 1910.

8. Dickinson, *Germany,* 464–65.

9. Paul Nathan, *Xanten-Cleve: Betrachtungen zum Prozeß Buschhof* (Berlin: H. S. Hermann, 1892), 1. Unless otherwise indicated, all translations are mine.

10. Zdenek Jaros, *Polná: Kulturne historicky pruvodce* (Jihlava: Muzeum Vysociny, 1989), 7–13.

11. Jaros, *Polná,* 15; also Bretislav Reyrich (Rérych), *Polná: Pruvodce po meste a okolí* (Polná: Club Cs. Turistu, 1927), 6; "Zidé a Polná," typescript, n.d. (Muzeum Vysocina, pobocka Polná), 37.

12. Václav Kotyska, *Uplny místopisny slovník Království Ceského* (Prague: Bursík and Kohout, 1895), 1044–45.

13. Bruno Schumacher, *Geschichte Ost- und Westpreussens,* 4th ed. (Würzburg: Holzner Verlag, 1959), 221, 281–82.

14. Ibid., 286.

15. Max Aschkewitz, *Zur Geschichte der Juden in Westpreußen* (Marburg: Johann Gottfried Herder-Institut, 1967), 178.

16. Jörg K. Hoensch, *A History of Modern Hungary, 1867–1986* (London and New York: Longman, 1988), 12.

17. Tibor Frank, "Hungary and the Dual Monarchy, 1867–1890," in *A History of Hungary,* ed. Peter F. Sugar (Bloomington: Indiana University Press, 1990), 259.

18. Frank, "Hungary and the Dual Monarchy," 259–60.

19. Andrew C. Janos, *The Politics of Backwardness in Hungary, 1825–1945* (Princeton: Princeton University Press, 1982), 127–28; Frank, "Hungary and the Dual Monarchy," 259; Hoensch, *Modern Hungary,* 23.

20. Janos, *Politics of Backwardness,* 127–28; Hoensch, *Modern Hungary,* 31. Hoensch writes that some 2 million people were "drawn into the Hungarian orbit" between 1880 and 1910. This number included not only the country's 700,000 Jews but also 600,000 Germans, 200,000 Slovaks, and 100,000 Croatians. Hoensch, *Modern Hungary,* 31.

21. Barbara Suchy, "Antisemitismus in den Jahren vor dem Ersten Weltkrieg," in *Köln und das rheinische Judentum: Festschrift Germania Judaica 1959–1984,* ed. Jutta Bohnke-Kollwitz et al. (Cologne: J. P. Bachem, 1984), 266–67.

22. Suchy, "Antisemitismus," 266.

23. August Rohling, *Der Talmudjude: Zur Beherzigung für Juden und Christen aller Stände* (Münster: Adolph Russell, 1871). On Rohling, see I. A. Hellwing, *Der konfessionelle Antisemitismus im 19. Jahrhundert in Österreich* (Vienna, Freiburg, and Basel: Herder, 1972), 71–183; Joseph S. Bloch, *My Reminiscences* (Vienna: R. Löwit, 1922–23), 61–67; Jacob Katz, *From Prejudice to Destruction: Anti-Semitism, 1700–1933* (Cambridge, MA: Harvard University Press, 1980), 219–20, 285–86. Publication and distribution figures are from Suchy, "Antisemitismus," 266; and *Acten und Gutachten in dem Prozesse Rohling contra Blochap* (Vienna: M. Breitenstein, 1890), 1:3.

24. See, for example, the report in the *Jewish Chronicle,* 29 July 1892, 5–6.

25. Ibid. The *Chronicle* goes on to say: "It is further pointed out that as Jews are labouring under an everlasting curse, their hatred to Christians is equally everlasting, and the inference that the writer leaves his readers to draw is that the Ritual

Murder is consequently a constant phenomenon in Jewish life. The discovery that this disgraceful work is now in circulation has produced considerable sensation in Germany, and Conservative organs like the *Kölnische Zeitung* join hands with Democratic newspapers like the *Frankfurter Presse* in severely condemning this literary outrage."

26. Schumacher, *Geschichte Ost- und Westpreussens,* 284.

27. Ibid., 284–85.

28. Victor Karady, "Religious Divisions, Socio-Economic Stratification and the Modernization of Hungarian Jewry after Emancipation," in *Jews in the Hungarian Economy,* ed. Michael K. Silber (Jerusalem: Magnes Press, 1992), 170, 179. Karady points out that "Magyarization," as it was called, was virtually complete (over 90 percent) in the northern and eastern counties, including Szabolcs.

29. On the place of Jews in the Czech-German national conflict, see Hillel J. Kieval, *The Making of Czech Jewry: National Conflict and Jewish Society in Bohemia, 1870–1918* (New York: Oxford University Press, 1988); Gary B. Cohen, *The Politics of Ethnic Survival: Germans in Prague, 1861–1914* (Princeton: Princeton University Press, 1981), 76–85, 168–83, 217–73; and Wilma A. Iggers, ed., *The Jews of Bohemia and Moravia: A Historical Reader* (Detroit: Wayne State University Press, 1992), 130–49, 182–319.

30. Reyrich, "Zidé a Polná," 37; *Polná: Pruvodce po meste a okolí,* 48.

31. On the Protestant orientation in Czech nationalism, see Tomás G. Masaryk, *The Meaning of Czech History,* ed., with an introduction by, René Wellek, trans. Peter Kussi (Chapel Hill: University of North Carolina Press, 1974); Milan Hauner, "The Meaning of Czech History: Masaryk versus Pekar," in *T. G. Masaryk (1850–1937),* vol. 3: *Statesman and Cultural Force,* ed. Harry Hanak (Houndsmills and London: Macmillan, 1990), 24–42; Karel Kucera, "Masaryk and Pekar: Their Conflict over the Meaning of Czech History and Its Metamorphoses," in *T. G. Masaryk (1850–1937),* vol. 1: *Thinker and Politician,* ed. Stanley B. Winters (Houndsmills and London: Macmillan, 1990), 88–113.

32. On the origins of the German-Jewish school system in Bohemia, see Hillel J. Kieval, "Caution's Progress: The Modernization of Jewish Life in Prague, 1780–1830," in *Toward Modernity: The European Jewish Model,* ed. Jacob Katz (New Brunswick: Transaction Books, 1987), 71–105. On Jewish acculturation in nineteenth-century Bohemia, see William O. McCagg Jr., *A History of Habsburg Jews, 1670–1918* (Bloomington: Indiana University Press, 1989), 65–82; Hillel J. Kieval, "The Social Vision of Bohemian Jews: Intellectuals and Community in the 1840s," in *Assimilation and Community: The Jews in Nineteenth-Century Europe,* ed. Jonathan Frankel and Steven J. Zipperstein (Cambridge: Cambridge University Press, 1992), 246–83; "The Lands Between: The Jews of Bohemia, Moravia and Slovakia to 1918," in *Where Cultures Meet: The Story of the Jews of Czechoslovakia,* ed. Natalia Berger (Tel Aviv: Bet Ha-tefutsot and Ministry of Defence, 1990), 40–48.

33. These arguments are developed more fully in Kieval, *Making of Czech Jewry,* 10–63.

34. On the legal, as well as political, underpinnings of Austrian nationality policy, see Gerald Stourzh, *Die Gleichberechtigung der Nationalitäten in der Verfassung und Verwaltung Österreichs, 1848–1918* (Vienna: Verlag der Österreichischen Akademie der Wissenschaften, 1985).

35. Bohumil Cerny, *Justicny omyl/Hilsneriada* (Prague: Magnet Press, 1990), 10. On the 1890 and 1900 censuses generally, see Kieval, *Making of Czech Jewry,* 60–63.

36. William O. McCagg Jr., *Jewish Nobles and Geniuses in Modern Hungary* (Boulder, CO: East European Quarterly, 1972), 223. Similarly, in *A History of Habsburg Jews* he described the "alliance between the Magyar-speaking nobility and the reformer Jews" that was cemented in the 1860s (135).

37. Janos, *Politics of Backwardness,* 112–18.

38. Macartney, *Hungary,* 216–17.

39. Andrew Handler employs both terms in describing Jewish-Gentile relations (36). It is he who provides the quotation from Eötvös. *Blood Libel at Tiszaeszlar* (Boulder: East European Monographs, 1980). Nathaniel Katzburg combines the two sentiments when he describes relations as "friendly, even if [they] contained a small measure of superiority." *Antishemiyut be-Hungariyah, 1867–1914* (Antisemitism in Hungary, 1867–1914) (Tel Aviv: Dvir, 1969), 107.

40. Paul Nathan, *Der Prozess von Tisza-Eszlár: Ein Antisemitisches Culturbild* (Berlin: F. Fontane, 1892), 93–97.

41. Géza Onody, *Tisza-Eszlár in der Vergangenheit und Gegenwart: Über die Juden im Allgemeinen-Jüdische Glaubensmysterien, Rituelle Mordthaten und Blutopfer-Der Tisza-Eszlárer Fall,* trans. Georg von Marczianyi (Budapest, 1883), 156. According to Andrew Handler, Onody had been forced to lease part of his estate (in fact, that part that lay outside of Tiszaeszlár) from its new, Jewish owners, Simon and Gyorgy Pöhm. This humiliating situation turned into "a passionate, implacable hatred of Jews in general." Handler, *Blood Libel,* 31.

42. Ibid., 36.

43. On the growth of the Jewish population in Hungary, see Victor Karady and Istvan Kemeny, "Les Juifs dans la structure des classes en Hongrie: Essai sur les antécédents historiques des crises d'antisémitisme du XXe siècle," *Actes de la recherche en sciences sociales,* no. 22 (June 1978): 28–29.

On the application and impact of the edicts of toleration on the Jews of Galicia and Hungary, see Michael Silber, "The Historical Experience of German Jewry and Its Impact on the Haskalah and Reform in Hungary," *Toward Modernity,* 107–57; Artur Eisenbach, "Das galizische Judentum während des Völkerfrühlings und in der Zeit des Kampfes um seine Gleichberechtigung," *Studia Judaica Austriaca* 8 (1980): 75–92; Josef Karniel, "Das Toleranzpatent Kaiser Josephs II. für die

Juden Galiziens und Lodomeriens," *Jahrbuch des Instituts für Deutsche Geschichte* 11 (1982): 55–89.

44. Karady and Kemeny, "Les Juifs dans la structure des classes en Hongrie," 29.

45. Onody, *Tisza-Eszlár,* 156.

46. Ibid., 157.

47. From the trial testimony, quoted in Nathan, *Der Prozess von Tisza-Eszlár,* 110.

48. Suchy, "Antisemitismus," 253, quoting from official police files. Suchy concludes from the investigation reports that the murder was sexual in character.

49. *Encyclopaedia Judaica* (hereafter cited as *EJ*), s.v., "Xanten"; general population figures (for 1910) from *Die Gemeinden mit 2000 und mehr Einwohnern,* 48–49. Though it always was a small community, Xanten was sufficiently important to serve as the meeting place for the Jewish Diet of the Rhine beginning in 1690. In 1787 a special building (also containing a synagogue) was set aside for the assembly's meetings. After 1890 the Jewish population declined steadily: in 1916 it stood at thirty persons; by 1930 barely fourteen Jews remained.

50. Nathan, *Xanten-Cleve,* 4–5.

51. See Julius H. Schoeps, "Ritualmordbeschuldigung und Blutaberglaube: Die Affäre Buschhoff im niederrheinischen Xanten," in *Köln und das rheinische Judentum: Festschrift Germania Judaica 1959–1984,* ed. Jutta Bohnke-Kollwitz et al. (Cologne: J. P. Bachem, 1984), 287, 297–98 (in which he quotes from the file of the district magistrate's office in Moers, Nordrhein-Westfälisches Hauptstaatsarchiv, Düsseldorf [HStAD], LA Moers, Nr. 547).

52. Aschkewitz, *Westpreussen,* 1; William W. Hagen, *Germans, Poles, and Jews: The Nationality Conflict in the Prussian East, 1772–1914* (Chicago: University of Chicago Press, 1980), 22.

53. Hagen, *Germans, Poles, and Jews,* 22–23; J. Perles, "Geschichte der Juden in Posen," *Monatsschrift für Geschichte und Wissenschaft des Judenthums* 13 (1864): 281–95, 321–34, 361–73, 409–20, 449–61; 14 (1865): 81–93, 121–36, 165–78, 205–16, 256–63.

54. See the account in Perles, "Geschichte," 14 (1865): 165–78.

55. Aschkewitz, *Westpreussen,* 23, 31–38, 177–79.

56. *Die Welt,* 21 September 1900, 1–2.

57. Aschkewitz, *Westpreussen,* 127.

58. The collusion of the landed estate in Jewish efforts to circumvent the effects of Vienna's restrictive legislation has yet to be studied closely. For now, see Josef Wertheimer, *Die Juden in Österreich* 2 vols. in 1 (Leipzig: Mayer und Wigand, 1842), 1:187–94; Ludvík Singer, "Zur Geschichte der Toleranzpatente in den Sudetenländern," *Jahrbuch der Gesellschaft für Geschichte der Juden in der Cechoslovakischen Republik* 5 (1933): 236–37; Karel Adámek, *Slovo o zidech* (Chrudim,

1899), 5–8; Adolf Stein, *Die Geschichte der Juden in Böhmen* (Brno: Jüdischer Buch- und Kunstlerverlag, 1904), 86–90.

59. Reyrich, *Polná: Pruvodce,* 34–36; Jaros, *Polná,* 11.

60. Reyrich, *Polná: Pruvodce,* 56.

61. On Jewish population figures, see Jirí Fiedler, *Jewish Sights of Bohemia and Moravia* (Prague: Sefer, 1991), 139–40; and Ruth Kestenberg-Gladstein, "The Jews between Czechs and Germans in the Historic Lands," *The Jews of Czechoslovakia* (Philadelphia: Jewish Publication Society of America, 1968), 1:29. On the application of the *Familiantengesetze,* see Anita Franková, "Erfassung der jüdischen Bevölkerung in Böhmen im 18. und in der ersten Hälfte des 19. Jh. und die Bestrebungen, den Anteil der jüdischen Bevölkerung einzuschränken," *Judaica Bohemiae* 6 (1970): 55–69; and Jaroslav Prokes, "Der Antisemitismus der Behörden und das Prager Ghetto in nachweißenbergischer Zeit," *Jahrbuch der Gesellschaft für Geschichte der Juden in der Cechoslovakischen Republik* 1 (1929): 41–262.

62. Jaros, *Polná,* 14.

63. On Jewish migration from the Czech countryside during the second half of the nineteenth century, see Kieval, *Making of Czech Jewry,* 10–17; Kestenberg-Gladstein, "The Jews between Czechs and Germans," 27–32 (with caution); Jan Herman, "The Evolution of the Jewish Population in Bohemia and Moravia, 1754–1953," in *Papers in Jewish Demography, 1973,* ed. U. O. Schmelz, P. Glikson, and S. Della Pergola (Jerusalem: Institute of Contemporary Jewry, Hebrew University, 1977), 191–206; "The Evolution of the Jewish Population in Prague, 1869–1939," *Papers in Jewish Demography,* 53–67. For Polná's population figures, see J. Fiedler, *Jewish Sights,* 139–40.

64. The records of the Kutná Hora Regional Court (Krajsky Soud Kutná Hora) as well as of the Prague Criminal Court (Zemsky Soud Trestní) are housed in the Státní oblastní archiv (SOA), Prague. SOA also maintains the records of the Hilsner murder investigations and trials—files generated by the Kutná Hora prosecutor (SZ Kutná Hora), the Písek prosecutor (SZ Písek), the chief prosecutor in Prague (VSZ Praha), and the Kutná Hora and Písek courts. I would estimate that the Kutná Hora and Prague courts together dealt with more than twenty criminal cases involving anti-Jewish agitation between 1883 and 1899.

65. The handwritten indictment and trial record are to be found in SOA, KS Kutná Hora, C 1893/48.

66. Marc Raeff, *The Well-Ordered Police State: Social and Institutional Change through Law in the Germanies and Russia, 1600–1800* (New Haven: Yale University Press, 1983).

67. SOA, KS Kutná Hora, C 1893/48.

68. Ibid.

69. Ibid.

70. The fifth electoral curia included all males over the age of twenty-four. On the parliamentary elections of 1897, see Cohen, *Politics of Ethnic Survival,* 238;

and Bruce M. Garver, *The Young Czech Party, 1874–1901, and the Emergence of a Multi-Party System* (New Haven: Yale University Press, 1970), 234–37.

71. SOA, KS Kutná Hora C 1897/68. File contains: arrest record, 1 March 1897 (German); writ of indictment, 5 March 1897 (Czech); trial protocol, 15 March 1897 (Czech); verdict, same date (Czech); trial protocol in German; personal statement of the accused, signed with three crosses, 1 March 1897; written statements of two policemen; and personal statements of Marie Veselá and Anna Finková.

72. *Namlouvat si* can have the more formal meaning "to court" someone, but the colloquial expression *namlouvat si dívky* means to chase, or run after, girls; cf. Josef Fronek, *Cesko-Anglicky Slovník* (Prague: Státní Pedagogické Nakladatelství, 1993), 266.

73. SOA, KS Kutná Hora, C 1897/68; writ of indictment; trial protocol.

74. Ibid., statements of Marie Veselá and Anna Finková.

75. Ibid., statement of Jan Musil.

Andean Two-Step: The Encounter between Bolivians and Central European Jewish Refugees

Leo Spitzer

The Anas

Two women—one quite young, in her early twenties, the other wrinkled, older, but probably no more than in her late forties—merge in my memory. Both, in my recollection, are named Ana, and I think of them as "the Anas," even though, in all likelihood, one of them probably had a different name.

Both of them are cholas, *the Bolivian term for urban-dwelling* mestizas *of Spanish-American and Indian-American descent, and both dress in traditional Aymara* chola *style.[1] They wear several layers of short* pollera *skirts tucked one beneath the other like crinolines, a blouse and woolen pullover, a vest jacket, and a woolen shawl. On the street they use a richly colored rectangle of hand-woven cloth, the* ahuayo, *as a carryall slung across their back and tied around the neck and wear a dark green, brown, or black bowler hat, the characteristic item of attire with which* chola *dress is most widely identified.[2]*

The older Ana worked for us first, but I cannot recall when she was initially hired by my parents as a sirvienta, *an all-around house "maid" to help with the cleaning, laundry, and cooking. I associate them both with our apartment on the Calle Mexico in La Paz, a place to which my parents moved in 1946, after the war ended, when my father decided to set up a plumbing and electrical shop of his own and our family's economic situation took a turn for the better. Neither one was a "live-in maid," but both spent long hours in our house for five or six days a week, and both worked for our family over a period of many years. Each used a tiny room in an interior courtyard of the house, near our apartment and my father's workshop, as a place to rest during the day and to sleep over on those rare occasions when they stayed overnight. Although I do not recall any interdiction about our presence in that room, my sister and I rarely entered it. Yet I do remember its inside quite vividly: a room no larger than a pantry, barely able to contain a cot and a stool, with cut-out pictures from magazines pasted on the walls and a small statue of the Virgin of Copacabana and a candle enshrined in a corner. I seem to have been both attracted and a little frightened by the dark, lair-like quality of the place.*

Despite the years that both of the Anas worked in our house, and the many hours they spent with our family and especially with my sister and me on an almost daily basis, we really knew remarkably little about them and their lives. While the older Ana was most probably married, a mother, perhaps even a grandmother—facts that my parents would certainly have been interested in and informed about—our knowledge and comprehension of Ana's home world and cultural milieu seem to have remained quite superficial and limited. Where she actually lived, what her family looked like, what they did on a daily basis, what they thought and spoke about—all this intrigued me as, I am sure, it did my mother and father. But a certain cultural distance remained unbridgeable between the Anas and my parents, reinforced in part by the hierarchical master-servant, employer-laborer division that underlay their relationship and in part by some unspoken, and perhaps unexamined, unwillingness by each of them to grant the other more than restricted access to their respective private and collective universe.

In one of our family albums there is a photo of the younger Ana, standing near the street entrance to our apartment with my sister, Elly, and me. Elly and I are dressed up in costumes—for Carnival perhaps. My sister is outfitted to look like an Andean "Indian boy," wearing coarse linen pants, a hand-woven indigenous cloth belt, a knit wool cap with ear flaps, a woven cloth ahuayo *slung across her shoulder. I am costumed as a "Mexican Indian peasant," with wide-brimmed "sombrero," poncho, pants tucked into boots, and I am carrying a miniature guitar. Ana, dressed normally in her everyday* chola *style but with her dark bowler hat set somewhat rakishly at an angle on her head, is between the two of us. She is laughing broadly, without apparent resentment—seemingly in good-humored amusement about the imitation "indios" in her company. Looking at the photo, I recall the time when this Ana took me along to see where she lived in a part of La Paz where I had never been before, into a crowded area of small shops and houses quite far from our apartment and the main concentration of refugee settlement. There, in the midst of her kinfolk, neighbors, and numerous children, I became an*

object of curiosity and display. I was stared at, examined, touched—a blonde,
hazel-eyed anomaly in a crowd of black-haired people.

"We Looked at Them . . ."

The Influx

In the mid-1930s and until the end of the first year of World War II thousands of refugees from Nazi-dominated Central Europe, the majority of them Jews, fled to Bolivia to escape an increasingly vehement persecution. Wealthier or "better-connected" refugees, who emigrated soon after the Nazis came to power, had acquired visas and found a haven in "countries of choice": Great Britain, the United States, Australia, Palestine, Argentina, Brazil. The tightening of immigration to these countries, however, virtually closed off entry for the large number of persons desperate to leave in the late 1930s.[3] By the end of the decade Bolivia was one of very few places to accept Jewish immigrants. Close to twenty thousand refugees from Germany, Austria, Czechoslovakia, and Hungary arrived between 1938 and 1940—a number that, when calculated as a percentage of Bolivia's total "non-Indian" population at the time, gives some sense of how substantial the demographic impact of this Central European immigrant influx must have been.[4] The new arrivals settled primarily in La Paz, 12,500 feet above sea level, as well as in Cochabamba, Oruro, Sucre, and in small mining and tropical agricultural communities throughout the land.

The region that had become Bolivia after its independence from Spain in 1824—Alto Perú—had once before been the refuge of persons seeking an escape from religious intolerance and persecution in Europe. In the course of the sixteenth century and during the extended, and often brutal, sway of the Spanish Inquisition, thousands of New Christians, or *conversos*—persons of Jewish origin who had been converted to Christianity by force or prudent choice of their own—left the Iberian Peninsula. Clandestinely or openly, many sought haven in Spain's Latin American colonies. Bringing badly needed technical and entrepreneurial skills with them, a number of *conversos* settled around the silver mining areas of Potosí and in centers of trade and commerce like Chuquisaca (later Sucre), Santa Cruz, and Tarija. Over the years some of these *conversos,* or their offspring, intermarried with local Christians and were increasingly integrated into the Catholic establishment. In the process the background religious "stain" that had made them identifiable as "outsiders" was blurred, if not eradi-

Fig. 1

cated. But traces of their Sephardi ancestry survived, discernible both in family names and in customs of Jewish origin, which were perpetuated for generations despite the loss of their original meaning.[5] Until well into the first decades of this century, for example, it was the custom for women in some families in Santa Cruz to light candles on Friday evening, a Jewish ritual inaugurating the Sabbath, and for persons associated with some of the oldest and most distinguished "colonial" families in Sucre to maintain a semi-secluded seven-day deep mourning for their dead, which, in form if not substance, bore great resemblance to the Jewish mourning period, *shivah*. Ancient candlesticks and silver objects of Sephardi origin, as well as incunabula inscribed in Hebrew, have been passed down within some of Sucre's families for generations.[6]

Yet, despite the early presence of *conversos* in Bolivia's colonial past and relics of Judaic practices and beliefs, few if any Jews seem to have emigrated to the country in the first century of its independence. In this respect Bolivia was quite different from its more accessible and economically attractive South American neighbors like Argentina and Brazil, whose governments periodically encouraged "white settler" immigration from Europe and in which substantial Jewish communities developed in the course of the nineteenth and early twentieth century.[7] Small numbers of East European Jews did trickle into Bolivia in the early part of this century, fleeing persecution in Poland or pogroms in Russia in the aftermath of the failed revolution of 1905 or in the aftermath of the Bolshevik Revolution of 1917. But, before the rise of Nazism in Central Europe and the massive influx of European refugees in the late 1930s, very few Jews, perhaps less than a hundred from Alsace, Poland, and Russia, had settled in this Andean land.

"The Moon Was More Real to Us . . ."

Before the refugees left Europe in the late 1930s, Bolivia had been little more than a place on a map of South America for them. They knew virtually nothing about its physical geography or climate and even less about its history, government, and economy. In their eagerness to find a land that would accept them, they had been ready to go anywhere that would permit them to live in safety. "Bolivia—quick, where is it?" was Egon Schwarz's response on receiving his visa through the Hilfsverein (Refugee Aid Society) from the Paris consulate. "We would have gone to the moon," Andres Simon recalled. "Bolivia was a closer possibility, but the moon we saw every night. It was more real to us." "I knew about Bolivia what you know about the North Pole," Renate Schwarz said to me. "Maybe you know more about the North Pole."[8]

If the refugees knew anything at all about the inhabitants of the country to which they were emigrating, it was either extremely limited or stereotypical. My father, like many others, met his first "real" Bolivian national at the consular office—in his case in Munich, where he had gone from Vienna to acquire the four visas that would permit him, my mother, and his parents to leave Austria. Many, perhaps most, refugees had only a remote and impressionistic sense of the cultural and ethnic milieu into which they were entering. *Spanish-speaking, Catholic, Indian*—these were the terms they vaguely associated with the inhabitants of the country offering them asylum. But these were broad, generic identifiers that hardly prepared the refugees for the immense cultural and social differences they would have to face. Their preconceptions of the land and its people were shaped by information that varied greatly in reliability and perspective. Some of it came from old, half-forgotten world geography and world culture lectures they had received back in school or from photographs and descriptions in widely circulated German travel books from the 1920s with intriguing titles like *Im dunkelsten Bolivien* (In Darkest Bolivia) and *Vom Urwald zu den Gletschern der Kordillere* (From the Jungle to the Glaciers of the Cordillera).[9] More up-to-date, but not necessarily more trustworthy, information came in letters from those who had preceded them to Bolivia or from the second- and thirdhand retelling of the contents of such letters. Some was acquired "post-visa," by looking up the entry "Bolivia" in encyclopedias and geographical atlases or information in the pamphlet *Jüdische Auswanderung nach Südamerika* (Jewish Emigration to South America), especially prepared in Berlin for emigrating Jews by the German Jewish Hilfsverein. In that publication they would have been able to read:

Bolivia is one of the poorest, least developed, and for a long time, least stable of the South American lands. The economic importance of the country derives predominantly from its abundance of valuable minerals, particularly tin. As a consequence, possibilities for professional employment are best for technicians, chemists, and others who might be retrainable for mining-related work; they are less opportune for manual workers and farmers.

Up to now, relatively few German-Jewish immigrants have reached the country. Owing to the extremely high altitude at which they are located, the most promising regions of this land can only be tolerated by persons with a very strong heart and healthy lungs. . . .

Bolivia is the country with the greatest percentage of pure-blooded Indians in its population. Indians and persons of mixed-racial background live in primitive cultural circumstances.[10]

But images of Bolivia and its inhabitants were also derived from widely disseminated, highly romanticized adventure literature—a literature that routinely represented the landscape and people of South America as mysterious, primitive, exotic, if not forbidding, and which simplified or blurred the particularity and diversity of both. Werner Guttentag, for example, emigrated from Germany to Bolivia via Holland in 1939. Before leaving Europe, he decided he would move to the city of Cochabamba (where he still resides) simply on the basis of its relatively central location on the map of Bolivia—which, he relates, he examined closely for the first time only after learning that he and his parents had received visas to go there. But, as was true with Heinz Markstein, Egon Taus, Julius Meier, and many other young refugees, his most vivid predeparture image of Bolivia's indigenous populations came from reading *Das Vermächtnis des Inka* (The Bequest of the Inca) and *In den Cordilleren,* two of the "South American novels" of the prolific and immensely popular German author of adventure books Karl May. May, best known for his numerous Wild West thrillers and for his hero "Old Shatterhand"—a fascinating mélange of Teutonic knight and pulp novel cowboy hero—visited North America only after his retirement as a novelist and never set foot in South America. Yet, although his colorful and seemingly authentic ethnographic representations of Indian peoples and their lives were largely invented—the imaginary creations of a fertile mind—they helped to enliven and strengthen popular Central European stereotypes concerning the "otherness" of American Indians. "One came away from May's novels," Werner Guttentag observed, "confirmed that the glories of the Indians' past were gone, that civilization had passed them by, and that they fit into one of three categories. They were either wild, backward, or noble." For those refugees whose preconceptions of indigenous people were influenced by this captivating author, it would undoubtedly have seemed highly ironic at the time to discover that Karl May's works had also been the favorite reading of the young Adolf Hitler—that, according to cultural critic Klaus Mann, Hitler had indeed considered May as one of his literary mentors.[11]

"So Strange, So Unbelievably Strange . . ."[12]

We absolutely didn't know what was awaiting us. We didn't know about the people, or their customs, or traditions. We did not expect the altitude to be so oppressive. On the train from Arica to La Paz, people's noses and ears were bleeding. Some were hemorrhaging.[13]

The Indios. We never had seen anything like them. Already on the train, at stops, a real novelty: we looked at them; they looked at us.[14]

What immediately impressed me about La Paz was the smell—a terrible impression. The streets smelled horrible. The Indians urinated and defecated in the streets. The women squatted right down in the street, lifted up their skirts, and did their thing. There were no public sanitary facilities. And they brought their llama herds through the streets. And the llamas spit and left their little traces.[15]

The Indian women wore multiple skirts and colorful mantas. They were sometimes beautifully dressed, richly dressed, with gold and silver pins and gold earrings. But they had no culture. They had no civilization.[16]

I noticed that I was in a black land. Not that the people were Negroes, but so many men and women were dressed in black or dark clothing. Only sometime afterwards did I learn that they were still in mourning clothes—mourning their dead, casualties in the disastrous Chaco War that Bolivia had fought with Paraguay.[17]

Music . . . the noise of a never-before-heard, never-ending, melancholy Indian music, whose monotone initially grates the nerves, but which one never again forgets after hearing it played night after night for months on end.[18]

[Here] practically nothing is as one knows it, either in society or in nature. The person who applies middle-European standards to what is seen and experienced will never understand.[19]

"Nothing is as one knows it, either in society or nature"—Egon Schwarz had said soon after his arrival in Bolivia. And, indeed, there was little in the Central European cultural background or experience of the refugees that would echo sympathetically and provide a familiar referent to help ease their integration into their new land. Neither the cities nor the countryside reminded those who had left Germany, Austria, or any of the Central European countries of the Austro-German *Kulturkreis* of places they had known before.

For incoming refugees the rugged, severe, physical environment in which they now found themselves was the first impediment to adjustment. When they arrived in La Paz, or anywhere in the Andean highlands, most of them felt the effects of altitude sickness—*soroche*—and suffered shortness of breath, sleeplessness, and aches in the head and body. Those with lung or heart problems generally found the altitude unbearable. If they moved to the semitropical or tropical lowlands, they encountered high temperature and humidity and faced the danger of contracting illnesses for which the temperate-climate disease environment from which they had emigrated had provided no immunity or tolerance. But, aside from the adjustment difficulties and medical dangers associated with their natural surroundings, it was the immense *foreignness* of the cultural environment that compounded feelings of alienation: they were truly outsiders, strangers in a strange land. The various indigenous people looked different, they dressed differently, their customs, practices, festivals, and foods were unfamiliar, they communicated in languages that none of the immigrants had ever heard before, their psychology and worldview seemed unfathomable:[20]

It is July 1941 in Cochabamba. Dr. Heinrich Stern, born almost sixty years earlier in Nordhausem am Harz, Germany, and a recent arrival in Bolivia, reflects in a note written to himself:

The path was rocky and rough, steep and lonely. Now I sit on a rock and look about me. Thorny shrubbery, thicket, tall cactus, stones and stones. In the distance, two, no three wretched huts; mountains all around, giant, furrowed mountains. The sun sinks lower, its rays bring a magic glow to the peaks. Loneliness, frightful loneliness; and strangeness. In the far distance two women, wrapped in red ochre shawls, climb uphill. Their appearance increases my sense of loneliness, of abandonment. Indianerlandschaft! *Indian landscape! My new homeland! Is this my new homeland?*

Dark thoughts waltz through my brain. They torment me, they repeatedly knock and sting against my forehead. They circle about the horizon and

want to penetrate the distant mountain wall; and they search and inquire:
The sky above me, is it not the sky of the old homeland? No, it seems to
be—or am I only imagining it—more glaring, more poisonous. Only the
clouds cast a smile of friendliness on me, reminders of other environs. But
the land remains hostile. A landscape of the uncivilized—Indianerlandschaft, *Indian landscape. Gigantic, strange, melancholy and lonely.*[21]

Bewilderment. Nostalgia. Yearning. Difference. It is not difficult to discern the sensibility of romantic poetry and of its emotional language in
this text: influences of Herder, the young Goethe, even of Wordsworth's
"spontaneous overflow of powerful feeling," seem to be embedded within
it.[22] The individual—here, Dr. Heinrich Stern, sitting on a mountainous
hillside at dusk—explores personal emotions in relation to the landscape
and the surrounding forces of nature while seeking to make a connection
and to establish some form of balance between them. Stern, after all, was
raised in a cultural milieu in which the literature and music of romanticism
had been vital elements within formal schooling and popular culture; his
generation was steeped in the subjective touchstones, in the "language of
the heart," of the romantic arts. But in Stern's contemplation the encounter
with Bolivian nature is a hostile and melancholy one. In his new setting, he
discovers, no romantic balance of forces between individual body and natural environment can be achieved. He perceives himself to be in an alien
world—in a world of others, in an *Indianerlandschaft.* Nothing in it, except
the clouds, seems familiar. Indeed, the only other human presences in the
forbidding landscape, two Indian women in ochre shawls, accentuate his
sense of difference and emphasize the cultural distance of his disconnec-
tion. He feels alone, abandoned. And the forbidding landscape itself —
that "landscape of the uncivilized," as he calls it—capped by the "glaring,"
"poisonous" sky above him, appears to reject him, to heighten his nostalgia, to increase his loneliness, his yearning for the homeland he has been
forced to relinquish. "Here I sit in captivity," he writes. "Nations, continents, an ocean separate me from my homeland. Coolly, I try to take into
account that hate, cruelty, and misery now reign there. But the heart over-
comes the mind. And the heart suffers."[23]

Images of Difference

Photographs from the earliest years of the immigration underscore and
further illuminate the widely shared character of refugee responses to the

physical environment and the people they encountered in Bolivia. In family albums especially, in which a sense of period and place is reflected through the principle of selection and arrangement, three types of pictures predominate.[24] The first, of individual refugees and their relatives, is no doubt meant both as a visual private record and as a way of telling about the past. These photos convey aspects of family history: birthdays, celebrations, leisure times, scenes of work, occasions with friends and acquaintances. They are images that connect generations, link the photographer, the subject, and the viewer, and seem to provide reassurance of survival, familial solidity, and endurance in the aftermath of persecution and forced departure. But many of the albums also contain numerous photos of nature: of the immense snow-capped peaks of the Cordillera Real, of the rugged starkness of the altiplano and the precipitous roads and pathways down from the *cumbres* to the lowlands, of Lake Titicaca, and of the junglelike vegetation and lush beauty of the tropical forests. And they all include photographs of indigenous peoples: snapshots of women carrying babies on their backs, of families with llama herds, of market women in bowler or stove-top hats, portraits of children and old people. Consistently, they also display images of women and men dressed in elaborate costumes, sometimes in exquisite masks, playing instruments, dancing, performing in fiestas.

Certainly, when examined at a surface level the numerous photographs of Bolivian landscapes and Indians simply attest to the intense fascination with which the refugees viewed the strangeness of the physical and human environment in which they found themselves. These photographs are all, in this sense, *tourist photos,* within a long tradition of souvenir representation inspired by picture postcards, illustrations in travel magazines, stereoscopic views, and landscape art. They were intended to convey the image "captured" by the photographer to the viewer—to "show it off" or to recall it as an event or to attest to "being present," to "having been there."[25] In Susan Sontag's words, as tourist photos they provide "a way of certifying experience" while actually limiting it "to a search for the photogenic."[26] But these photographs, as Victor Burgin has theorized, also carry a less visible yet profoundly ideological encoding within them. "The intelligibility of the photograph is no simple thing," Burgin cautions in this regard. "Photographs are texts . . . and the 'photographic text,' like any other, is the site of a complex 'intertextuality,' an overlapping series of previous texts 'taken for granted' at a particular cultural and historical conjuncture."[27]

Viewed in this light, it becomes apparent that the nature photos in the albums in fact subdivide into categories. One grouping depicts the refugees' actual physical presence in the landscape: it shows them "there," miniaturized, if not engulfed, by the immense scale and power of their natural surroundings. It also documents their physical involvement with nature: their recreational excursions into its terrain, their hikes and climbs, their explorations of its topography (see figs. 2 and 3). In contrast, a second grouping is marked by the virtual absence of the human subject—by a concentrated focus on dramatic, spectacular, extreme nature. Here, in photo after photo, it is a primal world that is being depicted—a landscape of towering, often volcanic, mountains and scrub-covered hills, of darkly opulent tropical rainforests, of lake view within (see figs. 4, 5, and 6).

It is precisely the persistence of these categories of pictorial representation, and the characteristics of each grouping, that seem to link them ideologically to earlier European imaginings of the South American continent, to discourses about a "wild and gigantic nature" and an "aesthetics of the sublime" that disseminated into German literature and the German popular consciousness through the impact of nineteenth-century romanticism and the epic writings of Alexander von Humboldt. It was Humboldt, after all, as Mary Louise Pratt has argued, who "reinvented South America first and foremost as nature" and who scaled down, if not totally erased, the human within it. It was through his immensely popular and influential works—volumes such as the *History and Geography of the New Continent,* his work *Views of Nature*—and the superbly crafted engravings of natural phenomena within them, that South America was reduced, in Pratt's words, "to pure nature and the iconic triad of mountain, plain, and jungle" (see figs. 7 and 8). Through Humboldt and the romantics the "image of [South America as] primal nature . . . became codified in the European imaginary as the new ideology of the 'new continent.'"[28] Despite the refugees' lack of specific knowledge about Bolivia and its peoples before their departure from Europe, therefore, it would seem that their impressions and representations of the Bolivian physical environment and its inhabitants were *translations,* rather than *quotations,* from the world in which they now found themselves. They were translations based on notions of nature and culture and on ways of seeing and explaining, which, like invisible baggage, they had brought with them to South America. Apparently, the "old geography books" and the "old school lectures" that many recall having informed them in a "general way" about their New World destination shaped their perceptions more profoundly than they actually realized. And, given the content of these perceptions, the refugees' photo-

Fig. 2

graphic fascination with their physical environment makes sense at still another level. "Wild nature"—"captured" in photos, reduced in size, sorted, situated, pasted into family albums, and given permanence—was turned by them into "wild nature, domesticated." With photographic images they supported an illusion of control.

It is another ideological encoding, however, a different discourse, that seems to have been reflected in the photos depicting refugees in their recreational excursions into the landscape (see figs. 9 and 10). Looking at these, one sees new immigrants—young persons like my father and mother, like

Fig. 3

Heinz Jordan, Lotte Weiss, Heinz Pinschower, Alex Deutsch, Ella Wolfinger, and many others—in a relaxed mode, normally in small groups, wading through rivers, climbing rocks, viewing waterfalls, sailing Lake Titicaca, challenging glaciers and mountain summits. They are usually dressed in makeshift hiking clothes—long-sleeved shirts, sweaters, jackets, long or short pants, heavy shoes—and some of them carry rucksacks or rope or grasp walking sticks. In a number of the pictures men wear felt hats, occasionally Tyrolean. It is a rugged and healthy engagement with the outdoors that is represented in these photos. They project youth, vigor, physical fitness, discipline, and a sense of camaraderie and personal fulfillment.

YAMPARI – BOLIVIA

FOT. F.T.

Fig. 4

Fig. 5

Fig. 6

Fig. 7

A View of the Mountains of Chimborazo and Carguairazo, in South America.

Pub.d by Longman Hurst Rees Orme & Brown Aug.t 1811.

Fig. 8

Fig. 9

Indeed, were it not for the fact that the persons being depicted were all recent refugees from Europe, almost all of them Jews, the photographs could be read as no more than souvenir snapshots—recollections of fun outings into the varied environments of nature. But shared history and the European youth movement background of so many of the younger refugees seem present within the photos as well. It was, after all, a central tenet of the Zionist organizations Ha-Shomer Ha-Tsair and Maccabi, to which many of these young immigrants had belonged in Germany or Austria, to advocate physical exercise, sports, muscular development, bodily discipline, and physical engagement with nature as a means of Jewish

Fig. 10

renewal.[29] Are the refugees, in their physical excursions into the rugged landscape, performing according to a notion of personal and social reha- bilitation in vogue in European Jewish (especially Zionist-socialist) youth circles in the 1920s and 1930s? Are they, in effect, representing themselves as examples of a superior "New Hebrew" physical type—strong, fit, self- confident Jews invalidating the negative image of the effete, weak, stooped "Yid" reviled by antisemites? And, paradoxically from our perspective, is there perhaps also in these refugee images a trace of the physicality ideal- ized by highly popular German and Austrian youth organizations such as the Wandervogel, from which Jews had been systematically excluded during the Nazi period? When I look at these photographs of refugee outings today, the tune and words of a song from my childhood in Bolivia repeatedly creep into my mind:

> Das Wandern ist des Müllers Lust, das Wandern,
> das Wandern ist des Müllers Lust, das Wandern.
> Das muss ein schlechter Müller sein,
> dem niemals fiel das Wandern ein, das Wandern,
> das Wandern, das Wandern, das Wandern.[30]

> [Hiking is the miller's pleasure, hiking,
> hiking is the miller's pleasure, hiking . . .]

This is Franz Schubert's "Das Wandern" from *Die Schöne Müllerin*—the song most closely identified with Wandervogel excursions in Europe and one that my parents and their friends often hummed and sang during our Sunday ramblings into Bolivian nature.[31]

But, while the refugees' photographic representations of the physical environment and their own engagement with nature reveal some of the ideological encoding structuring their relationship to the land in which they found themselves, their conceptions of the native "other," and of themselves in relation to that other, seem to emerge most sharply in the numerous photographs of indigenous people that their collections and albums also contain (see figs. 11, 12, 13, 14, and 15). Regardless of whether these photos depict Indians in everyday circumstances—working, caring for children, interacting in small groups, or alone—or show them costumed and masked at festival occasions, they all appear to share a particular quality. Like the photographs of the natural surroundings, they seem to reflect a sense of timelessness, a dehistoricized constancy of existence beyond the vicissitudes of the era in which they were taken. The people in these images, however, are not dehistoricized in the grand sense of a mythic nature or of geological time. Instead, they seem to have been photographed as though they were *ethnic objects* in an ethnographic deep freeze, removed and disconnected from a historical past and from any claims on a political present. Their diverse cultural background and the differences between them—whether they are Aymara or Quechua, rural or urban, *cholos* or campesinos—have been subordinated to a composite notion of "Indianness," a stereotype of racial uniformity in which traces of

Karl May's imaginary Winnetou and numerous representations of America's "Indians" in European popular culture can surely be detected.[32]

In looking at these photos, I would certainly not deny the legitimate pleasures that an encounter with indigenous people occasionally brought to refugees like my mother and father: that the aesthetics of the occasion, its novelty, color, adventure, or some such factor, may have stimulated their taking and keeping Indian photographs.[33] At the same time, despite the range of factors that might have inspired these photos to be made, it was a consistent characteristic of these encounters that the refugee photographers—European, white, generally bourgeois, and, most probably, male—were the spectators, the persons looking, the observers in possession of the power to record. Rarely in these early photos are refugees visible in the same frame with indigenous people. No relationship between them is depicted, no mutuality of observation. The Indians have been photographed as exotics, for the striking character of their difference. And in their lack of reciprocity to the camera's gaze the inequality of the encounter can be seen. They are the ones being observed; their images are the objects being collected. The refugees, out of the frame, behind the camera, gazing at the other, enhance their own identity in the perceived contrast. In the image of the difference they shore up their sense of "civilized" self and confirm a vision for themselves that many of them may have begun to question in the aftermath of their traumatic experience of displacement—a vision of European cultural modernity and of progress.[34]

Los Judios Alemanes

It is, of course, important to stress that neither the refugees nor the Bolivians whom they encountered were in any sense a homogeneous group. When the refugees arrived in the late 1930s, Bolivia was, as it remains today, the most Indian of the American republics. Only some 5 percent of Bolivia's approximately 3,250,000 native inhabitants at the time belonged to the Spanish-speaking, urban elite—the predominantly Catholic elite that identified itself as "white," was educated in the ways of European culture, and had ruled the country politically and economically since its independence from Spain. A larger population of mestizos, persons of Spanish and Indian parentage or descent, belonged to the urban lower-middle and lower classes or were rural freeholders and were located in the social hierarchy in a rung well beneath that of the dominant elite. Its members spoke

Fig. 11

Fig. 12

Fig. 13

Fig.14

Fig. 15

Spanish as well as one of the Amerindian languages, received less formal education and inculcation in European cultural ways and outlooks, dressed in Western but also in the uniquely *cholo* style, and practiced a Catholicism strongly influenced by the belief systems and folk religion of the indigenous populations. They, however, identified themselves as apart, and socially above, the largely subordinated and exploited Quechua- and Aymara-speaking Indian majority: different from the more than 70 percent of Bolivia's population that serviced the dominant groups as manual laborers, servants, workers, farmers, miners, and soldiers.

The refugees, in turn, sprang from broadly similar cultural and ethnic backgrounds, but their origins and social status had been diverse in Central Europe, ranging across generational, educational, political, and class lines and incorporating various professional backgrounds. They included persons who had at one time been engineers, doctors, lawyers, musicians, actors, and artists as well as a large number of both skilled and unskilled workers whose living had been interrupted by Nazi exclusionary decrees. The majority who came to Bolivia were Jews or married to Jews. Some, however, were non-Jewish political refugees: communists, socialists, and others persecuted by the Nazi regime. The Jews themselves differed greatly in the degree of their identification with their religion and its traditions. There were Zionists among them, atheists, orthodox believers, "High Holiday" Jews, and nonpractitioners. They shared a common identity as Jews only in the sense, perhaps, that they had all been defined as Jews from the outside—that the Nazis had "othered" them as Jews.

No matter what their background differences had been in Europe, however, the vast majority of refugees arrived in dire straits, with few personal possessions and very little money. This in itself had a leveling effect, cutting across previous class distinctions. But there were other factors, too, that helped the refugees to create a sense of collective identity, aiding their adjustment and survival. Despite differences of detail, their common history of persecution was certainly one of these. Each and every one of the refugees had been identified as undesirable, stripped of citizenship and possessions. They were all "in the same boat." The war back in Europe, as well as their separation from relatives and friends, was also an ever-present reality of which they were collectively conscious and which bonded them together. They kept themselves—one another—informed of news about the war from accounts in the press and radio, and they shared efforts to discover the fate of those left behind. In this regard the German language (which they still spoke at home and among themselves) served as a vehicle of inquiry, information, and unity. It allowed them to communicate intimately and to express themselves with a degree of familiarity that most could never attain in the Spanish of their surroundings. German permitted them to maintain a wider connection with refugees and immigrants in other countries and throughout Bolivia—by means of their own newspaper, the *Rundschau vom Illimani,* which Ernst Schumacher established in La Paz in 1939, or the important *Aufbau* of New York or the *Jüdische Wochenschau* of Buenos Aires.[35]

But it was memory—the employment of memory by the refugees to connect their present to a particular version of the past—that served as the creative tool of adjustment, helping to ease cultural uprootedness and alienation. No sooner had they arrived in Bolivia when a process began by which the immigrants recalled, negotiated, and reshaped their memories of Europe. They employed elements of these memories to re-create institutions, symbolic practices, and a style of life that they had previously shared. Collective memory became the basis on which they built a communal "culture" to serve their changing needs.

It was no doubt from their recollections of the Israelitische Kultusgemeinden of Berlin and Vienna that one of the first centers of collective immigrant activity, the Comunidad Israelita, was founded in La Paz in 1939 by refugees from Germany and Austria. This communal organization established a synagogue, a home for the aged, a *Kinderheim* serving as kindergarten, boarding, and day care center, and a school, La Escuela Boliviana-Israelita. But, from its inception, the Comunidad also fulfilled a very different social function. Its quarters became a clubhouse in which people could gather, eat meals, read newspapers, play cards, chess, or Ping-Pong—where they could gossip, socialize, exchange information, and reminisce about their lives, loves, and the past.[36] The Comunidad became a version of an institution that many of the immigrants would have remembered with nostalgia: the *Klublokal,* or coffeehouse, of Central Europe.

And, within a relatively short period, in 1939 and the early 1940s, the refugees created other organizations, established shops and restaurants, and developed cultural activities that reconnected them to a way of life from which they had been forcibly detached. A glance through the pages of the *Rundschau vom Illimani* and *Jüdische Wochenschau* of these years provides illustrative examples. The Hogar Austriaco (Austrian Home, as the Austrian club was called), the associations Das Andere Deutschland and Freies Deutschland, the League of Women of the Comunidad, and the

Macabi Sports Club; the Cafe Viena, Club Metropol, Cafe-Restaurant Weiner; the Pension Neumann, Pension Europa; the Haberdashery Berlin, Casa Paris-Viena, Peleteria Viena; the Buchhandlung La America advertising German editions of Franz Werfel, Paul Zech, Bruno Weil; the *Kleinkunstbühne* (cabaret theater) presenting scenes from Schnitzler, Hoffmansthal, Beer-Hoffmann, as well as readings of German classics; the Colegium Musicum with its chamber music concerts and recitals featuring Mozart, Beethoven, and Schubert played by musicians trained at conservatories in Vienna, Prague, and Berlin—these, and many others, attest to the range of the immigrants' economic and institutional adjustment in Bolivia and confirm the character of their symbolic reconnection with Central Europe.[37]

Children of the refugees like me, especially during the early years of the immigration, received both formal and informal tuition strongly influenced by cultural memories of Europe. The intended purpose behind the establishment of the Escuela Boliviana-Israelita, for example, was twofold: the school offered courses in Spanish, so that recently arrived children might learn the language of the land, and it instructed them in the three Rs as well as in Jewish religion and history. From its inception, moreover, Bolivian officials also required the school to hire a Bolivian teacher to instruct its pupils in local and national history, in what the Bolivians called *educación civica*.[38] Apart from the Spanish language classes and *educación civica*, however, the pedagogical methods and general curriculum of the Escuela Boliviana-Israelita differed little from those employed in elementary schools in Germany and Austria before the rise of Nazism. The examples the immigrant teachers used in their subjects of instruction derived, as one might have expected, from their Central European cultural background and experience.

Sifting through memorabilia of which I became the keeper when my mother died,

I look at my report cards for grades one through four from the Escuela Boliviana Israelita. Seeing my grades in geography and music, I try to recall if I was in my first or second school year when Dr. Asher first taught us to locate the Danube, Rhine, and the Alps on a map of Europe, and when it was that Mr. Aaron, who played a portable piano and the accordion, taught us to sing Ha-tikvah *as well as German folk songs.*

I find five of my childhood books. Two of them, Max und Moritz: Eine Bubengeschichte in sieben Streichen *(Max and Moritz: A Boys' Tale in Seven Episodes) by Wilhelm Busch (my copy published in Santiago de Chile), and H. Hoffman's* Der Struwwelpeter *(Shock-headed Peter), are cautionary tales that my parents and grandmother read aloud to me dozens of times. They contain my scribblings and, probably, the earliest existent sample of my nickname, Poldi, printed in pencil in my own hand- writing. It is, I am quite certain, because of the horrible penalty paid by Konrad in "Die Geschichte vom Daumen-Lutscher" (The Story of the Thumb-Sucker) and Paulinchen in "Die gar traurige Geschichte mit dem Feuerzeug" (The Truly Sad Story with the Lighter) that I never sucked my thumbs and was fearful about playing with matches. Two other books—an illustrated German children's edition of* Grimm's Fairy Tales *and Frida Schanz's* Schulkindergeschichten—*were also read to me by my grandmother Lina. The fifth, a children's book in Spanish and printed on wartime paper now yellowed by time, is* Beethoven, El Sacrificio de Un Niño. *Beethoven and Johann Strauss were my father's favorite composers.*

I discover that an undated Hogar Austriaco *cabaret program is also among the memorabilia. It introduces a show, "Radio Wien Sendet: Ein Wunschkabarett" (Radio Vienna Broadcasts: A Cabaret on Demand) and lists, among its entertainment numbers, "In einem Wiener Vorstadt- varieté" (In a Viennese Suburban Music Hall), "Ein Maederl aus Moedling" (A Lass from Moedling), "Frauen sind zum Kuessen da" (Women Are Made to Be Kissed), and various other skits in Viennese dialect.*

In spite of the persecution they had endured, therefore, and Nazi efforts to depict them as the other, it was Austro/German culture—and, in partic- ular, Austro/German Jewish bourgeois culture as it had existed in the cap- ital cities—that provided the refugees with a model for emulation and a common locus for identification. This held true even for persons, like my parents and others, who had come from a working-class background and whose political sympathies lay with Marxism. Commenting on the charac- ter of this identification with some irony, Egon Schwarz noted how often the immigrants began their sentences with the phrase "Back home in Ger- many . . ." or "Back home in our country . . ." and how one man, in a con- versation with him, had actually exclaimed: "Back home in our concentra- tion camp. . . ."[39] At the very time when that dynamic social and cultural amalgam, European Jewish bourgeois culture, was being ruthlessly and systematically destroyed by the Nazis, these refugees attempted to revive aspects of it in an alien land thousands of miles from their home: in a country that offered them a haven but in which many—perhaps most—of them felt they were mere sojourners.

"And They Looked at Us . . ."

Given the virtual absence of Jews in Bolivia before the refugee influx in the late 1930s, the appearance of large numbers of European immigrants was certainly a noticeable fact to the Bolivian inhabitants of the land. Not surprisingly, however, both Bolivian written and oral records of the encounter with the incoming refugees largely reflect the views and perceptions of persons belonging to the literate middle and upper sectors of society, a relatively small segment of the total national population. It is difficult to know what kind of impression the presence of this sizable group of new foreigners made on the highland Aymara and Quechua people who first met them or how they were viewed by persons belonging to smaller indigenous settlements in the tropical lowlands of the country. While it is indeed probable that memories of the refugees' appearance and early presence exist within the personal recollections of some of Bolivia's Indian inhabitants, these seem not to have been orally transmitted outside of the confines of family or small-group conversation. They appear to have remained unrecorded in writing or in other, more widely disseminated forms of popular representation, and, as such, they have been virtually inaccessible for analysis.

Quite possibly, of course, the immigrant newcomers made no *special* impression on the vast majority of the indigenous population. Indians, and even *cholos,* who worked for or with refugees and who had the opportunity to encounter them for a longer than casual basis might have noticed few if any physical and cultural distinctions between recent immigrants from Central Europe and other whites who had preceded them in Bolivia. Although the younger Ana who worked for our family as a domestic servant may have been a native of La Paz or have lived in the city for some time, many of the *sirvientas* and indigenous day wage laborers were themselves recent arrivals in Bolivia's urban centers—relatively new immigrants from the rural areas who had moved to the cities on a temporary or permanent basis in search of better living and working conditions.[40] They had come from a relatively isolated countryside where Aymara or Quechua, and not Spanish, was the predominant language, where herding and the slower seasonal demands of agriculture had influenced the tempo of social and familial life, and had emigrated to cities that operated on different time rhythms—places that must have seemed crowded by comparison, bustling with diverse people, and which offered material enticements that were only accessible through participation in a cash economy. As Antonieta Huanca recalled for the anthropologist Lesley Gill in the mid-1980s about her first impression of La Paz when she saw the city from the altiplano as a ten-year-old girl:

> All the houses looked so tiny, and I was afraid to get on a bus to go down. There were so many people, and the smell of gasoline made me sick to my stomach. My aunt and I didn't speak Spanish, only Aymara, so it took a while to find our way around and to learn the names of things.[41]

In the cities access to the cash economy—to jobs and material resources—was structured by work experience, skill, and a rigid, gender-based division of labor. Male newcomers from the hinterlands usually entered the cash economy at the very lowest rung, as day laborers employed as load carriers (*cargadores*) or as unskilled manual workers engaged in heavy physical jobs such as ditch digging, stone breaking, and road repair. In these jobs their contact with the European refugees was minimal, and the effect of the impact of the refugee influx on their everyday lives would, undoubtedly, have been extremely superficial. Indigenous men and *cholos* who had lived in the city for some time, however, found employment of a semiskilled and skilled nature—in construction jobs as mechanics, plumbers, electricians, bricklayers, painters, and the like—and they tended to have more extensive and closer contacts with European refugees who were employed in similar work. Photos from the earliest years of the immigration in our family albums, for example, show my father, my grandfather Nathan, my uncles, and other Central European refugees working at various construction sites together with indigenous Bolivians. In some of these photographs both Bolivian and European workers pose together smiling in a group, and, even though physical differences between "natives" and "foreigners" are clearly discernible, the cultural distinctions between individuals in the pictures seem submerged beneath the complementarity of their endeavor. And yet, despite the apparent leveling effect of joint enterprise—of engagement together in similar work over extended periods of time—no verbal remembrance from the Bolivian workers has come down to us to accompany the photos, and one is left wondering about the incompleteness of the represented encounter. How did these indigenous and *cholo* Bolivians regard the German-speaking gringos[42] with whom they worked—white men who actually got their hands dirty and did hard physical labor? What about competition within the job and over jobs? feelings of inequity? mutual exclusivity? misinterpretations based on linguistic and cultural differences? conflicts about notions of time and attitudes to work? Did they feel economically threatened by the arrival of so many European refugees over such a short period of time—or did they even notice that this was taking place?

Indigenous women and *cholas* had access to different spheres of the urban economy than did the men. Women either created work for themselves by selling agricultural or other merchandise on the streets or in the marketplaces, or they searched for positions as domestic servants. In the latter case they worked primarily in the homes of the Bolivian white and mestizo upper classes but also—after refugees began to gain some financial resources—in the households of European immigrants. Although factors such as class, ethnic background, and household composition influenced relations and expectations between employers and servants, domestic service, no matter where it was carried out, always placed the *sirvientas* in a subordinate position vis-à-vis their bosses.[43] Yet, here again, our inability to tap the recollections of domestic workers from the early years of the refugee influx limits any detailed understanding of *sirvienta* perceptions of immigrant employers. We are thus left to speculate how *sirvientas* processed the fact that refugee households were generally less affluent than those of Bolivian employers, that refugees tended to be Jewish rather than Catholic in belief, that refugee señoras, unlike their upper-class Bolivian counterparts, sought work outside of the home to supplement the household income, that among the relatively recent immigrants the male *patrón* exercised little power over family and household affairs, that wartime concerns and fearful insecurities characterized so many refugee conversations and interactions, that, indeed, the persons that employed them *were refugees:* persecuted outcasts who had been forced to flee from the countries in which they had been born. Despite the asymmetrical nature of the relationships involved in these situations of domestic service—despite differences in class, ethnic background, culture, and outlook—the intimacy and extended nature of the mutual encounter between servants and employers within the confines of a home would suggest that neither could have remained indifferent to the lives of the other.[44] And yet details about this interaction between refugees and *sirvientas,* unvoiced and unrecorded by the latter, seem destined to elude us.

But what about other Bolivians? How did members of the literate middle sector of society—the Spanish-speaking mestizos—as well as persons belonging to the europeanized white minority elite respond to the refugee influx?

Big Noses and Elders of Zion

In March 1939 the *Revista de Bolivia* published a photo of the first-prize winners in a Carnival contest for most humorous costume.[45] It shows a couple facing the camera: a "husband" dressed in a dark, shabby suit, wearing a fedora pulled nearly down to his ears, carrying a large carpetbag, and standing arm in arm with his "wife." "She," obviously a man dressed in women's clothing, is wearing a curly-haired wig and hat, dark glasses, smeared-on lipstick, an oversized overcoat, and is carrying an umbrella. The most conspicuous feature in the photo, however, is the husband's oversized nose, a beaklike protuberance overwhelming his face.

Entitled "Los judios," the picture requires little interpretation. The prize-winning couple is clearly parodying the forlorn appearance of many of the Jewish refugees entering Bolivia at the time—the shabbiness of their dress and the poverty of their material possessions. But it is the representation of a stereotype of Jewish physical appearance, the depiction of the grossly enlarged "Jewish nose" on the "husband," that is undoubtedly meant to trigger the viewer's guffaw. Jews are characterized and recognizable by their big noses, the costumed pair is reminding onlookers. See the funny-looking Jews!

A year later, in March 1940, the La Paz newspaper *El Echo Libre* printed a cartoon on its front page showing two opulent and corpulent Jews, each with a sizable nose, pulling a Bolivian citizen to a cross to crucify him.[46] In Cochabamba, Bolivia's second largest city, the newspaper *La Prensa* published a series of editorials and articles in November 1940 decrying the presence of "a Jewish beast" and of "rancid" Jews "with nauseous odor and a devilish attitude" and warning of a "Jewish pestilence [brought on by] . . . this race cursed by God and mankind." Focusing on "the typical smell of the Jews, the nauseous smell . . . somewhat stronger than that of the animals of the highlands," Dr. Cesar Herrera argued in the newspaper that this bodily odor revealed Jews to be hereditary carriers of leprosy—potentially fatal sources of infection to unaware Christians with whom they came in contact.[47]

In letters written during this period of intensive Jewish immigration, moreover, refugees also complained that the epithets "Judio" and "Sucio Judio" (Dirty Jew) were occasionally hurled contemptuously at them and that they were called "murderers of Christ." They told of being jostled and hassled in the streets, ignored or insulted by officials, and that graffiti proclaiming "¡Basta de Judios!" (No more Jews!) and "¡Fuera Judios!" (Jews Out!) would sometimes be scrawled on their doors and walls. Given their generally impoverished condition upon arriving in Bolivia, refugees also found it particularly ironic that some Bolivians considered them "money grubbers," identifying them with usury, unfair financial dealings, and "international Jewish capitalist" schemes for world economic domination.[48]

Many of the stereotypes behind these Bolivian antisemitic expressions did, of course, derive from the hoary Spanish-Catholic popular tradition blaming Jews for the killing of Jesus and from ancient images depicting Jews as avaricious, physically unattractive, and potentially dangerous "outsiders"—from anti-Jewish prejudices that had been brought to South America from Europe centuries earlier. They were, in this sense, the "invisible baggage" carried by Bolivians in their encounter with the refugees. But, since few "real" Jews lived in Bolivia until the mid-1930s, the fact that these stereotypes were retained so vividly within the consciousness of the dominant elites and the mestizo urban lower-middle and lower classes and that they reemerged with such frightening vehemence after the refugees' arrival reflects a peculiar characteristic of anti-Jewish prejudice throughout history—that in Europe, and in areas influenced by European colonial expansionism, antisemitism existed and persisted even where Jews were virtually absent.

It was clear, however, that the virulence of some Bolivian antisemitism in the late 1930s and during World War II was inspired by Nazi propaganda and activities—by efforts of German officials, pro-Hitler German residents, and fascist sympathizers within the Bolivian civilian and military elites to focus on Jewish refugee immigration and stir up antisemitic sentiment, as a way to further their own political and strategic agendas in this region of the South American continent. Two related examples confirm this.

The first centered on a scandal over the illegal sale of Bolivian visas to Jews in Europe uncovered in mid-1939, a few months before the death of President German Busch, the Chaco War hero who had been the most powerful supporter of the admission of Central European refugees to

Bolivia.[49] The discovery that a ring of consular officials in Europe, allegedly with the compliance and active involvement of Foreign Minister Eduardo Diez de Medina, had sold thousands of Bolivian immigration permits at the consulates in Warsaw, Hamburg, Genoa, Paris, and Zurich, pocketing millions of U.S. dollars from their dealings, was seized by a number of Bolivian politicians as a propaganda windfall. They utilized this scandal to rally and enlarge popular support against outsiders and against foreign domination of natural resources and the national economy.[50] They alleged that Diez de Medina was motivated by greed and sympathies stemming from his own "crypto-Jewish" familial background, his surname suggesting New Christian origins. Implying guilt by association, some hinted at an international conspiracy between Jews and capitalists to control Bolivia's wealth and exploit its people, singling out the Austrian Jewish tin mining magnate Mauricio Hochschild's central involvement in the economy and his role in facilitating refugee immigration as confirmation of their dire warnings.[51] Pointing to the influx of numerous refugees who, instead of complying with visa stipulations requiring their settlement as agricultural colonists, had remained in the cities in economic competition with Bolivians, a number of politicians called for an immediate cessation of refugee immigration. Others, seeking more drastic measures, demanded the expulsion of all newcomers. "Jews are an unhealthful element" because of their "selfish social, racial, and moral principles," declared the group of "independent" deputies who introduced an (ultimately unsuccessful) bill to bar Jews from the country in August 1940.[52] The newspapers *La Razon, El Echo Libre,* and *La Cronica* in La Paz and *La Prensa* and *El País* in Cochabamba joined the attack with an ongoing campaign of anti-Jewish articles and editorials.[53] And, in November 1940, when Diez de Medina was eventually put on trial for his alleged role in the sale of sanctuary to European refugees, spectators in the packed galleries of the Chamber of Deputies kept up a steady chant of "Down with the Jews! Death to the Jews!"[54]

Although the antisemitic agitation subsided by mid-1941, when President Enrique Peñaranda used the exposure of an alleged pro-Axis plot to overthrow his government to expel the German ambassador and crack down on fascist and other extremist political critics, it resumed with renewed intensity in September 1942 when the Chamber of Deputies debated another bill to exclude "Jews, Negroes, and Orientals" from the country.[55] In the course of the debate Deputy Zuazo Cuenca read aloud portions from *The Protocols of the Elders of Zion*—a tsarist forgery alleging a Jewish conspiracy to dominate the world—as well as from the Henry Ford–sponsored book *The International Jew.* In supporting him, Deputy Gustavo Chacón described the Jewish immigrants as "parasitical suckers of the national moneys," warning that they would bleed the country dry. Other deputies denounced the "international character of Judaism" as a potential threat to Bolivian institutions, maintaining that, wherever Jews penetrated in the world, they came to dominate the press, banks, and politics. The newspaper *La Calle,* in one of its many editorials supporting the exclusion bill, lamented the "inundation" of the country by immigrants "with very beaked noses," by members of the "Jewish race" who were waiting "to fall like a ravenous invading horde upon the cities of Bolivia" and planning to gain control of the government. Jews, another article declared, were "corrupter[s] of defenseless people" who, if not stopped at the gates, would cast a "noose" over the heads of Bolivians. Jews, as "a race," a number of influential members of the Bolivian political and press elites concluded, posed a danger to Bolivia's "nationality" and should be expelled.[56]

While it is possible, as some believed at the time, that documents implicating the German ambassador and Nazi officials in plans for a pro-Axis putsch were counterintelligence fabrications of the United States government, no such uncertainty exists about direct and indirect Nazi efforts to stir up antisemitic and anti-refugee resentments in Bolivia and bolster sympathetic Bolivian nationalist politicians in their pro-German, anti-American, anti-British stance.[57] Not long after Zuazo Cuenca read sections from *The Protocols of the Elders of Zion* to the galleries and into the record of the Chamber of Deputies, it was revealed that the portions he had "selected" came from the pamphlet *Ilustrativo y Informativo Material para Oradores* (Illustrative and Informative Material for Orators), published and translated by the German Office of Propaganda.[58] Until his expulsion Ernst Wendler, the German ambassador, had also been *Landeskreisleiter* of the Nazi party in Bolivia, which, according to official German records for the period, counted 170 active members and over 1,100 pro-Nazi supporters throughout the country.[59] It was also no secret that the German embassy had subsidized the two most malevolent antisemitic newspapers in La Paz, *La Razon* and *La Calle,* as well as *El Imparcial, El País,* and *La Prensa* in Cochabamba.[60]

It would, however, be a grand distortion to confine any survey of Bolivian middle-sector and elite responses to Jews during this period of intense refugee immigration only to examples of negative stereotyping and antisemitism. By far the most widely held reactions to the Jewish presence

ranged from indifference to tolerance to a welcoming, sympathetic acceptance. During the peak immigration months, in the late 1930s, and
throughout the war years and beyond, many Bolivians forcefully defended
the immigrants. Their voices and opinions, expressed publicly in forums
and in print, provided a strong counterpoint to antisemitic hate mongering
and worked to reassure the refugees of important support within Bolivian
establishment ranks. Indeed, from the earliest days of the refugees' arrival
in the country, goodwill and trust characterized the relationship of many
Bolivians toward them. Bolivians, in this respect, "made space" for the
immigrants, allowing them to set up businesses and to enter and participate in numerous entrepreneurial activities. They also made space physically and culturally, so the immigrants could establish their own social and
cultural institutions.

Refugees recalling their emigration to Bolivia in writing or oral testimony have been universally grateful to Bolivians for saving their lives.[61]
Bolivian antisemitism, despite its persistence, is usually remembered as a
relatively minor episode within a sojourn fraught with challenges and
difficulties but also characterized by relative tolerance. No matter how
brief or lengthy their residence in Bolivia would be, this Andean land
inserted itself into the memory of these émigrés as the place that gave them
refuge when all others had rejected them. "For better or for worse," Ilse
Hertz observed in her recollection of the emigration, "Bolivians permitted
us to live."[62] It was in Bolivia that the refugees survived the horrors of the
Nazi Holocaust. Consciousness of that overwhelming reality is the background against which their present-day memories have been constructed.

Apartness within the Contact Zone

In her recent work *Imperial Eyes* Mary Louise Pratt has coined the term
contact zone to identify the type of social space marking the encounter of
peoples previously separated by geography and history. Within a contact
zone members of encountering groups interact on an individual and collective basis, establishing ongoing relations with each other. Generally
speaking, contact zones have varied over time and from place to place.
Relations between encountering groups within them have, as during the
colonial era, for example, reflected situations of domination and subordination and "conditions of coercion, radical inequality, and intractable
conflict."[63] But relations within contact zones have also been characterized
by significant degrees of cultural reciprocity and hybridity and by the phe-

nomenon of "transculturation"—by the way encountering individuals and groups absorb as well as shape and influence their construction and constitution of one another.[64]

In the Bolivian contact zone within which the mutual encounter between Central European refugees and Bolivians occurred, there was significant economic interaction but relatively little cultural reciprocity and hybridity—little breakdown of the cultural, social, and political boundaries that distinguished refugee and host groups. Paradoxically, the very institutions the refugees created in Bolivia and the symbols and memories on which they relied for their collective identity in their land of refuge were instrumental in maintaining barriers between them and Bolivians. Thus, while one might have expected to find some greater degree of social and cultural interaction and interchange between the refugees and those Bolivians closer to them in social background—with the Spanish-speaking white and mestizo middle classes and with members of the professional and ruling elites—relatively little, in fact, took place. The immigrants' reconstituted culture—based on Central European Jewish bourgeois values, on the German language, on a certain conception of "modernity," literature, music, and hygiene, and on their liberal and materialistic worldview—proved irreconcilable with what they perceived to be a deeply rooted Catholicism, intensely private family lifestyle, social conservatism, and industrial "backwardness" of middle- and upper-class Bolivians.

The middle- and upper-class Bolivians, of course, also maintained largely impermeable barriers between themselves and the immigrants. Guarding access to Bolivian citizenship by means of lengthy residency and complex naturalization regulations, they relegated the vast majority of refugees to the legally much less secure status of "resident alien," which strongly discouraged and, in effect, generally impeded refugee participation in the political realm, which the Bolivian elites controlled. Personally as well, their social interactions with the immigrants were largely superficial. Certainly, flirtations and sexual encounters did occasionally occur. But marriages between Bolivians (the vast majority of whom were Catholic) and Jewish refugees were extremely rare and, in the few instances in which they did take place, were viewed by members of both groups as eccentric departures from the communal fold.[65] Despite business and professional dealings with the immigrants, moreover, it was highly uncommon for Bolivians to invite them to their house. Culturally and, in many respects, socially, Bolivians and refugees remained one another's other.

Appearances

Two young children, holding hands, are standing in a yard by a house. There are plants near them—not in the ground but in large tin cans. Nature contained. In the background a woman wearing a dress and apron and holding a pot is partially visible, her shoulders, neck, and head cut off by the top edge of the photograph. One of the children is Indian. She is dark complexioned, black haired, and is smiling broadly, looking directly at the photographer. A knit cap with ear flaps covers most of her hair, and she wears a torn gray-toned cardigan over an undershirt and a soiled, ripped skirt. She is barefooted. The other child, blond, fair complexioned, is wearing a light sweater, striped seersucker overalls with cuffs, and shiny black shoes, and has one of his hands in a pocket. He is also smiling—less broadly perhaps—and his eyes look off to the side, away both from his companion and the camera. The blond boy is Poldi—Leopoldo—now known as Leo. I no longer remember the name of the Indian child.

In my father's handwriting the printed caption above and beneath the photo in the album reads: "Sechzen monate! und hab' einen freund!" (Sixteen months! And hav'a friend!) Freund *is masculine in German.* Freundin *is a female friend. This ambiguity—between the Indian child's gender as identified by my father and gender as indicated by her?/his? worn skirt—is curious but possibly inadvertent. Either my father made a mistake in identification, or the child was indeed a boy. But other uncertainties—involving meaning, not identification—also accompany this photo. "Every photograph presents us with two messages," John Berger tells us: "A message concerning the event photographed and another concerning a shock of discontinuity. Between the moment recorded and the present moment of looking at [a] photograph, there is an abyss."[66] The photograph's ambiguities reside in this "discontinuity," in this "abyss between the moment recorded and the moment of looking."[67]*

What could the event in this photographic image have meant for the young Indian child? What was its meaning for Poldi? For the photographer? For the person later assembling the album? Were we truly playmates—friends—as the caption insists? Or, perhaps, could the photograph and its description really have been intended as a commentary on differences—on our "obvious" racial and class distinctions as manifested in our contrasting physical appearances and clothing? Did the picture's placement in the album imply that it was as absurd to maintain the possibility of real friendship between "these children" as it was to declare that, at the age of sixteen months, Poldi could really

SECHZEHN MONATE!

ICH KANN SCHON SCHREIBEN! UND HAB'EINEN FREUND!

Fig. 16

write? Alternatively, did this photo and its caption represent one of my par-
ents' immigrant fantasies—their "fairy tale" of New World acceptance and
integration: the child of refugees holding the hand of a child of Bolivia's
indigenous inhabitants? If so, it was a fairy tale that would be marred by a
frightening and violent reality. This young Indian child, whose name or gen-
der I am unable to recall, was killed not long after our photo was taken,
hurled to the street from a second story balcony by the crazed son of our land-
lord. Our picture together, smiling, holding hands, may be the only image in
existence of this child's appearance.

NOTES

This essay incorporates some material previously published in "Andean Waltz," in *Holocaust Remembrance: The Shapes of Memory*, ed. Geoffrey H. Hartman (Oxford: Blackwell, 1994), 161–74; and "Invisible Baggage in a Refuge from Nazism," *Diaspora* 2 (1993): 305–36.

1. "Cholo[a]" is a complex social category that originated during the colonial era in the Andean region as a designation for persons culturally and racially "in between" peninsular Spaniards and Indians. As Lesley Gill has indicated, "the category represents a vast social and cultural frontier between the racial divisions of 'Indios' and 'blancos' (whites); a classificatory schema that the descendants of the Spanish conquerors and other 'whites' have struggled to maintain for hundreds of years. Because of its amorphous character, the boundaries that separate 'cholos' from 'Indios' and 'whites' are constantly contested." See Lesley Gill, *Precarious Dependencies: Gender, Class, and Domestic Service in Bolivia* (New York: Columbia University Press, 1994), 4. Also see Linda J. Seligman, "To Be in Between: The Cholas as Market Women," in *Constructing Culture and Power in Latin America*, ed. Daniel H. Levine (Ann Arbor: University of Michigan Press, 1993), 269–70.

2. See M. Lissette Canavesi de Sahonero, *El Traje de la Chola Paceña* (La Paz: Los Amigos del Libro, 1987).

3. See the detailed account in Herbert A. Strauss, "Jewish Emigration from Germany: Nazi Policies and Jewish Responses," *Leo Baeck Institute Year Book* 25 (1980): 313–61, and 26 (1981): 343–409. Although a large number of refugees were admitted to Bolivia conditionally, as *agricultores*—with visas stipulating that the immigrants settle in rural areas and engage in agriculture or related occupations—the majority, coming from urban backgrounds, managed to remain and settle in the country's urban centers.

4. In 1942 a census of all foreign-born immigrants over the age of sixteen was carried out throughout Bolivia. No summary analysis of that census exists, but over fifteen thousand of the original individual census questionnaires, including

the immigrant's photo, birthplace, birthdate, date of immigration, occupation, marital/parental status, and place of residence in Bolivia, can be found in boxes marked "Censo de Extanjeros, 1942—Judios" at the Archivo de La Paz, La Paz, Bolivia.

5. The name Diez de Medina, for example. The name Sucre itself, of course, has been the subject of some controversy. The "Liberator" and founder of the Bolivian republic, Antonio José de Sucre, after whom the city of Sucre was named, is sometimes traced back to a Jewish ancestor named Zucker, who is said to have emigrated to Alto Perú from Uffenheim, Bavaria, in the eighteenth century. See "Bolivia," in *Comunidades Judias de Latinoamerica, 1971–1972* (Buenos Aires: Comité Judio Americano, 1972), 101. For early Jewish settlement in Bolivia, see Jacob Beller, *Jews in Latin America* (New York: J. David, 1969), 211–12; J. X. Cohen, *Jewish Life in South America: A Survey Study for the American Jewish Congress* (New York: Bloch, 1941), 111–21; Judith Laikin Elkin, *Jews of the Latin American Republics* (Chapel Hill: University of North Carolina Press, 1980), 3–24; Marc J. Osterweil, "The Meaning of Elitehood: Germans, Jews and Arabs in La Paz, Bolivia" (Ph.D. diss., New York University, 1978), 55–58; Jacob Shatzky, *Comunidades Judias en Latinoamerica* (Buenos Aires: American Jewish Committee, 1952), 100–101.

6. See Günter Friedländer, "Bolivia," *American Jewish Year Book* 59 (1958): 410–11; Beller, *Jews in Latin America,* 211–12; Marek Ajke, "Colectividad y Vida Comunitaria Judia en Bolivia," *Medio Siglo de Vida Judia en La Paz* (La Paz: Circulo Israelita, 1987), 17–18.

7. See Haim Avni, *Argentina and the Jews: A History of Jewish Immigration* (Tuscaloosa: University of Alabama Press, 1991); Jeffrey Lesser, *Welcoming the Undesirables: Brazil and the Jewish Question* (Berkeley: University of California Press, 1995); Susane Worcman, ed., *Heranças e Lembranças: Imigrantes Judeus no Rio de Janeiro* (Rio de Janeiro: Associacao Religiosa Israelita do Rio de Janeiro, 1991); Elkin, *Jews of the Latin American Republics;* Judith Laikin Elkin and Gilbert W. Merkx, eds., *The Jewish Presence in Latin America* (Boston: Allen and Unwin, 1987).

8. Egon Schwarz, *Keine Zeit für Eichendorff: Chronik unfreiwilliger Wanderjahre* (Königstein: Athenaum, 1979), 58; videotaped interview with Andres J. Simon, La Paz, Bolivia, 22 July 1991; videotaped interview with Renate Schwarz, Teaneck, NJ, 2 May 1991.

9. Rudolf Dienst, *Im dunkelsten Bolivien: Anden, Pampa und Urwaldfahrten* (Stuttgart: Strecker und Schröder, 1926); Theodor Herzog, *Vom Urwald zu den Gletschern der Kordillere: Zwei Forschungsreisen in Bolivia* (Stuttgart: Strecker and Schröder, 1923).

10. Hilfsverein der Juden in Deutschland, *Jüdische Auswanderung nach Südamerika* (Berlin: Jüdischer Kulturbund in Deutschland, 1939), 21, 23; my translation.

11. Videotaped interview with Werner Guttentag, Cochabamba, Bolivia, 31 July 1991; videotaped interview with Julio Meier, La Paz, 5 August 1991; videotaped interview with Egon Taus, Los Angeles, 21 April 1992; videotaped interview with Heinz Markstein, Vienna, 25 June 1992. See Karl May, *In den Kordilleren* and *Das Vermächtnis des Inka,* vols. 13 and 39 of the *Gesammelte Werke* (Bamberg: Karl-May-Verlag, 1961) Also see Christian Heermann, *Der Mann, der Old Shatterhand War: Eine Karl-May-Biographie* (Berlin: Verlag der Nation, 1988); Marin Lowsky, *Karl May* (Stuttgart: J. B. Metzlersche Verlagsbuchhandlung, 1987); Klaus Mann, "Karl May: Hitler's Literary Mentor," *Kenyon Review* 2 (1940): 391–400; Günter Scholdt, "Hitler, Karl May und die Emigranten," *Jahrbuch der Karl-May-Gesellschaft* (1984): 60–91; Ekkehard Koch, "Zwischen Rio de la Plata und Kordilleren: Zum historischen Hintergrund von Mays Südamerika-Romanen," *Jahrbuch der Karl-May-Gesellschaft* (1979): 137–68.

12. Videotaped interview with Heinz Markstein, Vienna, 25 June 1992.

13. Videotaped interview with Heinz Pinshower, Chicago, 10 April 1991.

14. Ibid.

15. Videotaped interview with Renate Schwarz, Teaneck, NJ, 2 May 1991.

16. Ibid.

17. Videotaped interview with Werner Guttentag, Cochabamba, Bolivia, 31 July 1991.

18. Schwarz, *Keine Zeit für Eichendorff,* 66.

19. Ibid., 65–66.

20. For an articulation of this feeling, see Schwarz, *Keine Zeit für Eichendorf,* 72–73.

21. Heinrich Stern, "Indianer-Landschaft," typescript, Cochabamba, Bolivia, July 1941; my translation.

22. William Wordsworth, preface, *Lyrical Ballads of Worsdworth and Coleridge,* 2d ed. (London, 1800).

23. Heinrich Stern, "Indianer-Landschaft."

24. For a stimulating discussion of representation in family albums, see Patricia Holland, "History, Memory and the Family Album," in *Family Snaps: The Meaning of Domestic Photography,* ed. Jo Spence and Patricia Holland (London: Virago, 1991).

25. Roland Barthes, *Camera Lucida,* trans. Richard Howard (New York: Hill and Wang, 1981), 80–81.

26. Susan Sontag, *On Photography* (New York: Farrar, Straus, and Giroux, 1989), 9.

27. Victor Burgin, "Looking at Photographs," in *Thinking Photography,* ed. Victor Burgin (London: Macmillan, 1982), 144.

28. Mary Louise Pratt, *Imperial Eyes: Travel Writing and Transculturation* (London: Routledge, 1992), 120–26.

29. *Encyclopaedia Judaica,* s.v. "Maccabi World Union"and "Ha-Shomer ha-Za'ir."

30. Franz Schubert, "Das Wandern" in "Die schöne Müllerin," *Franz Schuberts Werke: Kritisch Durchgeschene Gesamtausgabe,* ser. 20, vol. 7, 134.

31. See Edith Foster, *Reunion in Vienna* (Riverside: Ariadne, 1989) 131–32, for an interesting parallel recollection by a Jewish Viennese refugee of the *Wandervogel* and its hiking songs.

32. See Catherine Lutz and Jane Collins, "The Photograph as an Intersection of Gazes," *Reading National Geographic* (Chicago: University of Chicago Press, 1993), 187–216.

33. Fredric Jameson, "Pleasure: A Political Issue," in *Formations of Pleasure,* ed. F. Jameson (London: Routledge, 1983), 1–14.

34. I have been asked: "How else should the refugees have taken these photos?" Among others photographic representations of indigenous people *as historical actors*—in which their agency and the social and political context remain very much in evidence—can be found throughout the published works of the Brazilian photographer Sebastião Salgado. See, for example, Sebastião Salgado, *Workers: An Archeology of the Industrial Age* (New York: Aperture, 1993); *An Uncertain Grace: Photographs by Sebastião Salgado* (San Francisco: San Francisco Museum of Modern Art, 1990); *Fotografias* (Rio de Janeiro: Funarte, 1982). Also see Cornell Capa, *The Concerned Photographer* (New York: Grossman, 1972).

35. For a discussion of the *Rundschau vom Illimani* and Ernst Schumacher, see Patrik von zur Mühlen, *Fluchtziel Lateinamerika: Die deutsche Emigration, 1933–1945* (Bonn: Verlag Neue Gesellschaft, 1988), 217–19, 221–26. The Institut für Zeitungsforschung, Dortmund, has a microfilm copy of the *Rundschau* from 1939 to 1946. The importance of the *Aufbau* as a vehicle for refugee communication and as an instrument for fostering a refugee community during the war is highlighted by Schwarz, *Keine Zeit für Eichendorff,* 79. The Wiener Library in London and Tel Aviv has a complete run of the *Jüdische Wochenschau* on microfilm. Also see Lieselotte Maas, *Deutsche Exilpresse in Lateinamerika* (Frankfurt: Buchhändler-Vereiningung, 1978), 43–47, 81–83.

36. The *Circulo Israelita,* founded in 1935 by Polish and Rumanian Jews, was the first Jewish community organization in Bolivia. Although it would continue to exist as a separate entity throughout the war years and, in the 1950s, would absorb the, by then, much diminished *Comunidad,* it was the *Comunidad,* with its (at the time) larger Central European membership and its affiliated institutions, that dominated Central European immigrant community life. For a history of the *Circulo Israelita,* see *Medio Siglo de Vida Judia en La Paz.* Also see Schwarz, *Keine Zeit für Eichendorff,* 81.

37. *Jüdische Wochenschau* (monthly Bolivia sections of the Buenos Aires newspaper) and *Rundschau vom Illimani,* 1939–42.

38. *Medio Siglo de Vida Judia en La Paz,* 171–75.

39. Egon Schwarz, *Keine Zeit für Eichendorff,* 73.

40. Gill, *Precarious Dependencies,* 1–4, 58–77. Although her focus is largely on the post-1952 period, I am greatly indebted to Lesley Gill's wonderfully insightful study of gender, class, and domestic service in Bolivia for my discussion of indigenous perceptions of the refugees.

41. Quoted in Gill, *Precarious Dependencies,* 1. Like all names used in Gill's study, Antonieta Huanca is a pseudonym (see 11).

42. Although the term *gringo* is widely used throughout Spanish America to refer to Anglo–North Americans, its popular usage also often includes fair-haired or lighter-skinned Europeans.

43. Gill, *Precarious Dependencies,* 16.

44. Ibid., 6.

45. *Revista de Bolivia* (La Paz), no. 21, March 1939.

46. See A. Yarmush, "Anti-Semitic Agitation in Bolivia," American Jewish Joint Distribution Committee (hereafter cited as JDC), file 1075 (Bolivia), 1939–40.

47. See *La Prensa* (Cochabamba), 23, 24, 25, 26, 28, 29 November and 3 December 1940. English translations of these articles can be found as enclosures to Milton Goldsmith's report to the JDC. JDC file 1075, 1939–40.

48. See Milton D. Goldsmith, "Confidential Report on Bolivia to the JDC," JDC file 1076, 1941–44; A. Yarmush, "Anti-Semitic Agitation in Bolivia," JDC file 1084, 1939–40 (March); "Recent letter from a refugee, settled in La Paz, Bolivia," JDC file 1075, 1939–40; "Aus Bolivien," *Rundschau vom Illimani,* 5 April 1940.

49. President Busch, the son of a Bolivian woman and a German doctor who had emigrated to Bolivia in the early years of this century, made an agreement with the Austrian Jewish mining magnate Mauricio Hochschild permitting the admission of upward of twenty thousand refugees from Germany and Austria. But this agreement was predicated on the expectation that the immigrants would largely be agricultural colonists who would settle in and help to develop the underpopulated and economically backward Chaco and eastern lowlands regions of the country. Busch, however, died—ostensibly by suicide in August 1939 but under mysterious circumstances—and the personal agreement between him and Hochschild lapsed without being ratified by the Chamber of Deputies. For reference to the agreement, see letter of 7 March 1939 from M. Hochschild to Edwin Goldwasser of the American Jewish Joint Distribution Committee in New York, JDC file 1075, 1939–40. Also see Herbert S. Klein, *Bolivia: The Evolution of a Multi-Ethnic Society,* 2d ed. (New York: Oxford University Press, 1992) , 208–9; von zur Mühlen, *Fluchtziel Lateinamerika,* 212–13; Porfirio Diaz Machicado, *Historia de Bolivia: Toro, Busch, Quintanilla, 1936–1943* (La Paz: Juventud, 1958).

50. Interview with Walter Guevara Arze, La Paz, 17 March 1995.

51. Hochschild had emigrated to Bolivia in the early 1920s—long before the

panic immigration that followed the *Anschluss* of Austria by Germany in March 1938.

52. Klein, *Bolivia*, 208ff.; James M. Malloy, *Bolivia: The Uncompleted Revolution* (Pittsburgh: University of Pittsburgh Press, 1970), 115–18; "Immigrant Plot Exposed in Bolivia," *New York Times*, 25 May 1939; "Bolivians Bill to Bar Jews Wins Approval: Deputies Accept First Reading of Immigration-Permit Ban," *New York Times*, 9 September 1940; "Bolivia: Refugee Racket," *Time*, 30 December 1940, 25.

53. See the collection of Bolivian newspaper clippings (P.C. 2322b) in the Wiener Library, London. Also see report by Milton Goldsmith on Cochabamba and "German Fifth Column Activity" as well as his enclosures of clippings from the local press in JDC file 1075, 1939–40.

54. See "Bolivia: Refugee Racket," 25; interview with Walter Guevara Arze, La Paz, 17 March 1995.

55. For the background of the discovery of the pro-Axis plot and President Peñaranda's expulsion of the German ambassador, Ernst Wendler, see Alberto Ostria Gutierrez, *Una Revolución tras los Andes* (Santiago de Chile: Editora Nascimento, 1944), 131–95; and Porfirio Diaz Machicado, *Historia de Bolivia "Peñaranda"* (La Paz: Juventud, 1958), 53–65. For the renewed antisemitic agitation, see Jerry W. Knudson, "The Bolivian Immigration Bill of 1942: A Case Study in Latin American Anti-Semitism," *American Jewish Archives* 20 (1968): 138–59.

56. Knudson, "The Bolivian Immigration Bill of 1942"; *La Calle* (La Paz), 16 and 20 September, 28 October 1942; Joseph Bonastruo, "Bolivia Challenges the Jew," *Congress Weekly*, 30 October 1942, 9–10. Cuttings from contemporary newspapers focusing on antisemitic agitation and incidents can also be found in the YIVO archives, HIAS file, RG 245.4 XIII, 1943.

57. See Klein, *Bolivia*, 215; von zur Mühlen, *Fluchtziel Lateinamerika*, 214–15. Reiner Pommerin, *Das dritte Reich und Lateinamerika: Die deutsche Politik gegenüber Süd- und Mittelamerika, 1939–1942* (Düsseldorf: Droste Verlag, 1977), 250–58.

58. Knudson, "Bolivian Immigration Bill," 149.

59. See Reiner Pommerin, *Das dritte Reich und Lateinamerika*, 254. Although the members are not listed by name, it is likely that the majority were German residents in Bolivia.

60. Milton Goldsmith, "Report on German Fifth Column Activity in Cochabamba" (La Paz, 4 December 1940), in JDC file 1075, 1939–40; Klein, *Bolivia*, 215.

61. See, for example, Franz D. Lucas, "Wo und wie ich den Tag erlebte," in *Mensch, der Krieg ist aus!: Zeitzeugen erinnern sich*, ed. Werner Filmer and Heribert Schwan (Düsseldorf: Econ Verlag, 1985), 224–31; Renee Rosen (Renate Schwarz), *It Happened in Three Countries*, 3 vols. (New York, 1979); videotaped

interview with Julius Wolfinger, New York, 2 July 1990; videotaped interview with Andres J. Simon, La Paz, Bolivia, 22 July 1991; videotaped interview with Renate Schwarz, Teaneck, NJ, 2 May 1991; Jorge Knoepflmacher, "Acceptance Speech of 'Cóndor de los Andes' Award," Oruro, Bolivia, August 1962 (transcript from audiotape by Ulrich Knoepflmacher).

62. Ilse Herz, in videotaped interview, Arsdale, NY, 26 February 1991.

63. Pratt, *Imperial Eyes,* 6.

64. Ibid., 4–7.

65. Many of the persons I interviewed have referred to these: for example, Julius Wolfinger (3 July 1990), Henry and Liesl Lipczenko (12 August 1990), Heinz and Hani Pinshower (10 April 1991), Werner Guttentag (31 July 1991), Walter Guevara Arce Jr. (2 August 1991). Also see Schwarz, *Keine Zeit für Eichendorff,* 82–83; Arthur Propp, "[Auto]Biography to the End of the Stay at Sucre" (MS, Leo Baeck Institute, New York).

66. John Berger and Jean Mohr, *Another Way of Telling* (London: Writers and Readers, 1982), 86–87.

67. Ibid., 89.

Colonization and Decolonization: The Case of Zionist and African Elites

Dan V. Segre

At first sight there seems to be little in common between Zionism and the national movements of the Third World and, more particularly, of Africa. The diplomatic and economic links established by the State of Israel with new African states in the 1960s were impressive partly because they looked as if they were created ex nihilo. The speed with which the Israelis entered the "African game" and the equal speed with which they found themselves ejected from it in the 1970s and reaccepted in the 1990s tend to underline the superficiality of these links. There were, of course, politically interested rationalizations of this newly found "brotherhood": the historicomythological relations between King Solomon and the Queen of Sheba; the role of black "Zionist" and messianic African churches and sects; the possible latent influence of Jewish lore on certain African tribes, such as the Poeul or the Ashanti of Ghana.[1] More serious even if sporadic were efforts to look for possible connections between Jewish and African movements of emancipation, considering that in both cases the search for a national identity was linked less to a specific territory than to the consciousness of sharing a common tragic fate. Another common point seemed to be the similitude of self-images that had been influenced by diaspora and dependent conditions, in spite of different historical settings, conditions that were responsible for a rapid loss of indigenous culture and a willing acquisition of alien values drawn from metropolitan-prejudiced environments.

Africanism, like Zionism, is essentially a movement of ideas and emotions, directly influenced by efforts to combine redemption with return. Edward Wilmot Blyden (1832–1912), the West Indian–born Liberian diplomat and scholar, forefather of Pan-Africanism, went on pilgrimage to Jerusalem as early as 1866. He became an ardent admirer of political Zion-

218 / *Comparing Jewish Societies*

ism thirty years later because of his metapolitical view of both Jewish and African destinies. His essay *The Jewish Question,* which appeared in Liverpool in 1898, followed Theodor Herzl's *Der Judenstaat* by only two years. "There is hardly a man in the civilized world," he wrote, "Christian, Mohammedan or Jew, who does not recognize the right of the Jew to the Holy Land, and there are few who, if the conditions were favorable, would not be glad to see them return in a body and take their place in the land of their fathers as a great—leading—secular power."[2] He advised the Jews against aiming at political aggrandizement, believing that the primary contribution of the Jews to world civilization—as of blacks, inside and outside Africa—was the spiritual element lacking in a Western world "immersed in materialism." In 1919 W. E. B. Du Bois, promoter of the first Pan-African Conference, wrote: "The African movement means to us what the Zionist movement must mean to the Jews, the centralization of rare effort and recognition of a racial fount."[3] This assessment is not surprising, since both Zionism and Pan-Africanism were the outcome of processes of emancipation started by the Enlightenment and by moral, religious, and romantic reactions to the French Revolution. Moreover, both movements developed outside their "homelands" and strove, at least in the beginning, more for human dignity than for political independence. In both cases a messianic ideal, in which religious ingredients acted both as a coalescent factor of the new identity and solvent of foreign dependence, served to legitimize the revolt: some slave uprisings in nineteenth-century America were justified on the basis of biblical texts about God taking the Jews out of bondage.[4]

Zionists were certainly less interested in Africa than were Pan-Africanists in Zionism. Theodor Herzl, in his utopian novel on the revival of Jewish society in Palestine, mentioned the African colonial question, promising that the Jews, once independent, would come to the aid of blacks.[5] Conversely, an American black nationalist, Marcus Aurelius Garvey, leader of the unsuccessful "Back to Africa" movement between the two world wars, took pride in calling himself a "Black Zionist," although he knew little about the Jews and Palestine. All this may offer material for diplomats and propagandists to promote the idea that African, Jewish, and Zionist history have many points in common. In fact, the links between Israel and Africa are so thin that no comparison can be made between Zionism and African national movements in terms of their ideological development and even less in terms of their political organization and trials. What can be usefully compared is the psychology of the elites of Israel and those of the new countries of the Third World, especially in Africa, and the effect that their respective diasporas have had on them.

The most relevant similarity between Jewish and African nationalism is their exposure to the impact of Westernization, albeit in very different situations of political and cultural dependence. For an "enlightened" African as for an enlightened diaspora Jew, to become Westernized meant identification with a source simultaneously of prestige and oppression. One must be careful to avoid thesis mongering, that is, mixing ideology, political fashion, and academic evidence; differences in historical experiences must continuously be borne in mind. The impact of Europe on the Jews, even on those of Eastern Europe who kept a separate social identity much longer than did the Jews of the West, was totally different from the impact of European culture on African colonial societies. Geographical, cultural, political, and social environments are not comparable, and any attempt to apply emotion-loaded terms, such as *imperialism, colonialism,* or *slavery,* to the two cases will prove useless, if not self-defeating. The situation changes, however, when one looks at the psychological impact that Westernization and modernization have had on Jewish and African intellectuals faced with the problem of national revival. In matters concerning national identity, legitimacy, the relationship between modern and traditional social structures, the dilemmas and behavior of African and Jewish nationalist elites show some striking similarities. This is not surprising, considering the effort that both Jewish and African intellectuals, born in traditional societies, had to make in order to adapt to the exigencies of foreign centers of attraction while struggling to justify their claims to total independence. For both Africans and Jews identification with Western culture was a source of prestige and frustration simultaneously; for both it often meant a total break with their own national traditions; for both it meant the adoption of foreign images of themselves and the development of feelings of social and cultural marginality to parent and adopted society; for both this feeling of marginality manifested itself in expressions of self-hate and an irrational attraction to, as well as a rejection of, the West.

The relationship between colonized and colonizer has been the topic of many studies.[6] This is not the place to go into the subject. It may, however, be pointed out parenthetically that in works on colonialism, such as those of Frantz Fanon and Albert Memmi, Jews and blacks are constantly intermingled. The comparison attempted by these authors deals principally with the psychology of the colonized man in a colonial situation—Jew, African, whatever. The question is whether these similarities can be found after political independence is achieved. That is the main purpose of the first part of the present inquiry, while in the second, written thirty years later, I will try to show how African and Israeli societies have parted ways and thus cease to provide material for fruitful comparisons.

Among the scholarly studies of African political societies that have flooded the libraries of learned institutions in the past twenty years, the work of an African political sociologist, Peter P. Ekeh of Ibadan University, has special relevance to our subject. While Ekeh seeks to explain the effects of colonization on the elites of Nigeria,[7] his conclusions are relevant to many other new states, including Israel. Ekeh claims that "the experiences of colonialism in Africa have led to the emergence of a unique historical configuration: the existence of two publics instead of one public, as in the West." In the West the private realm and the public realm have common *moral* foundations: in Africa and in many new countries of the Third World they do not. There is one private realm, founded on indigenous tradition and culture, and two public realms, each with a different type of moral linkage to the private realm. One public realm, writes Ekeh, "can be identified with primordial groupings, sentiments, and activities which nevertheless impinge on the public interest. [It] operates on the same moral imperatives as the private realm" and is activated and legitimated by traditional culture. Next to it, however, is another public realm, which, at least in Africa, is historically associated with colonial administration and which has become identified with popular politics in postcolonial Africa. Although it provides essential civil structures, such as the military, the civil service, the police, its chief characteristic is that it has no moral linkage with the private realm. Peter Ekeh calls this the "civic" public and underlines the fact that in Africa this public lacks the generalized moral imperatives operative in the private realm and in the primordial public. "The native sector," he concludes, "has become a primordial reservoir of moral obligations, a public entity which one works to preserve and benefit. The Westernized sector has become an amoral civic public, from which one seeks to gain, if possible, in order to benefit the primordial public." Hence, the corruption that has permeated the political life of new states in Africa, the difficulty for new governments in mobilizing the masses for the benefit of the state, the contradiction between parallel manifestations of total involvement and the sacrifice of the individual and group for the benefit of the "primordial" public sector (the extended family, the clan, the tribe, etc.), and the apathy shown toward the civic administrative public sector by the same individuals or groups.

Ekeh also notes that the conflict between what he calls two "bourgeois groups," the foreign and the indigenous (I think the term *elites* would be more appropriate), is characterized by an acute sense of insecurity due to a crisis of legitimacy. In fact, the emerging indigenous ruling class is

> composed of Africans who acquired Western education at the hands of the colonizers and their missionary collaborators, and who accordingly were the most exposed to European colonial ideologies of all groups of Africans. [For this reason] although native to Africa, the African [elite] depends on colonialism for its legitimacy. It accepts the principles implicit in colonialism but it rejects the foreign personnel which ruled Africa. It claims to be competent enough to rule, but is has no traditional legitimacy. In order to *replace* the colonizer, it has to invent a number of legalistic theories to justify that rule.

Some elements of this analysis can be applied to the Israeli case but with one fundamental difference—namely, that most foreign ideas or institutions were not imposed from the outside but were freely adopted and developed by Zionists, who were more anxious to imitate non-Jewish ways than to preserve traditional Jewish values. The "civic public" was not founded either on Jewish political values or on Jewish "primordial groupings." Both before and after the establishment of the State of Israel, Jewish society in Palestine was strongly influenced by the cultures, customs, institutions, and ideologies brought by Zionist settlers from their lands of origin. In their thinking and behavior there was, of course, a strong element of original Jewish culture, but concepts such as socialism, democracy, secular nationalism, as well as institutions such as the cooperative farm, labor unions, political parties, theater, painting, school systems, and the like had little or no connection with the traditional culture of the diaspora.

It is legitimate to ask to what extent political values and traditions existed in a nation-in-exile. I have discussed this problem elsewhere;[8] it will be sufficient here to say that it is inconceivable that a dispersed nation could retain its homogeneity, its communal autonomy, and an extraordinary religious-cultural unity in spite of its geographical and bureaucratic decentralization, without some elements of a distinctive political identity. The history of the West and of Islam is full of instances in which Jews engaged in political action for their own or others' sake or for both. The idea that because Jews did not possess a nation-state there could be no Jewish politics or political thought or political institutions is as unfounded as the idea, held throughout the colonial period, that most African peoples had no history before the arrival of the Arabs or the Europeans. What is true is that in the wake of Jewish emancipation and the weakening of traditional society, from the eighteenth century onward, Jewish national consciousness and Jewish institutions experienced a deep crisis, like most colonized African polities in the eighteenth and nineteenth centuries. Conversely, the newly independent African states and the State of Israel adopted political concepts and institutions from the West, developing variations of social and political habits that often conflicted with more traditional ones.

This was already true of the Zionist immigrants who came to Turkish Palestine before World War I, the members of the wave of immigration known as the Second Aliyah, to which most of the state's future leaders—Presidents Ben-Zvi and Shazar, Premiers Ben-Gurion and Levi Eshkol, etc.—belonged. Although they grew up in traditional East European Jewish societies, they had little in common with the religious Jews of the old Palestine community. The discrepancy between the two types was so marked that, almost until the British victory over Turkey, the *haluts* (secular Jewish pioneer) was often regarded as anathema by the members of the nineteenth-century Jewish population in Palestine, religious and secular.[9] The process did not stop with the creation of Israel, because the immigrants, who came in the thousands to populate the new state, including most of those who came from Islamic countries, had been subject to varying degrees of Westernization, an influence that they and their fathers had been more than ready to accept. The Zionist elite of European origin drew its inspiration directly from the *haskalah* movement, the Jewish Enlightenment, which was in many senses a revolutionary development, giving birth to a new, secular Jewish elite in open opposition to that of traditional rabbinic culture and society. In certain cases visions of emancipation were carried to Jews in Eastern Europe on the muzzles of conquering guns, as was the case with Africans (by Napoléon in the former case, by European colonial powers in the latter). Napoléon, of course, gave his conquests a revolutionary and ideological dimension that was lacking in colonial conquests in Africa, the theory of the White Man's Burden notwithstanding. But some similarity, in the effects produced by the more or less violent encounter between Jewish and African traditional societies and the Westernization of the eighteenth and nineteenth centuries, can be seen in the ways in which Jewish and African elites absorbed the ideas and prejudices of the imported culture. In the Jewish case, as in many colonial societies, the Westernized intellectual believed that the elements he admired most in the West as holding the secret of power—science, political institutions, military organization—were "neutral" instruments that could be adopted without losing his own identity.[10] From this rational, neutral point of view both the African *évolué* and Jewish *maskil* (secular intellectual) criticized their own traditional societies and called for sweeping reforms. In the case of the Jews there was also a call for the "normalization" of the Jewish people, that is, a broadening of the Jewish occupational structure to eliminate its "lazy," unproductive elements—its peddlers, rabbinical scholars, petty financiers, and "miserable" middlemen.

If we look at the criticisms that both liberal Gentiles and enlightened Jews leveled at traditional Jewish society, we find that they were rather like those employed by European colonizers to discredit local indigenous societies and which African *évolués*—as well as American blacks—often internalized and accepted as part of their own collective self-image. This process of "self-hate" can be seen as an ultimate expression of the process of alienation to be found in every colonized society.

The difference between the alienated Jewish assimilationist and the alienated African *évolué* is, of course, considerable. Yet both suffered from the psychological dichotomy of the Westernized native; both sought to promote themselves by accepting and submitting to a foreign culture and its values and by legitimizing such dependence. For the assimilating Jew, as for the assimilating African, the abandonment of the "superstitions" of his own tradition and the acquisition of a foreign education were the conditions for joining the ruling colonial elite. In the colonies Western education also meant an escape from manual work, which was considered degrading. In the case of the Jews it was more a switch from one nonmanual work situation to another, but in both cases the perceptions of colonizer and colonized were similar: they identified Westernization and modernization with progress, superiority, promise of social advancement. The fact that Jews could avail themselves of Western educational facilities to a far larger extent than Africans was a question of quantity, not of quality. In both cases it produced two results: it helped to promote and preserve "the aura of charisma which formed the legitimacy for European rule," and it contributed to enlarging the cleavage between Western and traditional institutions, giving to the latter the connotation of naïveté[11] that was the basis of the condescending distinction between the Westernized and "naive" sectors in traditional societies.

The Africans, writes Ekeh, "claim to be competent enough to rule but have no traditional legitimacy." They are therefore compelled to "invent theories" to justify that rule. First, they accept that Western interpretation of African history that assumes that African history did not exist before the Europeans arrived. Next, they come to believe that colonization represents in the framework of society "what conception and education is in the family."[12] The belief is made acceptable to the native by a subtle presentation of scientific, philosophical, and ideological concepts about the values of colonization, all aimed at establishing European metropolitan cultural superiority over the colonized society. In the field of science belief in such superiority remains unshaken to this day.[13] At all events such efforts at cultural colonization met with no serious opposition.

The Jews went through a like process more quickly and more thoroughly than any other colonized people because of their high level of education and their longer contact with the culture of the West, to which they soon became active contributors.

The creation of the State of Israel did not halt this process. In fact, the success of Zionism increased the process of alienation from Jewish tradition in two ways. Imitation of the West, especially its military and economic prowess, was seen as the quickest way to catch up with the train of progress and modernity. Furthermore (and in this Zionism was a more assimilationist national movement than any in Africa), the creation of a state based, at least in principle, on the first secular Jewish community in history contributed to the belief that the "normalization" of the Jewish people, its becoming "like all the other nations," was indispensable to the consolidation of political independence.[14] The most important result was to divert an existing, powerful assimilationist trend from the individual to the collective level. It created a deep cleavage between a Jewish identity founded on a national religion, which does not need a national territory to survive, and a territorial state, with a majority of its population increasingly convinced that they do not need religion, in its traditional form, to exist.

Despite the many differences, the Westernized Jewish and the Westernized African nationalist fought on three similar fronts at once: against foreign political oppression (antisemitism and colonialism, respectively), against institutionalized traditionalism, and against the vested interest of those among their own people who had identified totally with the West. Two passages, taken at random from speeches made sixty years apart by a Zionist and an African nationalist intellectual denouncing the evils of cultural and psychological assimilation, will underline this point. The first speech was delivered in 1897, at the First Zionist Congress in Basel, by the Jewish physician and cultural critic Max Nordau; the second, in 1956, at the First Congress of Black Writers and Artists in Paris, by the black physician and theorist of liberation Frantz Fanon. Nordau told the delegates:

> Jewish misery has two forms, the material and the moral. In Eastern Europe, North Africa and western Asia—in those very regions where the overwhelming majority, probably nine-tenths of all Jews, live—there the misery of the Jew is to be understood literally. It is a daily disaster of the body, anxiety for every day that follows, a tortured fight for bare existence. In Western Europe the question of bread and shelter and the question of security of life and limb concern them less. There the misery is moral. It takes the form of perpetual injury to self-respect and honour, and of brutal suppression of the striving for spiritual satisfaction which no non-Jew is obliged to deny himself.

The Western Jew, continued Nordau, had bread, and yet he did not live by bread alone; the old forms of misery had been replaced by new ones, for Jews had misunderstood the inner character and purpose of emancipation. It was not a remedy for an ancient injustice but, rather, a logical consequence of the French Revolution. Revolutionary ideology decreed (although popular sentiment rebelled against it) that principles came before sentiment. Intoxicated with the ideals of the Revolution, Jews hastened to cut themselves off from the self-contained, culturally self-sufficient life of the ghetto. With the new outburst of antisemitism in the 1870s the assimilated Jew discovered his true situation.

> He had lost the home of the ghetto, but the land of his birth is denied to him as home. He avoids his fellow Jew because anti-Semitism has made him hateful. His countrymen repel him when he wishes to associate with them. He has no ground under his feet and has no community to which he belongs as a full member. . . . The emancipated Jew is insecure in his relations with his fellow beings, timid with strangers, even suspicious of the secret feelings of his friends. His best powers are exhausted in the suppression, or at least the difficult concealment, of his own real character. . . . He becomes an inner cripple.[15]

Frantz Fanon probably never read a line of what Nordau wrote about Jews, but as a psychologist he knew that "an anti-Jewish prejudice is no different from an anti-Negro prejudice." He was not thinking of Jews when he expressed ideas like those of Nordau:

> Exploitation, tortures, raids, racism, collective liquidation, rational aggression, take turns at different levels in order literally to make of the native an object in the hands of the occupying nation. This object—man, without means of existing, without a *raison d'être*—is broken in the very depth of his substance. The desire to live, to continue, becomes more and more indecisive, more and more phantom-like. It is at this stage that the well-known guilt complex appears. . . . The inferiorized group has admitted, since the force of reasoning was implacable, that its misfortunes resulted directly from its social and cultural characteristics. Guilt and inferiority are usually the consequences of this dialectic. The oppressed then tries to escape these, on the one hand by proclaiming his total unconditional adaptation to the new cultural model or on the other hand by pronouncing an irreversible condemnation of his own cultural study. . . . Having judged, condemned, abandoned his cultural forms, his language, his food habits, his sexual behavior, his way of sitting down, of resting, of laughing, of engaging himself, the oppressed flings himself upon the imposed culture with the desperation of a drowning man.[16]

It would certainly be both unfair and uncritical to compare these two speeches, so similar in their anguish and their analyses of national assimilation and dejection, without pointing out some obvious differences between the impact of cultural colonization on the Jew and on the African. The African *évolué,* with a few exceptions, such as the poet Sardar Senghor, former president of Senegal, remained on the fringes of the colonizing culture. The Jewish intellectual, because of his or her residence in the countries of the West and because of the common biblical past shared by Judaism and Christianity, has become a primary contributor to, and in fact an enlivening element of, Western culture. He or she has turned into a major interpreter—historically, artistically, psychologically, and politically—of the peoples among whom he or she dwells, often with tragic results, as recent German history shows.[17] Looked at from this perspective, the brain-drain currently taking place in the underdeveloped countries of the Third World correlates with that of the Jews insofar as contributions to Jewish culture are concerned. In spite of the differences, the Jew and the

Israeli, like the assimilated *évolués* of the colonized world, remain at one and the same time "inside" and "outside" the imported Western culture. It seems legitimate, therefore, to ask to what extent this cultural position continues to be relevant in a postcolonial era to the distinction between the "two publics" made by Ekeh and to serve as a source of public corruption.

In the case of Israel, considering the pluralism of its society and its high level of education, industrialization, military organization, social mobility, and civic motivation, it may seem inappropriate to talk of primordial and civic sectors in Ekeh's sense. Yet it is not difficult to perceive a profound dichotomy between the values of traditional Jewish culture and those of the imported Western or Islamic cultures of Israelis; between the legitimacy of an elite basing its claim to rule on the authority of alien institutions and ideologies and an elite, or several elites, contesting this authority on the basis of Jewish tradition, or of a new nativist one, itself already a mixture of several cultural trends.

This dichotomy has become more evident since the 1967 war and has fueled a national debate, which successive events, such as the war of 1973, the invasion of Lebanon in 1982, the Intifada, and the growth of religious fundamentalism, have increased. It heightened the debate on the legitimacy of the State of Israel by sharpening—inter alia, thanks to the historic opposition between Jewish tradition and secular Israeli nationalism—the ideological radicalism of the Palestinian Arabs. It raised the questions of how the state could remain democratic without conferring equal rights on those who had come under its control and how it could remain a Jewish state if those rights were indeed granted and accepted. It forced the country's leadership to face the dilemma of developing an economy entirely dependent on aid from and trade with the Western capitalist world but subject to all sorts of control imposed by wartime necessities, Marxist ideology, and the vested interests of its socialist power elites.

The financial scandals and the rapid rise of crime[18] that have marred Israeli society at an increasing pace since the Six Day War were, in a sense, an indication of the vitality of a pioneering society that had broken new ground in all directions and was now searching for new norms with which to comply. As in the case of the two publics in Africa described by Ekeh, it showed the existence of a dichotomy in collective behavior that had developed as a direct consequence of the Israeli public's divided dependence: on indigenous and on imported values. At the same time, political and military constraints contributed to strengthening traditional Jewish values, increasing the clash with modernization.

During and after the Yom Kippur War in 1973 these Jewish values became more dominant: they were expressed in the voluntarism of large strata of the civilian population, the passionate, almost masochistic need for collective self-criticism, the increased interest in Jewish studies, and continuous public and private debate about the identity and legitimacy of the Israeli state in terms of Judaism and Jewish interest. Politically, it contributed to the growth of extraparliamentary groups (such as *Gush Emunim* [Bloc of the Faithful], a nonparty organization devoted to the judaization and settlement of Judaea and Samaria) and of the religious establishment in general, to the defeat of the Labor coalition after thirty years in power in the 1977 elections, and to the unexpected rise to power of the Right and of Menachem Begin. I have discussed elsewhere the deep Jewish roots of this quasirevolution in Israel and the paradoxical support that the poorest classes of the country gave to the party that symbolized free enterprise and capitalism.[19] It will be enough to say here that the Begin phenomenon seems to be the result of the need to find an authoritative father figure to bridge the gap between the old, national, collective memories and values of the Jewish people and the new, national, collective memories and imported values of the Israeli nation. This gap is certainly different from the one analyzed in Ekeh's model of the two publics. But it is close enough to justify the claim that the dynamics of Israeli society cannot be understood *only* in terms of Western political experience.

In terms of social analysis Israel has elements in common with other Third World countries, but from every other point of view one cannot, today, find parallels with Africa. Many events are responsible for this change, but the most significant are the peace with Egypt (1979) and the massive immigration of Russian Jews ten years later. The sympathy of Africans and African Americans for Zionism, which in the past inspired a certain feeling of convergence, has turned sour as a consequence of the involvement of peoples of color in the Arab-Israeli conflict (inaccurately presented as a conflict between blacks and whites, rich and poor, colonialism and anticolonialism).[20]

The disenchantment of Israelis with previously very friendly African governments, due to their position in the Middle East conflict and their dwindling international role, diminished Israel's interest in the continent. But the major new divergences are to be found elsewhere.

One cannot speak any longer of similar African and Jewish expressions of self-hate; of "black souls and white masks," as did the fathers of Zionism (Pinsker, Nordau) and Pan-Africanism (N'Krumah, Fanon). Furthermore, it is no longer possible to relate to them in general terms as Africans and Jews. What, in the past, gave to both a certain feeling of similarity was their feeling of belonging to oppressed "families." Once foreign rule ended and antisemitism diminished, this common trait lost much of its relevance. It was replaced, in Africa, by old tribal rivalries and, among Jews, by weaker links between Israel and an increasingly assimilated diaspora.

No less important are the differences created by the cleavages of social geography. In Africa the worldview of the farmer has little in common with that of the African who can afford to travel by air to London or Paris. The climate and the productivity of those who can use air conditioners differ from those who cannot afford them. Climatic and transport restrictions similar to those prevailing in Africa persisted in Palestine up to World War II. Today, as far as habitat, physical conditions of work, internal movement, and travel abroad are concerned, the situation has radically changed in Israel, together with popular feelings of marginality.

This change has been accompanied in many cases by a new and often almost irrational attraction of the Israeli toward the Western world. But it is an attraction very different from that of the Jew of a century ago, since it is now a normal relationship of immigrants, not of unwanted aliens. Paradoxically, one could also observe an opposite anti-Western trend, due to the emergence of an Israel-centered Jewish self-consciousness, linked, as I said, in some fundamentalist circles with anti-Western currents.[21] There is the revival of the Hebrew language, which has increased cultural parochialism. There is the multitude of religious institutions, more numerous in Israel than in the whole diaspora prior to World War II and not particularly Western in their world outlook. There is also a change in the old Zionist political aspirations. Its most secular cosmopolitan trend, the socialist one, now favors a small Israeli state in order to maintain its Jewishness, whereas a large part of the nationalist religious camp favors a "Greater Israel," which, with its growing Palestinian population, would eventually lose its Jewish character and become a binational state.[22]

In Africa, and this includes Arab-African societies, Ekeh's analysis continues to be valid, with the possible exception of South Africa. Tribalism and Islamic fundamentalism—both in their own ways at odds with Westernization—are growing. So are corruption and political illegitimacy. The inability to preserve and develop the positive elements left by colonization or to replace them with valid new ones has contributed to disastrous economic and social situations, which, in turn, fuel tribal violence and religious radicalism. The tragedy of Somalia and Rwanda speak for themselves and have induced a renowned African political scientist, Ali Mazrui, to envisage for them some kind of international "recolonization."

Paradoxically, the one remaining similarity between Israel and Africa is a spectacular growth of population. But, while Africa tries desperately to export people, Israel makes efforts to import them—including non-Jewish manpower from Asia—through immigration. This is a direct outcome of the fact that 5.2 million Israelis produce and export more goods than all the states of black Africa put together, oil and South Africa excluded. (Not a unique phenomenon when one remembers that in 1959 South Korea and Ghana had approximately the same GNP.)

But what is making the greatest change between Israel and Africa is the information revolution. The collapse of the Soviet Union caused some four hundred thousand Russian immigrants (one-third of them not Jewish but with Jewish relatives) to come to Israel. The flow— today reduced to about sixty thousand immigrants a year and characterized by a high level of education and social problems—has radically changed the composition of the population. The new immigrants also serve to focus Israel's attention on the new states of the former Soviet Union and away from Africa. This shift away from Africa is reinforced by the opening of the immense Indian and Chinese markets after the establishment of diplomatic relations in 1991. At the same time, the transfer to Israel of almost the total Jewish population of Ethiopia, while enriching the already multicultural character of Israeli society, has not strengthened, at least for the moment, links with Africa.

The bifurcation of roles, structures, power, and aims between Israel and Africa thus seems irreversible. Israel is becoming the largest Jewish community in the world. Although not isolated, as before, it remains a solitary nation, without linguistic and religious kinship with other nations, a unique, fragile experiment in the coexistence of political rationality with political mysticism, of secularism with fundamentalism, of modernization with tradition.

Such an experiment has little in common not only with black Africa but also with the Arabs, the West, and the Jewish experience of the past. Such an experience will continue to carry the imprint of the encounters of Jews with many civilizations. The encounter of Israel with Africa retains only this in particular: it is one of the few cases in which the meeting between Jews and non-Jews—with the exception of some conflicts with Christianity in Ethiopia—has not been saddened, as elsewhere, by tragic memories.

NOTES

1. Historical relationships between Jews and Africa have been studied in a very erratic way. The relationship between Jews, Palestine, and Ethiopia is well-known: see Jean Doresse, *L'Empire du Prêtre-Jean* (Paris: Plon, 1957); Ernst Hammerschmidt, "Jewish Elements in the Cult of the Ethiopian Church"; and Sven Rubenson, "The Lion of the Tribe of Judah—Christian Symbol and/or Imperial Title?" *Journal of Ethiopian Studies* 3, no. 2 (July 1965): 1–12, 75–85. The links between Jews and other parts of East Africa are less certain. There are many oral traditions and a few historical documents concerning Madagascar; see Gabriel Ferrand, "Migration musulmane et juive à Madagaskar," *Revue d'histoire des religions* 52 (1905): 381–417; and Franas X. Razakandrainy, *Parenté des Hovas et des Hebreux* (Tananarive: Volamahitsy Amparibe, 1954); as well as the more contemporary Arie Oded, "Ha-Bayudaya u-meyasdah Semei Kakungulu" (The Bayudaya and its Founder Semei Kakungulu), *Ha-mizrah he-hadash* 17, nos. 1–2 (1967): 65–66. With regard to West Africa historical evidence of Jewish presence and influence is less rich and extensive than for North Africa and the Sahara. There is a vast literature on the Kahima and the Berbers; see *Encyclopaedia Judaica,* s.v. "Kahina"; as well as an interesting article by Israel Levi, "Le lait de la mère et le proselytisme," *Revue des études juives* 87 (1929): 94–95; and H. Z. Hirschberg, "The Problem of the Judaized Berbers," *Journal of African History* 4 (1963): 313–39. An acute study of the ancient presence and role of the Jews in West Africa is Raymond Manny, "Le Judaisme, les juifs et l'Afrique occidental," *Bulletin de l'Institut Français d'Afrique Noire* 11 (July–August 1949): 34. See also Sidney Mendelsshon, *The Jews of Africa, especially in the Sixteenth and Seventeenth Centuries* (London: K. Paul, Trench, Trubner, 1920); and J. J. Williams, *Hebrewisms of West Africa: From the Nile to Niger with the Jews* (London: Allen and Unwin, 1930).

2. Edward W. Blyden, *The Jewish Question* (Liverpool: Lionel Hart, 1898).

3. *Crisis,* February 1919.

4. Herbert Aptheker, *American Negro Slave Revolts* (New York: International Publishers, 1969).

5. Theodor Herzl, *Old-New Land* (New York: Bloch, 1960).

6. Those more relevant here are Albert Memmi, *Portrait d' un juif* (Paris: Gallimard, 1962); and Frantz Fanon, *The Wretched of the Earth* (New York: Grove Press, 1968). Another pertinent book, although relating to the special experience of Jewish Lebanese intellectuals, is Lucien Elia, *Les Rates de la diaspora* (Paris: Flammarion, 1969.) I found illuminating evidence for the common mentality of Jewish and African intellectuals in "Les Intellectuels Africans: où sont-ils?" *Réalités africaines* 6 (December 1963–January 1964).

7. Peter P. Ekeh, "Colonialism and the Two Publics in Africa," *Comparative Studies in Society and History* 1 (1975): 91–112.

8. D. V. Segre, *Israele e il Sionismo: dall' auto-emancipazione all' auto-colonizzazione* (Milan: Editoriale Nuova, 1979).

9. The first open clashes between the old Jewish residents of Palestine and the immigrants took place in 1889, significantly, over the request of the Jerusalem rabbis to let the fields lie fallow during that sabbatical year. In 1890 performance of the first Hebrew play, *Zerubavel,* by M. L. Lilienblum, was stopped by the Turkish authorities, who had received word that the play was subversive. The first Hebrew newspaper, *Ha-tsevi,* aroused such deep resentment among the Old Yishuv that its founder, Eliezer Ben-Yehuda, who is credited with reviving modern Hebrew, was denounced and then arrested by the Turks in 1894.

10. Jacob Katz, *Tradition and Crisis: Jewish Society at the End of the Middle Ages* (New York: Schocken Books, 1971), 262.

11. Hannah Arendt, *The Origins of Totalitarianism* (New York: Harcourt, Brace, 1951), 131.

12. Ekeh, "Colonialism and the Two Publics in Africa."

13. Y. Elkana and D. V. Segre, *Philosophical Queries on the Presuppositions Underlying Technical and Science Teaching in Developing Countries* (Jerusalem: Van Leer Jerusalem Foundation, 1972).

14. The question of the relevance of ancient, non-Western traditions to modern life in Third World nations is a central problem of the contemporary worldwide phenomenon of transculturation. I have dealt with the impact of Jewish tradition on modern Israeli society in "Jewish Political Thought and Contemporary Politics," *Shefa Quarterly: A Journal of Jewish Thought and Studies* 1, no. 2 (1977): 76–92.

15. Quoted in David Vital, *The Origins of Zionism* (Oxford: Clarendon Press 1975), 362–64.

16. Frantz Fanon, *Toward the African Revolution: Political Essays* (New York: Grove Press, 1969), 41–54.

17. Isaiah Berlin, "Jewish Slavery and Emancipation," in *Hebrew University Garland: A Silver Jubilee Symposium,* ed. Norman Bentwich (London: Constellation Books, 1952).

18. The two most publicized scandals were those of Michael Tsur and Asher Yadlin. The indictment of Tsur, managing director of the government-sponsored investment company, the Israel Corporation, and a former director-general of the ministry of commerce and industry, showed the intricate connections between international financial circles and Israeli bureaucracy. The indictment of Yadlin, a former secretary-general of Hevrat Ovdim, the holding company of the Histadrut's economic enterprises, underlined the corrupting interconnection of money, favoritism, and party policies in the socialist establishment. It led to the suicide of a cabinet minister (David Ofer, minister of construction, who, on his own written admission, committed suicide because he could no longer stand press accusations of complicity in the Yadlin case). For insights into the intricate play of money and

power in Israel and the diaspora, see Yuval Elitzur and Eliahu Salpeter, *Who Rules Israel?* (New York: Harper and Row, 1973), 220–40.

19. "The Symbolic Force of Begin's Power," *Washington Post,* 15 August 1977.

20. Paradoxically, for people like Marcus Aurelius Garvey to be a black Zionist meant, inter alia, to identify with that element of a social "whiteness" represented by American Jewry. Today there is an element of identification with white society in African Americans' imitation of white American antisemitism.

21. Emanual Sivan and Menachem Friedman, eds., *Religious Radicalism and Politics in the Middle East* (Albany: State University of New York Press, 1989).

22. Baruch Kimmerling, "Boundaries and Frontiers of the Israeli Control System: Analytical Conclusions," in *The Israeli State and Society: Boundaries and Frontiers,* ed. Baruch Kimmerling (Albany: State University of New York Press, 1989), 265–82.

Railway Workers and Relational History: Arabs and Jews in British-Ruled Palestine

Zachary Lockman

During the period of Ottoman rule over the Arab East, from 1516 until the end of World War I, the term *Palestine* (*Filastin*) denoted a geographic region, part of what the Arabs called *al-Sham* (historic Syria), rather than a specific Ottoman province or administrative district. By contrast, from 1920 to 1948 Palestine existed as a distinct and unified political (and to a considerable extent economic) entity with well-defined boundaries. Ruled by Britain under a so-called mandate granted by the League of Nations, Palestine in that period encompassed an Arab majority and a Jewish minority.

By now a fairly substantial historical and sociological literature on Palestine during the mandate period has accumulated. Broadly speaking, several features can be said to characterize this literature.[1] For one it gives disproportionate attention to elites and to diplomatic, political, and military history, to the disadvantage of other social groups and of the social, economic, and cultural dimensions of the development of the Arab and Jewish communities in Palestine. There is also, for a variety of reasons, a great quantitative (and to some extent qualitative) disparity between the published research on the policies and activities of the Zionist movement, its component parties and institutions in Palestine, and, more broadly, the development of the Yishuv, the pre-state Jewish community in Palestine, on the one hand, and the literature on the political, social, economic, and cultural history of Palestine's Arab community, on the other. I would also argue that many, if not most, of the historians, sociologists, and others who have contributed to this literature have worked from within (and implicitly accepted the premises of) either Zionist or Arab/Palestinian nationalist historical narratives. As a result, much of the published research, while often valuable and important in its own right, nonetheless fails to adopt a sufficiently critical stance toward the categories of historical analysis that it deploys.

These characteristics are to varying degrees related to the historiographical issue on which I would like to focus here, an issue central to the way in which the modern history of Palestine has been framed but which has only recently begun to be subjected to a serious critique. The paradigm of historical interpretation informing much of the literature has been premised on the implicit or explicit representation of the Arab and Jewish communities in Palestine as primordial, self-contained, and largely monolithic entities. The Yishuv, and to a lesser extent the Palestinian Arab community, are usually depicted as coherent and unconflicted objects that developed along entirely distinct paths in accordance with dynamics and as the result of factors largely unique and internal to each. The paradigm thus assumes that the Arab and Jewish communities in Palestine interacted only in very limited ways and only *en bloc* and certainly did not exert a formative influence on one another, as whole communities or through the interrelations of their component parts. By extension communal identities are regarded as natural, rather than as constructed within a larger field of relations and forces that differentially affected (or even constituted) subgroups among both Arabs and Jews.

We may call this the dual society model because it posits the existence of two essentially separate societies with distinct and disconnected historical trajectories in mandatory Palestine. This model manifests itself most clearly, perhaps, in the work of leading Israeli scholars, who start from the premise that the history of the Yishuv (and later of Israel) can be adequately understood in terms of the interaction of the Yishuv's own internal social, political, economic, and cultural dynamics with those of world Jewish history. The influence of the largely Arab environment within which the Zionist project and the Yishuv developed and of the matrix of Arab-Jewish relations and interactions in Palestine is defined a priori not as constitutive but as marginal and is largely excluded from consideration.

A classic example is S. N. Eisenstadt's 1967 study, *Israeli Society,* which promises to provide "a systematic analysis of the development of the Jewish community in Palestine from its beginning in the late 1880s up to the present day."[2] As Talal Asad (among others) has pointed out, Palestinian Arabs play virtually no role whatsoever in this analysis: the Yishuv seems to have developed in a vacuum, its evolution propelled by the articulation and triumph of values conducive to successful institution building.[3] Eisenstadt's students, Dan Horowitz and Moshe Lissak, embrace the dual society model even more explicitly in their influential work *Origins of the Israeli Polity: Palestine under the Mandate:*

> In Mandatory Palestine two separate and parallel economic and stratification systems of different levels of modernization emerged which maintained only limited mutual relations. Our contention is that this phenomenon arose due to the influence of ideological and political pressures exerted within each of the two national communities.[4]

The dual society model also informs most work on the mandate period by Palestinian and other Arab scholars, though it is usually not explicitly theorized. No Arab historian or sociologist suggests that the Zionist project did not, in the long run, have a tremendous impact on Palestinian Arab society. But that society is usually represented as a preexisting, preformed entity, which was then threatened, encroached upon, and, in 1947–49, largely destroyed by an aggressively expanding Yishuv. Interaction between Arabs and Jews is largely limited to the sphere of political and military conflict, rather than seen as having had a significant impact on the development of Palestinian Arab society in other spheres as well.[5] Many of the foreign scholars who have published research on the modern history of Palestine have also shared this focus on one or the other of the two communities, which are depicted as essentially separate and self-contained entities.

The dual society paradigm does, of course, allow for a single significant mode of interaction between Arabs and Jews in Palestine: conflict, violent or otherwise. This is one reason for the disproportionate attention in the literature to the political, diplomatic, and military dimensions of the relations between Arabs and Jews. The criticism that Avishai Ehrlich recently put forward, however, with regard to Israeli sociologists can also be extended to many historians of modern Palestine. Arab-Jewish conflict, Ehrlich argues,

> is not integrated analytically into the theoretical framework of the sociological discourse . . . . [It] is not perceived as a continuous formative process which shaped the institutional structure and the mentality of the Israeli social formation (as well as that of the Palestinian Arab society). At best, if at all, the Arabs and conflict are regarded as an external

addendum, an appendix to an internally self-explanatory structure: an appendix which erupts from time to time in a temporary inflammation.[6]

The scarcity of historians with a command of both Arabic and Hebrew has no doubt contributed to the prevalence and persistence of the dual society model, as have the insularity, self-absorption, and reluctance to challenge the prevailing consensus characteristic of (but, of course, not unique to) societies, many of whose members perceive themselves as still engaged in a life-or-death struggle to secure their collective existence against grave threats and realize their national(ist) project. But the dominance of this paradigm also reflects (and reinforces) the way in which most scholars have implicitly or explicitly conceptualized their object of study. The result has been a historiography that has hardly questioned the representation of the two communities as self-evidently coherent entities largely uninfluenced by each other. This approach has rendered their mutually constitutive impact virtually invisible, tended to downplay intracommunal divisions, and focused attention on episodes of violent conflict, implicitly assumed to be the sole normal or even possible form of interaction. It has also helped divert attention away from exploration of the processes whereby communal identities and nationalist discourses in Palestine were constructed (and contested), including the ways in which boundaries between (and within) communities were drawn and reproduced, and practices of separation, exclusion, and conflict articulated.[7]

The Emergence of a Relational Paradigm

In recent years the utility of this paradigm has been increasingly challenged by Israeli, Palestinian, and foreign scholars who have consciously sought to problematize and transcend, or at least to render more complex, both Zionist and Palestinian nationalist historical narratives and categories. This project of critique and reconceptualization has involved a move beyond the narrowly political to explore the social, economic, and cultural histories of each community. More important, it has also reflected a new commitment to relational history, rooted in an understanding that the histories of Arabs and Jews in modern (and especially mandatory) Palestine can only be grasped by studying the ways in which both these communities were to a significant extent constituted and shaped within a complex matrix of economic, political, social, and cultural interactions. This project has also sought to explore how each was shaped by the larger processes by which both were affected—for example, the specific form of capitalist development that Palestine underwent from the nineteenth century onward, markets for labor and land, Ottoman patterns of law and administration, and British colonial social and economic policies.

This turn to relational history was greatly facilitated by the new forms of interaction between Israeli and Palestinian societies that developed in the aftermath of Israel's 1967 conquest of the remainder of mandatory Palestine and the extension of Israel's rule to encompass fully one-half of the Palestinian people. The subsequent decades of occupation, conflict, and crisis have made it increasingly clear that at the core of the Arab-Israeli conflict lies the Zionist-Palestinian conflict. This has led Israeli Jewish intellectuals in particular to seek a new, demythologized understanding of their past as a way of making sense of the political, social, and cultural changes their own society has undergone as a result of this historic encounter. For their part Palestinian intellectuals and scholars in the occupied West Bank and Gaza and elsewhere have, since 1967, acquired a much deeper and more nuanced understanding of Israeli politics, society, and culture, which has opened the way to a better understanding of Zionist and Israeli history. Foreign scholars have also contributed innovative new work in recent years.[8]

One risk in adopting a relational approach, of course, is that the specificity of the histories of Arabs and Jews in Palestine may be lost sight of. It was this—or, perhaps more precisely, a concern that the history of the Palestinians would continue to be largely subsumed within a Zionist historical narrative, thereby denying them an independent identity and agency—that Palestinian political scientist Ibrahim Abu-Lughod seems to have been warning against a decade ago when he rebuked historians of Palestine for assuming that it is impossible to "study the historical development of the Palestinian Arab community at any particular point in modern times without taking immediate cognizance of the presence—effective or fictitious—of the Jewish community as represented by the Zionist movement." While admitting that it is "difficult to disentangle Palestinian history and culture from the endemic conflict between Palestinian and Zionist and Palestinian and British imperialist," Abu-Lughod insisted that "the Palestine of 1948 was a very different Palestine from that of 1917 and the difference is not solely the result of the impact of either imperialist or Zionist."[9]

Abu-Lughod is certainly right to argue that the very disproportionate attention paid to Zionism and the Yishuv, and the not unrelated neglect (and implicit marginalization) of Palestine's Arab majority, has had a distorting effect on our overall understanding of the modern history of Palestine. His assertion that "the social and cultural evolution of the Palestinians in modern times is in desperate need of study" is also entirely justified. Without question more (and better) research on the history of the Palestinian Arab community as a distinct (though, of course, not homogeneous or internally unconflicted) entity is urgently needed. At the same time, however, historians cannot avoid seeking to grasp how the development of Palestine's Arab community was shaped by a complex set of economic, social, cultural, and political forces, including those generated by the Zionist project and British colonialism. The same applies, of course, to historians of Zionism and the Yishuv. We must certainly recognize, though, that there will inevitably be some tension between the effort to achieve a relational perspective and respect for the historical specificity of each community.[10]

The project of reconstructing a relational history of Palestine is still in its initial stages, and many issues remain to be examined or reexamined. In the context of the preceding discussion and in order to illustrate the utility of a shift in focus from the internal dynamics of a single community (as the dual society paradigm would prescribe) to the domain of Arab-Jewish interaction, I briefly explore here one particular case from the British mandate period: the evolving relations between Arab and Jewish railway workers, especially those employed at the railway repair and maintenance workshops on the outskirts of Haifa.

Several factors make exploration of this group particularly interesting. Unlike nearly all Arab-owned enterprises and most Jewish-owned enterprises in Palestine, the Palestine Railways (an agency of the mandatory government of Palestine) employed both Arabs and Jews. It was, therefore, one of the few enterprises in which Arabs and Jews worked side by side, encountering similar conditions and being compelled to interact in the search for solutions to their problems. The Palestine Railways was also one of the country's largest employers, with a work force of about twenty-four hundred in 1924, reaching a war-swollen peak of seventy-eight hundred in 1943. This work force, composed of numerous unskilled Arab peasants hired to build and maintain roadbed and track, also included substantial numbers of skilled personnel in the running and traffic departments and at stations across the country and, in 1943, some twelve hundred Arab and Jewish workers employed at the Haifa workshops.[11] Indeed, until the proliferation of British military bases during World War

II, the Haifa workshops constituted Palestine's largest concentration of wage workers.

In addition, the railwaymen were among the first industrial workers in Palestine to organize themselves. An organization of Jewish railway workers was established as early as 1919, while Arab railway workers began to evince interest in trade unionism soon thereafter and would go on to play a key role in founding and leading the Palestinian Arab labor movement. Moreover, it was in large part the interaction of Jewish and Arab railway workers that first compelled the Zionist labor movement and the various left-Zionist political parties, as well as the largely Jewish but anti-Zionist communists, on the one hand, and various forces in the Arab community, on the other, to confront, in both ideological and practical terms, the question of relations between the Jewish and Arab working classes in Palestine.

The extent, duration, and character of the interactions among Arab and Jewish railway workers were exceptional, making them an atypical group in many respects. That very atypicality, that group's location astride communal boundaries, may, however, serve to highlight some of the problematic features of the nationalist and conventional scholarly narratives of the mandate period. It may also allow us to get beyond the usual counterposing of cooperation and conflict as mutually exclusive binary opposites, a dichotomization that tends to presume the prior existence of two distinct entities between which one or the other of these states obtains, thereby obscuring the larger field within which those entities are constituted and interrelate in whole or in part. The more open-ended concept of interaction may be of greater utility in exploring the ways in which relations among the members of this group (and others) took shape within a broader (and historically specific) economic, political, and cultural matrix. At the end of this essay I will point to some of the broader implications of this approach, which I believe may contribute to a rereading of the history of the Zionist-Palestinian conflict.[12]

Hebrew Labor and Arab Workers

Although Palestine's first railroad line, a French-financed project linking Jaffa on the Mediterranean coast to Jerusalem high in the hill country, was opened in 1892 and the subsequent two and one-half decades witnessed substantial railway development, very little is known about the railway workers themselves until after World War I. At that point the railway work force seems to have been drawn mainly from the local Arab population, along with many Egyptians conscripted for labor service with the British forces conquering Palestine from the Ottomans and a small number of Syrian, Greek, and other foreign skilled workers.[13] These workers were joined from 1919 onward by Jewish immigrants from Russia and Poland channeled into railroad jobs by agencies of the Zionist Organization and by the employment offices of the two labor-Zionist parties, the social-democratic Ahdut Ha-Avodah (Unity of Labor) and its nonsocialist rival, Ha-Poel Ha-Tsair (Young Worker).[14] The Zionist movement was anxious to lay the basis for the large-scale immigration and settlement finally made possible by the Balfour Declaration of November 1917, in which Britain had committed itself to supporting the establishment in Palestine of a "national home" for the Jews.

For the labor-Zionist parties and, from 1920 onward, for their creation the Histadrut (the General Organization of Hebrew Workers in the Land of Israel), which soon became not only the central institution of the labor-Zionist movement but also a dominant force in the Yishuv as a whole, placing new Jewish immigrants in jobs on the railroads was not simply or even primarily a matter of securing their individual livelihoods. It was part of the broader campaign for the conquest of labor (*kibbush ha-avodah*), a campaign the goal of which was the achievement of Hebrew labor (*avodah ivrit*).[15] These were central elements in the discourse and practice of the labor-Zionist movement. Though they had roots in the socialist ideology that adherents of labor Zionism brought with them from Eastern Europe, they were in large part the product of the Jewish workers' encounter with Palestinian realities in the decade before World War I.

Those immigrants' desire to proletarianize themselves and create a Jewish working class in Palestine that would both wage its class struggle and assert itself as the vanguard of the Zionist movement as a whole foundered on the fact that the gradual, though incomplete, integration of Palestine into the capitalist world market and the transformation of agrarian relations in the countryside from the late nineteenth century onward, coupled with rapid population growth, had created a growing pool of landless Arabs available for wage labor in the new Jewish agricultural settlements as well as in the towns and cities. The domination of the local labor market by large numbers of Arab workers willing to work for low wages and a severe shortage of employment opportunities owing to the country's underdevelopment posed a serious problem for the Zionist project. Unless employment in jobs with wages approaching European rates could be found or created, it was unlikely that Jewish immigrants would come to Palestine in significant numbers or remain there long, and the firm implantation of an ever-growing Yishuv would be very much in doubt.

Through a process of trial and error the labor-Zionist movement gradually developed two complementary strategies to deal with this situation.[16] To create employment opportunities and develop the Yishuv's increasingly self-sufficient economic base, the Histadrut, less a conventional trade union federation than a highly centralized instrument of the Zionist project, used funds supplied largely by the Zionist Organization (which until the 1930s was dominated by bourgeois Zionists) gradually to build up its own high-wage economic sector, in which only Jews would be employed, including a ramified network of industrial, transport, marketing, and service enterprises and new forms of collective and cooperative agricultural settlement (the *kibbutz* and the *moshav*). At the same time, the labor-Zionist movement engaged in a sustained effort to gain for Jews a larger share of the existing and newly created jobs in other sectors by trying to induce Jewish and other private employers and the British administration to hire Jewish workers instead of less expensive and (at least initially) less demanding Arab workers. This in turn required an effort to pressure Jewish workers who sought easier ways of making a living to accept and remain at even the most difficult and poorly paid occupations. The Histadrut leadership insisted that the fate of the Zionist project in Palestine depended upon the success of this relentless campaign for the conquest of labor and the achievement of maximal Hebrew labor (i.e., Jewish employment) in every sector of Palestine's economy.[17]

Joint Organization among the Railway Workers

Achieving the conquest of labor on the Palestine Railways proved particularly difficult, however. Few Jewish immigrants channeled into railroad jobs were willing to endure for very long the low wages, long hours, harsh conditions, and abusive treatment characteristic of railway work in Palestine, so, whenever better jobs were available elsewhere, the Jewish immigrants quit. The leaders of the first organization of railway workers in Palestine, the exclusively Jewish Railway Workers' Association (Agudat Poalei Ha-Rakevet [RWA]), founded in 1919, and leaders of the Histadrut, to which that union was affiliated, thus found that labor Zionism's struggle to strengthen Hebrew labor in this economically and politically vital sector conflicted with what most Jewish workers perceived to be their own self-interest.

244 / Comparing Jewish Societies

It soon became apparent that a significant number of Jews could be kept working as railwaymen only if wages and working conditions were significantly improved. The Jewish railway workers, however, though disproportionately represented among the skilled workers, accounted for only a small minority (ranging from 8 to 12 percent) of the railway work force as a whole. No matter how well organized, the Jewish railway workers could not hope to improve their wages and working conditions by their own efforts. This brought to the fore the issue of cooperation between the Jews and the Arab railwaymen, who constituted the great majority of the work force, especially the Arab foremen and skilled workers in Haifa. The issue became especially acute when, in the summer of 1921, Arab railway workers in Haifa (to which the Palestine Railways' main maintenance and repair workshops were being transferred from Lydda) approached their unionized Jewish coworkers about the possibility of cooperation; some even expressed interest in joining the Histadrut, attractive not only because of its apparent strength as a labor organization but also because it offered its members such services as health care, interest-free loans, and access to consumer cooperatives.

That the Haifa workshops were the scene of these initial contacts is not surprising. As noted earlier, before World War II these shops constituted the largest single concentration of industrial wage labor in Palestine, employing side by side hundreds of Arab, Jewish, and other workers, many of them skilled or semiskilled. In the 1920s a substantial Jewish minority lived alongside an Arab majority in Haifa, which was a rapidly growing and relatively cosmopolitan city already on its way to becoming Palestine's main port and industrial center.[18] In this atmosphere it was possible for Jewish workers, especially recent arrivals from Russia who had been radicalized by the October Revolution and its aftermath, to establish contact with an emerging stratum of relatively skilled and educated Arab workers and foremen interested in trade unionism. Some of the latter were no doubt influenced by the activities of the Jewish union, but others may already have become acquainted with trade unionism in their countries of origin (e.g., those from Syria or Egypt) or through contact in Palestine with non-Jewish European workers, mainly Greeks and Italians, who had their own mutual aid societies.

Thus, developments on the ground among the railway workers themselves first put the issue of relations between Jewish and Arab workers on the agenda of the Zionist labor movement and later kept it there. Well into the 1920s the question of joint organization (*irgun meshutaf*) was extensively (and often hotly) debated within and among the contending left-Zionist parties within the Histadrut. In these debates party leaders and Histadrut officials expressed a broad range of conflicting perspectives about joint organization, ranging from enthusiasm to strenuous opposition.

On the one hand, many left-Zionists professed loyalty to the principle of class solidarity across ethnic lines. As socialists standing at the head of what they regarded as a better-organized and culturally more advanced Jewish working class, they felt that they had a moral obligation to help their less class-conscious and largely unorganized Arab fellow workers—a sort of proletarian *mission civilisatrice*.[19] Although this perspective was tinged with paternalism and replete with contradictions and ultimately could not be separated from the broader issue of the Zionist project's implications for Palestine's Arab majority, it would nonetheless be a mistake to lose sight of the subjective moral impulse involved and of the extent to which even the most exclusivist practices were embedded in a discourse of socialism and proletarian internationalism.

Arguments based on morality and principle were complemented by more pragmatic arguments. Some labor-Zionist leaders argued that the best way to eliminate the threat that cheap unorganized Arab labor posed to expensive organized Jewish labor and enhance job opportunities for Jews was to help Arab workers organize themselves. Organized Arab workers would presumably be better able to raise their wages, eliminating or at least reducing the wage differential that led employers to prefer them to Jews. It is unlikely that such a strategy could have been effective in the labor market that existed in Palestine at that time, but it nonetheless had its proponents, among them (in the early 1920s, at least) David Ben-Gurion, the Histadrut's increasingly powerful secretary and preeminent leader of Ahdut Ha-Avodah.[20]

But labor-Zionist leaders also expressed anxiety about joint organization's possible consequences for the Zionist project. The admission of Arabs to the Histadrut or its constituent trade unions, or even their organization into separate unions under the Histadrut's tutelage, was likely to conflict with the long-term goal of increasing Jewish employment, and, once organized, the Arab workers might not be controllable. "From the humanitarian standpoint, it is clear that we must organize them," said one Histadrut official in December 1920, "but from the national standpoint, when we organize them we will be arousing them against us. They will receive the good that is in organization and use it against us."[21] Histadrut leaders were also well aware that in neighboring Egypt, for example, the trade unions were under the influence of the nationalists and played a significant role in the anticolonial struggle.[22]

In the end the most important factor prodding the Histadrut toward action was probably the fear that, if the Histadrut did not organize Arab workers, the Palestinian Arab nationalist movement—defined in labor-Zionist discourse not as an authentic national movement but, rather, as an instrument of exploitative and reactionary Arab landlords and clerics—might seize the initiative with potentially dangerous consequences for the Zionist project. In January 1922 the Histadrut majority, led by Ben-Gurion and his allies, endorsed joint organization among the railway workers, a decision reaffirmed and extended to encompass workers in other mixed workplaces at the Histadrut's third congress in July 1927. These resolutions also required, however, that any joint union of Arabs and Jews be composed of separate and largely autonomous national sections for each, with the Jewish sections to remain affiliated with the Histadrut.[23] From the standpoint of labor Zionism this approach had the apparent virtue of reconciling the demands of proletarian internationalism and Zionism: the Histadrut would demonstrate its commitment to helping Arab fellow workers unionize and improve their lot while at the same time preserving the exclusively Jewish character of the Histadrut and its trade union organizations, which would thus be free to carry out its national (i.e., Zionist) tasks, including immigration, settlement, economic development, and the struggle for Hebrew labor.

Abortive Unity

This position was not acceptable, however, to the Arab skilled workers and foremen who spoke for a substantial number of other Arabs employed in the Haifa railway workshops and elsewhere. As they became increasingly aware that the Histadrut was an integral part of the Zionist movement, the Arabs insisted that any joint union of Jews and Arabs not be divided into separate national sections and not have any links with the Histadrut. Ilyas Asad, one of the Arab workers' leaders, told his Jewish colleagues at a March 1924 meeting of the Railway Workers' Association council:

> I am striving to establish ties between the Jewish and Arab workers because I am certain that if we are connected we will help one another, without regard to religion or nationality. Many Arab workers do not wish to join nationalist organizations because they understand their

purpose and do not wish to abet a lie. They saw on the membership card [of the railway workers' union] the words Federation of Jewish Workers [i.e., the Histadrut] and they cannot understand what purpose this serves. I ask all the comrades to remove the word Jewish, and I am sure that if they agree there will be a strong bond between us and all the Arabs will join. I would be the first who would not want to join a nationalist labor organization. There are many Arab nationalist organizations, and we do not want to join them, and they will say we have joined a Jewish nationalist organization.[24]

As a result of these differences, negotiations between Arab and Jewish railway workers' leaders over the formation of a joint union for all the railway workers in Palestine were for years unsuccessful. In 1924, however, adherents of Poalei Tsiyyon Smol (Workers of Zion-Left), a party that occupied the extreme left end of the Zionist spectrum, won effective control of the RWA. Although committed to establishing a Jewish homeland in Palestine, this small but vigorous party simultaneously regarded itself as the authentic revolutionary vanguard of the world Jewish proletariat (and unsuccessfully sought admission to the Comintern as such); rejected participation in the Zionist Organization, which it regarded as an instrument of the Jewish bourgeoisie; and denounced the Histadrut majority's determination to build up a separate high-wage economic enclave for Jews in Palestine.[25] This party won growing support among the rank and file of the (still exclusively Jewish) railway workers' union because its call for militancy and class struggle was attractive to many disgruntled workers, whose already miserable wages and working conditions were being exacerbated by layoffs and management efforts to cut costs and who had lost patience with demands by the Ahdut Ha-Avodah–dominated Histadrut for self-sacrifice in the national cause. Poalei Tsiyyon Smol also advocated a position on the question of joint organization that seemed to offer a real prospect of achieving unity between Arabs and Jews, which many of the Jewish workers had come to see as an absolutely essential precondition for improving their situation. The party not only rejected the notion of separate national sections within the railway workers' union, but it also wanted the Histadrut itself to undergo what it termed a separation of functions: that is, to transfer its Zionist functions to a separate organization and transform itself into a Jewish-Arab trade union federation committed solely to the class struggle.

After an intensive effort the new railway union leadership came to terms with the leaders of the Arab workers in November 1924. The Arab unionists agreed to join their Jewish colleagues in a new international union with the understanding that they would play an equal role in running the union and that the new organization would disaffiliate from the Histadrut if it refused to accept the separation of functions. By the end of November 1924 several hundred Arab workers had joined the union (now known as the Union of Railway, Postal and Telegraph Workers [URPTW]), transforming an organization that had since its inception as the RWA been virtually all Jewish into one whose membership was roughly half-Jewish and half-Arab and encompassed some 20 to 25 percent of the railway work force.[26]

This joint union of Arabs and Jews survived for only a few months. Most of the Arab unionists soon concluded that their Jewish colleagues were not sincerely committed to achieving unity as originally conceived nor to developing a completely independent and apolitical trade union dedicated only to the interests of all the railway workers. The Arabs also grew impatient with what they took to be dissembling, if not outright deception, on the part of their Jewish colleagues, whom they came to believe were not being straightforward with them about their commitment to the Zionist project.

Their suspicions and doubts were not without basis in reality. Even as they spoke of proletarian internationalism and Arab-Jewish solidarity, the Jewish union leaders continued to work behind the scenes with the Histadrut to increase Jewish employment by incessant lobbying of railways management, the government of Palestine, and the Colonial Office—and by pressing Jewish foremen to hire only Jewish job applicants.[27] The Histadrut's campaign for Hebrew labor on the railways, to which even the new Poalei Tsiyyon Smol–influenced leadership was party, was a source of tremendous resentment among the Arab rank and file, who felt that they were being discriminated against in hiring and promotion and feared displacement by Jewish immigrants.[28]

The Arab unionists also felt that their Jewish colleagues were taking advantage of the Arabs' ignorance of Hebrew and limited understanding of Yishuv politics. That the Arab unionists did not fully grasp their Jewish colleagues' politics is suggested by the fact that, as late as November 1924, Hasanayn Fahmi, one of the Arabs co-opted onto the union's central committee, was asking his Jewish colleagues whether or not there was in fact any connection between the union he had just joined and the Zionist movement and whether or not they themselves were Zionists. In this and other instances Poalei Tsiyyon Smol activists tended to provide evasive or disingenuous responses in order to downplay their commitment to Zionism, avoid alienating the Arab unionists, and preserve the joint union. But there were also instances of deliberate deception. At a meeting of the union's council in January 1925, for example, the Jewish translator who was rendering the proceedings into Arabic for the benefit of the Arab delegates deliberately watered down the Zionist content of a speech by Ben-Gurion to make it more palatable to the Arabs.[29] These things made the Arab unionists vulnerable to criticism, from the Arab nationalist press and activists and from among the rank and file, that the Arab unionists were being duped and exploited by the Zionists. In the first months of 1925 most of the Arab trade unionists, who had joined the URPTW's leadership only a few months earlier, quit, taking most of the Arab rank and file with them.

The Jewish unionists and the Histadrut attributed the collapse of the joint union to sabotage by the communists, Palestine Railways management, or both. Activists of the still almost exclusively Jewish but strongly anti-Zionist Palestine Communist Party (known as the PKP, from its initials in Yiddish) had sought to alert the Arab railway workers that they were joining a union still closely affiliated with the Zionist Histadrut and led by committed Zionists, but at the beginning of 1925 the communists were in fact urging the Arab workers not to leave the joint union but, rather, to remain within it and struggle to reform it. Palestine Railways management had an obvious interest in keeping its work force divided and does seem to have used selective wage increases and equally selective dismissals to signal its antiunion attitude to the Arab rank and file. Yet the decision of most of the Arab workers to leave the union cannot be attributed solely or even mainly to management pressure. In fact, the Histadrut's attempt to pin the blame on "outside agitators" tells us less about the actual causes of the breakup in early 1925 than it does about labor Zionism's conception of its own project and of Arabs, which rendered it unable to come to terms with its own role in this failure.[30]

In the summer of 1925, a few months after the breakup of the joint union, the seceding Arab unionists joined forces with the leaders of a mutual aid society for Arab railway workers and established a new, exclusively Arab organization, the Palestinian Arab Workers' Society (PAWS).[31] Although PAWS initially consisted almost exclusively of Arab railway workers in Haifa, its new name and its program indicated its founders' ambition to make it the Arab counterpart of the Histadrut, an organization that would eventually encompass all the Arab workers in Palestine. Until the emergence of rival communist-led trade union federations in the 1940s, PAWS was indeed the largest and most important Palestinian Arab labor organization, uniting a fluctuating membership drawn from various trades and locales around a more stable core of Haifa railway workers, whose own organization would later be formally known as the Arab Union of Railway Workers (AURW).[32]

Tenuous Cooperation

From 1925 until the end of the mandate period, then, two separate unions were active among the railway workers. Relations between the AURW and the older, larger, and wealthier union led by Jews, soon back in the hands of supporters of Ben-Gurion and the Histadrut majority and known from 1931 as the International Union of Railway, Postal and Telegraph Employees in Palestine (IU), were often rocky, with alternating periods of cooperation and conflict.[33] The main impetus for cooperation was the glaringly obvious fact that, confronted by a highly intransigent management backed by a miserly colonial state, neither union was sufficiently strong on its own to achieve very much for its membership: The IU had some 250 dues-paying members in 1927 and the AURW even fewer. Chronic discontent by the rank and file over low wages and poor working conditions was periodically exacerbated by what the workers perceived as arbitrary and abusive acts by management, including wage cuts, layoffs, and short hours. The resulting sense of grievance and the understanding that disunity meant weakness generated demands from rank-and-file Arab and Jewish workers that their leaders put aside their differences and work together.

Typically, pressure from below and upsurges of rank-and-file militancy led the two unions' leaders to negotiate the formation of an ad hoc joint committee based in Haifa. This committee, which was comprised of representatives of both unions, would then proceed to organize protest meetings, draw up memoranda of grievances and demands, and represent the railway workers in talks with management. These joint committees tended, however, to be rather short-lived. After a few months they were increasingly undermined by conflicts between the two unions, ultimately resulting in the joint committee's dissolution and barrages of mutual recriminations, as each side accused the other of selfishly sabotaging unity and the workers' interests. As a result, relations between the two unions were not infrequently clouded by bitterness and mistrust.

In large measure this mistrust was generated by the steadfast insistence by the IU that it was the sole legitimate representative of all the railway workers in Palestine, Jewish and Arab. The Jewish-led union thus refused to regard its Arab counterpart as an equal partner that authentically represented the Arab railway workers and even launched sporadic drives to undermine it by directly recruiting Arab workers. The IU's claim to exclusivity was bolstered by its retention, until 1936, of a number of Arab members attracted by its much more effective and visible presence in the workplace and as a national organization, the perception that behind the IU stood the wealthy and powerful Histadrut, and an ability to offer its members access (via the Histadrut) to services that were totally beyond the AURW's means, including health care, loans, and legal aid.

For their part the AURW's leaders accepted the legitimacy of, and were willing to cooperate with, the IU but only as the representative of the Jewish railway workers. The Palestinian unionists enormously resented the IU's refusal to extend reciprocal recognition, its attempts to recruit Arab workers, and its continued commitment to Hebrew labor, manifested in constant lobbying to get more Jews hired. Arabs who joined the IU were denounced by AURW leaders as dupes or lackeys of the Zionists, if not outright traitors.

The rank and file's desire for cooperation was such, however, that neither leadership could afford to appear to be seen as openly opposed to unity. For example, even when IU leaders concluded that the benefits of cooperation were accruing disproportionately to the AURW, broke up joint committees, and initiated drives to recruit Arab workers, they sought to place the blame for the collapse of cooperation on their erstwhile Arab partners, whom they accused of inactivity or bad faith.[34] The Arab unionists displayed a similar concern for rank-and-file opinion: on several occasions in the late 1920s they went so far as to distribute leaflets in Hebrew to the Jewish railway workers to make known their version of what had led to the breakup of a joint committee and to accuse the IU leadership of acting in bad faith and undermining the workers' unity.[35] Moreover, at least until the outbreak in 1936 of a countrywide Arab revolt against British rule and Zionism, Arab railway unionists generally ignored or resisted pressure from the Palestinian nationalist movement to terminate cooperation with Jewish unionists. It is significant, too, that the dream of a single union for all of Palestine's railway workers remained very much alive among the rank and file right up to 1936, and in a more subdued way even beyond, though its realization was always blocked by the same issues that had undermined unity in 1925.

The extent to which this apparently widespread desire for cooperation at the institutional level was accompanied by the development of social relationships between Arab and Jewish workers at the personal level, within or outside the workplace, is unclear. In the early 1920s, at least, some Jewish railway workers lived in predominantly Arab neighborhoods of Haifa, and elsewhere the long shifts characteristic of railway work threw Jews and Arabs together, especially at remote locations. A report in 1928 of Arab workers attending the funeral of a Jewish coworker suggests some degree of social interaction.[36] In his memoirs Bulus Farah, an Arab unionist (and later a communist activist) who went to work in the Haifa workshops in 1925 as a fifteen-year-old apprentice, spoke of the "mutual understanding" that had prevailed there and suggested that the Jewish workers respected their Arab coworkers for their technical abilities.[37] This is not implausible, given that most of the Jews were new to industrial work, and some may have seen the Arabs as exemplars of the proletarian authenticity for which they were striving. Over the years Arab and Jewish union leaders do seem to have developed personal relationships: Yehezkel Abramov, a longtime Jewish railway union leader, would in his old age remember sitting around with colleagues from the AURW on the Tel Aviv beachfront after a joint meeting with management.[38]

Yet Abramov also conveyed his frustration that most of his fellow Jews could not be bothered to learn or use the names of Arab coworkers and instead referred to specific individuals simply as "the Arab."[39] Unlike his colleagues, Abramov took the trouble to learn Arabic and made a point of sitting with Arab workers during lunch breaks at the Haifa workshops. That he regarded himself as exceptional in this regard suggests a high degree of social separation: though Arabs and Jews may have worked side by side, apparently in their leisure time within and outside the workplace they generally kept to themselves. In the 1920s and the early 1930s the IU sponsored cultural and educational activities for its Jewish and Arab members, and the meetings that it sponsored jointly with the AURW were usually held in Arab coffeehouses. But there are no reports of Jewish workers frequenting Arab coffeehouses, the main site of leisure-time social interaction among men in urban Arab neighborhoods, and relatively few Arab workers took part in the cultural and social institutions sponsored by the Histadrut or other Jewish organizations.

In mixed cities like Haifa some degree of interaction in public spaces was inevitable and persisted until 1948. Despite Zionist campaigns to boycott Arab in favor of Jewish produce, many Jews (especially from the working class) continued to frequent Arab markets to take advantage of lower prices, and some Jews continued to live in Arab neighborhoods, where rents were lower. But Jews were increasingly concentrated in exclusively Jewish neighborhoods; the string of new workers' suburbs just north of Haifa, especially after outbreaks of violence in 1921, 1929, and, in particular, 1936–39, made mixed neighborhoods unsafe.

Wartime Resurgence and Postwar Militancy

In addition to exacerbating residential, social, and economic segregation, the intercommunal violence and tensions that accompanied the 1936–39 revolt made cooperation between Arab and Jewish railway workers even on purely economic issues all but impossible. By contrast, the period of 1940 to 1946 witnessed unprecedented solidarity between Arab and Jewish workers, not only among the railwaymen but in many other mixed enterprises as well. This may seem ironic in retrospect, since by the end of 1947 Palestine was engulfed in a full-scale civil war. But during World War II and immediately after it a short-lived conjuncture created new possibilities for militant joint action, though they were eventually eclipsed by escalating political tensions.

The Palestinian working class, Arab and Jewish, expanded very dramatically during the war. Disruption of the usual sources of supply stimulated development of the country's industrial base, as did the demand created by the enormously swollen British and Allied military presence. Military bases and related service enterprises proliferated, drawing tens of thousands of Arab peasants and townspeople into wage labor at work sites that also employed Jews. The railway sector shared in this expansion. After suffering during the 1930s because of growing competition from motor transport and then the Arab revolt, the war years witnessed the rapid extension of railroad lines, a tripling of freight tonnage carried per kilometer, and a large increase in the work force of the Palestine Railways.[40]

Labor shortages in many sectors strengthened the workers' bargaining position, while high inflation pushed them toward action. In Palestine, as elsewhere in Britain's domain during this period, the British colonial authorities moderated their hostility to trade unions, created a new apparatus to monitor and mediate labor disputes, and looked more favorably on labor legislation. In these circumstances there ensued an unprecedented wave of unionization and militancy that affected Arab workers most dramatically because they had hitherto been less active and less organized. The leaders of both the Histadrut and the PAWS regarded this development with some ambivalence. By contrast, this upsurge was encouraged by, and in turn benefited, newly reinvigorated left-wing forces in both the Arab community and the Yishuv, which implicitly challenged nationalist leaderships on both sides by advocating class solidarity and political compromise between Arabs and Jews.

During the war a new Arab Left emerged in Palestine, organized in the communist-led National Liberation League ('Usbat al-Taharrur al-Watani [NLL]). Left-wing trade union activists, among them veterans of the AURW, won significant support in unions hitherto under the control of the more conservative PAWS leadership as well as in newly organized unions, leading ultimately to a split in the Arab trade union movement and the establishment of a Left-led Arab Workers' Congress aligned with the NLL. In the Yishuv the initially kibbutz-based socialist-Zionist Ha-Shomer Ha-Tsair (Young Guard) movement, which advocated a binational Palestine and Arab-Jewish class solidarity and was trying to extend its influence among Jewish urban workers, now emerged as a serious force on the left flank of the Histadrut leadership. In a sense Ha-Shomer Ha-Tsair can be said to have replaced the defunct Poalei Tsiyyon Smol at the left end of the Zionist spectrum; it won significant support among militant Jewish workers, including railway workers, in what had become known as Red Haifa. The Jewish communist movement also resurfaced during and after the war. Largely discredited in the Yishuv because of its support for the 1936–39 Arab revolt, it now sought to gain legitimacy and support from the wartime popularity of the Soviet Union, whose Red Army the Yishuv hailed as the main force fighting the Nazis, and by trying to ride the wave of worker activism. The Jewish communists also moderated their long-standing hostility to Zionism and sought admission to the Histadrut, from which they had been purged two decades earlier.

Among the railway workers the changing circumstances were first manifested in unprecedentedly smooth relations between the IU and the AURW from 1940 onward. The IU tacitly recognized that under the prevailing circumstances recruitment of Arab workers was unrealistic and rapprochement with the AURW therefore unavoidable, while the paralysis of the Arab nationalist movement during the war years and strong rank-and-file pressure made the AURW leadership more amenable to cooperation.[41] A series of job actions and short strikes culminated, much to the unhappiness of the Histadrut and PAWS leaderships, in a three-day occupation of the Haifa workshops in February 1944.[42] Unrest continued after the end of the war in Europe, manifested during 1945 in a number of brief wildcat strikes by railway and postal workers, now among the most militant and experienced (and, of course, most integrated) segments of the Palestinian working class. The NLL's newspaper, *al-Ittihad,* hailed these incidents as "clear proof of the possibility of joint action in every workplace," provided that the workers steered clear of interference by both Zionism and "Arab reaction."[43]

The Arab communists' prescription seemed to find confirmation in April 1946, when a planned strike by Jewish and Arab postal workers in Tel Aviv spontaneously expanded to encompass some thirteen thousand Arab and Jewish postal, telegraph, railway, port, and public works department workers, along with ten thousand lower- and middle-level white-collar government employees. This general strike paralyzed the British colonial administration and won the support of much of Jewish and Arab public opinion. The Arab and Jewish communists naturally saw in it a wonderful manifestation of class solidarity, "a blow against the 'divide and rule' policy of imperialism, a slap in the face of those who hold chauvinist ideologies and propagate national division," but warned the strikers against "defeatist and reactionary elements, Arab and Jewish." Conservative newspapers on both sides were less enthusiastic. The conservative nationalist newspaper *Filastin,* for example, attacked PAWS for allegedly colluding in what it regarded as a politically motivated and Zionist-inspired movement. The right-wing Jewish daily *Maariv* hailed the strike at first but later denounced it as detrimental to the Zionist cause.[44]

The strikers ultimately won many of their demands, and their victory gave a strong boost to the fledgling Arab labor movement. The following year witnessed the rapid growth of unions and the spread of worker activism, especially in the army camps and at the oil refinery and the Iraq Petroleum Company's pipeline terminal in Haifa. In these workplaces Arab and Jewish workers often cooperated in pursuit of higher wages and better conditions, although relations between the Histadrut and the Arab unions were never entirely free of friction.

Civil War and Partition

That friction was exacerbated, and the postwar wave of activism ultimately brought to an end, by the rising political tensions that accompanied the escalation in 1947 of the three-way struggle among the Zionist movement, the Palestinian nationalist movement, and the British to determine the fate of Palestine. In 1944 the Zionists had launched a campaign to force

Britain, their erstwhile protector and ally, to open Palestine to Jewish immigration and move toward Jewish statehood, which in turn helped stimulate the revival of the Palestinian Arab nationalist movement. Unable to suppress opposition or achieve a negotiated solution, an exhausted and isolated Britain turned the Palestine issue over to the United Nations, whose General Assembly adopted a resolution on 29 November 1947 recommending the partition of Palestine into independent Arab and Jewish states. Partition was rejected by the leaders of Palestine's Arab community, still two-thirds of the country's population, who saw it as a violation of their right as the indigenous majority to self-determination in an undivided Palestine. Partition was accepted by most of the leaders of the Yishuv and of the Zionist movement, for whom a sovereign Jewish state, even if in only part of Palestine, was still a tremendous achievement.[45]

Violence between Arabs and Jews erupted almost immediately after the vote and quickly escalated into a cycle of terrorist violence and countervivolence directed mainly against civilians. By the end of December over three hundred and fifty people had lost their lives in the civil war engulfing Palestine. The single bloodiest incident of this first month of violence was touched off on 30 December 1947, when operatives of the right-wing Zionist Irgun Tsvai Leumi (National Military Organization, usually referred to in Hebrew by its acronym, Etsel), commanded by Menachem Begin, threw a number of grenades into a crowd of a hundred Arabs gathered at the main gate of the British-owned oil refinery on the northern outskirts of Haifa in the hope of finding work as day laborers. Six were killed and forty-two wounded in what Etsel claimed was an act of retaliation for recent attacks on Jews elsewhere in Palestine. Within minutes of the incident an outraged mob of Arab refinery workers and outsiders turned on the Jewish refinery workers, killing forty-one and wounding forty-nine before British army and police units arrived.[46]

News of the bloodshed at the oil refinery quickly reached the nearby repair and maintenance workshops of the Palestine Railways. Tensions were already high there because of the deteriorating political and security situation in the country, and now they soared to explosive levels as some of the younger Arab workers threatened their Jewish coworkers (of whom there were fewer than a hundred at the time) and tried to shut down the machinery. The railway workshops were, however, spared the orgy of bloodletting that had engulfed the oil refinery. The veteran Arab unionists, some of whom had been among the founders of PAWS, quickly intervened, faced down the hotheads, and kept the peace until buses could be brought to transport the Jewish workers home safely. The workshops were then shut for ten days, until relative calm had been restored in Haifa and security arrangements put in place.[47]

In the following months Palestine descended into full-scale civil war, but the railway workshops continued to function as normally as external circumstances allowed. The existence of Arab and Jewish union cadres with extensive experience of cooperation and a tradition of mutual respect allowed these workers to avoid, for a time at least, being drawn into the maelstrom of intercommunal violence. After April 1948, however, the question of relations between Arabs and Jews at the Haifa workshops became moot. The work force there was left almost exclusively Jewish, when most of the city's Arab population fled as Jewish military forces besieged their neighborhoods. The same transformation took place throughout the country. Though the work force of the Palestine Railways had been mostly Arab, the flight or expulsion from their homes of half of Palestine's Arab population during 1947 to 1949 left the work force of the new Israel Railways almost entirely Jewish.[48] Nearly four decades of interaction among Arab and Jewish railway workers thus came to an abrupt end.

Rethinking Palestinian History

There are students of the Zionist-Palestinian conflict who have pointed to instances of cooperation between Jews and Arabs in mandatory Palestine, especially cooperation among workers, as evidence that the conflict need not have taken the course it did, that a peaceful solution that met the basic needs of both Arabs and Jews might have been found had the voices of reason, compromise, and working-class solidarity on both sides prevailed. The history of the mandate period thus becomes a story of missed opportunities, or a morality tale in which the so-called bad guys on both sides triumph over the peacemakers, whose weakness and ineffectuality is somehow never really accounted for.[49]

I am not making that argument here. On the contrary, the Zionist and Palestinian nationalist movements clearly sought irreconcilable objectives and were on a collision course from the very start. Moreover, although during the mandate period Arab and Jewish railway workers were involved in persistent efforts to cooperate and developed a sense of solidarity that at times transcended (or at least moderated) national divisions, relations among them were profoundly affected by the dynamics of the broader

Zionist-Palestinian conflict, as the denouement of their interaction in 1948 conclusively demonstrated. In addition, as I noted earlier, the railway workers were in many respects an atypical group.

In the history recounted here one can find instances of both conflict and cooperation between Jews and Arabs. Instead of trying to locate the sole or essential meaning of relations among Arab and Jewish railway workers in either term, however, it may make more sense to shift our focus to the ways in which intercommunal as well as intracommunal identities, boundaries, and projects were constructed and reproduced and place in the foreground the contestation that always characterized those processes. Thus, among the Arab railway workers some unionists who certainly regarded themselves as nationalists strongly opposed to what they saw as Zionist encroachment on their homeland nonetheless defied the official nationalist line by embracing a discourse of worker solidarity across ethnic boundaries that promoted cooperation with Zionist Jews. Similarly, contending political forces among the Jewish railway workers put forward conflicting definitions of what it meant to be a Jew and a worker in Palestine and widely differing notions of how to relate to the Arab majority of the railway work force. More broadly, the existence of a more or less unified market for unskilled and semiskilled labor in Palestine, especially in the government sector, and the circumstances and exigencies that employment by the colonial administration generated, helped shape perceptions, strategies, and relationships among all members of the Palestine Railways work force. In this sense the Arab and Jewish railway workers not only "made themselves" (to borrow E. P. Thompson's imagery) but also "made" each other within a broader matrix of relations and forces.

It is not only with respect to the railway workers, however, that a relational approach that focuses on the mutually constitutive interactions between Arabs and Jews in Palestine may prove useful. For example, I suggested earlier that the urgent need to exit (at least partially) a labor market dominated by abundant low-wage Arab labor prompted the labor-Zionist movement to strive to construct a relatively self-sufficient, high-wage economic enclave for Jews in Palestine. This imperative also propelled the unrelenting struggle for Hebrew labor and other practices couched in the language of worker solidarity and class struggle but aimed largely at excluding or displacing Arab workers. These practices exacerbated intercommunal tensions but also facilitated labor Zionism's drive for hegemony over rival social and political forces *within* the Yishuv. By the mid-1930s this strategy, implemented mainly by the Histadrut (whose membership encompassed more than a quarter of the Yishuv's population in 1936) and its affiliated economic, social, cultural, and military institutions, had helped the Zionist labor camp become the dominant force within the Yishuv and the international Zionist movement. In this sense many of the institutions and practices that for an entire historical period, from the 1930s into the 1970s, were considered among the most distinctive features of the Yishuv and of Israeli society (e.g., the kibbutz, the powerful public and Histadrut sectors of the economy, the cult of pioneering, the role of the military) can be understood as directly or indirectly the product of the Zionist project's interaction with Arabs and Arab society on the ground in Palestine.

Similarly, while Israeli sociologists have conventionally explained the subordinate social location and status of Israel's Oriental Jews—the majority of the country's Jewish population, which derives from Arab countries or from elsewhere in Asia or Africa, as opposed to Eastern Europe—in terms of the failure of these culturally traditional people to adapt successfully to a modern society, recent critical scholarship has stressed their relegation to the bottom ranks of the labor market (where they displaced or replaced Palestinian Arabs) and official denigration of their culture, defined by the dominant groups in Israel as backward (Arab).[50] Before World War I some Zionist leaders had already envisioned Yemeni Jews as replacements for Palestinian Arab agricultural workers and actually sponsored Yemeni Jewish immigration to Palestine. After 1948 it was largely Jewish immigrants from Arab countries who filled the social vacuum created by the flight or expulsion of the vast majority of the Arabs who had lived within the borders of the new State of Israel. From this perspective, then, it can be argued that the matrix of Jewish-Arab interactions in Palestine played a central role in shaping ethnic relations within Jewish society in Palestine (and later Israel).

Arab society in Palestine was, in turn, profoundly influenced by the Zionist project in a variety of ways. There was, of course, the catastrophic displacement of 1947–49, but in the preceding decades Jewish immigration, settlement, investment. and state building had already had an important impact on Arab society. That impact can be seen in the direct and indirect effects of Jewish land purchases, settlement, and agricultural practices on Arab agrarian relations, the complex effects on the Arab economy of the large-scale influx of capital that accompanied Jewish immigration and development, and the effects of the economic and social policies implemented by a British administration committed to fostering a Jewish national home in Palestine but also concerned about alienating the country's Arab majority.

Most of the scholars who have so far deployed a relational approach have tended to emphasize the structural economic relationships between Arabs and Jews in Palestine, especially markets for land and labor. This emphasis has been extremely useful as a corrective to the conventional historiography, but it can marginalize questions of meaning and conduce to an economistic reductionism. Yet neither the evolution nor the content of a distinctly Palestinian Arab culture, identity, and national movement can be adequately understood except in relation to the specific character of the Palestinians' confrontation with Zionism. Nor can one make sense of the labor-Zionist project without taking into account not only labor market strategies but also the ways in which the Arab worker and the Arab working class in Palestine were represented and the roles they were made to play in labor-Zionist discourse. At a crucial stage it was to a significant extent in relation to those (always contested) representations of Arab workers that labor Zionism articulated its own identity, its sense of mission, and its strategy to achieve hegemony within the Yishuv and realize its version of Zionism.[51] The modes of interaction between the Arab and Jewish communities in Palestine and their mutually constitutive impact on one another must therefore be seen as discursive as well as material.[52]

As historians and others explore the history of modern Palestine in new ways, as the object of inquiry is reconceived, and as a different set of concepts and categories is deployed, it will become increasingly clear that the two communities were neither natural nor essentially monolithic entities, nor were they hermetically sealed off from each other, as the conventional historiography assumes. Rather, the two communities interacted in complex ways and had a mutually formative effect on each other, both as communities and through relationships that crossed communal boundaries to shape the identities and practices of various subgroups. These complex and contested processes operated at many levels and in many spheres, including markets for labor, land, agricultural produce and consumer goods, business ventures, residential patterns, manufacturing and services, municipal government, and various aspects of social and cultural life. These interactions also had an important but little explored spatial dimension manifested in shifts and reorientations in demographic, economic, political, and cultural relations and flows among and within different settlements, villages, urban neighborhoods, towns, cities, and regions of Palestine.

A number of recently published works already manifest new approaches to the histories of Arabs and Jews in Palestine. These approaches challenge conventional categories, cross hitherto unquestioned boundaries, and treat Palestine not as sui generis but as suitable for comparative study. This process will be furthered as more scholars frame and explore new and different kinds of problems while drawing on both Arabic and Hebrew source materials. In the long run, I hope, it will be possible to put the pieces together and move toward a new relational synthesis of the history of mandatory Palestine and, more broadly, of Palestinian history over the past two centuries. Such a synthesis will need to interrogate and transcend nationalist narratives on both sides, respecting what is specific to the histories of Arabs and Jews in Palestine even as it explores the ways in which those histories were (and remain) inextricably and fatefully intertwined.

NOTES

My thanks to Joel Beinin, Beshara Doumani, Joel Migdal, and the editors of *Comparative Studies in Society and History,* for their helpful comments on earlier versions of this essay. This version was completed while I was a Visiting Fellow at Princeton University's Shelby Cullom Davis Center for Historical Studies, for whose financial support and intellectual stimulation I am grateful.

1. Much of what follows also applies to the literature on Palestine in the late Ottoman period and to Israel and the Palestinians inside and outside what had been Palestine after 1948 as well. But it is especially relevant to the four decades during which Palestine existed as an administratively unified entity, before partition, war, Palestinian displacement, and massive Jewish immigration radically altered the terms of the interaction between Arabs and Jews in Palestine. For surveys of the field, see Kenneth W. Stein, "A Historiographic Review of Literature on the Origins of the Arab-Israeli Conflict," *American Historical Review* 96 (1991): 1450–65; Tarif Khalidi, "Palestinian Historiography: 1900–1948," *Journal of Palestine Studies* 10, no. 3 (Spring 1981): 59–76; and Beshara B. Doumani's important essay, "Rediscovering Ottoman Palestine: Writing Palestinians into History," *Journal of Palestine Studies* 21, no. 2 (Winter 1992): 5–28.

2. S. N. Eisenstadt, *Israeli Society* (New York: Basic Books, 1967), 1.

3. Talal Asad, "Anthropological Texts and Ideological Problems: An Analysis of Cohen on Arab Villages in Israel," *Review of Middle East Studies* 1 (1975): 14 n. 11. See also Gershon Shafir, *Land, Labor and the Origins of the Israeli-Palestinian Conflict, 1882–1914* (Cambridge: Cambridge University Press, 1989), 1–7.

4. Dan Horowitz and Moshe Lissak, *Origins of the Israeli Polity: Palestine*

262 I Comparing Jewish Societies

under the Mandate (Chicago: University of Chicago Press, 1978), 13; first published in Hebrew as Mi-yishuv li-medinah: yehudei erets yisrael bi-tekufat ha-mandat ke-kehilah politit (Tel Aviv: Am Oved, 1977).

5. For example, 'Abd al-Wahhab al-Kayyali, *Ta'rikh filastin al-hadith* (Beirut: Al-Mu'assasa al-'arabiyya lil-dirasat wa'l-nashr, 1970); or Muhammad Nakhlah, *Tatawwur al-mujtami' fi filastin* (Kuwait: Mu'assasat Dhat al-Salasil, 1983).

6. "Israel: Conflict, War and Social Change," in *The Sociology of War and Peace,* ed. Colin Creighton and Martin Shaw (Houndmills: The Macmillan Press, 1987), 131.

7. For example, research on the gendered character of those identities, discourses, and practices has gotten under way only recently.

8. The Israeli scholars who have pioneered what might be called the revisionist tendency of Israeli historiography include Baruch Kimmerling, Gershon Shafir, Michael Shalev, Lev Luis Grinberg, Tamar Gozanski, Shlomo Swirski, Ella Shohat, and the contributors to the now defunct journal *Mahbarot li-mehkar u-le-bikoret.* For a discussion of some of the revisionist works on the events of 1947–49 and of the political conjuncture out of which they emerged, see Zachary Lockman, "Original Sin," in *Intifada: The Palestinian Uprising Against Israeli Occupation,* ed. Zachary Lockman and Joel Beinin (Boston: South End Press, 1989); see also Laurence J. Silberstein, ed., *New Perspectives on Israeli History: The Early Years of the State* (New York: New York University Press, 1991).

Given the dispersion, statelessness, and subordination that characterize Palestinian life, the continuing centrality of the struggle for national self-determination and the limited resources at the disposal of most Palestinian scholars, explicit revisionism has perhaps not surprisingly been less in evidence among Palestinians. Nonetheless, a number of studies manifest what I call a relational approach, most notably Elia Zureik's *The Palestinians in Israel: A Study in Internal Colonialism* (London: Routledge and Kegan Paul, 1979). A number of other Palestinian scholars have produced studies that depart from conventional narratives in approach and choice of subject, including Salim Tamari, Musa al-Budayri, Mahir al-Sharif, 'Abd al-Qadir Yasin, Philip Mattar, and Muhammad Muslih. Various Palestinian research centers and institutions of higher education have in recent years also published important work in Arabic on aspects of Palestinian social and cultural history.

Among works produced by scholars who are neither Israeli nor Palestinian, pride of place belongs to Roger Owen's edited volume, *Studies in the Economic and Social History of Palestine in the Nineteenth and Twentieth Centuries* (Carbondale: Southern Illinois University Press, 1982), and especially to his introduction, which explicitly discusses various conceptualizations of Palestinian history. Innovative work has also been produced by Talal Asad, Theodore Swedenburg, Rachelle Taqqu, and Joel Beinin. This survey is, of course, by no means exhaustive.

9. "The Perils of Palestiniology," *Arab Studies Quarterly* 3 (1981): 403–11. The

subsumption of Palestinian identity, agency, and history is obviously related to the long-standing disparity in the relative power and status of Israeli Jews and Palestinians. While the former are citizens of an established nation-state, most of the latter live under alien (and often repressive) rule, whether within or outside their historic homeland, and as a people are still denied national self-determination in any part of Palestine.

10. The catastrophic disruption of Palestinian Arab society in 1947–49 and the consequent destruction of many of the source materials from which Palestinian social and cultural history might have been reconstructed, combined with the relative abundance of material on the Jewish side, make it very difficult to avoid privileging the history and perspectives of the Yishuv—a skewing that my own research presented here does not, I admit, entirely escape.

11. Palestine Railways, *Report of the General Manager.*

12. This discussion of the railway workers is drawn from a larger research project exploring interactions among Jewish and Arab workers, trade unions, labor movements, and leftist political parties during the mandate period.

13. The Syrians were not, of course, actually considered foreign until Britain and France divided up geographic Syria into the four new political entities of Syria, Lebanon, Palestine, and Transjordan. On the railway workers in the early postwar period, see Bulus Farah, *Min al-'uthmaniyya ila al-dawla al-'ibriyya* (Nazareth: al-Sawt, 1985), 40–46.

14. See the transcripts of interviews with Yehezkiel Abramov (9 April 1972) and Efrayyim Shvartzman (20 March 1972), Center for Oral Documentation, Archive of Labor and Pioneering, Lavon Institute for the Study of the Labor Movement, Tel Aviv (hereafter cited as "AL").

15. From its inception at the turn of the century and with diminishing consistency up to 1948, the labor-Zionist movement tended to use Hebrew (*ivri*) instead of Jewish (*yehudi*) to refer to itself and its project. This was an expression of labor Zionism's denigration and rejection of diaspora Judaism, which it associated with statelessness, powerlessness, and passivity, and its exaltation of the (suitably mythologized) ancient Hebrews as a socially normal and politically sovereign nation living in its homeland and working its soil. By conceiving of themselves as Hebrews, a new and different type of Jew living in the Land of Israel and free of the defects allegedly produced by two thousand years of exile, these Zionists meant to emphasize their authenticity and their rootedness in Palestine.

16. Gershon Shafir has analyzed most effectively how labor-Zionist ideology, and the practices and institutions associated with it, were strongly shaped by the markets for labor and land in which the immigrants of the Second Aliyah (wave of Jewish immigration) found themselves when they arrived in Palestine between 1903 and 1914 (see his book *Land, Labor and the Origins of the Israeli-Palestinian Conflict*).

17. For a classic statement of the doctrine of Hebrew labor, see David Ben-

Gurion, *Avodah ivrit* (Tel Aviv: Histadrut, 1932), translated into English and published in London as *Jewish Labour* at about the same time. Ben-Gurion went so far as to accuse Jewish private employers (mainly citrus farmers) who preferred Arab to Jewish workers of "economic antisemitism." On the campaigns to impose Hebrew labor on Jewish farmers, see Anita Shapira, *Ha-maavak ha-nikhzav: avodah ivrit, 1929–1939* (Futile Struggle: Hebrew Labor, 1929–1939) (Tel Aviv: Hakibbuts ha-meuhad, 1977).

18. Haifa's population rose from some 18,000 in 1918 to nearly 100,000 by 1936. On the city's development in this period, see Inlay Seikaly, "The Arab Community of Haifa, 1918–1936: A Study in Transformation" (Ph.D. diss., Oxford University, 1983); and Joseph Vashitz's uneven but useful study "Jewish-Arab Relations at Haifa under the British Mandate" (MS, kindly provided by the author).

19. Some went so far as to depict the Jewish proletariat in Palestine as the vanguard of a mighty movement that would liberate the oppressed workers of the entire Arab East, though this theme, not unpopular early in the decade, faded away thereafter. See, for example, Ben-Gurion's August 1921 theses for the Ahdut Ha-Avodah party congress, first published in issue 91 of the party organ, *Kuntres,* and later republished in *Anahnu ve-shekheineinu* (We and Our Neighbors) (Tel Aviv: Davar, 1931), a collection of his essays and speeches on the Arab question (61–62).

20. See, for example, his speech published in *Kuntres,* no. 106 (January 1922).

21. AL, protocols of meeting of the executive committee of the Histadrut (hereafter EC/H), 20 December 1920.

22. On the Egyptian labor and nationalist movements in this period, see Joel Beinin and Zachary Lockman, *Workers on the Nile: Nationalism, Communism, Islam, and the Egyptian Working Class, 1882–1954* (Princeton: Princeton University Press, 1987), chaps. 4–5.

23. *Din ve-heshbon la-veiydah ha-shlishit shel ha-histadrut* (Report on the Third Conference of the Histadrut) (Tel Aviv, 1927), 155.

24. *Kuntres,* no. 165 (4 March 1924).

25. The only serious study of this party is Elkana Margalit, *Anatomiyah shel smol: poalei tsiyyon be-erets yisrael (1919–1946)* (Anatomy of the Left: Poalei Tsiyyon in the Land of Israel) (Jerusalem: Y. L. Peretz, 1976).

26. The available figures are not entirely consistent or reliable, but at the end of 1924 the union apparently consisted of some 529 Jewish and Arab railway workers, out of a work force of almost 2,400. Almost all the Jews, but only 10 to 15 percent of the Arabs, employed on the railroad belonged to the union; most, if not all, of the Arab union members seem to have been skilled or semiskilled workshop workers, foremen, and other more or less permanent personnel from the running and traffic departments. On the size and composition of the union membership, see AL 104/25a, memorandum of the URPTW to the general manager, Palestine Railways; AL 208/14a, Central Committee of the URPTW to EC/H, 30 November

1924; AL 237/1; and also the figures given in *Din ve-heshbon,* 64. None of these figures include the unionized postal and telegraph workers, whose numbers were in any case much smaller.

27. On these ongoing efforts, see, for example, EC/H, 10 October and 7 November 1922; secretariat of the Histadrut executive committee (hereafter abbreviated as S/EC/H), 25 October 1925; Central Zionist Archives, S9/1424a, NURPTW to the Zionist Executive, November 1929; Meirowitz to the Labor Department of the Jewish Agency, 28 March and 27 April 1930.

28. On shop floor sentiments, see Farah, *Min al-'uthmaniyya,* 42–43.

29. AL 208/14a, CC/URPTW to EC/H, 30 November 1924; and *Haifa* 6 (1 January 1925): 43–44; interview with Avraham Khalfon, 29 January 1976, AL, Center for Oral Documentation.

30. I discuss this question more fully in "We Opened Up the Arabs' Minds: Labor-Zionist Discourse and the Railway Workers of Palestine, 1919–1929," *Review of Middle East Studies* 5 (1992): 5–32.

31. On the emergence of the PAWS, see *Haifa* 15 (30 April 1925): 117–18; *Filastin,* 6 March 1925; *al-Yarmuk,* 22 October 1925; al-Budayri, *Tatawwur;* and Yasin, *Ta'rikh.*

32. Though it may sometimes be anachronistic, for the sake of clarity and consistency I will use the acronym AURW throughout to denote the Arab railway workers organized within PAWS.

33. Though the Jewish-led union was known between 1927 and 1931 as the National Union of Railway, Postal and Telegraph Workers, for the sake of clarity I will henceforth refer to it as the IU.

34. See, for example, AL 237/24, Grobman to Ben-Tzvi, May 1928; AL 208/815a, Dana to S/EC/H, 6 January 1935 .

35. See, for example, AL 490/3.

36. In a Hebrew-language leaflet issued by PAWS, AL 237/21, 29 September 1928.

37. Farah, *Min al-'uthmaniyya,* 41.

38. Oral interview, 14 May 1987.

39. In our interview Abramov used the Yiddish term *der Araber,* reflecting the widespread use of that language among new immigrants from Eastern Europe. By contrast, Abramov noted, the Arabs were more respectful of Jewish coworkers and referred to them by name.

40. Paul Cotterell, *The Railways of Palestine and Israel* (Abingdon, Oxfordshire: Tourret Publishing, 1984), chap. 5.

41. AL 237/26b, Berman to EC/H, 3 May 1940; AL 237/16, IU, central committee meeting, 9 November 1940.

42. Ha-Shomer Ha-Tsair Archives, Aharon Cohen papers, 6 (5), "'Al ha-shevitah be-vatei ha-melakhah shel ha-rakevet" (On the Strike in the Railway Work-

shops); AL 208/3660, "Ha-shevitah be-vatei ha-melakhah be-haifa" (The Strike in the Haifa Railway Workshops); *Filastin,* 5 February 1944; *Mishmar,* 6 February 1944; *Haqiqat al-Amr,* 8 February 1944; *Palestine Post,* 6 February 1944.

43. *Al-ittihad,* 17 June 1945.

44. See the Palestinian press for April 1946; AL 425/33, joint leaflet of the PKP and NLL, 18 April 1946; AL, EC/H, 24 April 1946; Israel State Archives, 65/779, Arab Workers' Congress, *Bayan,* 25 April 25 1946.

45. This is not to say that the Zionist leadership actually desired or expected the establishment of a Palestinian Arab state. The Jewish Agency, the de facto leadership of the Yishuv, had in fact secretly reached an informal understanding with King Abdullah of Transjordan whereby the king would occupy and annex much of the territory assigned to the Arab state. See Avi Shlaim, *Collusion across the Jordan: King Abdullah, the Zionist Movement, and the Partition of Palestine* (New York: Columbia University Press, 1988).

46. See the report of the committee of inquiry appointed by Haifa's Jewish community, AL 250/ 40–3–9, and contemporary press accounts. Although the Jewish Agency promptly denounced the Etsel attack outside the Haifa refinery as an "act of madness," it also authorized its own military force, the Haganah, to retaliate for the massacre of Jews at the refinery by attacking and killing Arab civilians in the outlying village of Balad al-Shaykh on 31 December.

47. Oral interview with Efrayim Krisher, a former leader of the Jewish railway workers' union, 13 May 1987.

48. The best work on the causes of Palestinian displacement is Benny Morris, *The Birth of the Palestinian Refugee Problem, 1947–1949* (Cambridge: Cambridge University Press, 1987); on Haifa in particular, see 73–93.

49. Aharon Cohen's *Israel and the Arab World* (London: W. H. Allen, 1970) is a classic of this genre, as it contains much useful information.

50. See Shlomo Swirski, *Israel: the Oriental Majority* (London: Zed Press, 1989); and Ella Shohat, "Sephardim in Israel: Zionism from the Standpoint of Its Jewish Victims," *Social Text,* nos. 19–20 (Fall 1988): 1–35.

51. I explore this question in "Exclusion and Solidarity: Labor Zionism and Arab Workers in Palestine, 1897–1929," in *After Colonialism: Imperial Histories and Postcolonial Developments,* ed. Gyan Prakash (Princeton: Princeton University Press, 1995), 211–40.

52. Itamar Even-Zohar's work on the evolution of Hebrew culture in Palestine suggests one path along which a relational approach to Palestinian culture might be developed. See "The Emergence of a Native Hebrew Culture in Palestine, 1882–1948," *Poetics Today* 11 (1990): 175–91; and his other articles in that same issue.

The Viability of Ethnic Democracy as a Mode of Conflict Management: Comparing Israel and Northern Ireland

Sammy Smooha

Introduction

There is a striking difference in the achievements of the Jews in Palestine/Israel and the British in Ireland. The Jews' experience is a success story. They started to settle Palestine in 1881, built a state of their own, displaced most of the Palestinians who lived in the area that became Israel, have kept the internal Arab minority in check, and since 1993 have pursued a solution of territorial partition to the century-old conflict with the Palestinians. On the other hand, the British have repeatedly failed to control Ireland since occupying it in the eleventh century. They sent settlers to Ireland in the seventeenth century, annexed it, and in the nineteenth century enfranchised the Irish but were forced to cede most of the area by 1920. The northern counties remained under British control up to 1969, but since then Britain's control has become less firm, and it has been taking steps that are likely to lead to full withdrawal. The Jews succeeded, while the British failed, despite the late date at which their settlement began and their inferior resources when compared to those of the British.

The aim of the essay is to explain the success of the Jewish-Zionist project in Israel in building a viable "ethnic democracy," in which Jews enjoy institutionalized dominance, in comparison to the failure of the British-Protestant endeavor to form a similar political system in Northern Ireland. This comparison seeks to clarify the conditions sustaining or undermining ethnic democracy.

Ethnic Democracy as a Mode of Conflict Management

Highly pluralized societies—namely, societies with significant racial, ethnic, religious, linguistic, national, and other communal divisions—face the grave problem of little societal cohesion and political stability. Bosnia, Rwanda, Georgia, Nigeria, Cyprus, Iraq, and Lebanon are only a few examples of the many countries that are split by internal strife and civil war. Disruption is the most likely eventuality unless cohesion-building measures are undertaken.

The literature on deeply divided societies reveals a plethora of methods to manage internal conflicts. Liberal democracy is traditionally considered the best way to cope with ethnic diversity. Questioning this common assumption, Arend Lijphart suggests consociational democracy as the most effective strategy to stabilize plural societies.[1] Ian Lustick argues, however, that under certain circumstances control may work where consociationalism fails.[2] John McGarry and Brendan O'Leary offer a comprehensive classification, distinguishing between methods for eliminating ethnic differences and methods for preserving and managing differences.[3] The "eliminating set" includes genocide, forced mass-population transfers, partition and/or secession (self-determination), and integration and/or assimilation. The "managing set" includes hegemonic control, arbitration (third-party intervention), cantonization and/or federalization, and consociationalism, or power sharing.

With Theodor Hanf I suggested in 1992 another detailed classification, finding it useful on both a theoretical and normative level to distinguish between democratic and nondemocratic modes of conflict regulation.[4] Four democratic modes are discernible: territorial change, liberal democracy, consociational democracy, and ethnic democracy. Territorial change takes the forms of partition, repartition, and unification when done peacefully. This mode is becoming more and more workable and acceptable in the new world (dis)order—witness the peaceful, voluntary breakup of the Soviet Union and Czechoslovakia.

I have suggested that the term *ethnic democracy* be used to refer to a new type of democratic political system that combines democracy with institutionalized ethnic dominance.[5] It is my assumption and prediction that some ethnic states, like Azerbaijan and Estonia, would opt to democratize along the lines of ethnic, rather than liberal or consociational, democracy, since this would allow them to retain the dominance of the ethnic group that was in control earlier.

Control is a heterogeneous political strategy. A nondemocratic version is domination, as exemplified in colonial states and apartheid in South Africa. Another form of control is ethnic democracy, which includes a moderate or limited degree of control as part of its definition. Some control of the non-dominant minority is necessary to maintain ethnic democracy. Combining a real political democracy with explicit ethnic hegemony, this peculiar brand of democracy has its own tensions and self-contradictions.

Some elaboration of ethnic democracy as a general model is in order. The system qualifies as a democracy according to the standard criterion of the extension of rights to the entire population. Four kinds of rights are granted to all citizens: human rights (including dignity, physical safety, and equality), social rights (including entitlement to health, housing, employment, minimal income, and education), civil liberties (including rights of assembly and association, freedom of the press, and independent judiciary), and political rights (including right to vote and stand for election, a multiparty system, change of governments through fair elections, and lack of military or foreign intervention in the political process).

Yet ethnic democracy differs from other types of democracy in according a structured superior status to a particular segment of the population and in regarding nondominant groups as having a relatively lesser claim and loyalty to the state. Among the various manifestations of superior status are monopoly over the highest offices and over the character of the state (emblems, symbols, official language, religion, immigration policy). They may be written into the constitution and other laws expressly or incorporated into unwritten but clear social rules. Since the state is considered to be the expression of the national aspirations of the dominant group, the nation takes precedence over the state or civil society. Great caution is exercised in recruiting people to very sensitive positions of trust in the society (the security services and top political posts) because the loyalty of those not belonging to the nation is somewhat suspect.

The contradiction between the two principles of organization that are built into ethnic democracy is evident in various spheres. It is reflected in restrictions on certain individual and collective rights and on the full expression of the national identity of nondominant groups.

Ethnic democracy can readily be distinguished from related modes of conflict regulation. Being a genuine democracy for all, ethnic democracy is not a *Herrenvolk* democracy, which is by definition a democracy officially limited to the dominant group only, such as South Africa before 1994.[6]

Ethnic democracy also differs from *control* in being clearly democratic, which in most cases control is not. Whereas in systems of control ethnic dominance takes precedence over all other considerations, in ethnic democracy the contradiction between the democratic and ethnic principle is real, not always resulting in the victory of the democratic-egalitarian rule. Yet control is a necessary component of ethnic democracy. A certain degree of political regulation and some economic dependence of the minority are essential for keeping ethnic dominance. Control in ethnic democracy is, however, subtle, manipulative, and hidden. Since control is taken for granted, it remains effective as a deterrent.

Although it makes concessions to minorities, ethnic democracy is not consociational because in *consociational democracy* the state is by definition neutral and minorities are accorded equal status, proportional representation, and veto power in areas of vital interest to them. In contrast, ethnic democracy lacks the principle of equality, partnership, power sharing, compromise, accommodation, and bilateral conflict regulation that characterize consociationalism. The minority remains at the receiving end and must constantly fight for rights and entitlements.

Officially extending collective rights to the minority while denying it equal status, ethnic democracy differs from *liberal democracy.* It rejects the liberal principle of individual rather than group rights, meritocracy, nondiscrimination, imposition of a common culture and identity, and implicit pressure to assimilate.

Since introducing the ethnic democracy model in 1990, I have received several responses, especially from those who study the Arabs in Israel. First, ethnic democracy is not a useful model because it is rare among the established democracies of the West and because most deeply divided societies outside the West are nondemocratic. Let me respond to this objection. Among the countries that are considered close to the West, Israel and pre-1969 Northern Ireland, as will be shown, conform to the ethnic democracy model. More important, ethnic democracy may serve as a viable option for nondemocratic, deeply divided societies, some of which may choose to democratize politically without relinquishing ethnic dominance. For instance, if Egypt were to become a democracy without renouncing the official dominance of the Muslim majority, then it would be an ethnic democracy. More generally, ethnic democracy may be more appropriate and attractive than liberal and consociational democracy to societies in which the nation is defined in terms of ethnic descent, culture, and language and nationalism tends to be integral and exclusionary. This is the situation in some East European states, in the states of the former Soviet Union, the Arab states, Muslim countries, and certain states in Africa. Unlike Western countries, these states do not define the nation in terms of common territory and citizenship, nor does their evolving nationalism tend to be open, inclusive, and coterminous with citizenship. There is a strong possibility that some of these democratizing states will become ethnic democracies.

Another reservation about the ethnic democracy model is that it is not genuine democracy but, rather, a concept used to legitimize and disguise a system of nondemocratic control. It is argued that any system that falls short of bestowing full equal rights is not a democracy. This, however, is a Eurocentric view that limits democracy to the Western models of liberalism and consociationalism. Ethnic democracy is a non-Western system that is admittedly a second-rate yet true democracy.

Since the concept of ethnic democracy rests on a built-in contradiction, it can be argued that it is inherently unstable, that it will either decay and be transformed into domination (authoritarian or hegemonic control) or evolve upward into consociational democracy, but that it cannot remain as is over an extended period of time. This argument is partially valid. It is true that ethnic democracy is less stable than liberal democracy, but it is as stable as consociational democracy.

It is possible to spell out certain conditions that generate and sustain ethnic democracy:

1. The dominant group constitutes a solid numerical majority, capable of ruling alone without the necessary support of the minority. Lijphart lists this condition as militating against stable consociational democracy.
2. The dominant group perceives the minority as a threat. The threat may be directed against national security, culture, political order, or the well-being of the dominant group.
3. The dominant group espouses ethnic nationalism and believes in its inalienable right to a separate political entity. This national sentiment legitimates unequal statuses between majority and minority.
4. The dominant group opts for political democracy for all because of ideological commitment, expediency, or necessity. The dominant majority may reluctantly turn to ethnic democracy when it must extend democracy to the minority.

5. The dominant group is an indigenous majority, and the nondominant group is an immigrant minority. Indigenous status may serve as a basis for superior claims by the dominant majority.
6. The dominant group is a homeland community with a sizable diaspora. The need to protect and repatriate the diaspora can become a sufficient ground, in the eyes of the majority, to prefer the diaspora to the resident minority.
7. The dominant group enjoys ethnic dominance long before the introduction of democracy. It can force democracy to adapt to the long tradition of structured ethnic dominance.
8. The dominant group exercises flexible and extensive control over the minority.

Since most of these conditions prevailed both in Israel and Northern Ireland at the time of their foundation as political entities, it should not come as a surprise that they turned to ethnic democracy as a means to achieve stability and ethnic quiet.

The Problem Formulated

This conceptual framework of ethnic democracy can be applied to both Israel and Northern Ireland. Both countries established a system of ethnic democracy when they were founded; Israel has retained it, while Northern Ireland has not.

Israel's population within the cease-fire borders in 1994 numbered 6.7 million. Five major dichotomies characterize this population: noncitizen Palestinian Arabs on the West Bank and Gaza Strip versus Israeli citizens (the demographic ratio is 25:75); Arab versus Jewish citizens (15:85); Muslim versus Christian versus Druze Israeli Arab citizens (78:13:9); religious versus nonreligious Jews (20:80); and non-European versus European Jews (48:52). Since all the nondominant groups, with the exception of the non-European Jews, are nonassimilating minorities and different in important respects from the dominant majorities, Israel has had to cope with the problem of societal cohesion since its founding in 1948.

During the last half-century Israel has utilized diverse modes of conflict regulation to preserve ethnic tranquillity. It used military control to subdue the large Palestinian population in the occupied territories. This method proved a failure, triggered the Intifada (Palestinian uprising) in December

1987, and brought about gradual disengagement by Israel following the Oslo agreement of September 1993. But within its pre-1967 borders Israel has had a remarkable record in keeping law and order in the last five decades. It has preserved its political stability, European culture, and Jewish-Zionist character despite enormous shifts in its population. It has managed to escape unrest by skillfully exploiting ethnic democracy in handling its Arab citizens, consociational democracy in accommodating its religious Jews, and a mixture of mechanisms in gaining the cooperation of nondominant Jews from Arab countries.[7]

In contrast to Israel, Northern Ireland exemplifies the breakdown of social order. The Catholic minority, one-third of the total population, was no longer prepared to tolerate its inferior position in the ethnic democracy established in the northern counties following the partition of Ireland in 1921. A half-century of control was followed by violent disintegration in the late 1960s.

The cases of Israel and Northern Ireland illustrate several points. Since constituent groups in a given state population can be regulated in quite different ways, it is necessary to examine the entire structure of a society, in all its pluralistic complexity, before generalizing about its cohesion. Variations in the selection of cohesive mechanisms should also be taken into account. And of utmost importance is the need to explain why certain mechanisms succeed in a given situation and fail in others.

Israel proper and Northern Ireland can be compared in regard to three different periods: (1) Israel, 1948–75, will be compared with Northern Ireland, 1921–68, when stiff ethnic democracy dominated in both countries; (2) Israel, 1976–94, will be compared with Northern Ireland, 1969–94, when ethnic democracy relaxed in Israel and totally ceased to exist in Northern Ireland; (3) viable future options in both countries will be discussed in the light of intergroup discourse and politics. These comparisons aim to uncover the configuration of conditions that enabled Jews to make Israel a stable ethnic democracy while preventing Protestants from achieving the same goal in Northern Ireland.

Ethnic Democracy in Its Prime: Israel, 1948–75, and Northern Ireland, 1921–68

Let us first discuss the nature of majority-minority conflict that gave rise to ethnic democracy in the two countries, then the features of ethnic democracy in each country, and finally the differences in the machinery of control and other conditions that accounted for Israel's success and Northern Ireland's failure.

Forming Ethnic Democracy

From their inception Israel and Northern Ireland were established as ethnic democracies. Other options were not even considered. Zionism accorded membership in the Jewish people on the basis of ethnic descent and religion. This ethnoreligious criterion was determined by the fact that Jews at the time lived in scattered diaspora communities, in which they were defined as an ethnoreligious minority rather than a homeland majority. Zionist settlers built the New Yishuv (modern Jewish community in Palestine) as a separate society for Jews. They viewed Palestine as the Jewish homeland, hoping to found a Jewish state there and thus solve the "Jewish problem" through mass resettlement of all Jews.

The Zionist project of establishing a Jewish state in Palestine was accepted by the West but rejected by the Arabs. When Britain lost effective control over Palestine after World War II and turned the fate of the country over to the United Nations, the latter body voted to divide it into two states—one Arab and one Jewish. The Arabs opposed the creation of a Jewish state, rejected the United Nations decision, insisted on building a single state with an Arab majority, and went to war to destroy the new State of Israel.

The newly proclaimed Jewish state did its utmost to minimize its Arab population and to make Israel as Jewish as possible while keeping it democratic. During the War of Independence most Arabs residing in territory under Jewish control either fled or were forced out. Israel threw open its doors to Jewish immigration and quickly achieved a Jewish majority. It declared itself a Jewish state, enacted the Law of Return, which offered unrestricted immigration and automatic citizenship to all Jews, made Hebrew an official and dominant language, adopted the Jewish calendar, hebraized the names of various sites, settled Jews throughout the land, and introduced many other policies and laws that favored Jews. Political democracy was extended to Arabs in accordance with the Zionist commitment to democracy and the need to obtain international legitimacy, but a machinery of control was imposed in order to prevent Arabs from undermining the new order.

The circumstances leading to ethnic democracy in Northern Ireland were different. England occupied Ireland in the eleventh century but failed to retain control over it. It attempted to incorporate it through English and Scotch settlement in the seventeenth century. The Protestant settlers concentrated in the North and displaced and subordinated the Catholic Irish there. In the nineteenth century Britain attempted to annex Ireland, a move that Irish nationalists, who wished to secede and establish an independent state, opposed. Beginning in 1886, the British government tried several times to grant Ireland home rule, but the Protestants blocked the effort. They feared that Irish autonomy would reduce them to a minority and cost them their dominant position. ("Home Rule Is Rome Rule"). The movement against home rule consolidated Protestant solidarity not as a separate nationalism but, rather, as an ideology of Unionism and Protestant supremacy.

The Ireland Act of 1920 provided for the partition of Ireland into an independent state in the south and an autonomous province (Ulster) in the north. This compromise only partially satisfied all the parties: the British achieved a certain degree of disengagement, the Irish a state of their own, and the Protestants a province of their own within the United Kingdom.

Unlike the Jews, who wanted an independent Jewish state, the Protestants wished to remain part of Great Britain and opposed the creation of an independent state of Ulster. The partition law provided for a liberal democracy in the province. Partition was designed, however, to make the Protestants a majority in the north while allowing the British to disengage from the conflict. There was nothing in the Ireland Act of 1920 nor in subsequent British policy to impose or even encourage power sharing between Protestants and Catholics in Northern Ireland. Thus, from the start Ulster was de facto, though not de jure, an ethnic democracy. The Protestants regarded Ulster as their patrimony, employed their numerical superiority to institute a majority dictatorship, discriminated against the Catholics, excluded them from power and privilege, and thus neutralized them as a threat to the regime.

To understand better how ethnic democracy operated, we must look into patterns of conflict in Israel and Northern Ireland during this initial period. Specifically, we must look at "potentiality for conflict" (the conditions leading to conflict), "intensity of conflict" (concrete expressions of conflict), and "machinery of control" (mechanisms used to handle conflict). I will show that the two countries are similar in regard to the first two points but different in regard to the effectiveness of the machinery of control. Hence, only the difference in the way conflict is handled can explain the difference in the degree of political stability of the two systems.

Potentiality for Conflict

Let us first compare the Arab and Catholic minorities in regard to the overall potentiality for conflict.

Nature of Minority Status. As seen and experienced by the nondominant groups, Israel and Northern Ireland are European settler societies. In both the present minorities were part of a larger indigenous population that claimed exclusive rights to the territory, viewed settlers as foreign intruders, and opposed partition compromises. When Britain imposed partition in both former colonies, it triggered internal wars and created minority problems in both. Arabs and Catholics alike emerged as defeated enemies, a very inauspicious beginning for peaceful coexistence. Both populations endured great difficulties in adjusting to a status reversal in which they shifted from a numerical majority to a subordinate minority. Resigning themselves to their new minority status was especially hard because of its inconsistency and contestability. Although reduced to minorities, Arabs (since 1948) and Catholics (since 1921) have remained majorities in their regions. These larger majority populations withheld recognition of partition and aspired to restore majority status to the minorities by revamping the political system. In consequence, Arabs and Catholics belong to a category known as "a disloyal (or enemy-affiliated) minority" (like Japanese Americans during World War II) and are considered potential fifth columns by their respective dominant groups.

Cultural Diversity. Language barriers, divergent lifestyles, and discrepancies in identity may strain group relations. Such cultural differences are significant in both countries, though more so in Israel. Arabs and Jews differ in all momentous cultural parameters. They have separate ethnic origins, speak mutually unintelligible languages, belong to and practice independent religions, and are of mutually exclusive nationalities. They diverge in family patterns as well. Arab families are larger and less egalitarian than Jewish families. Among Arabs the extended family (*hamula*) fulfills notable functions in mate selection, residence, politics, solidarity, and leisure, compared to its limited significance among Jews. Arabs have over the years adopted bilingualism and biculturalism, a common trend among cultural minorities in industrial societies, making Israeli culture a central subculture in their lives and dealings with Jews.

Cultural differences in Northern Ireland are smaller. On the one hand, Catholics and Protestants differ in ethnic descent (Gaelic vs. Scotch and English), and, although both are Christians, they belong to rival churches. Irish nationalism also separates the majority of Catholics from the majority of Protestants. On the other hand, both communities speak English and maintain a similar nuclear family structure. Although variations in lifestyle do exist (e.g., on average Catholics have larger families), they are far milder than those differentiating Arabs and Jews.

Cultural heterogeneity is conducive to group conflict in both societies but more so in Israel. The spread of a unifying modern culture to minorities is less marked in Israel. Arabs are in many respects part of a Third World underdeveloped society in comparison to Jews. The period of minority-majority coexistence is much shorter in Israel (sixty years as compared to three and a half centuries in Northern Ireland). Consequently, feelings of cultural affinity are stronger in Northern Ireland. While 81 percent of the Catholics in a 1968 survey felt that Ulstermen of the opposite religion were about the same as themselves, only 16 percent of the Arabs in a 1976 survey felt closer to the Jews; an additional 36 percent felt as close to the Jews as to the Arabs in the West Bank and Gaza Strip.[8] On the other hand, sectarian nationalism is equally divisive in both countries. Some 70 percent of the Arabs and 66 percent of the Catholics chose religion and nationality as their most significant self-identities.[9]

Social Separation. The greater the social separation, the fewer the crosscutting affiliations that can contain intergroup conflict. The available evidence indicates that social separation is considerable in both societies.

Israeli law provides for religious endogamy, separate Arab schools, and Arabic-language mass media. With the minor exception of the Druze population Arabs are exempted from compulsory military service. Special departments in various government offices, Histadrut (the General Federation of Labor), and major political parties also deal with Arab affairs. About 90 percent of the Arab population is concentrated in three geocultural contiguous regions (the Galilee, the Little Triangle, and the Negev); within them Arabs reside in totally separate Arab localities. The remaining 10 percent live in mixed towns but in separate neighborhoods. Apart from the universities schooling is segregated. Since very few Arabs belonged to the Zionist political parties before 1976 and few participate in other voluntary associations, de facto separation in these areas exists as well. While most Arabs meet Jews at work and public facilities, these contacts are technical or hierarchical. Friendships are not common. Mixed marriages are rare also and considered socially deviant.

Such extensive separation between Jews and Arabs is by and large voluntary. In the 1976 Israeli survey the majority of Arabs and Jews endorsed social and institutional separation. This should not come as a surprise, because the Arab right to separate identity is recognized in Israeli society and separation is considered necessary to maintain cultural and social pluralism.

Social separation in Northern Ireland prior to the civil war was similarly marked. The law provides for separate Catholic schools but otherwise does not regulate group relations. Separation is almost complete in three areas: marriages (96 percent marry within the group), schools (five-sixths attend exclusively Protestant or Catholic schools), and major political parties (95 percent of the Unionist supporters are Protestant, and 99 percent of the Nationalist supporters are Catholic).[10]

Although opportunities for work, neighborly, and other social contacts exist,[11] field studies show that Catholics and Protestants constitute almost completely self-contained communities. Religion, observes Gary Easthope, "subsumes all other identities except that of gender. If the religious affiliation of any individual is known, then the probability is that in a small social area one knows also where he lives, his occupation and place of work, the schools he attended, his kin, the sports he plays and follows, his taste in music and his position as a Republican or a Loyalist."[12] All significant interactions are confined within the group. Contacts with members of the opposite religion are reserved, and "the greatest efforts are made to prevent any controversial topic from being discussed."[13]

Unlike Arabs and Jews, Catholics and Protestants expressed unexpectedly substantial readiness for institutional integration before the outbreak of violence. "Surveys show a clear majority—64 percent of adults and 65 percent of youths—favor educating Protestant and Catholic children together. Among Catholics, 69 percent approve of integrated education." In addition, 69 percent of the Catholics and 27 percent of the Protestants in the 1968 survey said that, in principle, uniting the Protestant and Catholic churches was desirable.[14]

Socioeconomic Gaps. A variety of indicators suggest that inequalities in socioeconomic status are far sharper in Israel than in Northern Ireland. The inequality in the distribution of socioeconomic resources between

Jews and Arabs can be put at a rough overall estimate of two or three to one. Discrepancies of such magnitude are characteristic of those between the modern and backward sectors in nonindustrialized societies and hence should be considered appreciable in a more egalitarian and industrialized state like Israel.

It suffices to quote some statistics on standard of living, employment, and education to illustrate the Jewish-Arab gap. In 1977 the annual per capita income among urban Jews (16,342 Israeli pounds) was about twice the average of Arabs (8,814 Israeli pounds), but inequality was greater in the rural population.[15] Only 14 percent of Arab households, as compared to 55 percent of Jewish households, had a decent housing density of one person or less per room.[16] In 1976 only 13 percent of the Arabs, as compared with 44 percent of the Jews, were employed in high-status, white-collar occupations (scientific, technical, professional, managerial, and clerical jobs).[17] In fact, 37.5 percent of all employed Arabs in 1976 were concentrated in construction and agriculture, in comparison to only 12 percent of Jews.[18] In 1976 Jewish farmers earned 5.5 times more per cultivated unit than Arab farmers.[19] Education presents a similar picture. According to the 1972 census, 22 percent of Arab men and 51 percent of women were illiterate, in comparison to 6 percent of Jewish men and 13 percent of Jewish women.[20] In 1977 the average Arab, age fourteen and over, had 6.2 years of schooling, while the average Jew had 9.8 years; 5 percent of the Arabs and 19 percent of the Jews had at least some college education.[21] Differences in school attendance rates reveal that Jews enjoyed some advantage in compulsory primary education: the attrition rate among Arabs was 8 percent, while there was virtually no attrition among Jews.[22] The Jewish rate in post-primary education is two to three times greater, and in universities it is five to six times higher.[23]

Comparative figures in regard to Northern Ireland disclose smaller inequalities. In 1968 the weekly earnings of a median Catholic family were 85 percent of those of the median Protestant family (16.8 and 19.7 pounds, respectively).[24] Differentials in per capita income were, of course, greater because of larger families among Catholics. The greater Catholic need, however, did not make Catholics feel significantly greater economic deprivation: 68 percent of the Catholics and 78 percent of the Protestants considered their standard of living satisfactory.[25] Some 37 percent of the Catholics and 45 percent of the Protestants owned their homes.[26] Occupational inequality was similarly moderate to small. Among Catholics 9 percent were classified as business and professional, 24 percent as lower middle class, 53 percent as working class, and 9 percent as other social levels. Among Protestants the respective figures were 16 percent, 29 percent, 48 percent, and 6 percent.[27] With respect to education 59 percent of Catholics had received primary education; 35 percent, high school education; and 4 percent, college education, as compared to 47 percent, 44 percent, and 9 percent, respectively, among Protestants.[28]

Power Disparities. In societies like Israel and Northern Ireland, in which pluralism (cultural diversity and social separation) is institutionalized, differentials in ethnic power are reflected in two interrelated areas: representation in positions of power in society at large and institutional autonomy (the minority's control of its separate institutions). Arabs are much weaker than Catholics on both counts.

Arab representation in national decision-making bodies was virtually nil. The decision makers in government, the Jewish Agency, Histadrut, and major political parties in the 1970s were all Jews.[29] The proportion of Arabs among the owners and managers of the national economy was insignificant. Nor did Arabs enjoy institutional autonomy. Although elected Arab leaders head most Arab localities, it is difficult to speak of Arab community control at the time. This is because of the centralistic character of the government in Israel, frequent outside intervention in local affairs, and the presence of sectarian and kinship-based local feuds. Arabs did not control their other separate institutions. Arab education, religious bodies, radio and television stations, and the various departments of Arab affairs were all controlled by Jews. There was no Arab industry, while Arab agriculture was marginal. Nor did they command other independent organizations.

Like Arabs, Catholics were either entirely excluded from or uninfluential in the cabinet, the parliament, the courts, the police force, and the top echelons of the civil administration. They did have a considerable degree of institutional autonomy, however, much of it centered around the Catholic Church. Another stronghold is the school system, which is free from Protestant influence despite being funded by the state. The Catholics also have independent national parties and elect their own leaders to parliament. Although underrepresented, Catholics enjoy influential positions in local government. They have some industry of their own. They also maintain an independent press, clubs, and many voluntary associations. The Irish Republican Army (IRA) provides Catholics with retaliatory and disruptive powers, despite being outside the control of the organized Catholic minority. Israel and Northern Ireland are thus plural societies. In both the minorities emerged involuntarily, cultural discontinuities are substantial, and social separation is enormous. Ethnic stratification also exists, and power sharing is nonexistent. The potential for conflict between Arabs and Jews is by no means smaller than that between Catholics and Protestants.

Intensity of Conflict

The actual intensity of conflict—apart from violence—is also high in both countries. In Israel this is reflected in Jewish attitudes and behavior toward Arabs. Given the Jewish-Zionist character of the state, most Jews view Arabs as outsiders. Surveys indicate virulent anti-Arab feelings of disdain, distrust, and rejection among Jews. In the 1976 survey 44 percent of the respondents declared their firm belief that Arabs would not reach the level of progress of Jews, 83 percent thought that it would be better if there were fewer Arabs in Israel, 58 percent believed that Arabs are not trustworthy, 74 percent agreed that surveillance of Arabs should be expanded, and 76 percent did not like the idea of having an Arab superior at work.

Differential treatment of Arabs is also common. The white-collar job market in the Jewish economy is virtually closed to Arabs. There are no vacancies for Arabs who, due to housing shortages in the Arab sector, seek housing in Jewish neighborhoods. Arab local councils receive much less funding for development, subsidies, and other public assistance than comparable Jewish local councils.[30] In comparison to Jewish schools in the development towns, Arab schools are allocated smaller budgets, fewer facilities, and fewer programs of compensatory education.[31] It is estimated that, as a result of massive land expropriations, Arabs lost 40 to 60 percent of their landholdings between 1948 and 1967 and have lost a bit more since then.[32] Likewise, the Galilee Development Project aims to develop the northern region of the country without attending to the needs of the Arabs, who make up a large proportion of the population there.

For their part Arabs in Israel have strong reservations about Israel as a Jewish-Zionist state. In the 1976 survey of the Arab population 21 percent denied and 29 percent were reserved about Israel's right to exist, 64 percent held that the Zionist movement was racist, 64 percent favored the repeal of the Law of Return, and 70 percent thought that Arabs could not be equal citizens in Israel nor identify themselves with the state.

Feelings of deprivation and alienation are widespread among Arabs. Half of the respondents to the 1976 Israeli survey were dissatisfied with their Israeli citizenship, and 64 percent maintained that Arabs did not enjoy equal job opportunities. Arabs also felt relative deprivation. Sixty-four percent thought that Arab socioeconomic achievements should be compared to Jewish standards; 61 percent viewed the Arab-Jewish socioeconomic gap as large, while an extra 36 percent thought it to be medium; and 58 percent charged that government policies had the effect of widening the existing gap.

A great majority of the Arabs desired institutional autonomy. Over 80 percent held that it is important for Arabs to control Arab local councils, Arab education, and Arab departments in the central government. A majority ranging from 63 to 74 percent unreservedly favored forming independent Arab-based organizations such as a university, mass media, a trade union, industry, and a national party.

Palestinization of Arab identity is becoming widespread. While 51 percent of the Arabs polled thought the term *Israeli* described them well, 58 percent felt the same about the term *Palestinian*. When forced to choose the most appropriate self-identity, 46 percent opted for Palestinian identity, 12 percent for Arab identity, and 41 percent for Israeli-Arab identity. Forty-two percent maintained that Arab education should be oriented toward Palestinian nationalism.

Arabs in Israel strongly support the Palestinian cause. A majority of 85 percent felt that the Arab refugees should be given the right of repatriation, 75 percent favored a Palestinian state alongside Israel, 59 percent thought that the United Nations partition borders of 1947 (which did not award the Galilee and the Triangle, where most Arabs today live, to the Jewish state) were the most desirable boundaries for Israel, and 28 percent thought the same about the pre-1967 borders. Regarding their future, 57 percent preferred a separate-but-equal status in Israel, but 26 percent wanted to be part of a Palestinian state alongside Israel, and 17 percent wanted to live in a democratic-secular state in which Arabs and Jews had equal rights.

As for the proper strategies of change, a majority believed in an activist democratic struggle. Two-thirds thought it possible to improve the Arab situation by acceptable democratic means such as propaganda and political pressures. Between 61 to 69 percent endorsed the extraparliamentary use of boycotts, protest actions abroad, and general strikes.

All these opinions are considered extremist by Israeli standards, as a systematic comparison with Jewish attitudes shows. To illustrate: 62 percent to 74 percent of the Arabs as against 8 percent to 20 percent of the Jews favored the formation of independent Arab organizations. About 42 percent of the Arabs versus 7 percent of the Jews defined Arabs in Israel as Palestinian, and, consequently, 42 percent versus 0 percent advocated "Palestinian education" in Arab schools; 87 percent of the Arabs, as compared to only 8 percent of the Jews, were in favor of the pre-1967 or the 1947 partition borders for Israel; 61 percent to 64 percent of the Arabs versus only 1 percent to 6 percent of the Jews agreed to the use of boycotts, protest actions abroad, and general strikes as acceptable strategies in the Arab struggle. The plural structure of Israeli society is made abundantly clear by these figures: on fundamental matters a majority of Arabs hold views that are incompatible with the views of a majority of Jews.

The Arabs' very resentful attitude toward their subordinate minority status in Israel forms a sharp contrast with their fairly accommodating behavior. Of course, some protest actions occurred before 1976. They included a mass protest vote for the Communist Party, open criticism of the state, some cases of litigation, occasional clashes with the police, and limited participation in terrorist attacks. The overall picture, however, is one of Arab acquiescence. From 1948 to 1975 Arabs did little to challenge Jewish domination, resigning themselves to eighteen years of military government. Attempts to organize a national Arab party or other opposition movements were glaringly few and unsuccessful. In all national elections before 1976 a majority of at least two-thirds of the Arabs voted for Zionist parties or for their allied Arab lists.[33] Arabs did not act as a fifth column during the four Israeli-Arab wars of 1948, 1956, 1967, and 1973. Collaboration with the enemy and terrorism have been minimal, and there have been no Arab riots. Casualties and property losses as a result of violence were negligible. What there was of Arab opposition caused no significant change in government policies, which remained more or less the same until the mid-1970s. Arab resistance did not raise the cost of maintaining law and order, nor did it make the status of the Arab minority a major issue in Israeli politics or a problem in Israel's foreign relations.[34]

Conflict in Northern Ireland is equally intense. If racism is taken to involve discrimination based on a belief in the biological determination of behavior, it is doubtful whether this is the case in Northern Ireland. De Paor's statement that in Northern Ireland "Catholics are blacks who happen to have white skin"[35] is an indication of the gravity of the conflict, not a testimony to biological racism. Protestants scorn Catholics for being ignorant adherents of corrupt popery. Catholics are stereotyped as shiftless parasites who exploit social security benefits to raise large families. Protestants also believe that "99 per cent of Catholics are traitors or potential traitors, that they reject the Northern Ireland constitution, that they will always use 'their might and power' to overthrow the Protestant order. By virtue of being born Catholics, they are born disloyal."[36] This virulent ethnocentrism feeds on the exclusively sectarian nationalism that is entrenched on both sides.[37]

Under these conditions Protestants monopolized power and privilege, treating Catholics as outsiders and second-class citizens in many areas. They deliberately excluded them from policy-making positions. Discriminatory practices against Catholics in the areas of employment, public housing, local representation, regional development, and educational funding were very much in evidence until 1968. Police mistreatment of Catholics was also widespread.

Catholics expressed their antagonism in the militancy of their views. While most regard themselves as part of the Irish nation and define their identity as Irish, most Protestants see themselves as part of the British nation and perceive their identity as British.[38] Furthermore, in the 1968 public opinion survey two-thirds of the Catholics had reservations about or rejected the Northern Ireland constitution, two-fifths favored the use of illegal demonstrations, three-fourths made charges of anti-Catholic discrimination, and a clear majority opposed the status quo—which a clear majority of Protestants approved.[39]

Catholic disaffection was openly defiant and sometimes violent. Catholics hold annual celebrations whose function is to protest against Protestant hegemony. Their backing of nationalist parties is overwhelming. Significantly, a sizable minority of Catholics is involved in resistance movements, including strikes, banned street demonstrations, secret societies, and Sinn Fein political activities. It is estimated that the Irish Republican Army enjoys the support of about one-third of the Catholic population.[40]

In short, the high intensity of conflict in plural societies is clearly evident in both Israel and Northern Ireland. Discord on fundamental issues, sectarian nationalism, hostility, and discrimination divide minority and majority. It also appears that, violence aside, the conflict between Arabs and Jews is by no means less intense than the conflict between Catholics and Protestants.

Machinery of Control

It is apparent from the foregoing discussion that Israel and Northern Ireland have adopted ethnic democracy with a built-in machinery of control, rather than liberal or consociational democracy, as the main device for overcoming their minority problem. The greater political stability of Israel is explained by the greater effectiveness of its control, rather than less potentiality for conflict or less intensity of conflict.

The machinery of control is more fully documented in Israel than in Northern Ireland. In 1973 I suggested that Arab-Jewish relations in Israel should be conceptualized in terms of "an exclusionary domination model."[41] Later I expanded this initial analysis.[42] In a study of the Arab minority Ian Lustick presented a detailed description and explanation of the "system of control" over Arabs in Israel.[43] The following account builds on these works but offers a somewhat different interpretation.[44] Although Northern Ireland has been approached from various theoretical perspectives (a binational state, a religiously divided society, a plural society, a colony, etc.),[45] there has not yet been a systematic attempt to investigate the operation of the machinery of control there. The following analysis of the machinery of control in Israel is thus more elaborate than that for Northern Ireland.

From the outset Israel has enjoyed special conditions conducive to effective control of minorities. These conditions are either absent or weaker in Northern Ireland. The first and by far the most crucial factor is that Israel is an independent, sovereign state and Northern Ireland is not. Israel can manipulate the entire state apparatus (laws, internal security services, central administration, etc.) to effect control. Northern Ireland, on the other hand, is quite restricted in dealing with its minority. This is because it lacks certain state powers and is accountable to the British government.

Israel's second advantage in coping with minority issues is its centralization of political and economic power relative to levels of centralization in other Western democracies. Until the change in government in mid-1977 the ruling Labor Party was responsible for decision making in the central government, the Jewish Agency, and the Histadrut and served as distributing agency for the vast amount of capital from abroad. By coordinating policies, allocating resources, and dispensing patronage, the ruling elite could control various groups politically and economically. As far as can be determined, the ruling elite in Northern Ireland did not hold such power.

It further appears that Israel's ideology of legitimizing its control of minorities is apparently more convincing. Concerns about sectarian nationalism and the potential disloyalty of the minority provide the rationale for dominating the minorities in both societies. As for sectarian nationalism, the ideology of a Zionist-Jewish state is not perceived as any more acceptable than the ideology of Protestant supremacy. Israel, nonetheless, usually underplays sectarian nationalism in its dealings with the Arab minority, emphasizing, instead, the dangers for national security. It seems that national security is a more credible justification in Israel than in Northern Ireland. The Israeli-Arab dispute has proved to be more threatening to Israel's survival than the border dispute with the Irish Republic has proved to be threatening to Northern Ireland's survival. It provides a latent and practical legitimization of the inferior status of the Arabs in Israel and significantly undermines their demands for full equality.

Another advantage Israel has is the special vulnerability of the Arab minority as compared with the relative strength of the Catholic minority. This factor is probably as crucial in containing the Arabs as is Israel's sovereignty. The great vulnerability of the Arab minority results partially from the conditions prevailing prior to and immediately after the creation of the State of Israel. Of the 1.2 million Arabs in Palestine in 1947 only 160,000, or 13 percent, remained in Israel in 1949. The remaining Arab minority was on the whole more accommodating than the departing majority. This was because more of the militant, urbanized, and educated Arabs left than stayed. The new Arab minority remained virtually without an elite and also without leaders. It was cut off from the Palestinian population and the Arab world outside Israel. As a result, the local and national institutions, as well as the economy, of the Arab minority—all of which were not very strong during the British Mandate—collapsed during the transition to Israeli sovereignty.

There are further components of Arab vulnerability. As a Third World minority in a European-transplant society, Arabs have from the very beginning had fewer competitive resources, such as money, education, experience with urban life, exposure to Western culture. In addition, they have been handicapped by a divisive social structure in which kinship and religious cleavages have split them both locally and regionally.

Arab vulnerability contributed considerably to the machinery of control in the Arab sector. To expedite the process the authorities imposed military rule on the Arab minority during the years 1948 to 1966. The official justification was national security considerations. In sociological terms, however, the military government functioned as an effective machinery of control under optimal conditions. The military governors and their staff did not confine themselves to enforcing law and order (issuing passes and job permits outside the village, closing areas, detaining suspects, court-martialing defendants, etc.).[46] They were mostly engaged in building institutions and selecting leaders who would win over Arabs to the Jewish majority. Their task was greatly facilitated by the vulnerability of the Arab population. More specifically, the collapse of the old Arab institutions made it possible to found new ones more compatible with Jewish dominance. The vacuum left by the exodus of Arab professionals and leaders enabled the recruitment of persons acceptable to the authorities. Arab poverty encouraged dependency on Jews, while internal feuds made it easier to prevent the emergence of Arab organizations.

In contrast to the weak Arab minority, Catholic institutional autonomy survived partition well. The Protestant shift from minority to majority status in Northern Ireland in 1920 did not enable the Protestant authorities to destroy independent Catholic bases of power (in autonomous institutions), let alone impose a military government on them.

As for the machinery of control, it rests on the two bases of economic dependence and political domination. The function of economic dependence in plural societies is to deprive the subordinate group of an independent economic base for genuine leadership and political struggle. This situation existed in Israel.

As indicated earlier, the Arab economy declined after 1948. Arab agriculture has been continually the loser in its competition with Jewish agriculture, which enjoys all the advantages of better land, more water, greater mechanization, and better techniques of cultivation and marketing, not to mention government subsidies. Its production value reached a record low of 7 percent of the total agricultural production value in 1977.[47] Whereas about one-third of the Arabs still draw some income from agriculture (i.e., they are "residual peasants"),[48] only about one-tenth of all employed Arabs remain independent farmers. Most Arabs have become wage earners.

The degeneration of Arab agriculture was not accompanied by the creation of Arab industry. The overwhelming majority of Arab wage earners work in Jewish localities. They spend their earnings on food, manufactured goods, and improvement of housing accommodations. Little is left for economic investment. The Jewish power structure (i.e., the government, Jewish Agency, and Histadrut) hardly makes any effort to establish Arab-owned or Arab-managed industries. Arab neglect contrasts strongly with the encouragement of industry through tax deductions, easy credit, land appropriations, and other aid in the Jewish development areas.

The substantial rise in the Arab standard of living through higher wages and social security benefits has not appreciably transformed the backward infrastructure of the Arab localities. The traditional Arab villages up to the early 1970s were inadequately supplied with basic facilities such as piped water, electricity, a sewage system, health clinics, recreational halls, large commercial centers, etc. While some headway has been made in all these areas, Arab villages have not yet become urbanized communities in need of a sizable professional and trained service manpower. Once again the Arab minority has few resources, and the Jewish majority is not willing to make the enormous investment necessary to enable it to reach a higher stage of development.

Given the absence of an independent Arab industrial base and the continued underdevelopment of the Arab localities, the Arab minority cannot provide employment for the majority of Arab wage earners, professionals, and would-be militant leaders. The Arabs depend on the Jews to make a living, therefore, and cannot afford a serious struggle.

The large-scale incorporation of Arab workers, as a lower stratum, into the Jewish economy has made Jews unavoidably dependent, up to a point, on Arabs. More and more Arabs replace Jews in low-status, blue-collar service jobs. Yet the exact proportions do not suggest appreciable Jewish dependence. Arabs constitute, overall, only 9 percent of the Israeli civil labor force. They make up 24 percent of all agricultural workers and 27 percent of construction laborers[49] and are mainly the less-skilled workers in these two branches of the economy. Nevertheless, the control of these sectors, like others, is in the hands of Jewish trade union leaders and industrialists. By threatening summarily to dismiss any Arab who participated in the Land Day strike in 1976, they managed to dissuade the majority of Arabs from striking. In more protracted Arab-Jewish confrontations Arab families would, quite quickly, lose their livelihoods, whereas the Jewish economy, given the high proportion of non-European Jews in the lower stratum, noncitizen Arabs from the West Bank and Gaza Strip, and the option of importing foreign workers, could readjust easily by redistributing its manpower. It is not unwarranted, therefore, to propose that the exceedingly asymmetric Arab-Jewish economic interdependence makes Arabs in Israel quite vulnerable.

The other mainstay of the Jewish machinery of control is political domination. Whereas economic dependence prevents the minority from political struggle indirectly by dispossessing it of an economic base, political domination achieves this goal more directly.

The political means employed in Israel are diverse. To begin, there exists a legal basis for political regulation of dissenting minorities. Such a body of laws is of prime importance in Western democracies, in which civil liberties are officially universal and the administration of justice is largely impartial.

The Defense Regulations of 1945, which are still in force in Israel, make it possible for the government to declare any area in the country closed, impose a military government, proclaim a curfew, issue administrative detentions, etc. These special powers may be applied at any time to any locality or person. They have proved useful in dealing with the Arab minority since the official lifting of the military government in 1966. Thus, for example, military government was reinstated for a short time in Arab villages during the 1967 war. Certain villages were placed under curfew on Land Day in 1976, and from time to time restrictions are imposed on the movements of some Arab dissenters. The deterrent capability of the Defense Regulations of 1945 is considerable, as the prime minister's advisor on Arab affairs has testified.[50]

Intelligence gathering and surveillance in the Arab sector are extensive. The numerous Arab departments at the time openly gathered and assessed information from the Arab population. The secret services and the police still have their own Arab departments. Much of their efficiency is due to the fact that paid informers, well-placed members of the major *hamulas,* know a great deal about local affairs. Their collaboration is easily enlisted by offering them and their kinfolk jobs, help in competition with other *hamulas,* and protection. The effective ability of the authorities to prevent, detect, and punish is probably the most important mechanism in the machinery of Jewish control.

The authorities have taken territorial steps in order to strengthen political control. During and after the 1948 war some Arab border villages were demolished, and their residents were evacuated to the interior of the country. A program to settle the widely dispersed Bedouin population and prevent their movements across the cease-fire borders has been gradually implemented. And, more important, a sustained effort has been made to break the contiguous territorial basis of the Arabs in the northern Negev, Little Triangle, and the central-western Galilee. Within these densely populated Arab regions numerous Jewish settlements have been established: military bases, Nahal settlements (kibbutz-like military units), kibbutzim, *moshavim,* and development towns. A sizable proportion of Arab lands, absentee and expropriated, were made available for these Jewish settlements. The two development towns, Nazareth Illit and Carmiel, are the two best examples. The chief aim of this project to develop the Galilee is the demographic judaization of the area.

The Jewish authorities realized from the start that they needed to control Arab institutions in addition to checking their economic and territorial bases of power. The massive municipalization of Arab villages (only 13 percent of the Arab population in 1976 still lived in localities without municipal status),[51] the reorganization of Arab religious bodies, and the rebuilding of the Arab educational system by the authorities opened these major institutions to Jewish control. In fact, many decisions of local councils in Israel have to be approved by central government offices. Many officials in the Arab religious bodies are nominated by the authorities. Control of Arab education is very tight. Jews determine the curriculum, budget, and staff appointments (supervisors, principals, and teachers). While the curriculum is devoid of Arab or Palestinian nationalist content, it exposes Arab pupils to Zionism and Jewish culture.[52] Deviations by Arab educators are in most cases punished.

At the same time the authorities discouraged attempts to mobilize Arab public opinion and political support. As a result of Jewish intervention and Arab passivity, no Arab-based press, radio or television station, youth movement, university, trade union, or political party emerged. The best-known effort to establish an Arab national party (Al-Ard) in the years 1958 to 1965 was put down by the authorities.[53] Rakah, the Communist Party, tried to supply Arabs with an organizational base and leadership. It was tolerated because, as a mixed Arab-Jewish party and, at the time, a Soviet satellite, its contribution to Arab institutional autonomy was limited.

The continuation of the centuries-old cleavages within the Arab community along kinship and sectarian lines is another component of Jewish control.[54] A divided community is less likely to form autonomous institutions and to agree on concerted action. Surveillance is much easier to apply in a divided than in an atomized community. While internal divisions were intentionally encouraged by the authorities, they were also reinforced by impersonal forces. The most important factor was proletarianization without urbanization (migration) of the Arab masses. Economic dependence on Jews made Arabs insecure and forced them to fall back on kinfolk and coreligionists in crisis situations. As long as voluntary associations remained few and underdeveloped, the *hamula* and religious groups that serve social functions could not be undermined.

Control of the elite and its leaders was another efficient means of political domination. It took several forms. Traditional *hamula* elders were encouraged to enter local politics and to serve as mediators for the dispersal of benefits by the authorities. Over half of the Arabs with postsecondary education were schoolteachers and thus fully dependent for their livelihood on the government. Another segment of the Arab intelligentsia was tied to the government by direct or indirect work contacts. Self-employed professionals were few. Quite a few disenchanted educated Arabs who could have become genuine protest leaders left Israel voluntarily, and in certain cases they departed because of pressure from the authorities.

Control is also effective because it is judicious, calculated, and predictable. It is neither excessive nor arbitrary. Arabs are given civil rights, but their potentially threatening political activity is checked. They are granted all the institutional arrangements necessary for the preservation of their separate culture but are prevented from achieving institutional autonomy. They are not expected to be patriots but law-abiding citizens. They are allowed to express national feelings and to criticize the government but must refrain from disloyal actions. The departments for Arab affairs made a standard distinction between "positive" and "negative" Arabs and applied it in their daily activities. Positive Arabs—as individuals, organizations, or villages—receive benefits, and negative Arabs suffer. Random terror, lynching, and undue harassment, which tend to backfire, are virtually absent. The police protect Arab suspects against Jewish mobs in the aftermath of terrorist attacks. Briefly, since Jews control resources and distribute them in a predictable fashion, Arab compliance pays off.

The weaknesses of the machinery of control in Northern Ireland are striking when seen against the backdrop of Israel's system of control. Ethnic stratification in Northern Ireland is not sufficiently pervasive to make Catholics economically dependent on Protestants. A certain appeasement of Catholics has been sustained over the years due to a steady improvement in living conditions. This was possible owing to the increasing industrialization and economic growth of Northern Ireland and the benefits of the British state's welfare services. But without economic dependence such material gains could not provide control for long.

Protestant political domination was precarious, too. Despite the fact that Northern Ireland has the legal apparatus to subdue minority opposition (the Special Powers Act of 1922, which is similar to the Defense Regulations of 1945 in Israel), the absence of state sovereignty limited its freedom to exercise authority. The Stormont government always feared the reactions of the British government. For this reason it did not use its powers to intern suspects without trial during the crucial years 1968 to 1970.[55]

The Protestant authorities lacked internal security services for effective intelligence gathering, detection, and deterrence. The police force harassed the Catholic community instead of penetrating it.

Political domination could not succeed as long as Catholics maintained full-fledged institutional autonomy. Catholics used their churches, schools, political parties, and media as an independent base of power around which to build public support. Protestants were unable to contain Catholic organizations. Community control gave a sense of unity to the Catholic minority and made resources available to prevent the defection of the Catholic elite and leadership.

To conclude, the vast superiority of the Jewish machinery of control over the Protestant one should be clear on the basis of the evidence presented here. Ethnic democracy functioned better in Israel than in Northern Ireland thanks to the more effective machinery of control built into it.

The Transformation of Ethnic Democracy

The differences in the functioning of ethnic democracy in Israel through 1975 and in Northern Ireland through 1968 also account for the changes that have occurred since then. The sharp rise of the minorities in Israel since 1976 and in Northern Ireland since 1969 evoked strong countermeasures in both countries, leading to the liberalization of ethnic democracy in Israel and its breakdown in Northern Ireland.

The Liberalization of Ethnic Democracy in Israel

The first Arab general strike (30 March 1976), which protested the government's plan to expropriate some Arab lands, constitutes a watershed in Arab-Jewish relations. As part of its judaization project in the Galilee, the government announced its intention to confiscate 20,000 *dunams* (a *dunam* is one-fourth of an acre), of which only 6,300 were owned by Arabs, for public use. The amount of Arab land earmarked for takeover was an insignificant fraction, compared with the over half-million *dunams* confiscated from acquiescent Arabs earlier. The Arab response was vehement and largely unexpected. The Committee for the Defense of Arab Lands was established and called for a general strike. The government threatened to take firm actions against persons attempting to enforce the strike, and the Histadrut declared its support for the dismissal of strikers. None of the Jewish political parties, not even the Zionist Left, backed the strike. In view of this Jewish intimidation an unprecedented 64 percent of the Arabs fully endorsed the strike, and 44 percent took part in it. The government used heavy police force and in several places even declared a curfew and deployed army units to put it down. This showdown between the Jewish State and the Arab minority was marked by scores of clashes between protesting Arabs and the security forces, which left six Arabs dead and many more wounded.[56]

The 1976 Land Day strike and the many protests that have followed it testify to changes in the status of the Arab minority in Israel. Does it mean that control over the Arabs has finally collapsed? Has Israel's ethnic democracy irreparably eroded? The impressive Arab protest movement of 1976 certainly shows that, despite control and inferior status, the minority has managed in three decades to emerge from its marginal position. The benefits of Israel's formal democracy, exposure to modern culture, full employment and a subsidized economy, and welfare services steadily increased Arab resources. The numerical strength of the Arabs grew, their education and standard of living rose, their class structure became differentiated, with a sizable middle class and an educated elite, their kinship and sectarian ties weakened, their identity turned increasingly Palestinian, their contacts with the Arab world intensified, and their political culture became more sophisticated. The more Arabs accumulated resources, the less accommodating they became. As a result, control was increasingly resisted and became ever more costly for the Jews.[57]

These significant changes, however, modified rather than destroyed ethnic democracy and the control embedded in it. Although Israeli Arabs have continued to enjoy social, civil, and political rights and the status of an ethnic minority, Israel has essentially remained a prototype of ethnic democracy since its proclamation in 1948. It is a state of and for Jews, and it is so recognized internationally. Although both Hebrew and Arabic are official languages, Arabic is quite marginal in the public domain. All state symbols, holidays, heroes, historical sites, and national institutions are still Jewish. The Law of Return that admits Jewish immigrants freely and grants them citizenship automatically, but excludes Palestinians completely, has remained in force, allowing the entry of over a million Jews since the early 1970s. The state has continued to offer official recognition and entrust state functions to the Jewish Agency and the Jewish National Fund, which by virtue of their constitutions serve Jews alone. The Arab minority has also remained for the most part a culturally and socially nonassimilating minority, a working-class community in a middle-class society, a group excluded from the national power structure, untrustworthy in the eyes of Jews and the state, an ideologically dissident population.

Against the backdrop of this fundamental continuity the transformations in Arab-Jewish relations are striking indeed. While ethnic democracy has survived various changes, its control component has shrunk substantially. Israel has become strikingly more democratic for all its citizens. The Emergency Regulations of 1945 were relaxed, freedom of the press was expanded, the Supreme Court became much more active in defending civil rights, a number of basic human and civil rights laws were enacted, a two political bloc system was established, and the security services were subjected to closer scrutiny. National security has also lost much of its power as a justification for the control of citizens. Control of Israeli Arabs was also reduced as a result of the lifting of the military administration in Arab areas in 1966. After the 1967 war the Shin Bet (Israel's secret service), rather than military intelligence, was entrusted with the role of overseeing the occupied territories. This new, overwhelming task necessitated the shifting of staff that dealt with Israeli Arabs to the new areas. The Arab community has also become more educated, economically secure, politically conscious, aware of its rights and familiar with the ins and outs of the Israeli system, and, hence, significantly less amenable to penetration and control.

Some observers have grossly misinterpreted this appreciable diminution of control. Lustick, for instance, who provided the best detailed documentation of the system of control of the Arab minority and predicted its persistence, became convinced that by 1987 the system had collapsed and Israel was on the road to binationalism.[58] In fact, Israel has neither abolished control over the Arabs nor ceased to be an ethnic democracy. Control, rather, has shifted from a micro to a macro level, been used more selectively, become more subtle, and been reserved for more serious dissenters and extremists. The change can generally be characterized as a shift from routine close surveillance to remote but ultimate control. The Arabs know that

> Jewish control is firm, even when restrained and remote; that more liberal treatment by the authorities is not a compromise of Israel's Jewish-Zionist character; that any Arab defiance will be detected and severely punished; that they have real, pervasive stakes in Israel; that they are bound to lose by destabilizing Israel; and that they do not have a better, viable alternative to life as a minority in a democratic, Jewish state. Convinced of effective, ultimate Jewish control, Israeli Arabs have nilly willy

[*sic*] become more expedient, pragmatic, and moderate in their orientation toward Israel.[59]

The other overall noticeable change was "Arab politicization"—as distinct from "Arab radicalization." Arab politicization means that Arabs have become politically conscious and active, less tolerant of discrimination and deprivation, and more active in striving for peace and equality. They have also become more Israelized: more bilingual and bicultural, more accepting of Israel's political and territorial integrity, more resigned to their minority status, and more inclined to judge themselves by Israeli standards. The Arabs see their fate and future firmly tied to Israel. They have become increasingly fragmented along political lines, disagreeing about the best strategy to improve their situation in Israel. Arab politicization is reflected in the emergence of independent Arab leadership and organizations and in ongoing Arab protests. The co-opted traditional leaders have disappeared, replaced by new, educated, young, militant leaders who regularly challenge the Jewish establishment. Hundreds of independent Arab voluntary associations with funding from abroad have emerged. Several Arab or predominantly Arab parties have been established, winning over half of the Arab vote and completely displacing the traditional, pro-establishment Arab election lists. With the formation of the National Committee of Heads of Arab Local Councils and the Supreme Follow-Up Committee, the Arabs have national bodies that articulate positions in the name of the entire Arab minority, declare general, well-observed strikes, and take other actions at a national level. The level of Arab mobilization has reached the point that it effectively deters the authorities from making blatantly anti-Arab statements or taking blatantly anti-Arab actions. For instance, since the first Land Day strike in 1976 the authorities have refrained from further land takeovers in the Galilee.

Arab politicization has taken place, however, without radicalization. This means that Arabs have not turned against the state, have abstained from violence and terrorism, have not turned to civil disobedience, have not renounced Israeli citizenship and identity, have not shunned elections to the Knesset, and have not boycotted Jews and Jewish institutions. The radical segment among the Arabs is very small and cautious about not antagonizing the authorities. The Islamic movement that emerged in Israel in the 1970s, though radical in certain respects, is quite pragmatic and certainly law abiding when compared to Hamas and Islamic Jihad in the West Bank and Gaza.

In a complementary fashion the Jewish side has become increasingly more accessible, open, considerate, and compromising toward Israeli Arabs. Not only has control diminished, but the state is also less discriminatory in allocating funds to the Arabs. In 1992 the government even adopted a small-scale affirmative action program to recruit eighty qualified Arabs annually to mid- and high-level positions in the civil service. Jewish institutions, notably Jewish political parties, opened their ranks to full Arab membership. At the attitudinal level the Jewish public has become less ethnocentric toward the Arabs in Israel. Growing Jewish accessibility, not continued intransigence, characterizes the Jewish side. The intense Arab protest has not caused Jewish backlash, repression, and threats to disenfranchise or expel the Arabs. There is little evidence of Jewish violence (e.g., mob or vigilante) against Israeli Arabs. Kahane's racism was universally censured and opposed by the Jewish public and leadership.

Another development is the widening divergence between Israeli Arabs and other Palestinians. In 1967 Israeli Arabs were reunited with the Palestinian people and the Arab world from which they had been cut off in 1948. They have become increasingly Palestinian in their identity and solidarity. They have fought to advance Palestinian causes in Israel, and their political bodies have served as lobbies for the PLO when it was defined by Israel as a terrorist organization. They supported the Palestinian Intifada, demonstrated on its behalf, and sent relief to rebellious Palestinians in the occupied territories. Since 1976, however, Israeli Arabs have emerged as a distinct segment within the Palestinian people. They act and are perceived as Israeli Palestinians who, as outsiders, peacefully support the Palestinian struggle. They registered solidarity with the Intifada without participating in it. It is agreed upon by all sides that an independent Palestinian state would be for Palestinians in the West Bank, Gaza Strip, and abroad, not for Israeli Arabs. They are in Israel to stay, committed to fighting for equality, not for secession or sovereignty.

Finally, it is remarkable that the momentum of peacemaking between Israel and the PLO has proceeded with utter disregard for the Arab minority. This issue is treated as completely domestic by Israeli Arab leaders, the PLO, and Israel. Many Israeli Arabs feel that full settlement of the Palestinian question should also include their own vital interests (including return of or compensation for confiscated lands, the right to reconstruct scores of Arab villages destroyed in 1948, recognition of many squatter settlements as permanent villages, family reunions, international protection of collective minority rights) and that the PLO has abandoned them.

Yet they realize that their inclusion in the peace agenda may severely hurt them by casting doubt on their full Israeli citizenship and by overburdening the negotiations with additional hurdles. The continued handling of the Israeli Arab question as strictly domestic is probably the best indicator of persistent political stability and ethnic tranquillity in Israel.

The Collapse of Ethnic Democracy in Northern Ireland

These trends in Israel—that is, the persistence of ethnic democracy with a reduction in its control component, the politicization (rather than radicalization) of the minority, the growing accessibility (rather than intransigence) of the majority, the divergence of the minority from the rest of its people, and the continued treatment of the minority problem as internal and restrained (rather than international and urgent)—make a sharp contrast with developments in Northern Ireland during the same period.

The civil rights movement of 1968 constituted the turning point in Catholic-Protestant relations. It was modeled after the civil rights movement in the United States in terms of both its goals and tactics. Rather than negating Ulster's right to exist and calling for the unification of Ireland, the protesters demanded an end to job discrimination, equal access to public housing, and one-man, one-vote. Peaceful demonstrations, marches, sit-ins, and other legal means of extraparliamentary politics were employed by middle-class Catholics and some Protestant sympathizers. Despite their moderate, integrationist demands and the sympathy of Ulster's reformist prime minister at the time, the Protestant community as a whole resisted change and remained intransigent. The police repressed the protesters, a mass countermovement emerged, the prime minister faced accusations of appeasement and was forced from office, and rioting flared up. "The troubles," as the continued unrest is known, soon spun out of control, leading to violence by all sides.[60]

The most striking change in Northern Ireland was the deployment of British troops in Northern Ireland and the institution of direct rule from London in 1972 when it became clear that the Stormont government had lost control. The true meaning of this dramatic move is the loss of ethnic democracy, which was established in 1921. How can this rupture of the system be explained? The seeds of the final breakdown of the machinery of control in Northern Ireland were sown in the early years of partition. The Catholics never lost their institutional autonomy and independent leadership. Although the Protestants established a "majority dictatorship," they could not subordinate Catholic institutions and leadership as long as they lacked the powers vested in a sovereign state. It was, therefore, only a matter of time until the Catholics revolted.

The process of breakdown has been accelerating in Northern Ireland since World War II.[61] Increasing British intervention in the Ulster economy weakened Protestant domination. Catholics also became more independent of Protestants as more jobs became available to them through British investors. Growing British welfare services improved Catholic well-being and made the Stormont regime more tractable to British pressure for reforms. The Catholic middle class has grown rapidly as a result of the expanding educational system and the mounting demand for trained and professional workers. Instead of leaving Ireland for greener pastures abroad, as traditionally had been the case, more and more Catholics moved to booming urban centers. Catholic social climbers, however, soon experienced blocked mobility as the public sector remained closed to them. Influenced by the civil rights movement in the United States, they made reformist demands for greater equality and integration while refraining from challenging Ulster's legitimacy. With the strongest vested interest in the status quo, the Protestant working class spearheaded the counteropposition. The regime proved to be too weak to gain the cooperation of the defiant Protestant majority and the dissident Catholic minority. The already ineffective machinery of control finally collapsed.

Protestant supremacy was entrenched until 1968. The Protestants exercised a tyranny of the majority, monopolized the state apparatus, harnessed the security forces to keep the Catholics in check, appropriated to themselves a disproportionate share of societal resources (positions of power, employment, public housing), and legitimized their hegemony by attributing disloyalty, parasitism, corrupting papal influences, and inferiority to the Catholics. These ingredients of ethnic democracy could not survive the British takeover after 1968. The Protestants have suddenly become one of two communities vying for power, rather than the group in charge. Although initially sent to protect Catholics, British troops eventually employed security measures (such as massive house-to-house searches, internment, and juryless courts) that antagonized both communities. With the deterioration of law and order both sides felt increasingly insecure, distrusted the British army, and sought protection from their own, expanded paramilitary forces.

The British have failed to reduce violence to an "acceptable level." As many as 3,168 persons died from 1969 to 1994, while considerable property was damaged.[62] Protestants and Catholics alike have suffered, but in the end the British have been responsive to Catholic demands. Almost all civil rights inequities have been rectified. Gerrymandering was terminated, allowing Catholics to take control of towns in which they constitute a majority. Discrimination in the allocation of public housing was corrected with the formation of more accountable boards. An antidiscrimination employment law was passed in 1976, and an affirmative action law regulating recruitment by companies with 250 or more employees was enacted in 1989. The police forces were reorganized, and a complaints commission was established, which Catholics were encouraged to join. Catholics also benefited greatly from the expansion, with British funding, of the educational system, bringing their achievements to a level on par with those of Protestants. The growth of the public sector and the enforcement of an antidiscrimination policy caused Catholic employment in the civil service to rise to a level proportionate to their demographic strength. The Catholic middle class also enjoyed greater opportunities to enter technical, professional, and managerial positions.

The British took another significant step toward power sharing. Several attempts to form a coalition government during the periods 1972–74 and 1991–92 have failed because of Protestant opposition. The Anglo-Saxon political culture of "winner takes all," the large Protestant majority, the absence of overarching values, and the lack of a common nonsectarian identity have continued to block power sharing.

To the Protestants' great dismay the British also went much further in meeting Catholic nationalist demands. In 1985 the Anglo-Irish Agreement was signed, allowing for the first time for a consultative role for the Irish government in Northern Ireland in exchange for measures to curb terrorism from across the border. Dublin was deeply involved also in the talks over power sharing held in the years 1991–92.

Throughout the 1968–94 period the Protestants have remained publicly intransigent. They have objected to all the British reforms, whose aim is to dismantle their hegemony, appease their Catholic opponents, and turn Northern Ireland into a consociational democracy. They have found themselves as the main losers. On the sensitive question of the Irish Republic's involvement, Protestant leaders were not even consulted. From a Protestant perspective the British have not only failed to contain terrorism but have rewarded it with surrender. The poor and the working class, who are hurt the most by Catholic gains, constitute a solid social base for Protestant intransigence and extremism.

Paradoxically, despite all the democratizing and equalizing efforts on the part of the British, the Catholics have remained disaffected and have become increasingly radicalized. The basic problems have not been resolved: the unemployment rate among Catholics has remained 2.5 times that of Protestants; the labor market has continued to be split; physical safety has continued to be fragile; distrust of the security forces (British troops, the predominantly Protestant police) has lingered on; power sharing has not been installed; and the participation of the Irish government in the internal affairs of Northern Ireland has not produced any tangible gains. Catholic radicalization has been expressed by appreciable support for the Provisional IRA and Sinn Fein, whose primary concern has been unification of Ireland, rather than the provision of equality of rights and opportunities and proportional representation in the national power structure.

It appears that the pressing of nationalist claims and the official participation of Ireland in the domestic conflict have contributed to a greater convergence between the Irish people on both sides of the Northern divide. Irish identity and nationalism among the Catholics in the north have drawn them toward their brethren in the south and away from the Protestants.

Another development to be considered is the internationalization of the internal Catholic minority problem. While the fact that there are four parties to the minority-majority conflict in Northern Ireland (the Catholics, the Protestants, the British, and the Irish) was relatively dormant during the 1921–68 period, it has come to the fore and even been officially institutionalized. The long-term effect of this change is that any internal, bilateral solution would be insufficient.

By the end of 1994 a breakthrough in the stalemate and political violence in Northern Ireland took place. Secret and open talks during 1988–94 involving both political parties and paramilitaries in Northern Ireland and mediators (the British and Irish governments, Irish Americans) produced a cease-fire, a more relaxed atmosphere, discussions and negotiations, and a set of proposals for reforms that the British and Irish governments published in February 1995 as the Joint Framework Documents.[63]

The suggested framework introduces consociational democracy only indirectly. It conceives of Catholics and Protestants as diverse segments of the single "people of Ireland" and calls for the formation of an accountable government in Northern Ireland. The proposed package consists of a collective executive that includes representatives of the major political parties, a legislative assembly that needs special majorities to pass controversial legislation, control of the assembly's ten committees overseeing government departments by the various political parties, a bill of rights, a new police force, and novel relations between Northern Ireland on the one hand and the Irish Republic and Great Britain on the other. The British and Irish governments agreed to amend their laws (the Ireland Act of 1920 and the Irish Constitution of 1937) to ensure that unification of Ireland can come about only if a majority in Northern Ireland and a majority in the Republic accept it. The two governments would also serve as protectors, mediators, and arbiters for the two communities of Northern Ireland.

The Joint Framework Documents endorse a set of principles that officially terminate ethnic democracy in Northern Ireland. First, the conflict is recognized as national, and the Irish right to self-determination (i.e., to a united Ireland) is acknowledged. Second, the option of united Ireland has to be implemented through consent, not force. Third, the institutions of accountable government are designed to prevent majority dominance. Fourth, individual and collective rights will be protected by a constitutional charter of rights. And, fifth, the conflict is defined as "international," and hence North-South and East-West institutions are construed as part of the solution.

The Future Viable Options

The contrast between Israel and Northern Ireland can be further demonstrated by examining the viable options in each case: a liberalized ethnic democracy in Israel and a united Ireland in Northern Ireland.

Israel's ethnic democracy has proven to be a flexible and adaptable system. It has improved over the years by liberalizing its treatment of the Arab minority. The positive change has taken place as a result of the general democratization of society at large and in response to a sustained, militant struggle by the Arabs. The question is whether ethnic democracy in Israel will continue to liberalize, collapse, or evolve into a Western-style democracy.

Some analysts feel strongly that ethnic democracy does not stand a real chance in Israel. Oren Yiftachel argues that it is unlikely for an indigenous minority in a biethnic society, like Israel, to resign itself to the limitations and inequities of ethnic democracy, and hence escalation and confrontation are inevitable.[64] He points to various indications of Arab mobilization and radicalization. Yoav Peled also underscores the contradictions inherent in the Israeli system and the injustices caused to the Arabs, although he does not consider ethnic democracy as fragile and unstable as Yiftachel.[65] Both agree, however, that Israel's ethnic democracy is not viable in the long run, and for Israeli democracy to survive it should shift to consociational democracy as quickly as possible.

Israel is expected to practice increasingly a policy of nondiscrimination, recognize the Arabs as a Palestinian national minority, grant them institutional autonomy, and allow Arab parties and politicians into coalition politics and the national power structure. These probable moves may be misconceived by interpreters such as Yiftachel and Peled as the transformation of the Israeli political system from ethnic to consociational democracy. They are, however, only additional steps in the ongoing liberalization of ethnic democracy, a process that leaves Israel as a Jewish state, a state of Jews and for Jews, even after making substantial concessions to Israeli Arabs. Israel will continue to take measures to keep and increase its Jewish majority, promote its ties with the Jewish diaspora, and confer certain privileges on its Jewish citizens. It will remain Jewish in heart and substance.

Ethnic democracy will prevail in Israel for the foreseeable future because the Jews wish it and have the power to impose it, while the Arabs reject it but lack the power to do away with it. Since consociational democracy would mean a binational state and a liberal democracy would be a secular-democratic, non-Jewish state, both are rejected by the Jews. The transformation of Israel into consociational or liberal democracy would require two fundamental but related changes: a shift of Zionism from integral and exclusive to open and inclusive nationalism; and the separation in Judaism between ethnicity, nationality, and religion. Both are unlikely developments in the near future.

Of the three types ethnic democracy is not the worst for the Arabs. The worst, rather, is liberal democracy, since it poses the threat of assimilation to an Arab minority committed to Palestinian Arab ethnonationalism. Since the best option for the Arabs is obviously consociational democracy, it enjoys the widest Arab support, so that Arab intellectuals and activists increasingly speak in favor of transforming Israel in this direction.

Israeli Arabs cannot count on the Arab states or a new Palestinian state to intervene on their behalf in fighting Israel's ethnic democracy, not only because of fear of Israeli retaliation but also because they themselves are nondemocratic ethnic states, and a future state of Palestine will in all probability be at best an ethnic democracy like Israel. An ethnic democracy that leans toward consociationalism seems to be the most likely compromise under the given circumstances, especially with Israel's transition to the peace era.

While the settlement of the Palestinian question will be achieved by further liberalization of ethnic democracy within Israel, retreat from most of the area of the West Bank and Gaza Strip, and the formation of an independent Palestine alongside Israel, the settlement of the Irish question looks less certain. The case of Northern Ireland is indeed peculiar insofar as all three types of democracy are impractical for it. Richard Rose carefully discusses a dozen or so possibilities to restore peace in Northern Ireland but finds all of them unworkable.[66] He concludes that "the problem is that there is no solution."[67] Since the early 1970s the British have tried in vain to institute consociational democracy, and many still believe that this is the most probable solution, if any.

The 1995 Joint Framework Documents ushered in a new era. Paramilitaries stopped their violence, and political parties accepted the Framework as a basis for negotiations over a newly restructured Northern Ireland. What are the options for a permanent settlement? One possibility is that the quasiconsociational democracy proposed by the Joint Framework will evolve into a full-fledged consociational democracy. This is quite unlikely because nationalists both in Northern Ireland and the Republic would reject this arrangement as permanent.

It is more likely that the long-term settlement in Northern Ireland will be accomplished by ending partition and effecting unification of the north with the south. By 1995 only the Protestants continued to oppose this solution. This option, however, will be less and less resisted as Ireland, a member of the prospering European Community, will enjoy economic growth, expand its welfare state, and become more secular. Since Ireland has remained irredentist in its constitution and political behavior (although it has agreed to obtain the consent of a majority in the north for unification), it has to bear the cost of change if it wishes to absorb the Protestants. The Joint Framework makes it conceivable to expect that the Protestants, who are declining numerically and politically, will reluctantly become in the foreseeable future a distinct, sizable, protected minority (around 30 percent of the total population), benefiting from institutional autonomy and tolerance, in a united Ireland.

Conclusions

Israel after independence in 1948 and Northern Ireland after partition in 1921 faced a similar, severe, minority problem. The Arab and Catholic minorities were part of a larger population with which the new political entities were and continued to be in intense conflict. They were defeated, enemy-affiliated minorities. They neither accepted the legitimacy of the new regimes nor their minority status. The sharp discord on terms of coexistence was exacerbated by further cleavages. The minority and majority were clearly divided in culture and identity, separated in interpersonal and organizational frameworks, and unequal in terms of the distribution of resources.

Along with other plural societies Israel and Northern Ireland encountered the dilemma of how to govern without consensus. The dangers of minority unrest and political instability were present and clear. Theoretically, there are three democratic ways to achieve cohesion in Israel and Northern Ireland, as in other plural societies. One method is liberal democracy through privatization of ethnicity and formation of overarching values. The other possibility is consociational democracy that reconciles group differences through power sharing and compromise politics. Still another solution is to institute an ethnic democracy that combines rights for all with structured dominance of the majority and control over the minority. These three options are applied with a varying degree of success to cope with diverse minority situations.

Liberal democracy is not a viable option for Israel and Northern Ireland. It requires that two conditions be met: a strong willingness to shed primordial traditions and the creation of a new social order maintained by a national consensus. Yet these conditions are lacking altogether in Israel and Northern Ireland. Arabs and Catholics are nonassimilating minorities and are equipped with all the necessary institutional arrangements to keep their separate identity. Individual incorporation is regarded as neither desirable nor possible. Both the minorities and majorities are committed to exclusionary, sectarian nationalism. That is, they insist on a political entity in which their nationality and religion predominate. There is no room in their ideologies for fully equal-but-different national groups. For this reason Jews and Protestants can be considered involuntary majorities as much as Arabs and Catholics can be considered involuntary minorities. Furthermore, as far as the dominant majorities are concerned, the minorities are expendable ideologically, economically, and politically. In light of the distinct plural nature of both countries, the liberal democracy option is simply impractical.

The consociational alternative is equally impractical. Lijphart indicates the reasons for the failure of consociationalism in Northern Ireland,[68] and his explanation holds true for Israel as well. The main reason for not even trying the consociational solution is the opposition of the dominant majorities among both the leadership and ordinary people. Two of the three factors favorable to consociational democracy are lacking in Israel and Northern Ireland. One is "a multiple balance of power." Jews and Protestants are permanent majorities and do not need the electoral support of the minorities in order to stay in power. The other condition is "some degree of national solidarity." In fact, the reverse holds true in Israel and Northern Ireland, where sectarian nationalism is the major divider and there is no "overarching consensus." A third condition that Lijphart sees as essential is the "acceptability of the grand-coalition form of government as a normative model." It is absent in Northern Ireland but present in Israel. The Protestants who emulate the British type of government do not accept coalition government, but this is the rule in Israeli politics.

The Israeli case suggests, however, a fourth fundamental condition for consociational democracy: the dominant group's belief that the minority is able to disrupt the system while the majority is unable to prevent it from doing so. This is the prime factor underlying "the religious status quo" in Israel—that is, the consociational power-sharing arrangement between the nonreligious dominant majority and the religious nondominant minority. This belief is absent in Northern Ireland, and, as far as Israeli Arabs are concerned, it is also lacking in Israel.

In light of these constraints ethnic democracy suggests itself as the only practical solution. The conditions favoring ethnic democracy exist in Israel and Northern Ireland. The major ones are the lack of general consensus on fundamental matters, the lack of crosscutting affiliations, the lack of an objective need for power sharing due to the presence of permanent majorities, the existence of a keen sense of threat among the dominant group, and the belief that control can avert the nondominant group from realizing the threat. Under these circumstances ethnic democracy is superior to the largely impractical liberal and consociational options. This is the way the dominant majorities in both countries have defined the situation and, hence, opted for ethnic democracy.

Ethnic democracy indeed produced the best results for the Jews and Protestants for relatively long periods—fifty years in Northern Ireland and thirty years in Israel. During this period a harsh and inconsiderate form of ethnic democracy, depending mostly on control, was employed. It dealt directly with the immediate and concrete danger of subversion. But, if control is to be effective for a long run, at least one prerequisite must be met: the dominant group must have the capacity to manipulate the institutions and/or the leadership of the nondominant group. Otherwise, the minority can accumulate power and undermine the system. This possibility is particularly real in formal democracies in which the impatience with domination and the opportunity for organizing resistance are appreciable.

It is precisely on this point that Israel and Northern Ireland differ markedly. The Israeli machinery of control owes much of its effectiveness to special historical and current conditions that enabled Jews to subordinate Arab institutions and leaders. The post-statehood Arab minority was small, poor, leaderless, disorganized, and defenseless. The entire apparatus of the new sovereign Jewish state could be harnessed to make Arabs economically dependent on Jews, to subjugate the reconstructed Arab institutions to Jewish authority, to stifle any attempt to form independent Arab organizations, to neutralize rising Arab leaders, to impose surveillance on the Arab population, and to set up a judicious reward system sanctioning Arab compliance.

In contrast, the seeds of the final breakdown of the machinery of control in Northern Ireland were sown in the early years of partition. The Catholics never lost their institutional autonomy and independent leadership. Although the Protestants established a "majority dictatorship," they could not subordinate Catholic institutions and leadership as long as they lacked the powers vested in a sovereign state. It was, therefore, only a matter of time until the Catholics revolted.

In 1968 the Catholics initiated the civil rights movement to end discrimination. By that time their rising educational and socioeconomic standards increased their resources, reinforced their sense of relative deprivation, and strengthened their institutional autonomy. The Protestants perceived the protest as a direct threat to the system of ethnic democracy and reacted with intransigence. But they grossly misjudged the balance of power, underestimated the Catholic disruptive capability, overrated their control, and belittled the ability and willingness of the British to intervene. Their intransigence and relative weakness brought about the irreversible breakdown of ethnic democracy in the early 1970s and the proposed transition to accountable government in 1994.

Similarly, the Arabs of Israel also challenged ethnic democracy in 1976 and have continued to do so since then. Yet they have failed to undermine the system of ethnic democracy. The disparity in power between Arabs and Jews is still considerable. Despite improvement in their condition, the Arabs still lack institutional autonomy and sufficient resources, while the Jews can use the ample machinery of control of the sovereign state to keep the Arabs in a subordinate position. The Jews also feel strongly—and in this enjoy the backing of the international community—that they are entitled to keep Israel an ethnic democracy ("Jewish and democratic state"). The reality of the external threat also gives much more credence to Jewish claims than to Israeli Arabs demands. Furthermore, the Jews have shown flexibility in handling the Arab protest. Since 1976 they have essentially liberalized the system, relaxing control, eliminating some restrictions, reducing discrimination, dispensing more benefits, while still punishing illegal activities severely. This configuration of factors, which is absent in Northern Ireland, accounts for the survival of ethnic democracy in Israel.

The Jews' successful strategy cannot be divorced from their position on the wider Palestinian issue. All Israeli governments have adopted the same policy of keeping Israeli Arabs apart from their Palestinian brethren in the West Bank, Gaza Strip, and abroad. Jews agree that Israel cannot maintain political stability and ethnic peace if it fully annexes the occupied territories and enfranchises the Palestinians. In this case the Palestinians would turn into a prohibitively large and strong minority that could easily disrupt Israel's ethnic democracy. Given this Jewish national consensus, the bitter disagreement hinges on how to get rid of the noncitizen Palestinians: the radical Right advocates population transfer or depopulation, the Right bloc proposes retention of the territories without enfranchising the residents, while the Left bloc is willing to cede most of the area in order to dispose of the Palestinians. This controversy should not obscure the shared understanding that Israeli Arabs must be left a small and weak minority in order to meet the necessary condition for preserving Israel's ethnic democracy.

What does the future hold in store for the two cases? In the long run the probable solution is a united Ireland—largely nonsectarian, federal or confederal, increasingly prosperous through its integration into the European Community, and sufficiently secure to protect the individual and collective rights of Protestants and guarantee them institutional autonomy.

And what is the future of ethnic democracy in Israel? Will it finally fail as it did in Northern Ireland? Ethnic democracy stands on firmer foundations in Israel precisely because it has shown remarkable flexibility. On the one hand, ethnic democracy inescapably engenders structural contradictions. The inherent incompatibility between democracy for all and the Jewish-Zionist character of the state is becoming clearer and less tolerable for a growing number of Arabs. On the other hand, Israel is amply capable of adapting and positively responding to pressures to soften its ethnic nature. Israel will "normalize" as it moves to the peace era, integrates into the prosperous capitalist core, and increases its Jewish majority as a result of continuing immigration. Jews will feel more secure both as individuals, a community, and a state in the region. They will become less mobilized, less nationalistic, more individualistic, and hence more willing to treat Arabs equally as both individuals and a national minority. Enhanced Jewish security will allow for the recruitment of Arabs into the security forces, their admission into coalition governments, and the extension of institutional autonomy to them. While the new system will continue to be ethnic democracy, it will be much more liberal and tolerable to Arabs, especially if a Palestinian state, with ethnic democracy or nondemocracy, lives peacefully alongside the Jewish state.[69]

More generally, the Israeli case shows that ethnic democracy is indeed a viable and adaptable political system, no less than liberal and consociational democracies. As the case of Northern Ireland demonstrates, however, ethnic democracy is not viable in the long term if the central government is weak, the dominant majority is intransigent, and the nondominant minority enjoys wide institutional autonomy and accumulates power.

Ethnic democracy is the kind of democracy prevalent among certain deeply divided societies. While it has survived in Israel, it has broken down in Northern Ireland. It has been in operation in Malaysia since the early 1970s, and it is slowly emerging in the new states of the former Soviet Union as well as in some other states in Eastern Europe. Grounded on institutionalized ethnic dominance, ethnic democracy is clearly less democratic than Western-style liberal and consociational democracies. It is a better alternative, however, than a nondemocratic ethnic state, a state that uses nondemocratic, *Herrenvolk* means to control and exclude the minority. Advocates and opponents of this political form should seriously consider findings from comparative studies that shed light on the conditions conducive to ethnic democracy, its degree of stability, its advantages and disadvantages to the majority and minority, and the availability of realistic alternatives.

NOTES

1. Arend Lijphart, *Democracy in Plural Societies* (New Haven: Yale University Press, 1977).

2. Ian S. Lustick, "Stability in Deeply-Divided States: Consociationalism versus Control," *World Politics* 31 (1979): 325–44.

3. John McGarry and Brendan O'Leary, eds., "Introduction: The Macro-Political Regulation of Ethnic Conflict," *The Politics of Ethnic Conflict Regulation* (London: Routledge, 1993).

4. Sammy Smooha and Theodor Hanf, "The Diverse Modes of Conflict-Regulation in Deeply Divided Societies," *International Journal of Comparative Sociology* 33 (1992): 26–47.

5. Sammy Smooha, "Minority Status in an Ethnic Democracy: The Status of the Arab Minority in Israel," *Ethnic and Racial Studies* 13 (1990): 389–413.

6. Pierre L. van den Berghe, *Race and Racism* (New York: Wiley, 1978).

7. Sammy Smooha, *Israel: Pluralism and Conflict* (London: Routledge and Kegan Paul, 1978).

8. Sammy Smooha, *The Orientation and Politicization of the Arab Minority in Israel* (Haifa: Jewish-Arab Center, Haifa University, 1984); Richard Rose, *Governing without Consensus: An Irish Perspective* (Boston: Beacon Press, 1971), 214. The Israeli survey, which was conducted by Smooha in 1976, was based on a national representative sample of 722 Arabs (most were adults, but some were fifteen to seventeen years old) and a sample of 148 adult Jews from two towns. The surveys were supported by funds from the Institute for Research and Development of Arab Education at the University of Haifa and from the Ford Foundation, received through Israel Foundations Trustees. It is worth noting that the 1976 survey figures quoted here differ slightly from those reported in later publications, in which Arabs under eighteen were excluded in order to make the 1976 survey comparable with the 1980–87 surveys of Arab adults. The Irish survey was taken by Richard Rose in 1968, just before the civil war broke out. It was based on interviews with a representative sample of 757 Protestants and 534 Roman Catholics.

9. Rose, *Governing without Consensus,* 389.

10. Ibid., 341, 336, 235.

11. Ibid., 305–7.

12. Gary Easthope, "Religious War in Northern Ireland," *Sociology* 10 (1976): 431.

13. Rosemary L. Harris, *Prejudice and Tolerance in Ulster* (Manchester: Manchester University Press, 1972), 146.

14. Rose, *Governing without Consensus,* 336, 508.

15. *Statistical Abstract of Israel,* no. 29 (Jerusalem: Central Bureau of Statistics, 1978), 303.

16. Ibid., 315.

310 / *Comparing Jewish Societies*

17. *Statistical Abstract of Israel,* no. 28 (Jerusalem: Central Bureau of Statistics, 1977), 301.

18. Ibid., 313, 315.

19. Ibid., 360, 369.

20. Ibid., 595.

21. *Statistical Abstract of Israel* (1978), 652.

22. Ibid., 678.

23. These are rough estimates based on figures in ibid., 54, 668–69, 688.

24. Rose, *Governing without Consensus,* 289.

25. Ibid., 503.

26. Ibid., 293.

27. Ibid., 280.

28. Ibid., 500.

29. Sammy Smooha, *Arabs and Jews in Israel,* 2 vols. (Boulder, CO: Westview Press, 1989 and 1992), 1:40, table 3.4.

30. Majid Al-Haj and Henry Rosenfeld, *Arab Local Government in Israel* (Boulder, CO: Westview Press, 1990).

31. Sami K. Mar'i, *Arab Education in Israel* (Syracuse: Syracuse University Press, 1978).

32. Ernest Stock, *From Conflict to Understanding* (New York: American Jewish Committee, 1968), 46.

33. In the 1977 national elections the Arab vote for the non-Zionist, Rakah-dominated election list surpassed the 50 percent mark for the first time.

34. The controversy among Jewish political parties concerning whether to abolish military government in the Arab sector affected Arabs only partially. The welfare of the Arab minority was only one factor among several.

35. Liam De Paor, *Divided Ulster* (Baltimore: Penguin Books, 1970), 13.

36. Robert Moore, "Race Relations in the Six Counties: Colonialism, Industrialization, and Stratification in Ireland," *Race* 14 (1972): 37.

37. Hamish Dickie-Clark, "The Study of Conflict in South Africa and Northern Ireland," *Social Dynamics* 2 (1976): 53–59.

38. Michael Gallagher, "How Many Nations Are There in Ireland?" *Ethnic and Racial Studies* 18 (1995): 715–39.

39. Rose, *Governing without Consensus,* 189, 194, 272, 372.

40. Conor Cruise O'Brien, *States of Ireland* (London: Hutchinson, 1972), 128–29.

41. Sammy Smooha, "Pluralism: A Study of Intergroup Relations in Israel" (Ph.D. diss., University of California, Los Angeles, 1973).

42. Sammy Smooha, "Arabs and Jews in Israel: Minority-Majority Group Relations" (Hebrew), *Megamot* 22 (1976): 397–423; *Arabs and Jews in Israel.*

43. Ian S. Lustick, "Arabs in the Jewish State: A Study of the Effective Control of a Minority Population" (Ph.D. diss., University of California, Berkeley, 1976);

Arabs in the Jewish State: Israel's Control of a National Minority (Austin: University of Texas Press, 1980).

44. Beyond differences in detail and conceptualization, my analysis of the "machinery of control" differs in one key point from Lustick's analysis of the "system of control." Lustick presents control as a consistent structural, institutional, and programmatic system. Its constituent parts of segmentation, dependence, and co-optation are conceived as functional prerequisites much as in Parsons's system. Components reinforce one another, and the implication is that the system will cease to exist in the absence of any one of its components. Faithful to his watertight conception, Lustick explains away any deviation from the model as an "aberration." This view seems to me overdrawn and unduly rational. My account of the machinery of control makes no such firm assumption. Control in Israel, as any other institutional pattern, has its own structural contradictions and wears out over time. Various mechanisms contribute to its efficiency, but none is indispensable.

45. Arend Lijphart, "The Northern Ireland Problem: Cases, Theories, and Solutions," *British Journal of Political Science* 5 (1975): 85–95.

46. Sabri Jiryis, *The Arabs in Israel* (New York: Monthly Review Press, 1976).

47. *Statistical Abstract of Israel* (1978), 409.

48. Henry Rosenfeld, "From Peasantry to Wage Labour and Residual Peasantry: The Transformation of an Arab Village," in *Process and Pattern in Culture,* ed. Robert A. Manners (Chicago: Aldine, 1964), 211–34.

49. *Statistical Abstract of Israel* (1977), 301.

50. Raphael Bashan, "An Interview with Shmuel Toledano, the Prime Minister's Advisor on Arab Affairs" (Hebrew), *Maariv,* 28 November 1969.

51. *Statistical Abstract of Israel* (1978), 46.

52. Yochanan Peres, Avishai Ehrlich, and Nira Yuval-Davis, "National Education for Arab Youth in Israel: A Comparative Analysis of Curricula," *Jewish Journal of Sociology* 12 (1970): 147–64.

53. Jacob M. Landau, *The Arabs in Israel: A Political Study* (London: Oxford University Press, 1969); Jiryis, *Arabs in Israel.*

54. Khalil Nakhleh, "The Direction of Local-Level Conflict in Two Arab Villages in Israel," *American Ethnologist* 12 (1975): 497–516.

55. Rose, *Governing without Consensus,* 432.

56. Eli Rekhess, "Arabs in Israel and the Land Expropriations in the Galilee: Background, Events, and Implications, 1975–77" (Hebrew), mimeo, *Sekirot,* no. 53 (Tel Aviv: Shiloah Center, Tel-Aviv University, 1977).

57. For more details and bibliography on the following discussion of Arab-Jewish relations, see Smooha, *Arabs and Jews in Israel,* vol. 2.

58. Ian S. Lustick, "Creeping Binationalism within the Green Line," *New Outlook* 31, no. 7 (July 1988): 14–19; "The Changing Political Role of Israeli Arabs," in *The Elections in Israel, 1988,* ed. Asher Arian and Michal Shamir (Boulder, CO: Westview Press, 1990), 115–31.

59. Smooha, *Arabs and Jews in Israel,* 1:16–17.

60. On the post-1968 period, see John Whyte, *Interpreting Northern Ireland* (Oxford: Oxford University Press, 1990); T. Wilson, *Ulster: Conflict and Consent* (Oxford: Blackwell, 1989); Brendan O'Duffy, "Containment or Regulation? The British Approach to Ethnic Conflict in Northern Ireland," in *The Politics of Ethnic Conflict Regulation,* ed. John McGarry and Brendan O'Leary (London: Routledge, 1993); Brendan O'Leary and John McGarry, *The Politics of Antagonism: Understanding Northern Ireland* (London: Athlone, 1993); O'Leary and McGarry, eds., "A State of Truce: Northern Ireland after Twenty-Five Years of War," special issue, *Ethnic and Racial Studies* 18 (1995).

61. R. S. P. Longman and John Hickie, *Ulster: A Case Study in Conflict Theory* (London: Longman, 1971); Michael Farrell, *Northern Ireland: The Orange State* (London: Pluto Press, 1976); Ian McAllister, *The Northern Ireland Social Democratic and Labour Party* (London: Macmillan, 1977).

62. Brendan O'Duffy, "Violence in Northern Ireland, 1969–1994: Sectarian or Ethno-National?" *Ethnic and Racial Studies* 18 (1995): 741.

63. For an analysis of the meanings and conditions leading to the Joint Framework Documents, see Brendan O'Duffy, "Introduction: Reflections on a Cold Peace" and "Afterword: What Is Framed in the Framework Documents?" *Ethnic and Racial Studies* 18 (1995): 695–714, 862–72.

64. Oren Yiftachel, "The Concept of 'Ethnic Democracy' and Its Applicability to the Case of Israel," *Ethnic and Racial Studies* 15 (1992): 125–35.

65. Yoav Peled, "Ethnic Democracy and the Legal Construction of Citizenship: Arab Citizens of the Jewish State," *American Political Science Review* 86 (1992): 432–43.

66. Rose, *Governing without Consensus,* 390–95; *Northern Ireland: A Time of Choice* (London: Macmillan, 1976), 139–66.

67. Rose, *Northern Ireland,* 139. Rose's somber realism is more justified than Barritt's and Carter's wishful belief in consensus building through the integration of communities or the establishment of a consociational democracy in Northern Ireland. Denis P. Barrit and Charles F. Carter, *The Northern Ireland Problem: A Study in Group Relations,* 2d ed. (London: Oxford University Press, 1972), 155, 166. Lijphart's inclination to consider repartition as practicable seems also ill founded. Lijphart, "Northern Ireland Problem," 105–6.

68. Ibid., 99–102.

69. Sammy Smooha, "Arab-Jewish Relations in the Peace Era," *Israel Affairs* 1 (1994): 227–44.

Religion and Communal Life in an Evolutionary-Functional Perspective: The Orthodox Kibbutzim

Aryei Fishman

My purpose in this study is to refine understanding of the functional role of conventional religion for the viability of communal life.[1] I shall endeavor to do this by broadly coordinating Talcott Parsons's evolutionary perspective of human society with that of Robert Bellah on religion[2] and applying them to the formation and development of the Religious Kibbutz Federation (RKF) in Israel. By examining the historical experience of the groups that formed religious communes during the mandatory period in Palestine, I shall attempt to demonstrate that religion can play a dysfunctional as well as a functional role in a communal system.

Settlement Patterns and Religious Streams

By the time that the RKF was created in Palestine, in 1935, by members of Jewish religious pioneering movements, almost fifty secular kibbutzim had already settled on the land. Ever since the first kibbutz was founded in 1910, and especially since the institutionalization of this social format within the framework of the secular kibbutz movement in the early 1920s, the kibbutz had been recognized by the Zionist movement as the most effective social instrument for serving its goals. The RKF founders had adopted this highly structured form of settlement because it allowed for the highest degree of self-realization within a national framework. The founding members opted for the kibbutz also because its socialist values meshed with their own strong social awareness.

Apart from their religious orientation the first groups to set up RKF kibbutzim differed from the original secular groups in one unexpected way:

geographic origin. While the secular pioneers had come from Eastern Europe, it was pioneers from Germany that by and large established the norms that still prevail in the religious kibbutzim. And, while some orthodox pioneering groups did come from Eastern Europe (notably Poland but also Romania and Czechoslovakia), they encountered great difficulties in adapting to kibbutz life. An internal survey of the eight religious kibbutzim in the RKF in 1944 indicates that Germans constituted an absolute majority in five, a definite majority in a sixth, and were almost evenly divided with East Europeans in a seventh. Only in the eighth kibbutz did the latter enjoy an absolute majority (see table 1). The population of a ninth kibbutz, Massuot Yitshak, which was not then a member of the RKF, was also almost entirely of East European origin.

As early as the 1920s, it was clear that orthodox pioneers from Eastern Europe found it difficult to relate to kibbutz life. This was the decade during which the religious Zionist pioneering movement in Palestine, composed almost entirely of immigrants from Eastern Europe, took shape within the framework of Ha-Poel Ha-Mizrahi, the orthodox labor organization.[3] While this organization also championed a shared life pattern of settlement, it rejected the kibbutz for the more loosely structured *moshav,* or smallholder cooperative settlement,[4] which secular pioneers had initiated in 1921. This preference for the *moshav* is particularly striking when viewed against the background of secular Zionist settlement in the 1920s. Of the twenty-nine secular pioneering groups that settled on the land in that decade (virtually all from Eastern Europe), twenty (69 percent) opted for the kibbutz and only nine for the *moshav.*[5] The two religious pioneering groups that settled on the land in the 1920s, however, as well as those awaiting their turn to settle (with one exception that I will discuss), opted for the *moshav.*

It has been suggested that the difference between the East European and the German orthodox pioneering groups vis-à-vis their ability to adjust to the kibbutz lies in the historical background of the two groups. The German Jewish community became integrated into modern life in the nineteenth century as a result of emancipation, but only after World War I were most East European communities exposed to full-scale modernization. Inasmuch as the institutionalized form of kibbutz life was fashioned by modern, objective patterns of thought and organization, the German groups would have been better prepared than the East Europeans for the developed form of the kibbutz economy, grounded as it is in advanced technology. This explanation weakens, however, in light of the fact that the kibbutz movement was established by secular pioneers from the traditional communities of Eastern Europe.

TABLE 1.   Distribution of Members in the Kibbutzim of the Religious Kibbutz Federation by Country of Origin, 1 August 1944 (in percentage)

	Germany	Poland	Czechoslovakia	Romania	Austria	Italy	Palestine	Other
Yavne (N = 138)	62	9	4	4	7	3	1	10
Tirat Tzvi (N = 130)	45	32	—	12	3	1	—	7
Sdei Eliyahu (N = 114)	60	3	5	2	9	9	3	9
Be'erot Yitzhak (N = 88)	67	1	26	—	4	—	—	2
Kfar Etzion (N = 98)	2	73	18	2	—	—	1	4
Emunim[a] (N = 90)	77	3	2	—	14	—	—	4
Alumin[b] (N = 70)	43	14	10	9	4	—	14	6
Shluhot (N = 39)	67	2	5	—	26	—	—	—

Source: Toward the Third Council of the Religious Kibbutz Federation (Tel Aviv; HaKibbutz HaDati, 1944), 58. (In Hebrew.)

[a]Name later changed to Ein HaNatziv.

[b]Name later changed to Sand.

We therefore suggest that the difference in ability to accommodate to the kibbutz pattern derives from the divergent religious backgrounds of the German and East European founders of the RKF—Torah-im-Derekh Erets and Hasidism, respectively. The viability of a communal system hinges on the commitment of its members to a pervasive set of ultimate values that is ordinarily associated with religion. Only a supreme ideal can motivate individuals to subdue their personal needs and desires and subject themselves to a collective life that is dedicated to the daily realization of these values.[6] In the case of the secular kibbutzim, as we shall see, Jewish national revival constituted such a supreme ideal. In the case of the religious kibbutzim Judaism was challenged to provide such a footing for kibbutz life.

Torah-im-Derekh Erets and Hasidism represent two types on Bellah's scale of religious evolution, and each coordinates with one of the two basic stages that sociologists of the kibbutz delineate in the evolution of kibbutz life: (1) the inchoate "Bund" and (2) the institutionalized "Commune" stages.[7] Taking shape around different structural types of collectivities, each stage is real inasmuch as it is characterized by different empirical traits, and each is functional for the evolution of the kibbutz.

Parson's Theory Applied to Kibbutz Evolution

Parsons's theory of universal social evolution is particularly helpful for analyzing the evolution of the kibbutz system in a functional perspective as well as for evaluating the crucial role of a religious culture in sustaining the system. According to this theory, the social system in its primitive state embeds the behavioral, personality, and cultural systems at the human level of its environment, while natural and transcendent realities infuse a second level; the system as a whole is dependent on the process of differentiation for exercising control over its personal-natural environment. Once the cultural system gains autonomy from the social system, it plays a superordinate role in controlling it and its environment. And this is particularly true of a religious culture, which provides ultimate meaning to the social system.[8]

The Bund and Commune Stages

The development pattern of the kibbutz as a communal system may be regarded as an ontogenetic manifestation of the evolution of human society. New communes arise out of dissatisfaction with the existing order in that they represent an attempt to recreate society in accordance with utopian standards. This is usually accomplished by reverting to the largely undifferentiated state of reality that is manifest in the Bund stage of the kibbutz.

The Bund—formed as it is by individuals drawn together by a common vision of national and social regeneration who decide to join in the effort to realize their visions in a pioneering framework—constitutes a close-knit group embedded within transcendent and natural realities. While the Bund experience focuses on the individual inner life, the shared ideological symbols of group members fuel intense interpsychic relations that lead to a psychic collectivity with a consciousness of its own; this group consciousness, in turn, cultivates the values and commitments necessary for kibbutz life and dominates individual consciousness. By participating in the psychic collectivity, the individual seeks personal regeneration and "perfection." In this vein physical labor is conceived primarily as a means for communing with the natural world and cultivating the inner life. The dominant ethos of the Bund stage is the pursuit of harmony with fellow group members and with nature.

In this stage the cultural system is embedded within the collective consciousness; that is, intense interpsychic relations, mediated by shared symbols, cause transcendence to become "real" in the collective consciousness. Indeed, transcendent reality constitutes the significant reality of the social system in the Bund stage, and communal life is conceived as both a means of cultivating the transcendent reality and an empirical extension of that reality. The "family" feeling induced by the shared experience of transcendence[9] establishes the criterion that only those who embody the transcendent symbols are considered worthy of membership. And membership calls for commitment to roles that render individuals capable of merging psychically with their fellows, thereby intensifying the transcendent reality in the collective consciousness. At this stage the solidarity of the group is "mechanical";[10] that is, it is based on role homogeneity, diffuse relationships, and an undifferentiated consciousness.

The Bund addresses two functions basic to the social system:[11] cultivating values within the nascent cultural system while motivating members to realize them and integrating members into the larger life of the kibbutz through the psychic collectivity.

But the exigencies of the kibbutz social system, reinforced by the pressure of national and social values, led the accent of reality to shift to external life. When this happened, the natural-behavioral environment began to assume primary significance and the work ethic to intensify and focus on objective economic results. Kibbutz populations grew in size, and formal roles were adopted for regulating and defining the relationship between individual members and the kibbutz. Specific behavioral roles began to overshadow diffuse psychic roles, and a centralized authority organized societal roles into rational patterns centered on collective goals. The individual was now called upon to cultivate self-awareness in fulfilling his specialized roles.[12]

This process led to the emergence of an empirical collectivity—the Commune—from the psychic collectivity of the Bund stage. Based on differentiated roles and norms, the Commune displaced the inner-oriented personality as the focus of kibbutz life. It also addressed another two functions basic to the kibbutz social system: the development of a polity and an economy.[13] While the polity of the Commune penetrates the economy through its control of the means of production and of economic roles, the vigorous work ethic encourages the economy to develop an autonomous dynamic of its own. The functional interdependence of self-aware individuals fulfilling differentiated organizational and, particularly, economic roles fosters "organic" solidarity[14] as the prime integrative mechanism of group life. Thus, the Commune stage is characterized by a rational organizational-economic ethos aimed at transforming the natural-personal environment, rather than by an ethos primarily aimed at the pursuit of harmony.

In attempting to account for the viability of the secular kibbutz social system in religious terms, Siegfried Landshut argues that, for this system, the Jewish national revival constituted the functional equivalent of a conventional religion.[15] While it is beyond the framework of this essay to analyze the religious role Zionism played in the kibbutz context, we should note that, as part of the transition from the Bund to the Commune stage, national and social values were abstracted from the psychic collectivity, eventually attaining ideological autonomy. This ideology legitimated the empirical collectivity through the socialist values of equality and shared living, particularly as expressed in the rational patterns of production and consumption. But at a higher level it grounded this collectivity in the superordinate value of national revival. The fact that the collectivity was conceived primarily as a pioneering community led the criteria for group membership to place greater weight on performance in organizational, especially economic, roles. Thus, in the Commune stage the accent shifted from personal values to universalistic norms. The autonomous cultural framework enabled the social system to coordinate and control the personality and behavioral systems of its members and adapt them to the severe structural constraints of communal life.[16]

Individually delineated socialist and national values became the prime movers of the organizational-economic ethos. At the socialist level the shift in focus from individual psyche to empirical collectivity was translated into moral terms; the ethical format of the collectivity, as expressed in equality and shared living, was regarded as a social mold for perfecting interpersonal behavior. The individual was enjoined to seek salvation via a political ethic, that of rationalized behavior directed toward the empirical collectivity. At the national level the socialist structure constituted a community vehicle for the rational pursuit of national goals. The centralized authority made it possible to direct community life effectively, reorganizing societal roles when necessary in order to further the pioneering mission. Rationalized behavior was cultivated in terms of national duty and service. Indeed, at this level the political ethic constituted the preeminent means for pursuing salvation. The economic ethic, systematized and harnessed to the political ethic, was directed toward transforming nature.

The tension that accompanied the transition from the Bund to the Commune stage is reflected in the pages of *Ha-kevutsah,* a collection of protocols of meetings of kibbutz representatives in 1923 and articles expanding on their deliberations.[17] The latter reflect the fear that the institutionalization of kibbutz life would "impair the perfection of the inner life," "kill the 'over soul,'" "foster egoism," and "cramp esthetic farming." But in general speakers and contributors favor the cultivation of autonomous roles, individual responsibility, and economic achievement as well as the adoption of a prescribed set of regulations.[18] Indeed, the move toward greater differentiation between the kibbutz social system and its environmental constituents advanced the system's evolutionary state by enhancing its adaptive capacity. Kibbutzim in which such differentiation did not take place simply disintegrated.[19]

Parsons conceptualizes a number of processes that supplement differentiation in enhancing the social system's capacity to adapt to its environment.[20] As our analysis implies, the transition from Bund to Commune stages also involved enhancing the system's efficiency and productivity through the heightening of individual awareness and the specialization of collectivities and roles, broadening the scope of membership by giving greater weight to behavior, fostering a higher mode of integration via a universalistic normative system that allowed for more efficient interrelation and coordination of social roles, and modifying the original societal values to legitimate differentiated roles, the polity, and the economy, thereby extending the scope of commitment to a wider range of activities.

Two Types of Judaism on Bellah's Evolutionary Scale

When the orthodox pioneering groups opted for kibbutz life, they proceeded to apply their religious culture to the existing communal system. In contrast to the members of the secular pioneering groups who, having shed traditional religion, had been able to employ their autonomous emotive and cognitive capacities to cultivate the Bund and Commune stages of the kibbutz on the grounds of a national and socialist ideology, the orthodox pioneers, for whom Judaism continued to constitute the essential core of their meaningful world, felt constrained to give it a governing role in sustaining the kibbutz system. This was to be done via two evolutionary modes—Hasidism and Torah-im-Derekh Erets—whose respective states of differentiation are congruent with those of the Bund and Commune stages. These modes correspond, respectively, to the "historic" and "early modern" stages on Bellah's scale of religious evolution.

Bellah theorizes five stages in religious evolution—primitive, archaic, historic, early modern, and modern—which are distinguished by their relative states of differentiation, at three levels. In Bellah's own summary: "First and most central is the [1] evolution of the symbol systems which . . . move from 'compact' to 'differentiated.' In close conjunction with evolution, [2] religious collectivities become more differentiated from other social structures and [3] there is an increasing consciousness of the self as a religious object."[21] Religions of both the historical and early modern types are salvation religions that conceive of the world as dualistically structured between empirical and transcendent realities. These two types differ markedly, however, in their relative states of differentiation. The historic type downgrades the personal organism and the empirical world, blurring the boundaries between the latter and transcendent reality; it conceives of salvation as mediated through ritual or mystical experience and is realized by a core self with a relatively weak self-awareness. The early modern type, on the other hand, makes a distinct separation between empirical and transcendent worlds, regarding the former as an arena for working out salvation through earthly activities performed by autonomous individuals and collectivities.

Although Hasidism[22] was created much later than rabbinic Judaism, it constitutes a "regressive" mode of Judaism on the evolutionary scale. Derogating the world,[23] Hasidism interweaves a heavy residue of the mythological pattern characteristic of the primitive type of religion into its basic historic type.[24] It distinguishes between a primordial "perfected" world, in which all elements are in harmony in the godhead, and the actual "defective" world, in which divine "sparks" are embedded within man and nature.[25] Centering on the spontaneous core self, this mode of Judaism perceives the elements of the physical and social worlds as capable of merging into one seamless religious cloth. Hasidism enjoins the individual to pursue salvation through an ethic of love,[26] through communing affectively with the divine sparks scattered in empirical reality—in effect, through restoring primordial harmony. In this design the preeminent vehicle for attaining salvation is the psychic collectivity centered about the pneumatic leader, the *tsaddik.*[27] Hasidism may be said to define reality by an appreciative standard, the pursuit of harmony.

In contrast to Hasidism, Torah-im-Derekh Erets (literally, Torah and civic life)[28] is world affirming. Created in nineteenth-century Germany by Samson Raphael Hirsch, one of the fathers of modern Jewish orthodoxy, and projecting the "transformative potentialities"[29] of rabbinic Judaism vis-à-vis the modern world, this mode of Judaism posits a distinct gulf, although a direct relationship, between a transcendent Lawgiver and self-aware man. Torah-im-Derekh Erets conceives of *halakhah,* religious law, as rationally structured and directly related to the empirical world; it enjoins man to study the law by employing the logical canons of hermeneutics and to apply the law to empirical reality in order to sanctify this reality.[30] Thus, in this mode of Judaism the empirical community is the foremost arena for applying the law. Indeed, in the tradition of rabbinic Judaism the halakhically ordered community is regarded as bearing a transformative ethos for mastering the world religiously and thereby improving it; it is only as a member of such a community that the individual can attain salvation.[31] Torah-im-Derekh Erets, then, defines reality by a cognitive standard within a rational-empirical context. Its religious legitimation of the physical environment, of the autonomous behavioral and personality systems,[32] as well as the empirical collectivity and its component roles,[33] is a corollary of its religious worldview.

While Hasidism and Torah-im-Derekh Erets both cultivate individualism, Hasidism emphasizes emotive individualism, regarding collectivization at the psychic level as the means for attaining true selfhood, and

322 / *Comparing Jewish Societies*

Torah-im-Derekh Erets cultivates rational individualism in relation to the empirical religious community and among the individuals involved in its realization.

Returning to the difference between the East European and German religious pioneering groups in their adaptations to kibbutz life, the dominant component of Judaism for the former was Hasidism and for the latter Torah-im-Derekh Erets. We suggest that Hasidism was capable of sustaining the Bund stage of kibbutz life but incapable of supporting the Commune stage and that adherence to Torah-im-Derekh Erets patterns enabled the German groups to persevere in this stage. Employing the existential-phenomenological approach, which regards the human consciousness as its field of research,[34] we shall turn to the ideological literature of the East European and German religious pioneering movements and groups in order to discern their respective worldviews. And, by enlisting the ideal typological method of inquiry,[35] we shall proceed to abstract the value orientation patterns of Hasidism and Torah-im-Derekh Erets from their literature to demonstrate their disparate abilities to accommodate structurally to and govern the kibbutz system in the Bund and Commune stages.

Hasidism's Influence on the Orthodox Pioneers

East European Groups

The orthodox pioneering youth of Eastern Europe departed from the traditional passivity of institutionalized Hasidism when they elected to adopt the active Zionist orientation to the world. They did, however, draw upon Hasidic concepts and symbols to provide the religious structure for their image of reality and the pioneering social ethos. Indeed, Hasidic elements formed a central component of Torah and Labor, the religious ideology that championed manual labor as a preeminent means for building the new Jewish society. Evolved by Ha-Poel Ha-Mizrahi in the 1920s,[36] this was the ideology promulgated within religious Zionist pioneering circles in the diaspora. But underlying this ethos was the Hasidic animus to perfect the world by restoring primordial harmony. Thus, while the pioneer was called upon to cultivate his immanent talent, as well as the immanent creative forces of nature, via his work ethic, he was also enjoined to pursue fusion of his core self with nature. In the words of a leading member of Ha-Poel Ha-Mizrahi in 1928:

The goal of existence is the harmony and perfection of creation; the goal of man is complete and absolute fusion in the wholeness of existence and the world. Man is not external to the world and to nature, and he does not utilize them to fulfill his practical, scientific and esthetic needs. He exists within the world . . . he is part of the world's soul. . . . The mission of man is not only to reveal the creative forces within nature and to cultivate them as a creative force for perfecting creation; it is especially to contribute from his specific talents, with which the Creator endowed him, to the world. . . . We have adopted the slogan of "Torah and Labor" out of the desire for unity and harmony, for fusion with the entire cosmos. . . . The goal of "Torah and Labor" is to remove dualism . . . to attain wholeness and harmony within all of creation.[37]

The social ethic of East European youth was also directed toward perfecting the core self, the essential social model being the psychic collectivity of Hasidism—minus the *tsaddik*. Members of the pioneering groups sought inner perfection by endeavoring to divest themselves of their physical personalities and self-awareness and lose themselves in the group psyche. This was to be accomplished by cultivating religious love for one another, a process described succinctly by Moshe Krone: "For those for whom 'Love thy neighbor as thyself' constitutes a foundation stone, the private 'I' is dissolved in relation to the collective 'I.'"[38] Indeed, it was through the sense of exaltation, aroused by the group and nurtured by the dense symbolic field relating to a transcendent reality, that the psychic collectivity constituted an agent for "elevating" the individual psyche in its quest for salvation. Personal regeneration was attained by experiencing the exalted reality that allowed the psyche to feel that "the spark of the oversoul . . . could wear wings . . . and transcend the material nature of the lower world."[39]

The Hasidic social ethic was reinforced by that of the Musar movement, which enjoins study of traditional ethical literature, self-criticism, and ethical conduct as the road to a pure inner life.[40] Accordingly, the symbolic world of East European youth was highly expressive and "compact." Pioneering, social, and religious values were enmeshed in a dense and complex affective pattern directed toward self-perfection. Physical labor was conceived as a means for "bringing perfection to base reality" and, at the same time, for "elevating man and drawing him close to the source of love."[41] Similarly: "Just as we seek to reclaim our arid soil and harsh land . . . so we seek to reclaim ourselves, to uproot self-love from our hearts and instill instead abounding love for our fellow man."[42]

This combination of Hasidic and Musar values readily legitimated the shared life pattern of settlement. In the words of a leading Ha-Poel Ha-Mizrahi figure this pattern of settlement expressed "the Hasidic concept in the sense of mutual influence and fusion of one member with the other and with the collectivity and the Musar movement in its emphasis on a moral ethic."[43]

Why, then, was it in the *moshav* rather than in the kibbutz that expression of this pattern crystallized? It appears that, while East European pioneering groups adopted the communal format as a framework for consolidating the group, they did not extend it beyond the Bund stage; the differentiated structure of kibbutz life in the Commune stage repelled them. The secular empirical collectivity, with its formalized behavioral roles and rigid collective restraints, jarred the core self of these orthodox pioneers in their quest for spontaneous uplift. In the words of a letter from 1925: "In the large Commune the individual is no more than a cog in the whole machine . . . there are no psychic connections between all members, and the possibility of self-development is automatically voided."[44] Thus, the goal of self-perfection cultivated by those pioneers influenced by Hasidism was more amenable to the values of the *moshav,* in which "each individual can live his own life and do his work in those spheres that he and the group mark off in advance . . . without being constrained by anyone's will."[45]

The one exception, which may prove the rule, was Kvutsat Ha-Natsiv. Established in 1924 as a pioneering group intending to pursue the communal life pattern, it was, however, oriented solely to the psychic mode of this pattern; its members explicitly dissociated themselves from the political dimensions of communal life and downplayed the economic dimension, perceiving the Commune as the preeminent framework for cultivating the inner life.

One should seek the path leading to the perfection of the individual in the social body, not in the political, but in the communal sense. A collective group that is permeated by the idea of moral purification and improvement of character traits and is united in its life pattern to the extent that its members feel a friendly, familial relationship towards one another and even more—such a group by common effort can reach the height to which it aspires. "Everyone will help his neighbor and encourage his brother" [Isa. 41:6]. Egoism dissolves and faults and imperfections are corrected and improved by mutual criticism.[46]

The few extant descriptions of daily life within Kvutsat Ha-Natsiv strongly suggest that its psychic collectivity proved incapable of grounding the differentiated reality of pioneering life. The external and objective aspects of this life appear to have enervated the group's religious ethos. In 1925 a member wrote: "Religious feeling weakens anew every time. . . . I hardly pray with intention. . . . Everything has become a matter of rote."[47] Kvutsat Ha-Natsiv dissolved in 1927.

It was only in the 1930s, under the inspiration of Rodges, the first German religious communal group in Palestine, that religious pioneering youth in Eastern Europe began to identify with the kibbutz social pattern. These youth were more deeply involved in the general society than their Ha-Poel Ha-Mizrahi predecessors of the 1920s. Having grown up in newly emancipated East European communities, virtually all of them had received a secular education, and some had graduated from *Gymnasia.* Nonetheless, they continued to cultivate Hasidic-Musar values as the religious underpinning of their pioneering and social outlook. Indeed, within the Bund reality of the pioneering training farms in their countries of origin, they conceived of the kibbutz as the prime social structure for realizing these values. "The only way to create a harmonious and just society is to uproot evil . . . and attain goodness. . . . This can be done only in the kibbutz."[48] Similarly: "Kibbutz life constitutes our goal: the sole life framework leading to the refinement of man and his perfection."[49] In other words, the East European orthodox youth of the 1930s regarded the kibbutz as a socialist society that emerges from inner-perfected individuals.

German Pioneering Groups

Hasidism also provided the religious grounding for the Bund reality of religious pioneering groups from Germany. Orthodox Jewish youth were influenced by the same existential ferment that led German youth at the start of the century to create neoromantic youth movements.[50] Within the framework of their own youth movements Jewish youth, too, experienced the urge to realize a new human identity, a "whole person," through primary interpersonal relations in the framework of the *Gemeinschaft* and the return to nature.[51] Indeed, the Jewish religious Bunds[52] constituted one component of the "Panorama of Bunds"[53] of this period. A description of an orthodox summer camp experience in 1928 captured the movement's neoromantic mood:

> Life in the *Gemeinschaft* fused the comrades together. . . . The camp was built by those who participated in it, but even more, the participants were built by the life in the *Gemeinschaft.* Academics, workers, eastern and western Jews, rich and poor alike—all differences vanished. . . . To experience the *Gemeinschaft,* to experience the other . . . could engulf people and create them anew.
>
> The forces of nature also influenced us. . . . Against the backdrop of the forest, the rapport of all those who shared our aspiration was an experience. Perhaps, even more, it was an expression of the *Gemeinschaft* living among us and within us.[54]

The religious pioneering movement in Germany included a considerable number of East European immigrants among its members. It was the established German members, however, raised in the spirit of Torah-im-Derekh Erets, who set the tone for the new movement. Indeed, the existential ferment of orthodox Jewish youth was largely a reaction to Torah-im-Derekh Erets. At one level it expressed a protest against the "cold" rationalism of German orthodox Jewry; at this level the ferment was cast into Hasidic symbolic and social patterns. German Jewish youth became sensitized to Hasidism through the works of Martin Buber and also through encounters with Hasidic groups of Polish origin that migrated to Germany, especially after World War I.[55]

But at a second level the ferment was directed against the dualism of German orthodox Jewish life, between a religious life confined to the ritualistic sphere and another, all-embracing general life. After several generations of emancipation German orthodox youth were well versed in modern life and possessed a high awareness of the universal component of their identity. To them becoming a "whole person" involved participating in a social system that integrated Jewish religious and universal life. And Zionism offered them an opportunity to attain such integration.[56] Their identification with socialism was a corollary of this universal self-awareness. Influenced in the 1920s and early 1930s by the Christian socialism of Paul Tillich and others,[57] orthodox Jewish youth were encouraged to seek the religious roots of Jewish socialism.[58]

Commune Reality in the Religious Kibbutz Federation

The transition from the Bund to the Commune stage came about when the pioneering groups moved from their training farms in Europe to Palestine and, following the pattern created by secular kibbutzim, set up farming work camps for further training and in anticipation of permanent settlement sites. When their populations grew from several to many dozens, roles became differentiated, specialized, and objectified. Empirical collectivities were shaped along rational patterns that organized behavior within the framework of the polity and its constituent economy. The work ethic intensified, and physical labor became the overriding feature of daily life. In other words, as the rational organizational-economic ethos came to the fore, the religious kibbutz member was called upon to individualize and objectify his personality. Once the kibbutz settled on the land, the rational ethos heightened.

The differentiating thrust of kibbutz evolution, honed by pioneering values, tended to subdue the spontaneous psychic self. This is exemplified by the impact of the economic ethic upon two kibbutz institutions—daily meals and prayer meetings. Whereas both institutions are deemed highly functional for stimulating the psychic collectivity, and therefore are usually sustained in a collective setting in religious communes,[59] the intense economic ethic of the religious kibbutz weakened their effectiveness.

Thus, on weekdays morning and noon meals were shortened by being taken individually, in order to accommodate the work schedules of the various economic branches. Similarly, the prescribed thrice-a-day prayer service, which ideally is held in public, often took place with a bare quorum, as most members prayed by themselves. Only on the Sabbath and religious holidays did the community assemble for joint meals and prayers. But, in the words of a member whose group was in the first year of settlement on the land, "Our Sabbaths [and holidays] have become mere days of rest; their sacredness is not felt; even for the singing of hymns [at the dinner table] it is very difficult to open one's mouth."[60] While in the course of time members did become more adjusted to hard physical work, Sabbath celebrations remained restrained.

Nor were there means to stimulate the psychic collectivity at the end of each workday. In time even the evening meal became formally structured. Torah and secular classes held on weekday evenings and on the Sabbath were attended by a minority of members. And the format of the "general meeting," usually held once a week, was devoid of specific religious content.

It follows that the Commune stage of kibbutz life offered few arrangements to stimulate the inner life. "From the religious standpoint, the religious man in our [kibbutz] society will be rigorous, dry, lacking in religious succulence and warmth."[61] But these were the very traits that eventually abetted accommodation to Commune life.

Difficulties of the East European Groups

The core Hasidic values of the East European groups hampered their adaptation to the pioneering values of the Commune. The poor fit between Hasidic value orientations and Commune realities created a strain that may be demonstrated by focusing on Kfar Etsion,[62] the one religious kibbutz whose members were almost all from a Hasidic background. Expressions of the inner strain in the social system of this kibbutz are found in its bulletin and other writings, from the time a work camp was set up in 1935 until the kibbutz was destroyed in 1948.

The pioneer work ethic was minimized in the first year of this group's independent work camp existence because it impaired cultivation of the inner life. In a letter sent in 1936 to leaders still in Poland it was noted: "In Palestine, physical labor takes up most of one's time. . . . Our outlook, however, is not grounded in this reality and . . . we must wage an offensive against such a trend. . . . If we are unable to remove this *evil reality* in its entirety, we must weaken its influence as much as possible."[63] Two articles from the kibbutz bulletin four and five years later suggest that the general membership had not yet been able to internalize the rational organizational-economic ethos.

> I look through our bulletin. . . . Again a lyrical article . . . nature, God . . . the renewal of the soul. . . . Is it a healthy phenomenon that . . . such a publication is full of lofty ideals and does not deal with some of the most necessary considerations, such as those of the farm economy? Interestingly enough, we cannot find anyone who will write about a plan for our economic future.[64]

> For all practical purposes, the community has almost ceased to constitute a collectivity oriented toward shared living, and has become an association of individuals. . . . Due to the lack of appreciation for the individual . . . he experiences a sense of isolation. . . . Instead of warmth

and sympathetic intimacy, the member often finds an exaggerated formalism that borders on bureaucracy.[65]

Not only were the members of Kfar Etsion unable to adapt to the Commune reality, but the environmental input of that reality acted to devitalize their core value orientations in that it deflected the individual from the accepted Hasidic road to personal salvation within an otherworldly sphere. Kfar Etsion fostered the study of Musar for a number of years and, in different periods of its existence, held a Hasidically fashioned *seudah shlishit* (third meal) late on Sabbath afternoons to stimulate both quiet meditation and ecstatic enthusiasm through lyrical hymns and wordless tunes. Such study and ritual, however, could not offset the dampening effect of the organizational-economic ethos on the inner life. Thus, he laments:

> The external factors throw us into the whirlpool of life until it appears that one cannot halt for a moment to listen to the stirrings of the soul, which demands an internal-moral stock-taking.[66]
>
> Dry realism has cut off every possibility of following the thrust of a vision. We have forgotten that there is a truth transcending [empirical] "reality," which has become the sole yardstick of our thinking. . . . We do not know how to integrate the dream into reality through everyday conduct.[67]

After the group settled on its permanent site in 1943 its vigorous application to the development of a full-fledged farm economy muted Hasidic value orientations still further. One young Kfar Etsion member complained to a group leader that overemphasis on economic activities "comes at the expense of the inner content, the soul." Highlighting the salience of pioneering values in the group's culture, the leader's response alludes to organic solidarity as an alternative source of satisfaction: "The very construction of the first Hebrew settlement in the area between Jerusalem and Hebron can also provide inner satisfaction and content."[68] The specific roles that required rational, self-aware individuals functioning in a framework of organic solidarity could not be institutionalized, however, in religious terms.

The inability of the core Hasidic value orientation patterns to legitimate individualism, as well as the general malfunctioning of the social system, was made evident in one of the last issues of the Kfar Etsion bulletin:

We are confronted with the undermining of our partnership in fate and in mutual responsibility. . . . Individualism gains in strength from year to year. . . . The romantic past with its vision of the negation of the "self" will no longer return. . . .

How our farm economy suffers because the member lacks psychic satisfaction! It has been said that every branch of the farm has some member who is concerned with it, but the quintessential farm—man— is left to himself.[69]

The editorial in that same issue summarizes the crisis: "For us, kibbutz life is becoming increasingly divested of its essence, and there is no one to imbue it with new content."

The inability of Hasidism to sustain a meaningful kibbutz life in its Commune stage induced those pioneers of East European Hasidic background who wanted to continue in that life to assimilate into the German group. As for Kfar Etsion, the tragic end that it met in the Arab-Jewish War of 1948[70] preceded what would seem to have been its inevitable dissolution as a kibbutz. A survivor of the group told me that, had not Kfar Etsion been destroyed, its members were certain to have converted the settlement into a *moshav shitufi* (a combination of *moshav* and kibbutz). Indeed, Massuot Yitshak, the other religious kibbutz whose members originated almost entirely from Eastern Europe and was largely of Hasidic background, converted into a *moshav shitufi* in 1950.

Structural Compatibility of Torah-im-Derekh Erets

Orthodox German pioneering youth, although they grounded their Bund stage in Hasidism, had no misgivings about discarding the Hasidic pattern when they encountered the environmental challenge of Commune reality. This reality was precipitously thrust upon Rodges, the first German pioneering group in Palestine. Rodges members established their kibbutz in 1931, and for several years it constituted the major absorption framework for religious pioneers who opted for kibbutz life.

The pedestrian life in Rodges in the early years of the kibbutz is vividly brought out in a comparison between Rodges and another religious communal group that was established next to it a half-year after its founding. Composed of members of Bnei Akiva, the local Palestinian orthodox Zionist youth movement, this group was grounded in the Hasidic-Musar ethos. A Bnei Akiva leader observed at the time that there was a "continuous turnover" at Rodges, where "the heart is bleak and the weary face dejected, where people live together . . . but nevertheless are alone on the holidays, on the Sabbath, on the six work days." The writer contrasts the "cold" atmosphere at Rodges with that of the "hot, seething" Bnei Akiva group, with its "youthful enthusiasm and faith." He concludes that "the future belongs to Bnei Akiva," as "it is evident that sentence has been passed" on Rodges.[71] Yet it was the Bnei Akiva group that disbanded, in 1933, while Rodges became Kibbutz Yavne in 1941.

The ethos of Rodges is outlined in a 1934 report of one of its leaders:

What . . . we find in our circle is no more than a weak image of an already decadent Hasidic milieu complemented by youth memories that are incongruent with the non-romantic reality of the Jewish worker. As long as our group . . . consisted of twenty to thirty members and every-thing, as they say, took care of itself, there was at least an atmosphere of *Gemutlichkeit.* But the moment that we passed the hundred mark all that changed. Then the problem of shaping the life of the *Gemeinschaft* confronted us mercilessly, in all its acuteness.[72]

Indeed, when faced with Commune reality, the German pioneers had no qualms about reverting to the patterns of Torah-im-Derekh Erets, the mode of Judaism within which it had been socialized—for Torah-im-Derekh Erets, grounded in the perception of religious law as the central element of Jewish religious life, affirmed the environmental and societal elements that had to be upgraded in the Commune stage. Citations from the ideological literature of the German-bred pioneers indicate their abil-ity to legitimate these elements in religious terms and thereby to control their Commune environment. It should be noted that some of these pas-sages were written as a foil to the Hasidic perspective.

The inclusion of material life within the sphere of Jewish religion signifies the affirmation of that life. . . . Just like the "spirit" and the "soul," man's body is part of the divine image. Accordingly, Judaism determines man's way of life and the tasks incumbent upon him. . . . This is expressed in the determination of *halakhah* as the basis of reli-gion.[73]

Man's reason and moral concepts are implanted in him by God, and they, no less than nature, are to be developed by man. . . . It is not through the divestment of the "I" that religious man is judged, but through the development of his psychic and rational capacities. . . . Jewish religion is revealed to us . . . as a law given to us by a supreme Lawgiver in order to rule the community and shape the life of the individual therein. . . . The purpose of this religious perception . . . is to establish order in reality and to ground the Jewish community on a firm basis.[74]

It seems that religious legitimation of the empirical collectivity and the rational personalities that composed it allowed the German-bred pioneers to cultivate organic solidarity through the individual "who maintains his [rational] autonomy" and also "accepts the yoke of responsibility for the group enterprise."[75] Furthermore, the stress in rabbinic Judaism on objective performance, on observing the law rather than on psychic intentionality, fits the strong behavioral dimension of Commune life. In 1960 one religious kibbutz member articulated this aspect of the halakhic ethos in the context of kibbutz life:

We cannot rest content with uplifting religious experiences. We attribute significance to the act of the individual within his community, for his community, and together with his community in the drabness of everyday life. If one can add a deep feeling and an exalted intention, so much the better. But we will not forgo the act, even if it is not always accompanied by exalted thought.[76]

Within this rational-conceptual framework German orthodox pioneers cultivated a religious ethos of transforming reality by means of a legal ethic. Nurtured by a dynamic cognitive and practical perception of the law, this ethic enjoins man to reshape reality by actively adopting a rational approach to both religious law and empirical reality. Thus, the study of the Torah was not viewed solely as sheer intellectual activity; its major role was to be one of guidance toward innovation through uncovering new laws[77] and toward acting on reality by defining norms of behavior for realizing divine law in empirical life: "Study lacks influence and an abiding validity if it does not participate in creating social life in its entirety. Study lacks purpose if it does not lead to action. According to our outlook, study exists for its practical application to all aspects of practical life."[78]

The capacity of the German pioneers to generalize their kibbutz culture was crucial to their ability to cope with the differentiated reality of the Commune stage. By placing the accent of religion on the practice of the law, they were able to disengage pioneering and socialist values from religious values and to rationalize the former in a unified and integrated system of ideas around a central halakhic core. Such rationalization enhanced the autonomy of these ideas in relation to the social system, thereby bringing the pioneering and socialist values of the secular empirical collectivity within the parameters of the religious culture, which, in turn, strengthened commitment to these values. In short, for those grounded in Torah-im-Derekh Erets it was rationalization, through conscious ideas, that enabled religious culture to exercise its superordinate role in controlling the Commune system and its environmental constituents and to influence social action thereby.[79]

This rationalization was achieved by investing the socialist and pioneering dimensions of the secular empirical collectivity with the valence of the halakhically ordered community. Thus, the socialist structure of the kibbutz was regarded as the contemporary manifestation of the biblical ethos of world transformation, of "the reality-perfecting and social aspiration of the Jewish religion which was most pronounced in the words of the prophets and which *halakhah* in its entirety aims to validate and actualize . . . in everday life."[80] The pioneering structure was interpreted as a national framework for renewing the community in which *halakhah* ordered virtually all areas of life that had existed in traditional Jewish society and that nineteenth-century emancipation had circumscribed.[81]

In effect, the imposition of halakhic order upon the secular collectivity constituted a de-differentiating process. The awareness that the two were distinct entities, however, promoted their functional interpenetration and interaction. The secular collectivity provided the comprehensive differentiated social life upon which the halakhic order could be imprinted. In turn, the ultimate value represented by the latter legitimated the secular collectivity, thereby enhancing the motivation for its effective functioning. The secular collectivity thus constituted an instrument for reshaping the world in accordance with religious ideals.[82]

To sum up, by shifting the dominant component of the orthodox core of RKF culture from Hasidism to halakhic Judaism—from a love ethic to a legalistic ethic—the German-bred pioneers were able to reaffirm the superordinate role of religion in the religious kibbutz system and enable it to sustain and legitimate the Commune stage of the system. It enhanced the environmental-adaptive capacity of the religious kibbutz system in accordance with Parsons's aforementioned processes. It provided a religious grounding for rational individuals as well as specialized collectivities and roles, thereby enhancing their efficiency. It shifted the religious criterion for membership from belief to normative halakhic behavior, thereby including a wider group of members. It reinforced the higher universalistic normative mode of integration, thereby strengthening the interrelation of the political and economic roles. And, finally, it generalized the religious culture, thereby extending the range of commitment to a wide spectrum of societal activities.

The Functionality of Religion

The pattern of life created in kibbutzim established by orthodox German youth in the 1930s and 1940s still endures in the sixteen RKF settlements of the 1990s. One may enquire whether the religious grounding of these kibbutzim enhances their viability as compared with that of secular kibbutzim. The generally accepted criterion of longevity cannot be applied here, since secular and religious kibbutzim continue to exist. There is, however, one cardinal sphere of kibbutz life that seems to have benefited from the singular impact of religious culture: economic achievement. Recent studies of the economic performance of the RKF and of the secular kibbutz federations between 1958 and 1982 indicate that in this period the RKF increasingly surpassed the other federations in economic achievement,[83] notwithstanding such handicaps as adherence to ritualistic-legal norms, a higher birthrate, and less industrialization than in the secular kibbutzim. The widening gap between the performance of the religious and secular federations came to a head in the mid-1980s, when, in the wake of a series of economic blows, the secular federations found themselves enmeshed in a staggering debt and had to seek a government bailout, while the RKF remained solvent.[84] It appears that the higher level of self-rationalization, together with the religious political ethic, enhances the ethic of duty and service and accounts for the successful economic performance of the orthodox kibbutzim.[85]

Discussion

Inasmuch as the RKF communal system did not derive directly from a religious frame of reference, its experience can sharpen our understanding of the functional relationship between religion and communal life.

This study demonstrates that for a religion to fulfill its superordinate role in a communal system it must possess both of the evolutionary salvation modes: the historical one and the early modern one. It is the combination of these two modes that allows the religion to establish elective affinities with the functional needs of the system as they evolve. In other words, the religion must be capable of cultivating emotional and rational individualism as well as of sustaining and legitimating the communal structure as both an extension of psychic unity and an empirical collectivity in its own right; it must be capable of promoting mechanical *and* organic solidarity.[86] A religion that cannot provide such diverse resources to meet the functional needs of a communal system will be dysfunctional for the system.

In Peter Berger's terminology the two modes of salvation religion involve two modes of religious experience: "interiorized" and "confrontational."[87] The thrust of the interiorized mode is toward unity and that of the confrontational mode is toward differentiation. In Judaism the interiorized mode of religious experience can produce a communal system informed by an ethic of love. Induced by its relationship to an immanent mode of the Jewish divinity and focused on the individual psyche, this system is oriented toward recapturing an ideal reality that existed in the past. The confrontational religious experience can produce a communal system informed by the ethic of duty. Informed by its relationship to a transcendent mode of the Jewish divinity and focused on an empirical collectivity, this system is oriented toward realizing an ideal reality in the future.

A Comparative Afterthought: Application to Christian Communes

John Humphrey Noyes, who studied the nineteenth-century American communal scene, was the first to point out the functional relationship of religion to a communal system.[88] Noyes supports, in very general terms, the conclusion that this relationship is contingent upon two evolutionary modes of religion. Basing his evaluation on a distinction between the "spiritual and intellectual excitement" in the formation of new movements and "the institutions that arise out of it," he analyzes why revival movements that might have formed communal systems never did so and why the systems formed by such rationalist societies as the "socialistic" Owenites and Fourierists failed.

The revivalists had for their great idea the revival of the soul. The great idea of the Socialists was the regeneration of society. . . . Both failed in their attempt to bring heaven on earth because . . . they would not put their two great ideas together. The Revivalists failed for want of regeneration of society and the Socialists failed for want of regeneration of the heart.[89]

Noyes notes that his own Perfectionist society "issued from a conjunction" between revivalism and socialism.[90] (The Perfectionist communal movement existed for thirty-eight years, ultimately dissolving because of the decline in its religious beliefs.)[91]

Indeed, the viability of Christian communal living seems to draw nourishment from the two ideal types that Ernst Troeltsch indicates as corresponding to the interiorized and the confrontational types of religious experience: (1) a "religious communion of love" nourished by mysticism and conveying the reality of "one heart and one soul" derived from the Gospel ethic; and (2) a "kind of Christian socialism" induced by an ascetic worldly ethic and focused on the empirical community, which is regarded as an instrument with which to transform the world.[92]

It is hypothesized that the application of a combined Parsons-Bellah evolutionary model to a systematic study of Christian communal societies of relatively high viability might reveal that their social systems became differentiated in the course of their evolution and that the religious cultures that nourished them shifted the focus of communal life from Troeltsch's first to second type.

This seems to be borne out by the two longest-enduring Christian communal systems, the Hutterites and the Shakers. Both those groups grounded their communal systems in Troeltsch's two religious types. Like the kibbutz social system, the communal system of the Hutterites and the Shakers originated in a matrix of intense interpsychic experience focused on a transcendent world, through which the individual sought regeneration.[93] In the course of their evolution these systems, again like the kibbutz system, differentiated from their environmental constituents, thereby allowing articulate ideologies and highly ramified empirical collectivities to emerge.[94] The autonomous behavioral and personality systems of the Hutterites and Shakers are evident in their technological prowess and economic efficiency.[95] A recent study of the Hutterite system points to a functional correlation between its fused and differentiated stages and the two modes of religious salvation.[96] This study tends to confirm that a religious culture within a communal system must be structurally congruent with the evolutionary state of the system in order to sustain it.

NOTES

1. For a good historical discussion of this topic, see William S. Bainbridge, "Utopian Communities, Theoretical Issues," in *The Sacred in a Secular Age,* ed. Phillip E. Hammond (Berkeley: University of California Press, 1985), 21–35.

2. Talcott Parsons, *Societies: Evolutionary and Comparative Perspectives* (Englewood Cliffs, NJ: Prentice-Hall, 1966); *The System of Modern Societies* (Englewood Cliffs, NJ: Prentice-Hall, 1971); Robert N. Bellah, "Religious Evolution," *American Sociological Review* 29 (1964): 358–74.

3. See Aryei Fishman, *Judaism and Modernization on the Religious Kibbutz* (Cambridge: Cambridge University Press, 1992), 55–65.

4. Aryei Fishman, "On the Influence of Hasidism on the Initial Social Doctrine of Ha-Poel Ha-Mizrahi" (Hebrew), *Bar-Ilan Yearbook* 9 (1972): 392–412.

5. Alex Bein, *The Return to the Soil: A History of Jewish Settlement in Israel,* trans. I. Schen (Jerusalem: Zionist Organization, 1952), 555–72.

6. Siegfried Landshut, *The Kevutsah* (Hebrew) (Jerusalem: Zionist Organization, 1944), 7–8.

7. For these two stages, see Yonina Talmon, *Family and Community in the Kibbutz* (Cambridge, MA: Harvard University Press, 1972), 2–3; Erik Cohen, "The Structural Transformation of the Kibbutz," in *Social Change,* ed. George K. Zollschan and Walter Hirsch (New York: John Wiley, 1976), 703–42.

8. See Victor Lidz, "Religion and Cybernatic Concepts in the Theory of Action," *Sociological Analysis* 43 (1982): 387–405.

9. Talmon, *Family and Community,* 3.

10. Emile Durkheim, *The Division of Labor in Society,* trans. G. Simpson (New York: Free Press, 1964), 70–110.

11. Talcott Parsons, "An Outline of the Social System," in *Theories of Society,* ed. T. Parsons et al. (New York: Free Press, 1961), 1:38–40.

12. Cf. Philip E. Slater, *Microcosm: Structural, Psychological, and Religious Evolution in Change* (New York: John Wiley, 1966), 229.

13. Parsons, "Outline," 39–40.

14. Durkheim, *Division of Labor,* 111–32.

15. Landshut, *Kevutsah,* 52.

16. For such constraints, see Talmon, *Family and Community,* 203–10.

17. *Ha-kevutsah* (Tel Aviv: General Federation of Labor, 1924).

18. Ibid., 28, 57, 26, 83, 25, 23, 83–84, 55–66.

19. See the analysis in Henrik F. Infield, *Cooperative Living in Palestine* (London: Kegan Paul, Trench, Trubner, 1946), 19–20.

20. Parsons, *Societies,* 21–23.

21. Bellah, "Religious Evolution," 358.

22. See Martin Buber, *Hasidism and Modern Man,* trans. M. Friedman (New York: Horizon Press, 1958); *The Origin and Meaning of Hasidism,* trans. M. Fried-

man (New York: Horizon Press, 1960); Gershom Scholem, *Major Trends in Jewish Mysticism* (New York: Schocken Books, 1961), 325–50.

23. See Gershom Scholem, "Martin Buber's Interpretation of Hasidism," *Commentary* 32 (October 1961): 305–16.

24. Cf. Bellah, "Religious Evolution," 366; Peter L. Berger, ed., *The Other Side of God* (Garden City, NY: Anchor Books, 1981), 11–12.

25. Buber, *Origin and Meaning of Hasidism,* 83–88.

26. Buber, *Hasidism and Modern Man,* 225–56.

27. Ibid., 256.

28. The most comprehensive discussions of this movement are in Mordechai Breuer, *Modernity within Tradition: The Social History of Orthodox Jewry in Imperial Germany,* trans. E. Petuchowski (New York: Columbia University Press, 1992); and Isadore Grunfeld, "Samson Raphael Hirsch—The Man and His Mission," in *Judaism Eternal: Selected Essays from the Writings of Rabbi Samson Raphael Hirsch,* 2 vols. (London: Soncino Press, 1956), 1:xii–xlvii. See also Fishman, *Judaism and Modernization on the Kibbutz,* 33–44.

29. Cf. Shmuel N. Eisenstadt, "The Implications of Weber's Sociology of Religion for Understanding the Processes of Change in Contemporary Non-European Societies and Civilizations," in *Beyond the Classics?* ed. Charles Y. Glock and Phillip E. Hammond (New York: Harper and Row, 1973), 136.

30. Fishman, *Judaism and Modernization on the Kibbutz,* 40–41.

31. Ibid., 42.

32. S. R. Hirsch, *Explanation to the Pentateuch,* trans. I. Levy (New York: Judaica Press, 1971), 1:29–33, 194–96.

33. Hirsch, *Judaism,* 2:97–114.

34. For this approach, see Edward A. Tiryakian, "Structural Sociology," in *Theoretical Sociology,* ed. J. C. McKinney and E. A. Tiryakian (New York: Appleton, 1970), 112–35.

35. For this method, see Max Weber, *The Methodology of the Social Sciences,* ed. and trans. Edward A. Shils and Henry A. Finch (New York: Free Press, 1949), 90.

36. Fishman, *Judaism and Modernization on the Kibbutz,* 55–64.

37. Cited in Aryei Fishman, ed., *Ha-poel ha-mizrahi, 1921–1935* (Tel Aviv: Tel Aviv University, 1979), 186–87.

38. *Orhot: Vignettes—Benchmarks—Fragments of Thought,* ed. Moshe Krone (Warsaw: Ha-Shomer Ha-Dati, 1938), 108.

39. Ibid., 55.

40. Dov Katz, *The Musar Movement,* trans. Leonard Oschry (Tel Aviv: Orly Press, 1975).

41. Krone, *Orhot,* 49, 78.

42. *Hayyenu,* Iyar 5694 [1934], 11. Hebrew periodicals referred to in this essay and the groups that published them are as follows: *Alonim* and *Amudim,* RKF sec-

retariat; *Ba-tirah,* Tirat Tsevi commune; *Be-mahaneinu,* Kfar Etsion commune; *Ha-ohela,* the "left wing" of Ha-Poel Ha-Mizrahi; *Hayyenu,* Slavkov training farm in Poland; *Netivah,* executive of Torah and Labor movement in Palestine; *Ohaleinu,* Ha-Shomer Ha-Dati youth movement in Poland; *Zeraim,* Bnei Akiva youth movement in Palestine.

43. Cited in Fishman, *Ha-poel ha-mizrahi,* 201.

44. *Netivah,* 9 Nisan 5695 [1935], 8.

45. Cited in Fishman, *Ha-poel ha-mizrahi,* 200–201.

46. Ibid., 198–99.

47. *Ha-ohela,* 2–3 (ca. 1925), 44–45.

48. Cited in Krone, *Orhot,* 146.

49. *Ohaleinu,* Tevet-Shevat 5696 [1936], 13.

50. Howard Becker, *German Youth: Bond or Free?* (London: Kegan Paul, Trench and Trubner, 1946).

51. German youth articulated the thrust of its value orientations in terms of a "return to the *Gemeinschaft.*" The relationships that it cultivated, however, were in terms of the Bund, the designation that characterized this type of group. Indeed, Schmalenbach's concept of the Bund derived from the social reality generated by the German youth movements. See Herman Schmalenbach, "Communion—a Sociological Category," in *Schmalenbach on Society and Experience,* ed. Guenther Lueschen and Gregory P. Stone (Chicago: University of Chicago Press, 1977).

52. See Walter Z. Laqueur, *Young Germany* (New York: Basic Books, 1962), 163.

53. This is the name of a chapter in Laqueur's book. Ibid., 155.

54. Eugen Michaelis, "Zur Entwicklung des Tora wa'awoda Gedanken in Deutschland," *Chayenu* 23 (January 1938): 6–8.

55. Fishman, *Judaism and Modernization on the Kibbutz,* 73.

56. Ibid., 74–75.

57. See Laqueur, *Young Germany,* 118–19.

58. Mosche Unna, "Die jüdische Form des religösen Sozialismus," *Zion* (Berlin) 6, no.1 (January 1934): 4–7.

59. See, for example, Edward D. Andrews, *The People Called Shakers* (New York: Dover Publications, 1963), 182; John H. Hostetler, *Hutterite Society* (Baltimore: Johns Hopkins University Press, 1974), 168; Benjamin Zablocki, *The Joyful Community* (Chicago: University of Chicago Press, 1980), 47–48, 154.

60. *Ba-tirah,* 4 Sivan 5698 [1938], 3.

61. *Alonim,* Tishrei 5700 [1939], 6.

62. The name of this group until it settled on the land was Kvutsat Avraham.

63. *Ohaleinu,* Tevet-Shevat 5696 [1936], 15; emphasis added.

64. *Be-mahaneinu,* Tevet 5700 [1940], 15.

65. Ibid., Sivan 5701 [1941], 3.

66. Ibid., Tammuz 5699 [1939], 6.

67. Ibid., Sivan 5701 [1941], 9.

68. Ibid., Erev Rosh Ha-Shanah 5704 [1943], 8.

69. Ibid., Tishrei 5708 [1947], 4, 6.

70. Dov Knohl, ed., *Siege in the Hills of Hebron,* trans. I. HaLevy-Levin (New York: Thomas Yosselof, 1958).

71. *Zeraim,* Kislev-Tevet 5697 [1937], 4.

72. Rudi Herz, "Tora wa'awoda," *Zion* (Berlin) 6, no. 6 (October–December 1934): 76.

73. Moshe Unna, *In the Paths of Thought and Action* (Hebrew) (Tel Aviv: Moreshet, 1956), 16–17.

74. *Alonim,* Nisan 5702 [1942], 4, 9.

75. Naftali Bar-Giora, *Sedei Eliyahu* (Jerusalem: Zionist Organization, 1956), 66.

76. *Amudim,* no. 164 (Tevet 5720 [1960]), 8.

77. Fishman, *Judaism and Modernization on the Kibbutz,* 117–18.

78. Cited in ibid., 106–7.

79. Cf. Ann Swidler, "The Concept of Rationality in the Work of Max Weber," *Sociological Inquiry* 43 (1973): 36–41.

80. Cited in Fishman, *Judaism and Modernization on the Kibbutz,* 108.

81. Ibid., 98–99.

82. Ibid., 108–9. Cf. Judith Porter, "Secularization, Differentiation and the Function of Religious Value-Orientations," *Sociological Inquiry* 43 (1973): 69–70.

83. Aryei Fishman and Yaakov Goldschmidt, "The Orthodox Kibbutzim and Economic Success," *Journal for the Scientific Study of Religion* 29 (1990): 505–11; Aryei Fishman, "Judaism and Modernization: The Case of the Religious Kibbutzim," *Social Forces* 62 (1983): 18–26.

84. Fishman and Goldschmidt, "Orthodox Kibbutzim."

85. Fishman, *Judaism and Modernization on the Kibbutz,* 140.

86. Cf. Philip Abrams and Andrew McCulloch, *Communes, Sociology, and Society* (New York: Cambridge University Press, 1976), 152–88.

87. Berger, *Other Side,* 6.

88. John Humphrey Noyes, *History of American Socialisms* (Philadelphia: J. B. Lippincott, 1870), 655.

89. Ibid., 21–22, 26–27.

90. Ibid., 615.

91. Maren L. Carden, *Oneida: Utopian Community to Modern Corporation* (New York: Harper Torchbooks, 1969), 89–111.

92. Ernst Troeltsch, *The Social Teaching of the Christian Churches,* trans. O. Wyon, 2 vols. (New York: Macmillan, 1931), 1:62, 2:602.

93. Ibid., 2:694–705; Lawrence Foster, *Religion and Sexuality: Three American Communal Experiments of the Nineteenth Century* (New York: Oxford University Press, 1981), 17–19.

94. John W. Bennet, *Hutterian Brethren: The Agricultural Economy and Social Organization of a Communal People* (Stanford: Stanford University Press, 1967), 23–52; Foster, *Religion and Sexuality,* 17–18, 45–46.

95. Bennet, *Hutterian Brethren,* 159–98; Andrews, *People Called Shakers,* 94–135.

96. Karl A. Peter, "The Certainty of Salvation: Ritualization of Religion and Economic Rationality among Hutterites," *Comparative Studies in Society and History* 25 (1983): 220–40.

The Situational Analysis of Religious Change Revisited

Shlomo Deshen

In the early 1960s I served as a consultant to Israeli government officials on Jewish immigrants from Tunisia and Morocco who had recently arrived en masse in Israel. I studied the immigrants in what were in those days straggling, newly established towns and villages in a peripheral region of the country. They stemmed from the hinterlands of North Africa—the Atlas Mountains of Morocco and the Gabes-Jerba region of Tunisia—which were little affected, relative to the coastal areas of North Africa, by French colonial culture. Not only was the French language foreign to the immigrants, but they were, for the most part, also immersed in the old-time religion and culture of their Judeo-Maghrebi communities of origin. For many of these immigrants resettlement in Israel was their first move out of the places where they had been born and where their ancestors had lived since time immemorial.

The scene where the immigrants met Israeli government officials was marked by a highly centralized, paternalistic bureaucracy. The officials who administered state policy viewed themselves as efficient, Western, educated, socialist, humane, devoted. The immigrants partially acquiesced to this view, considering themselves very different from the administrators, but they were not as emphatic about this as were the latter. The views of the administrators, while not unrelated to reality, sharpened and exaggerated the actual differences between them and their immigrant clients.[1]

I arrived on the scene, a newly minted sociologist on the staff of the Israeli administration, in a town I named Ayara. I shared many of my colleagues' values and much of their self-image, but some I rejected. I was an observant orthodox Jew and felt attracted to the religious practices of the immigrant clients, while those same practices virtually repelled most of my colleagues, both administrators and social scientists (amazingly, even the anthropologists of that time), who were distant from religion.[2] Also, I did not share the collectivist socialist ideology of my administration colleagues and harbored quiet reservations about the wisdom of policies rooted in that ideology. Third, my sociology training made me suspicious and curious about some of the pronouncements of both my administrator colleagues and my immigrant clients.

I was marginal to the administration officials and, because of the religious factor, to my social science colleagues as well. After about three years I resigned my administrative position, shifted to academic anthropology, and immersed myself in regular fieldwork in a community of immigrants in Ayara. This is the background to the ideas I presented in my 1970 essay in *Comparative Studies in Society and History,* "On Religious Change: The Situational Analysis of Symbolic Action," and in a related essay "The Varieties of Abandonment of Religious Symbols,"[3] both of which I subsequently developed in my ethnography of North African Israelis (jointly with Moshe Shokeid) in 1974.

The sharply dichotomized social images that the administrators held dovetailed with the equally sharp unidimensional theoretical dichotomies, *modernism* versus *traditionalism,* for example, that were much in vogue in the late 1950s and 1960s. That academic fashion vanished rather abruptly, but other dichotomies, particularly that of *secularism* versus *religiosity,* were more resilient and at times still continue to figure in social science discourse. The concepts of religiosity and secularism entail notions of inherently distinct and opposed styles of thought and practice. Social scientists who accept this ramified dichotomy are led to use the blanket concept *secularization* and, more frequently, *revitalization, intensification,* and other similar terms to discuss changes that occur on the religious plane.

The *CSSH* essay stemmed from my grappling with indications of religious change that I observed among the North African immigrants. Initially, I sought to conceptualize changes among the immigrants in conventional terms[4] drawn from the conditions I outlined, which entailed two dimensions, the administrative-personal dimension and the theoretical-cognitive. But my effort led to futility: I came to realize that the assumption that secularism prevails in contemporary society obstructs the posing of nuanced questions that might advance more deeply our understanding of the nature of contemporary religion. Crude blanket concepts, I came to realize, were not helpful in acquiring knowledge about the variety of contemporary belief and ritual and, specifically, about the details of change.

To advance such questions and, more particularly, to understand the religious doings of the new immigrants of Ayara, I felt the need for a set of concepts that avoided the obfuscating assumptions that I had learned at university and that prevailed among my colleagues at the time. On a personal level, as a result of my own grappling with religiosity, I was uncomfortable with the notion of consistent secularism prevailing.

I then sought abstract concepts that were distant from the culture being studied so that they might provide perspective on the culture from beyond it and serve as an external point of departure from which to delve into that culture. In comparative studies in society and history the issue of concepts being abstract is cardinal. Concepts such as "Westernization" are evidently ethnocentric, embedded in a particular culture, and it is dubious to use them cross-culturally. Such usage entails a priori a particular solution to questions of culture change. The same is also true in regard to concepts in which the cultural bias is less overt, such as the dichotomy between "religiosity" and "secularism" in the sociology of religion. Stemming from liberal Protestant theology, these concepts are laden with a particular heritage of discourse, which is foreign to certain other varieties of religion in the Judeo-Christian-Islamic traditions, not to mention Oriental religions and others farther afield. On the personal level I needed sensitive and refined concepts that meshed with my waverings and doubts.

Let me offer an example of the problems that arise when one approaches phenomena of religious change with such ethnocentric concepts. In examining Anglican decisions about birth control, Brian Wilson conceptualizes the church's increasingly permissive rulings as secularization.[5] A comparable examination of increasing permissiveness in other cultures—namely, Judaism—might lead to a similar conceptualization of phenomena as evidence of secularization. Thus, medieval and early modern Jewry over time increasingly relaxed the ancient biblical prohibition against the taking of monetary interest in commerce. But viewing this as secularization, one intuitively feels, would be absurd, for medieval Jewry in general was anything but a secular society. Moreover, medieval Jewry governed itself through a religiolegal system that enabled the legitimation of many cultural changes by casuistic reasoning. Such, to take one instance, was the case of the relaxation of the prohibition on taking interest.[6] An understanding of the nature of particular changes in religiocultural practice thus requires consideration of the broader context in which these changes occur.

Intuition about the general nature of the context, however, is not sufficient. Returning to the issue of birth control, one might engage in a comparative examination of the matter in Anglicanism and Judaism and discover similarly permissive trends in both. Yet conceptualizing the Jewish instance as simply another case of secularization would be dubious because, phenomenologically, the two cases might be different. In Judaism certainly, in Anglicanism perhaps occasionally, some changes of practice can be legitimized through religiously sanctioned casuistic mechanisms. Sometimes, of course, practitioners effect changes without such legitimization.

Hence, the analysis of religious change requires information on the specifics of the way in which tradition was changed, the details of the arguments, and the rationalizations and the motivations of those who initiated it. Information about the bare outcome of religious debates, divorced from socioreligious context, provides little insight. Moreover, religious change is not illuminated by latching on to a blanket catchall concept. Worse, one might conclude that a religious culture that exhibits the kind of religiously sanctioned flexibility of Judaism is inherently secular, and hence religiously inferior, to a culture that does not permit change in this way. To do so, however, would allow the religious-secular dichotomy to serve age-old Christian prejudices about Jewish legalism, materialism, and lack of spirituality. Clearly, we are left with the need for a new set of concepts that are abstract and not rooted in the discourse of a particular religious tradition.[7]

One solution to this problem is to forge conceptual tools of a more abstract analytical nature. These tools must illuminate the central question of the study of religious change: "How does religion change?" The concepts, which must be derived from the study of religion itself, should permit the differentiation of particular phenomena within the sphere of religiocultural action. And the field of inquiry must be narrowed down to elemental components of religiocultural action.

This brings us to the need for a working definition of *religion*. Drawing on Clifford Geertz,[8] let me offer the following definition: a religion is (1) a system of symbols (2) that refers to problems of ultimate meaning and (3) thereby formulates an existential order. "Symbols" are expressions of sentiments through concrete forms (such as declaring articles of belief and practicing rituals). "Problems of ultimate meaning" are problems that confront people, and remain with them, when they have reached the limits of understanding. Such problems arise when stress is experienced or at times of moral reckoning, and they include questions of suffering and moral consistency. Problems of ultimate meaning are found in situations in which chaos is felt to threaten to intrude and shatter an ordered conception of existence. By "formulation of an existential order" I have in mind a systematic configuration of symbols—that is, an effective mechanism through which individuals order experiences. This definition of religion is broad and encompasses phenomena of symbolic action in fields other than religion as traditionally conceived, such as art and ideology. This is reasonable, provided that the symbolic actions are related to the formulation of an existential order vis-à-vis problems of ultimate meaning.

Defining religion along these lines leads to a sociological understanding of religion that entails primarily the examination of symbols, and systems of symbols, in relation to the varied and changing situations of the people who carry the symbols. Coming to the problem of religious change, one would want to know how and why particular practitioners change the meanings that they attribute to religious symbols and how particular religious changes are related to particular life situations and social roles. Our analytical categories will therefore be constructed by focusing on the actions of religious practitioners in relation to particular symbols.

The typology of symbolic actions that I now suggest is an attempt to refine the tools used and to arrive at greater clarity. The typology, rooted in the previous definitions of religion and symbols, seeks through a high degree of abstraction to encompass phenomena cross-culturally. It consists of the following categories: (1) eradication, (2) effacement, (3) creation, (4) innovation, and (5) profanation. The first three categories contain acts that pertain to the formal expression of symbols. Eradication and effacement are diametrically opposed to creation. The former two are acts whereby symbols are abandoned, whereas by an act of creation a new symbol is wrought. In acts of innovation and profanation the formal expression of the symbol undergoes no change; the acts, however, impinge on the meaning and content of existing symbols.

Eradication

An act of eradication consists in the separation of a symbol from the range of existential experiences to which the symbol traditionally applies. This occurs when the practitioner ceases to carry out the action that a living relationship with the symbol implies: the symbol thus loses relevance to experience. When practitioners refrain from a ritual action, they eradicate the ritual so far as their personal religiosity is concerned; also, when practitioners cease to express belief in a particular article of faith, they eradicate the set of symbols that composes that article of faith. Stated concretely, it means, for example, that when tribal Africans cease to relate anxieties to the power traditionally attributed to witchcraft they eradicate witchcraft.

Effacement

This category of action is superficially similar to eradication. Like the latter, it entails the abandonment of a particular symbol or cluster of symbols. But, as I indicated earlier, in the discussion of birth control and commercial practices, overt abandonment may be accompanied by a variety of meanings. Whereas some acts of abandonment warrant conceptualization as radical eradication, some do not, and they constitute a different type of phenomenon. An example from my field observations follows. The setting is that of the synagogue congregation of southern Tunisian immigrants, Tsidkat Hayyim, in Ayara. Back in Tunisia the religious status of southern Tunisians had been high, because most religious functionaries in Tunisia and Tripolitania came from there, particularly from the island of Jerba. More than other North African immigrants, the southern Tunisians in Ayara, particularly the adult generation, adhere strongly to traditional practices. But to their chagrin much has changed in matters of secondary importance in their lives.[9] They are now deeply aware of decline in their religious stature. The leader of the synagogue, when describing how elaborate the preparations for festivals had been abroad in comparison with the current hasty preparations, remarked succinctly, "The grace (*zekhut*) of Abroad has left us!" Many people, including some who themselves abandoned various customs, are nostalgic about the traditional life they have lost, and there is a pervasive feeling of dejection and failure. They have sunk, in their conception, to the level of others. I focus now on two religious changes among these pious people.

Beard Shaving

Practically all the congregants shave regularly, at least once a week. In southern Tunisian Jewish culture growing a beard is associated with piety, and many did so abroad. This is attested by verbal evidence and by photographs. But in Ayara even devout congregants and highly respected religious functionaries are clean-shaven. This is in marked contrast to people's generally slovenly, disheveled appearance. Elsewhere in Israel several rabbis from Jerba with whom I am acquainted are also clean-shaven, though they are very traditional in their ideas and in their personal style of living.

Abandonment of the *Nefilat Appayim* Rite

In the traditional Jewish liturgy the morning and afternoon weekday services include the *nefilat appayim* (falling on the faces) rite, which begins: "Merciful and Compassionate One, we have sinned before You; have mercy on us and save us!" It was customary to recite this and other verses while reclining with the head buried in the arm. According to the *kabbalah,* which greatly influences the ritual of southern Tunisia, the rite of *nefilat appayim* is invested with profound mystical power: while performing it, the worshiper is believed to lower his soul into the somber depths of evil and by an act of concentration of thought to rectify some of the evil of primal creation. But the rite is also believed to endanger the souls of the unworthy, and therefore only confident, righteous, scholarly men practiced it. I was informed that in Tunisia the number of persons who performed the rite was not large but more than in Israel. In Ayara no one does it. Elsewhere in Israel I have seen two southern Tunisians performing the rite of *nefilat appayim,* and I have been told of a third who does so.[10]

I interpret these changes in the context of pervasive feelings of religious self-depreciation. The acts of growing a beard and *nefilat appayim* are seemly for Jerbans of high religious stature, not for pious people who conceive of themselves as unworthy. Now, they explain, they are "ashamed" (*mitbayesh*) to appear overtly pious. The two symbolic acts are incongruent with the depreciated self-image of the practitioners, and by abandoning them they harmonized their existential situation. But their changed self-image and their ensuing abandonment of symbolic acts do not touch the bases of their religious beliefs, in contrast to the category of eradication. On the contrary, the doings of the pious Ayara people reflect a vital attachment to the values in which the symbols are rooted. Such abandonment is best referred to by the weak term *effacement.*

Creation

An act of creation consists in relating a range of existential experience(s) to a symbol that is either newly created or adopted from an alien tradition. Great historical figures of traditional religions sometimes created symbols, and acts of creation can particularly be found in religious conversions.

Many theologians and social commentators term phenomena of religious creation as *pseudoreligion* or *secular religion*. But, viewed phenomenologically and not ethnocentrically, the use of these derogatory terms is unfounded. There is no reason to consider the symbolic acts and beliefs of modern religions to be different from those of traditional religions, provided that the experience of the symbols is genuine, in the sense of the definitions already given. Also, to attribute a diffuse symbolic value that relates to problems of ultimate meaning to artistic activities is theoretically an act of religious creation.

Innovation

An act of innovation consists in changing the range of experience to which a symbol applies. The symbol becomes infused with new content that pertains to a range of experience previously not expressed by the symbol. The general category to which the newly symbolized range of experience belongs has previously been expressed by the symbol; now, however, the symbol has widened its connotative scope, since it also comprehends the new range of experience.

To cite a Jewish example: traditionally, the study of the *mishnah,* an ancient rabbinic legal text, was seen as an act of piety expressive of a desire to commune with the realm of the divine. In late medieval Jewish mysticism, however, the act of studying *mishnah* became imbued with additional content. It was now deemed to benefit the souls of the dead, and it therefore became a central part of the ritual of memorialism. The desire for communion with the realm of the divine evolved into the particular desire of communion with the souls thought to inhabit that realm. The general category of ranges of experience relevant to both the traditional and the mystical study of *mishnah* is the same. But in late Judaism there is a difference of detail within that general category. Such acts of religious change I categorize as innovation.

Profanation

Like innovation, profanation is an act that changes the range of experience to which a symbol applies; the symbol becomes infused with new content that pertains to a range of experience it previously did not express. In the case of profanation, however, the general category to which the newly symbolized range of experience belongs has not been previously expressed by the symbol, and that is the difference between profanation and innovation. I use the value-oriented, loaded term *profanation* deliberately because the actions it covers are illegitimate when seen from the perspective of the traditional religion. The question of the degree of traditional legitimization of any particular act of religious change is of analytical importance. In stating that the general category of experience now conveyed by the symbol has previously not been expressed, I do not refer merely to a far-reaching stage of religious innovation; rather, I seek to isolate a type of religious change that is so radical that the traditional religion has no mechanism to legitimate it.

Pivotal to this presentation have been the concepts of "symbol" and "existential experience" and the idea that the analysis of acts relating to symbols must take into account the relevant existential experience of the actors. Symbolic acts and the social situations of the actors compose a single unit; religious change must be examined in the light of that one unit, forming a single field of inquiry. The necessary technique is to handle ethnographic data through "situational analysis." Situational analysis consists of examining series of related data and deducing from them patterns of regular action. Empirically, the data are examined as units, such as "extended cases" and "social situations."[11] Following this, I illustrate the phenomenon of profanation with my own field observations.

A Case Study—A Torah Scroll Presentation

During the 1965 general election campaign in Ayara political parties vied with one another to dispense favors to potential voters.[12] Pai, one of the parties that ran in the election, presented a Torah scroll to a congregation of recent immigrants from Morocco, Shevah Yisrael. Torah scrolls are the most valued artifacts of Judaism. Each synagogue is required to have at least one. There was a shortage of Torah scrolls in Israel at the time because hundreds of new synagogues had been built since the onset of mass immigration in 1948. One of the main ways of obtaining scrolls was through custodians of the property of diaspora communities that had become defunct, either as a result of massacre during World War II or as a result of assimilation. Political parties frequently helped to provide synagogues with scrolls through contacts with the custodians, seeking thereby to influence the vote of the congregants.

On the evening appointed for the Torah scroll presentation the Shevah Yisrael congregants and many other Moroccan immigrants were assembled outside the Pai branch office at the far end of the town. Children and adults held lighted torches made from tin cans secured to sticks and filled with kerosene-soaked rags. The Torah scroll was carried in the center of the throng, and the men pushed toward it to have the privilege of carrying it a few yards. Throughout the procession the festive Sabbath eve hymns were chanted. Women along the way stopped and piously raised their hands to their eyes and kissed them. The flicker of the torches in the dark and the excited chatter of the children who milled on the periphery of the crowd radiated an atmosphere of solemn rejoicing and restrained emotion.

The crowd arrived at the synagogue, and, to the sound of devotional chanting, the scroll was placed in the ark. Then people sat down to listen to political speeches: Pai helps people to maintain their beliefs; here in Ayara a scroll is brought to the synagogue; the same is done elsewhere; everywhere Pai helps people to remain religious vis-à-vis secularism. The last speaker brought the speeches to a climax, closing his harangue with an impassioned call: "Hear O Israel the Lord is our God, the Lord is One [*ehad*]! This is the D, the great D, the D of Pai! Vote D!" The crowd then proceeded to the regular evening service, which included this verse, a pivotal part of the regular prayer service.

The symbolic act on which I now focus is the worshipers' expression during the service while reciting this ancient monotheistic declaration. Two distinct sets of actors are engaged in this symbolic act—the Pai politicians and the congregants of the synagogue. They are, however, involved in contrasting social situations, which mold differentially the meaning and the character of the symbolic act, in which both sets of actors are united. The verse, known as the *shema,* is the central credo of the Jewish faith. This is one of a small number of prayers that the observant is obliged to recite with concentration (*kavanah*). Throughout Jewish history intense religious fervor has been focused on the *shema.* Emotions erupted particularly at times of crisis and ultimate sacrifice, and generations of martyrs died with it on their lips.

The obscure phrases lend themselves to manifold interpretations. The verse is recognition of the one God, a supplication to Heaven, an assertion of identity with Jewry, a cry of defiance at tormentors, an affirmation of moral life in the face of death—and it may be all of these, and more, simultaneously. There is a traditional form in which the credo is written in Torah scrolls: the final letters of the first and last words of the verse are written in larger characters than the rest. All prayer books have adopted this form, and these letters are printed in a type bolder than the rest. The election symbol of Pai—the Hebrew character for *d*—happens, coincidentally, to be the same letter that is made prominent in the credo.

The politician thus trod on emotional ground when he appealed to his audience to vote for the *d* of the credo. The speech was timed so as to climax a religiopolitical ceremony—the procession and the Torah scroll presentation—in a way, to be the opening to the regular evening service that included the recitation of the credo. All the worshipers, both the congregants and the politicians, were observant Jews and ritually obligated to focus their attention on this recitation. It may be presumed that the particular political interpretation that had just been suggested was on the minds of the worshipers and impressed itself further in the course of the ritual recitation. Thus, an analysis of the ritual must take into account the election speech that preceded it.

Let us now examine the symbolic act of the recitation of the credo at the evening service from the point of view of the politicians. The notion they wanted to convey with the political speech was essentially this: the ancient credo, like the Torah as a whole, is pregnant with hidden meanings, which are constantly revealed to new generations that seek to immerse themselves in Holy Writ. And Pai, whose election symbol *d* coincides with the *d* of *ehad,* is the party that represents all that is right and good in the eyes of the Lord. In effect the speaker manipulated the credo for purposes of electioneering by interpreting in a homiletic manner the boldly printed *d* character of *ehad.* It could now be seen as related to the election symbol of the party, which coincidentally happened to be the letter *d.* The election speech was delivered after religious emotions had been stirred by the procession, the hymns, and the presentation of the Torah scroll, and it preceded a religious service in which the credo must be recited with concentration.

The aim of Pai, a religious party, aside from mundane aspirations for political power, was to execute religious policies, and the motivation of the politicians was essentially religious. They fired emotions by a homiletic interpretation of the credo that suited propaganda purposes. It is a characteristic feature of traditional Jewish homiletics to use symbols, particularly biblical verses, as vehicles to convey topical socioreligious messages. The aim of these messages is to enhance loyalty to traditional Judaism. Preachers change the meaning of the symbols, albeit in a traditionally legitimate manner, because the constant uncovering of new meanings in Holy Writ is inherent in Jewish homiletics. Rabbinic homiletics are in effect a mechanism for religious innovation in Judaism. The speech of the Pai politician, wherein he attributed political content to the credo, is in this context a religious innovation. This analysis also applies to the politicians' declaration of the credo in their own prayers at the evening service.

I turn to the worshiping congregation. Based on a general knowledge of the people involved, I maintain that the congregants did not see the aims of the religious party in the same light as the politicians.[13] The congregants were all newcomers to Israel, to whom party politics and democratic elections were novel. They were not in a position to differentiate clearly detailed differences among the religious and other parties. All parties and politicians were strange to them, and the phenomenon of religious parties was baffling. From their point of view their experience of the symbol of the credo was colored by an interpretation they could not relate to anything traditional. All the activities connected to the elections were new to them. They were confronted with an interpretation of the symbol that related to a strange political context. When the congregants came to practice their devotions at the evening service, the political interpretation that had just been suggested must have been on their minds. Seen from this aspect, the ritual action that took place at the evening service was an act of profanation.

These ritual acts took place within a single social field—public prayer in a synagogue—but they involved two distinct sets of actors whose general social situations were very different. These situations caused the meanings of the acts to be analytically different for the various people. This level of detailed analysis is possible when clearly delimited acts, and the social situations in which they are enacted, are conceptually embraced and discussed as a unit.

My 1970 essay concluded with a flourish:

Analysis of ritual action that does not also confront the complexities of social situations affords understanding only at an abstract and general level. In approaching the incidents discussed in this case study with the conventional terms of sociology of religion, one might characterize the incident as a whole, the speech and the prayers of both politicians and congregants, as "secularization." But in fact, as we have seen, the sociocultural contexts are such that the actions are diverse. Only by distorting the diversity can the actions be encompassed by a single analytical concept. The situational analysis of the symbolic action generates analytical tools . . . that are incisive enough to conceptualize particular phenomena of religious change. We are relieved of the burden of ethnocentric concepts and are able to analyze phenomena in more universal terms.

Conclusion

How has the essay weathered the years? A quarter of a century later the intellectual terrain is very different from what it was in 1970. The study of symbolism in cultural anthropology has expanded immensely, practically engulfing the discipline. We now have innumerable ethnographies, books, and journal articles focused on ritual and symbolism, as well as attempts at conceptualization and theory. But many of the ethnographic writings are parochial, not very successful in illuminating broad issues of humankind. And of the attempts at theory more than a few are idiosyncratic, wavering between banality and obscurity.

The criticisms of functionalist anthropology that gave rise to tendencies that currently prevail were indeed to the point. But many of the alternatives offered leave much to be desired. One may well wonder whether anthropology in the 1990s is more vigorous, insightful, and illuminating of the human condition than was anthropology in the heyday of functionalism. Therefore, the challenge of wedding detailed field observations with broad issues of anthropological understanding is still with us, and that is what I tried to address, in an ever so delimited way, in my old *CSSH* essay.

The past quarter century has seen the highly salient development of "reflexive anthropology." In Israel there has emerged "a critical sociology" of Israeli social science.[14] These have helped me become aware both of the roots of my approach and of that which it criticizes in the situation of social commentators in Israel, myself included, in the 1960s. It is rather commonplace now to indicate that both the social scientists and the administrators of the early years of Israeli statehood conceptualized their social environment according to their own worldviews. It has even become something of a fashion to denigrate the sociologists and anthropologists of that period as subservient to the then dominant ideologues and wielders of power. Be that as it may, my own criticism in the 1960s, and the approach that I consequently developed, did not stem only from reflection, pure and rarefied. My very first publication, boldly entitled "A Case of Breakdown of Modernization," written in 1963 and published in 1965, was embedded within the theoretical paradigm that then dominated my personal ambience and Israeli social science.

By the end of the decade, however, I had become exposed to British social anthropology of the Manchester variety at an interesting juncture in the history of that distinguished anthropology department.[15] The department was in the hands of the last generation of adherents to functionalist theory. But, while functionalism still dominated, it was of the revised version formulated by Max Gluckman, and that too was challenged by the emergence of the first generation of "symbolic anthropologists," such as Victor Turner, Mary Douglas, Edmund Leach, and Clifford Geertz (then at Chicago but influential also in Britain and Israel). Crucially, the last generation of British functionalists had become self-conscious and apologetic about their theoretical orientation. While the neofunctionalist orientation of Gluckman and his remaining associates was solid, they did not identify themselves as functionalists anymore. The label applied to them, but it had become unfashionable and embarrassing. The Manchester intellectual climate, as I experienced it, was thus one of unease and questioning. Consequently, I was enabled to articulate my own discomfort about bold and clear-cut social categories and expressed a critical view of some of the concepts that buttressed the categories of social science of the time in my *CSSH* essay. The more refined concepts that I suggested meshed with the marginal, rather hesitant positions that informed my personal life.

I readily acknowledge the subjective conditions that lie at the root of this essay. But this is not just a personal matter. Social reflection, ethereal and pure, unaffected by the existential conditions of people, probably never existed anywhere. And it behooves "critical sociologists" and "reflexive anthropologists" to be aware of that in relation to themselves, and not just in relation to those whose work they criticize.[16] As an academic project, "situational analysis of religious change" has not been a success. Among leading anthropologists only Raymond Firth[17] and one or two others took note of the essay. Both in social science and in history situational analysis in the comparative study of religion has remained untried. General and Jewish subjects could be studied productively through situational analysis. A Jewish example would be the study of the details of the dissolution of traditional Judaism in various societies in the wake of modernization or the reassertion of various modern orthodoxies in Israel and the diaspora in the past few decades. The potential is there, and, particularly within the delimited domain of comparing Jewish societies, situational analysis remains to be tried.

NOTES

I gratefully acknowledge the comments of participants in Todd Endelman's fall 1994 Comparative Studies in Society and History (CSSH) seminar and, in particular, those of Zvi Gitelman.

1. For elaboration, see ethnographies of the period such as Dorothy Willner, *Nation-Building and Community in Israel* (Princeton, NJ: Princeton University Press, 1969); Alex Weingrod, *Reluctant Pioneers: Village Development in Israel* (Ithaca, NY: Cornell University Press, 1966); Moshe Shokeid, *The Dual Heritage: Immigrants from the Atlas Mountains in an Israeli Village* (New Brunswick, NJ: Transaction, 1985); Harvey Goldberg, *Cave Dwellers and Citrus Growers: A Jewish Community in Libya and Israel* (Cambridge: Cambridge University Press, 1972); Shlomo Deshen, *Immigrant Voters in Israel: Parties and Congregations in a Local Election Campaign* (Manchester: Manchester University Press, 1970). There are additional ethnographies of the 1960–70 immigrant scene, full volumes and shorter essays, by many other scholars, mainly anthropologists. Myron Aronoff, Erik Cohen, Don Handelman, Gilbert Kushner, Len Mars, Emanuel Marx, Henry Rosenfeld, and the late Dov Weintraub and Yitzhak Eilam are just some of them.

2. It is notable that aside from my own writings, and with the single exception of Moshe Shokeid, religious activities were virtually absent in the ethnographies of my irreligious anthropological colleagues. See further comments on these matters in my essay "The Study of Religion in Israeli Social Science," in *Israeli Judaism: The Sociology of Religion in Israel*, ed. Shlomo Deshen et al. (New Brunswick, NJ: Transaction, 1995), 1–18.

3. In *Journal for the Scientific Study of Religion* 11 (1972): 33–41.

4. See Shlomo Deshen, "A Case of Breakdown of Modernization in an Israeli Immigrant Community," *Jewish Journal of Sociology* 7 (1965): 63–91.

5. See Brian Wilson, *Religion in Secular Society* (London: Watts, 1966).

6. For details, see Jacob Katz, *Tradition and Crisis: Jewish Society at the End of the Middle Ages,* rev. ed., trans. B. D. Cooperman (New York: New York University Press, 1993), chap. 8.

7. These formulations imply criticism of the category of "ritualism" (or "formalism") that is often used in theological discourse, in which *ritualism* means adherence to traditional forms that lack content. The term is used derogatively, implying legalism, pettiness, lack of religious thought and feeling. I suggest that what appears superficially as ritualism will emerge, upon close examination, as traditional symbolic actions that have undergone changes. I categorize these at present as either "profanation" or "innovation." For elaboration of these arguments and further examples, see my formulations in the original version of the essay, *Comparative Studies in Society and History* 12 (1970): 260–74; and Shlomo Deshen and

Moshe Shokeid, *The Predicament of Homecoming: Cultural and Social Life of North African Immigrants in Israel* (Ithaca, NY: Cornell University Press, 1974).

8. Clifford Geertz, "Religion as a Cultural System," in *Anthropological Approaches to the Study of Religion,* ed. Michael Barton (London: Tavistock, 1966), 1–46.

9. One instance is that in Jerba many congregants participated in Torah study groups, whereas in Ayara attempts to organize such groups failed. For elaboration, see Deshen and Shokeid, *Predicament of Homecoming,* chap. 6.

10. I was acquainted during the 1960s with most of the Jerban communities in Israel and can attest that altogether the number of practitioners of the rite was negligible. See Deshen and Shokeid, *Predicament of Homecoming,* chap. 6, for elaboration and for another example of effacement.

11. See J. Van Velsen, "The Extended-Case Method and Situational Analysis," in *The Craft of Social Anthropology,* ed. A. L. Epstein (London: Tavistock, 1967), 129–49; James Clyde Mitchell, *The Kalela Dance* (Manchester: Manchester University Press, 1956); Victor Turner, *Schism and Continuity in an African Society* (Manchester: Manchester University Press, 1957); *The Forest of Symbols* (Ithaca, NY: Cornell University Press, 1967); Max Gluckman, *Politics, Law and Ritual in Tribal Society* (Oxford: Blackwell, 1965).

12. For elaboration, see Deshen, *Immigrant Voters in Israel.*

13. For elaboration, see ibid.; and, particularly, Moshe Shokeid and Shlomo Deshen, *Distant Relations: Ethnicity and Politics among Arabs and North African Jews in Israel* (New York: Bergin and Praeger, 1982), chap. 8.

14. Uri Ram, *The Changing Agenda of Israeli Sociology: Theory, Ideology, and Identity* (Albany: State University of New York Press, 1994).

15. For a memoir of the social ambience of Manchester anthropology in the late 1960s, see Moshe Shokeid, "The Socialization of an International Student in Manchester: Paul Baxter's Role," in *A River of Blessings: Essays in Honor of Paul Baxter,* ed. David Brokensha (Syracuse: Syracuse University Press, 1994), 307–13.

16. See the trenchant comments of Moshe Shokeid, in "Commitment and Contextual Study in Anthropology," *Cultural Anthropology* 7 (1992): 464–77.

17. Raymond Firth, *Symbols Public and Private* (London: Allen and Unwin, 1973).

Glossary

aggadah: nonlegal materials in the Talmud and other rabbinic texts.

converso: Spanish or Portuguese Jew who converted to Christianity, irrespective of his or her motives and subsequent attachment, or lack of attachment, to Judaism.

dhimmi: non-Muslim, subordinate, "protected" subject of a Muslim state.

galut: diaspora, exile.

halakhah: Jewish law.

Hanukkah: winter festival commemorating the victory of the Maccabees and the rededication of the Second Temple in 165 BCE.

hasid (sing.), *hasidim* (pl.): adherents of mystical, pietist, revivalist movement that originated in the second half of the eighteenth century in southern Poland and Ukraine.

haskalah: the Jewish enlightenment in Central and Eastern Europe.

herem: ostracization, or excommunication, of an individual from the Jewish community.

kabbalah: Jewish mystical tradition.

kashrut: system of dietary laws and regulations.

kevutsah: small, pioneering collective agricultural settlement in the Land of Israel, precursor to the larger, village-like kibbutz

Lag ba-Omer: minor spring festival on the thirty-third day of the seven-week period (from the second day of Passover to Shavuot) of the counting of the *omer* (a sheaf cut in the barley harvest).

landsmanshaft (sing.), *landsmanshaftn* (pl.): mutual aid societies in East European immigrant communities in the late nineteenth and twentieth centuries, their membership drawn from the same town or region in the Old World.

maskil (sing.), *maskilim* (pl.): adherent of the Jewish enlightenment.

mellah: Jewish quarter in North African cities, orginally established to protect Jews, later intended to isolate, stigmatize, and penalize them.

millet: system that developed in the nineteenth century for governance of minority communities in the Ottoman Empire.

mishnah: earliest compilation of rabbinic teachings and discussions (ca. 200 CE); with later material (the *gemara*) constitutes the Talmud.

mitsvah (sing.), *mitsvot* (pl.): divine commandment.

moshav (sing.), *moshavim* (pl.): cooperative (but not collective) village of smallholders in the Land of Israel.

shekhinah: the manifestation, or in-dwelling, of the divine presence in the life of the Jewish people.

shema: monotheistic credo of Judaism recited every morning and evening.

shivah: seven-day period of mourning.

shtibel (sing.), *shtiblekh* (pl.): small, informal, unpretentious conventicle, or prayer room, of East European Jews.

Shulhan arukh: sixteenth-century code of Jewish law and practice compiled by Joseph Karo, authoritative to this day within traditional Judaism.

tefillin: leather straps and boxes, containing biblical texts, worn by Jewish males age thirteen and over during the weekday morning prayer service.

Torah-im-derekh erets: observance of Jewish law combined with acceptance of civil culture, credo of the modern orthodox movement in Germany.

tsaddik: charismatic leader of Hasidic sect.

tsitsit: fringes on ritual prayer shawl.

yeshivah (sing.), *yeshivot* (pl.): academy for the study of Jewish law.

Contributors

Shlomo Deshen is Professor of Social Anthropology at Tel-Aviv University. He is the author or coauthor of six books on the Jews of the Middle East and North Africa. His most recent books in English include *The Mellah Society: Jewish Community Life in Sherifian Morocco* (1989) and *Blind People: The Private and Public Life of Sightless Israelis* (1992).

Todd M. Endelman is William Haber Professor of Modern Jewish History at the University of Michigan. He is the author of *The Jews of Georgian England* (1979), *Radical Assimilation in English Jewish History* (1991), and *The Jews of Britain* (forthcoming). He is currently writing a history of conversion and other forms of radical assimilation in Europe and America from the Enlightenment to the present.

Aryei Fishman is Associate Professor in the Department of Sociology and Anthropology at Bar-Ilan University. He has written extensively on religious Zionism, in general, and on the religious kibbutzim, in particular. His *Judaism and Modernization on the Relgious Kibbutz* has appeared in both Hebrew (1990) and English (1992) editions. He is presently at work on a book that expands the theme of his contribution to this volume.

Nancy L. Green is Director of Studies at the École des Hautes Études en Sciences Sociales in Paris, where she teaches modern Jewish history and migration studies. She has written a history of Jewish immigrant workers in the French capital, *The Pletzl of Paris* (1986), and a comparative history of garment workers in Paris and New York, *Ready-To-Wear and Ready-To-Work* (1977). She is currently editing a collection of documents on East European Jewish immigrant workers in Europe and North and South America.

Hillel J. Kieval is Professor in the Department of History and the Henry M. Jackson School of International Studies at the University of Washington, Seattle. A specialist in the history of Hapsburg Jewry, he is the author of *The Making of Czech Jewry: National Conflict and Jewish Society in Bohemia, 1870–1918* (1988), as well as numerous articles on the social and cultural history of the Jews of East Central Europe. His current project is a book-length study of ritual murder trials in Central and Eastern Europe at the turn of the century.

Zachary Lockman is Associate Professor of modern Middle Eastern history in the Department of Middle Eastern Studies at New York University. He is the author of *The Egyptian Working Class, 1882–1954* (1987) and *Comrades and Enemies: Arab and Jewish Workers in Palestine, 1906–1948* (1996), coauthor, with Joel Beinin, of *Workers on the Nile: Nationalism, Communism, Islam, and the Egyptian Working Class, 1882–1954* (1987), and editor of *Workers and Working Classes in the Middle East: Struggles, Histories, Historiographies* (1994).

Dan V. Segre served in the Israeli diplomatic corps and taught political science at Bar-Ilan University, the Technion, and Haifa University. He is currently President of the Institute for Executive Seminars in Turin. He has written books on Africa, Zionism, and Israel, as well as his autobiography, *Memoirs of a Fortunate Jew* (1987), which has been published in six countries.

Stephen Sharot is Professor of Sociology at Ben-Gurion University of the Negev. He is the author of *Judaism: A Sociology* (1976), the first comparative sociological study of modern Judaism in a global context, *Messianism, Mysticism, and Magic: A Sociological Analysis of Jewish Religious Movements* (1982), and, with Eliezer Ben-Rafael, *Ethnicity, Religion, and Class in Israeli Society* (1991).

Sammy Smooha is Professor of Sociology at Haifa University. A specialist in comparative ethnic relations, he has published widely on internal political and social divisions in Israel. His books include *Israel: Pluralism and Conflict* (1978) and *Arabs and Jews in Israel* (2 vols., 1989 and 1992).

David Sorkin is Frances and Laurence Weinstein Professor of Jewish History and Thought at the University of Wisconsin, Madison. A specialist in German Jewish history, he is the author of *The Transformation of German Jewry, 1780–1840* (1987) and *Moses Mendelssohn and the Religious*

Enlightenment (1996). He is currently completing a comparative study of the eighteenth-century religious enlightenment, among Jews and Christians, in Germany, Austria, France, Scotland, and England.

Leo Spitzer is Professor of History at Dartmouth College. He worked initially in the comparative history of Africa and Latin America but in recent years has turned to studying individual and collective memory in the twentieth century. He is the author of *The Sierra Leone Creoles: Responses to Colonialism, 1870–1945* (1975) and *Lives In Between: Assimilation and Marginality in Austria, Brazil, West Africa, 1780–1945* (1990). He has just completed a book, *Surviving Memory,* that examines Austrian-Jewish refugee immigration to Bolivia and the reconstruction of Central European Jewish culture in Latin America during World War II.

Index